Food for Thought

Food for Thought

ESSAYS ON EATING AND CULTURE

Edited by Lawrence C. Rubin

Foreword by John Shelton Lawrence

McFarland & Company, Inc., Publishers
Jefferson, North Carolina, and London

rather than gastronomic consumptive habits, those that have brought me to the table of thoughts and ideas, rather than food. And it is to my parents, Esther and Herb, that I am grateful for instilling this hunger for understanding and thirst for knowledge. Their early exhortations to clean my plate because there were children starving in some remote corner of the globe have over the years been transformed into an insatiable curiosity.

I want to acknowledge my family: my wife, Randi, whose versatility in the kitchen sustains my body, but whose insightful recipes for living nourish me at a far deeper level; my son, Zachary, a self-professed thirteen-year-old *cheeseatarian,* who continually reminds me that love for life is the source of all nourishment; my daughter, Rebecca, who at eight has unlocked the secrets of the universe by tying the movement of the stars and planets to the rumblings in her tummy.

I thank the contributors to this book, fine cooks in the kitchen, all.

Chef Lawrence

Table of Contents

Foreword

by John Shelton Lawrence

Getting Eating Right

What greater pleasure for young parents than to see their new infant take its first sucks of milk from the mother's breast? The child lives, loves something, craves to sustain itself. At such moments, we recognize the vital kinship between human progeny and other mammals such as the kitten, the piglet, the puppy. All seem to crave a place at the banquet of sweet, primal pleasures.

A self-respecting household cannot indulge infant instincts too long because the growing child soon shows streaks of messiness. The little hand in the pureed carrots cannot resist stuffing a dollop into baby's own ear. The fingers thrust into the beans impulsively reach for the head, where the slithery paste mats the hair, producing a delightful sensation. And how about tossing this bowl of oatmeal at that watchful dog?

In these patience-stretching scenes, the splat mat beneath the high chair is too small to protect the surrounding spaces — the rug, hardwood, or linoleum. Weighed against such childish fun are the parents' awareness of cleaning tasks and the waste. Nutrition can be scarce, expensive. An imperative quickly comes to focus in adult consciousness. Cultural norms must be learned! Conformity to a respectful way of eating becomes the youngster's price of sitting at the table! So begins but one of society's varied projects to shape the universal need to consume food.

Social efforts to shape the cycles of hunger and satisfaction are doubtless older than civilization itself. History, much of it archeological, presents us with an array of significant markers: the hearth, cooking and eating utensils, field crops, animal husbandry, banquets, restaurant dining, franchise chains, dietary fads, eating disorders, eating contests — to mention just a few. This book assembled by Lawrence C. Rubin and his able contributors illuminates

1

significant values and meanings associated with recently emerging food markers. Since the articles have a strong contemporary emphasis, this foreword briefly suggests a historical frame for these phenomena by recalling some important early literary and philosophical explorations of hunger, eating, and social symbolism. These traces remind us that differences associated with food culture surfaced as quickly as *Homo sapiens* began to develop practices that suited their circumstances and eating styles that gratified their aesthetic sense. They also suggest that our creativity will adapt to evolving physical conditions for food production as well as to inventing new understandings of nutrition and styles of preparation.

Eating Toward Humanity

Thousands of years ago, the unknown authors of *Gilgamesh*, an epic narrative inscribed on stone tablets about 2000 BCE, symbolically conveyed the imperative to push eating in the direction of *Homo sapiens* who could walk and sit in an upright position. The story tells how Enkidu, at first a shaggy monster of a wild man, was rendered acceptable for intimate camaraderie with Gilgamesh, the king of Uruk. It was part of a divine plan to make a better ruler of Gilgamesh by giving him the companionship of someone with comparable physical strength. But before undertaking his counterbalancing role to the king's aggressive temperament, Enkidu had to be civilized. In describing his ways of eating, the epic poem repeatedly tells us that "He ate grasses with the gazelles, / and jostled at the watering hole with animals; / ... his thirst was slaked with (mere) water."[1] After being lured away from animal friends by a temple prostitute, who first got his attention with seven uninterrupted days of sex, he was firmly guided to eat as humans do. Quoting from the text of *Gilgamesh*:

> The harlot spoke to Enkidu, saying: / "Eat the food, Enkidu, it is the way one lives. / Drink the beer, as is the custom of the land." / Enkidu ate the food until he was sated, / he drank the beer — seven jugs! — and became expansive and sang with joy! / He was elated and his face glowed. / He splashed his shaggy body with water, / and rubbed himself with oil, and turned into a human.[2]

Thereafter, the animals, who had earlier nurtured Enkidu with their milk and shared forage, shunned him. They recognized his transit from feeding to eating as an alienation from their kind. Despite the existential pain of separation he sometimes felt, Enkidu remained human until his death.

In our times, we are constantly urged to lament how the "the natural" loses out to some new form of the artificially "processed." What we see in *Gilgamesh*, by contrast, is a "progressive" impulse to regard the products of field labor (the milled grain of bread[3] and beer) and artisan's craft (baking and brewing) as human advances beyond hunting and gathering food in the forest. Already we see a conceptual foundation for the split between organic food traditionalists and process-inclined food progressives that has continued to our day.

Eating with Gods

Numerous other cultural values have been attached to eating besides tidiness and socialization for companionship at the table. The books of Leviticus and Deuteronomy in the Hebrew bible formulate several distinctions between the "clean" and the "unclean," steadily guided by the admonition "not [to] eat any abhorrent thing."[4] Looking at Greek epics such as Homer's *Iliad* and *Odyssey* (around 800 BCE), attentive readers will notice much prayerful gratitude for food and wine. Commenting on the pattern, the archeologist Susan Sherratt observes that "Homeric feasting takes place as a matter of course every day, whenever named heroes and their companions prepare and eat a meal together, whenever they arrive somewhere and hospitality is offered and before they depart, before and at the conclusion of every heroic enterprise, and whenever they want to win the gods to their side. Feasting is ubiquitous and constant — it is what Homeric heroes do in company at every opportunity."[5] Whenever meat is roasted, a portion is sacrificed to the gods. Whenever wine is drunk, a libation is tossed on the ground in tribute to them. In a typical display of this attitude, Achilles and Diomedes complete their bath: "And rinsing off, their skin sleek with an olive oil rub, / they sat down to their meal and dipping up their cups / from an overflowing bowl, they poured them forth —/ honeyed, mellow wine to the great goddess Athena."[6]

Sometimes the meaning of a food sacrifice is that of a prayerful gratitude; in other cases it is appeasement — or outright manipulation of the gods' favor. Hesiod, another Greek poet, speaks frankly to this in his *Works and Days* (around 700 BCE): "In proportion to your means offer the gods sacrifices / that are pure and unblemished, and burn choice thighs for them. /... so that you win their favor for your affairs, / not having to sell your land, but buying more from others."[7] Plato presents an ironic display of such beliefs in the person of Euthyphro, the Athenian man in the street who tries to offer instruction to Socrates on the art of holiness. He remarks to him that sacrifices amount to "gods and men ... doing business with one another" — where the object is to profitably exchange lesser goods for greater ones: "holiness is learning how to please the gods in word and deed, by prayers and sacrifices."[8] So food can be a chip you play, one that permits you to buy others rather than seeing yourself sold.

In this exchange we can see Plato as rationalist (with Socrates as his avatar) rethinking the magic element of sacrificial food rituals. Since the gods are presumed to be vastly superior to humans, how could lowly humans bestow any benefit upon the gods by sharing their food? Here is a theme of conflict, so prevalent in the present, between secular and religious outlooks. Within the religious framework, existence is something we owe to other powers who expect to be recognized for their role in the gift of life. Accordingly, we should be grateful in the presence of food, bringing the gods to our table so that they can take their symbolical share of our good fortune and recognize the humility that we owe toward them. For Homer's heroic demi-gods, there can never be too much of the thanksgiving spirit. And that is very different from Euthyphro's clumsily rendered notion that we sacrifice our food and wine merely to gain the favors of the gods. With clever critical jabs, Socrates ironically deflates Euthyphro's rendition of Homer and Hesiod's wisdom; in so doing, he neglects to consider the existential gratitude that many would want to express ritually in the presence of their food.

Food as Way of Life

Some ancient creators focus acutely on the element of style that expressed the food fashions of an individual or group. One of the best-known plays on this theme is Aesop's "The Town Mouse and the Country Mouse," a moralistic tale from ancient Greece around 600 BCE. In that narrative, the Town Mouse boasts that while Country Mouse "lives like ants," his house is full of "luxury" and "dainties." When Country Mouse comes to sample "bread, barley, beans, dried figs, honey, raisins ... and cheese," he feels charmed until the residents of the house show up. Rejecting such dangerously acquired fare, Country Mouse declares, "I prefer my bare plowlands and roots from the hedgerow, where I can live in safety, and without fear."[9] Here the type of food is intertwined with the perpetual conflict between city slickers and country bumpkins, between luxury-traded-for-danger versus simple tastes prudently accepted as the price of safety.

Of greater fame and historical significance for antiquity is the "Dinner with Trimalchio" chapter in *The Satyricon*, a novelistic Roman tale. William Arrowsmith, a classics scholar who gave the book a rollicking translation, suggests that its author, Petronius, had functioned as "consul and intimate of the emperor Nero,"[10] who ruled from 54–68 CE. Petronius had thus witnessed eating practices in Rome's highest circles during a period of egregious decadence. In the picaresque episodes of the novel, hapless young men experience revelatory moments in Roman life. The most fully developed scenes occur at the banquet of Trimalchio, a freed slave who had speculated his way into fabulous wealth after inheriting his master's estate. The banquet is a vulgar display meant to impress his guests with the food novelties and his own limitless wealth in setting it before them. On one tray, for example, "lay fat capons and sowbellies and a hare tricked out with wings to look like a little Pegasus. At the corners of the tray stood four little gravy boats ... with phalluses for spouts and a spicy hot gravy dripping down over several large fish swimming about in the lagoon of the tray."[11] He offers up a huge boar, apparently unprepared, and then slices it open to disgorge not entrails but tasty sausages and meat puddings. As he performs his culinary stunts Trimalchio constantly proclaims his wealth and his generosity, and insists upon the merits of the startling dishes as well as the unsurpassed quality of his barrels of Falernian wine. The satirizing Petronius tells us that Trimalchio, so intoxicated by his wealth, is merely a clod who aspires to be an imposing snob. His food is a symptom of his rank vulgarity. *The Satyricon* thus gives us one of our first cultural snapshots of food as one-upsmanship — social aggression that targets groups deemed insufficiently sophisticated. These are the non-nutritional values that food yields for assertive personalities and cliques.

Where Will Food Culture Take Us?

Reflecting on food's early appearance as a topic for imaginative response, we can anticipate steady evolution in production techniques and the attribution of extra-nutritional values to food. Some changes will come from objective factors affecting food production (droughts, tsunamis, and so on) while others will derive from inventiveness regarding food's meaning and optimal ways to prepare it. The contributions of this book focus on food as a scene for the economic, social, and expressive values. Features in this territory are convincingly shown to be shaped by science, pseudoscience, cultural norms of beauty or longevity, and new forms of consumer-culture marketing. So, as much as being about the recent past and present, these essays intelligently guide us toward the future.

John Shelton Lawrence is an emeritus professor of psychology at Morningide College in Sioux City, Iowa.

Notes

1. Maureen Gallery Kovacs, trans., *Gilgamesh* (Stanford: Stanford University Press, 1985), 6. Parentheses are the translator's.
2. Ibid., 16.
3. Several translators, such as N. K. Sandars, employ the words *bread* instead of *food* and *wine* instead of *beer*. See her *The Epic of Gilgamesh*, rev. ed. (New York: Penguin, 1964), 67.

There the harlot speaks these words: "Enkidu, eat bread, it is the staff of life; drink wine, it is the custom of the land."

4. *The Holy Bible*, New Revised Standard Version (New York: American Bible Society, 1989), Deuteronomy 14:3.

5. Susan Sherratt, "Feasting in Homeric Epic," *Hesperia* 73 (Spring 2004) 301–337. Available on line http://www.findarticles.com/p/articles/mi_m0SDG/is_2_73/ai_n13493393 (accessed January 15, 2007).

6. Homer, Robert Fagles, trans, *The Iliad* (New York: Penguin, 1990), 295; Book X, ll. 667–70.

7. Apostolos N. Athanassakis, trans. and ed., *Hesiod: Theogony, Works and Days, Shield* (Baltimore: Johns Hopkins University Press, 2004), ll. 336–41, 72.

8. B. Jowett, trans. and ed., *The Works of Plato*, vol. 3, *The Trial and Death of Socrates* (New York: Dial Press, 1936), 85, 84.

9. Aesop, "The Town Mouse and the Country Mouse," in *Fables*. (University of Virginia Electronic Text Center http://etext.virginia.edu/toc/modeng/public/AesFabl.html Accessed January 31, 2007.

10. William Arrowsmith, trans., *The Satyricon of Petronius* (Ann Arbor: University of Michigan Press, 1958), viii.

11. Ibid., 33.

Works Cited

Aesop. "The Town Mouse and the Country Mouse," in *Fables*. Available online at the University of Virginia Electronic Text Center, http://etext.virginia.edu/toc/modeng/public/AesFabl.html. Accessed January 31, 2007.

Arrowsmith, William, trans. *The Satyricon of Petronius*. Ann Arbor: University of Michigan Press, 1958.

Athanassakis, Apostolos N., trans. *Hesiod: Theogony, Works and Days, Shield*. Baltimore: The Johns Hopkins University Press, 2004.

Holy Bible, New Revised Standard Version. New York: American Bible Society, 1989.

Homer. Robert Fagles, trans. *The Iliad*. New York: Penguin, 1990.

Jowett, B., trans. *The Works of Plato*, vol. 3, *The Trial and Death of Socrates*. New York: Dial Press, 1936. Available online at MIT Media Lab http://classics.mit.edu/Plato/euthyfro.html.

Kovacs, Maureen Gallery, trans. *Gilgamesh*. Stanford, CA: Stanford University Press, 1985.

Sherratt, Susan. "Feasting in Homeric Epic." *Hesperia* 73 (Spring 2004): 301–337.

Available online at http://*www.highbeam.com*. Accessed January 10, 2007.

Introduction

Lawrence C. Rubin

Welcome to the Table

Every book has an origin story, anchored in either a long and circuitous intellectual or experiential journey or in a seemingly simple and seminal moment of insight. The latter was the case for this volume. I was channel surfing and happened upon a most curious and seductive display that I later discovered went by the name of Professional Competitive Eating or PCE. It was the 2006 Krystal Square Off III, the third annual Krystal Burger eating competition, cosponsored by the International Federation of Competitive Eaters (IFOCE),[1] broadcast live from Chattanooga, Tennessee. I sat in awe, transfixed as a slender Japanese contender, Takeru Kobayashi, ranked by the IFOCE as *the number one eater in the world,* inhaled 97 of the bite-size burgers in eight minutes. I believed that, in this spectacle many would regard as profane, I was witnessing something if not sacred, then at least profound, or at the very least, worthy of study. While my thinking would only later coalesce into one of the chapters in this volume ("Beyond Bread and Circuses") this event clearly contained elements of organized sport, feast, spectacle and orgy. However, and most compellingly, it was in many ways a powerful and provocative ritual, with all of the power of "creating a complete and condensed, if somewhat artificial world ... a type of microcosmic portrayal of the macrocosm."[2] And it was in this microcosmic universe of potentialities that I believed there to be important and revealing discourse about the larger issues of food, eating and culture.

I trained as a clinical psychologist, and my first impression of professional competitive eating was filtered through psychopathology with a focus on this strange group of so-called professional eaters or "gurgitators," as they are referred to on the circuit. However, my fascination with cultural studies, particularly all things popular, raised the larger question, "Does this spectacle of organized debauchery and sanctioned bulimia reveal something deeper about industrialized culture?" I came to appreciate the possibility that in the United States, and perhaps other industrialized first-world nations, there is a *national eating disorder* as "we seem bent on reinventing the American way of eating every generation in great paroxysms of neophilia and neophobia."[3]

What else could explain the endless plethora of diets and diet books; cook books, cooking shows and networks devoted to food and eating; nutrition and health gurus and governmental guidelines; food movements, both fast and slow, organic revolutions; epidemics of obesity, bulimia and anorexia; media and advertising feeding frenzies, and, of course, the complex legacy of the transition from natural to industrialized food supply, distribution and consumption? Faced with this "dietary cacophony"[4] of information on what, how, when, where and why to eat, it is no small wonder that Americans are confused about how to feed themselves, so much so that "instead of relying on the accumulated wisdom of cuisine or even the wisdom of our senses, we rely on expert opinion, advertising, government food pyramids and diet books and we place faith in science to sort out for us what culture once did with rather more success."[5]

In a previous volume,[6] I offered the notion of *psychotropia,* the chemically-gated community, or wall-less asylum[7] around societies created by the media and pharmaceutical industries in order to satisfy the consensual need for emotional well-being (and to garner vast profits). Just as the proliferation of psychotropic drugs through marketing and advertising — what I refer to as the psychotropic cacophony — has made it difficult for consumers to regulate themselves emotionally, the dietary cacophony deadens our inherent capacity to regulate our physical well-being in the most fundamental of ways — through eating. The legacy of both the psychotropic and dietary cacophonies can be found in all aspects of the national eating disorder. The laboratory replaces the hearth, the individual becomes a consumer, fads and trends promising well-being in a pill or diet proliferate, food and eating are commodified, media dictates appetite, gender and class become targeted rather than served, and special interest groups assert their political agenda up and down the food chain.

Beyond the provocative nature of professional competitive eating and the compelling notions of psychotropic and dietary cacophony and a national eating disorder, I would like to now go back to a discourse on food and eating as we prepare to feast on the chapters ahead. In preparing this feast for you, no grand attempt has been made to define or categorize foods and eating practices, nor has effort been directed towards validating or refuting any particular theory that has come before. While I maybe guilty of taking a more developmental than structural[8] perspective in choosing the chapters to follow,

I value each in that they offer unique perspectives on food and eating practices, both contemporary and historic, literal and symbolic, as well as local and global. Regardless of the theoretical underpinning of any of these chapters, it is clear that, since eating is the most fundamental of all human activities[9] and expenditures on food typically constitute the largest single category in the world at large,[10] the study of food and eating is, in essence, a study of ourselves. Almost every academic discipline has had something to say about it, and it has therefore been my hope to present a number of critical thinkers who have focused their attention on the challenging issues related to food, eating and culture-past, present and future.

* * *

Part I, "From Pre-Modernity to the Hypermodern Age," offers insights into food and eating practices that stretch from the Industrial Revolution to the rapidly unfolding era called the Hypermodern Age. In Chapter 1, "Man, Machine and Refined Dining in Victorian America," Hillary Murtha laments that, for all their futility of design, mechanical Victorian dining objects expressed a utopian yearning for mechanized modernity. She then observes that as the nineteenth century drew to a close the modernity that they heralded killed them by degrees. In Chapter 2, "Shopping for What Never Was: The Rhetoric of Food, Social Style and Nostalgia," Carlnita Greene argues that a key way we construct our identities today is through the rhetoric of social styles or the use of commodities, language, performances, and aesthetics to communicate who we are, who we want to become, and how we want to be perceived by others. She analyzes how the text Martha Stewart, as a multimedia brand, functions rhetorically in this manner to create a social style steeped in nostalgia that harkens back to a mythic past. In Chapter 3, "All You Can Eat: Sociological Reflections on Food in the Hypermodern Era," Simon Gottschalk combines sociological insights about the discourse of excess with those about McDonaldization and hypermodernism to articulate opposing trends that drive the current moment and shape the social psychological dispositions that characterize it. He then turns his attention to alternative ways of approaching food and the social relations surrounding the practice of eating.

Part II, "Eat Locally, Think Globally," explores several contemporary phenomena affecting not only the local but the global marketplace. In Chapter 4, "Raising the Bar: The Complicated Consumption of Chocolate," Ellen E. Moore examines chocolate as a form of unequal exchange that takes place between producers in "developing" nations and "first-world" consumers through an analysis of the way in which chocolate companies represent themselves and their products. In so doing, she deals with the politics of representation, demonstrating how media analysis of a single cultural object can shed light on the cultural and economic significance of the disconnect between production and consumption. In Chapter 5, "The Espresso Revolution: Introducing Coffee-Bar Franchising to Modern China," Jackie Cook and Robert Lee outline field research undertaken in China as a partnership of venture capitalists investigate the potential for coffee-bar franchising in the more remote mainland Chinese provinces such as Sichuan, where teahouse tradition is still very much intact. They address the new positioning of today's "global" coffee bars within the "creative industries" redesign of postdigital "information hub" cities, the so-called "*incubator effect.*" In Chapter 6, "Mass Agrarianism: Wal-Mart and Organic Foods," Dawn Gilpin analyzes Wal-Mart's entry in the organic food market, and by using textual and discursive analysis focusing on reports from a variety of media sources, explores the social and cultural tensions reflected in competing definitions and perceptions of what organic foods are and what they represent.

Part III, "Hungering for Entertainment," explores several unique representations of food and eating practices in the media. In Chapter 7, "'Everybody Eats': The Food Network and Symbolic Capital," Megan Mullen draws form the work of sociologist Pierre Bourdieu, television historian Todd Gitlin, and cultural historians Barbara Ehrenreich and Loren Baritz (among others) to build a theoretical framework within which television's mediation of social class can be examined. She derives evidence from three primary sources: an interview with Food Network founder Reese Schonfeld, the network's interactive Web site, and the network's schedule and programs. In Chapter 8, "Semiotic Sound Bites: Toward an Alimentary Analysis of Popular Song," Christopher Westgate explores popular song from the repertoires of Dean Martin, Patti Smith and others in an analysis of how food produces sound and how sound produces food. In Chapter 9, "Hunger and Satiety in Latin American Literature," Santiago Daydi-Tolson argues that starting with the writings of Christopher Columbus, Latin American letters has shown continuous interest in the subject of hunger and food. He then addresses Pablo Neruda's poetic treatment of food and how it has brought together the basic elements that characterize the Latin American fascination with food and hunger.

Part IV, "We Are Where We Eat," looks at the oftentimes complex relation between food, eating and place. In Chapter 10, "Reengineering 'Authenticity': Tourism Encounters with Cuisine in Rural Great Britain," Craig Wight argues that within a culture where food and cuisine are enigmatic, tourism destination marketing is often based upon constructed "culinary tourism." He does this by addressing how the increasingly global competitive tourism environment exploits the tacit, undersold regional culinary strengths within the UK. In Chapter 11, "Passing Time: The Ironies of Food in Prison Culture,"

Jim Thomas explores the meaning of food within the prison culture as a symbolic and tangible element of the prison life by drawing from phenomenological and interactionist perspectives to demonstrate how food becomes integrated into the time consciousness of incarceration as a form of cultural capital. In Chapter 12, "Selfish Consumers: Delmonico's Restaurant and Learning to Satisfy Personal Desire," Heather Lee focuses on the early history of Delmonico's, purportedly New York's first restaurant, to explore the rituals and meanings of dining out and how they sustained a strain of sociability that contributed to the formation of urban identity. In Chapter 13, "Is It Really Better to Travel Than to Arrive? Airline Food as a Reflection of Consumer Anxiety," Guillaume de Syon proposes that food, as a central feature of both entertainment and community became neither when associated with air travel, thus reflecting consumer anxiety about an air age reminiscent of "bowling alone." In so doing, he suggests that fine dining, like that found aboard ocean liners, created an illusory experience that failed to last.

Part V, "Come Join Us," explores select issues of race and culture in food and eating practices. In Chapter 14, "Deconstructing the Myth of the Dysfunctional Black Family in the Film *Soul Food*," Tina M. Harris uses a popular culture approach to deconstruct the stereotypical belief that the Black family is a dysfunctional interpersonal system destined for eternal failure through the narrative text illustrated in the dinner ritual in the movie *Soul Food*. In Chapter 15, "Cultural Representation of Taste in Ang Lee's *Eat, Drink, Man, Woman*," Ming-Yeh T. Rawnsley uses Ang Lee's comedy film, which shows various characters preparing meals for different people for a variety of reasons, to argue that many of the relationships portrayed in the film are actually manifested by food and drink. This, she indicates, is consistent with the perception that the Chinese are a food-oriented people.

Part VI, "Eat, Drink and Be Public," focuses on the significance of eating in public places. In Chapter 16, "Snacking as Ritual: Eating Behavior in Public Places," Phillip Vannini draws upon symbolic interaction and dramaturgy theories to examine the ritualistic aspects and the broader cultural significance of snacking in public places — from popcorn in movie theaters to cotton candy at county fairs. He believes that such practices bespeak social relations based on deep-rooted habits of behavior and tradition. In Chapter 17, "Beyond Bread and Circuses: Professional Competitive Eating," I link this newest craze to its historical precedents in feasting and ritual to examine the role it plays for the contestant, the spectator and the culture.

Part VII, "Self-Reflection in a Fun-House Mirror," explores the relationship between food, eating and identity, with an emphasis on gender. In Chapter 18, "'Gourmandizing,' Gluttony and Oral Fixations: Perspectives on Overeating in the *American Journal of Psychiatry*, 1844 to the Present," Dr.

Mallay Occhiogrosso examines the treatment of overeating and people who are overweight in one of the dominant journals of academic psychiatry to reveal a progression that mirrors that of the general scientific community. She highlights the extent to which even a seemingly objective scientific culture is highly embedded in and interdependent on its greater societal context. In Chapter 19, "Having It His Way: The Construction of Masculinity in Fast-Food TV Advertising," Carrie Packwood Freeman and Debra Merskin look at the gendering of meat through an interpretive textual analysis of American fast-food advertising, particularly the hypermasculinized 2005–2006 Carl's Jr. and Burger King campaigns. Their findings reveal two major themes of meat's role in providing (1) freedom from constraint and (2) loyalty to a heterosexual male group identity (often by disempowering women), both of which have significant consequences for men's health and social relations between men, women, and other animals.

Notes

1. See http://www.ifoce.com.
2. Catherine Bell, *Ritual: Perspectives and Dimensions* (Oxford: Oxford University Press, 1997), 160.
3. Michael Pollan, *The Omnivore's Dilemma* (New York: Penguin, 2006), 299. Pollan's notion of a national eating disorder is offered to explain why Americans have been so vulnerable to food fads and diets.
4. Harvey Levenstein uses the term *dietary cacophony* to describe the loud and clashing sources of information about food, eating and nutrition from a number of sources, both industrial and governmental, during the 20th century. The term is attributed to Claude Fischler, in his *L'Homnivore* (Paris: Odile Jacob, 1990), 194.
5. Pollan, 303.
6. Lawrence Rubin, *Psychotropic Drugs and Popular Culture: Essays on Medicine, Mental Health and the Media* (Jefferson, NC: McFarland, 2006).
7. See Erving Goffman, *Asylums: Essays on the Social Situation of Mental Patients and Other Inmates* (New York: Anchor, 1961).
8. Roy Wood attempts to categorize theories of food and eating into structural (food and eating, rooted in the present as symbol and signifier) and developmental (the evolution of food and eating practices).
9. Sidney Mintz and Christine DuBois, "The Anthropology of Food and Eating," *Annual Review of Anthropology* 31 (2002): 102.
10. Paul Rozin, "Toward a Psychology of Food and Eating: From Motivation to Module to Model to Marker, Morality, Meaning and Metaphor," *Current Directions in Psychological Science* 5 (1996): 19.

Works Cited

Bell, Catherine. *Ritual: Perspectives and Dimensions*. Oxford: Oxford University Press, 1997.
Fischler, Claude. *L'Homnivore*. Paris: Odile Jacob, 1990.
Goffman, Erving. *Asylums: Essays on the Social Situation of Mental Patients and Other Inmates*. New York: Anchor, 1961.

Levenstein, Harve. *The Paradox of Plenty: A Social History of Eating in Modern America.* Berkeley: University of California Press, 2003.

Mintz, Sidney, and Christine DuBois. "The Anthropology of Food and Eating." *Annual Review of Anthropology* 31 (2002): 99–119.

Pollan, Michael. *The Omnivore's Dilemma.* New York: Penguin, 2006.

Rozin, Paul. "Toward a Psychology of Food and Eating: From Motivation to Module to Model to Marker, Morality, Meaning and Metaphor." *Current Directions in Psychological Science* 5 (February 1996): 1–7.

Rubin, Lawrence C. *Psychotropic Drugs and Popular Culture: Essays on Medicine, Mental Health and the Media.* Jefferson, NC: McFarland, 2006.

Wood, Roy. *The Sociology of the Meal.* Edinburgh: Edinburgh University Press, 2005.

1

Man, Machine and Refined Dining in Victorian America

HILLARY MURTHA

Celebrating the Machine

To the eyes of English visitor Anthony Trollope, mid-nineteenth-century America presented a spectacle of technological virtuosity. "The great glory of the Americans is in their wondrous contrivances;— their patent remedies for the usually troublous operations of life ... soda-water bottles open themselves without any trouble of wire or strings. Men and women go up and down stairs without any motive power of their own.... Everything is done by a new and wonderful patent contrivance," he wrote in his travel account *North America*.[1] Many Americans would have smugly agreed, pointing to their triumphant display of machinery at the 1852 New York Crystal Palace Exhibition (a forerunner to the world's fairs of the twentieth century), to the railroads already crisscrossing the nation, and at the factory smokestacks rising along the nation's waterways. Our once technologically backward country was booming with improvements in the industrial arts. In 1850, the United States Patent Office granted only 986 patents, but ten years later there was a more than fourfold increase in the number of patents granted, totaling 4,588, and by 1867 that number had quadrupled again to 21,276.[2] Americans wholeheartedly embraced the conceit of being a technologically gifted people, and described their new mechanical creations with terms of delirious lyricism: their engines were sublime, poetical inventions, "triumphing over time and space, outstripping the winds in speed, [and] annihilating every obstacle."[3]

Industrial production brought many new objects into the genteel middle-class home, but few that alleviated the burdens of housekeeping. For, while America gloried in its busy beehive of productive labor, the work of maintaining the domestic household was swept out of sight. Ostensibly leisured, the ideal lady-wife made her home a tranquil and uplifting refuge for her husband and children, concealing and deprecating her housewifely labors. For those visitors privileged to penetrate the private sphere, it was instead the refinement of the home's familial inhabitants that took center-stage.

No domestic setting was more revelatory of individual gentility than the formal dining room. As the author of one 1883 etiquette manual declared, it was the arena in which social misfits were betrayed into "instant detection." Another writer concurred: "Nothing indicates a well-bred man more than a proper mode of eating his dinner. A man may pass muster by *dressing well*, and may sustain himself tolerably in conversation; but if he be not perfectly 'au fait' *dinner* will betray him."[4] For in a time of greatly increased geographic and social mobility, elaborate new rules of dining etiquette helped draw the line between "true" members of the gentry class and social upstarts.

But on the middle-class dining table, technology and gentility met and comingled, not only in the display of factory-produced, mass-manufactured silver-plate, ceramics and damask cloth but also in the presence of mechanical dining objects. Why *mechanized* dining objects? There were many reasons. Mechanical dining objects stood as emblems of much that nineteenth-century Americans admired and desired. They stood as metaphors for progress and modernity, small domestic evidences of human mastery over nature through the machine — the machine technology they found so new and so wonderful.

At the same time, on the dining table, mechanized objects served as concrete reminders of the genteel ideal of a machinelike control over the animal appetites, and further distanced users from the act of eating. It was during the Victorian era that table manners first became markedly self-conscious; it was then that forks and spoons first became the essential, the *only* proper implements for conveying food to the mouth.[5] Food was not to be spoken of at the table, even in praise; and indeed, all references to the act of eating itself were tabooed. As a writer for *Harper's New Monthly Magazine* observed of well-bred diners, although "taking sustenance proves them akin to the beasts of the field, the beautiful manner in which it is performed appears almost to exalt them above mankind."[6] Anyone wishing to be part of polite society needed to display equally impeccable manners.

The stagy mechanics of mechanized objects also disguised and compensated for inadequate domestic service. Ideally, a genteel couple kept a sufficient number of servants to give the lady of the house a life of leisure, but this ideal was rarely, if ever attained. Well-trained waiters rendered their services as impersonally and unobtrusively as possible, and mechanical dining objects made symbolic substitution for the ideal servant as silently assistive presences.[7]

The foods so dramatically presented by mechanical hollowares were at least small luxuries to their middle-class consumers: butter, tea and coffee were expensive, no matter how commonly consumed.[8] The costly condiments in the "castor" (cruet) set, the pure iced water in the tilting pitcher, all these were foods to be exhibited pridefully, spectacularly. And as part of the greater display of glittering silver-plated and ceramic wares on the table, mechanical dining objects numbered among the hosts' emblems of social status.

A Glittering Centerpiece

The castor set, so-called because users cast its contents forth from it, was one of the first essentials to the well-set table at mid-century. These were metal frames for sets of bottles holding salt, pepper, mustard, vinegar, soy sauce and other condiments; occasionally one also sees them referred to as cruet frames. When these objects first appeared in eighteenth-century America, the condiments they contained were far too costly for regular consumption by middle-class consumers, but that had changed by the mid-nineteenth century, and fancy castors of patented designs had become both widely available and very popular.[9] The most common form of mechanized castor revolved (Figure 1). The mechanism was of the simplest kind possible: the circular carousel holding the castor bottles had a hole in the center. Resting upon a flange, this carousel fitted loosely over the metal shaft that ran vertically up the length of the castor frame, to form a handle at the top. The carousel turned like a merry-go-round, allowing diners easy access to all the bottles.

Or did it? Writing in 1841, Catharine Beecher advised hostesses to "set the castors in the exact center of the table. Some prefer to have them on

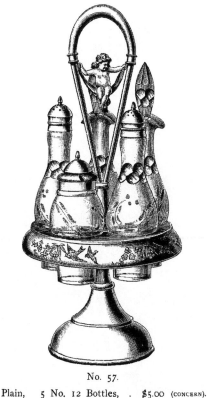

No. 57.

Plain,   5 No. 12 Bottles,   . $5.00 (concern).
Chased, 5 No. 12 Bottles,   .   5.50 (concert).

Figure 1. Revolving castor with bottles (1886–87 catalog, Meriden Britannia Company).

a side-table, and handed around by waiters, but the table looks better to have them set at the center." Her accompanying illustration of a well-set table, however, typically reveals that no guest could have reached the castor without reaching over platters or around other diners, an unpardonable rudeness. "If they [castors] are put on the sideboard," continued Beecher, "the celery stand may be placed in the center of the table instead."[10] It was the gorgeous symmetry of having a round, revolving object in the exact center of the table that apparently appealed to Beecher, and presumably to others as well, for other illustrations are similar. Indeed, one very ingeniously designed mechanical castor, produced by the Meriden Britannia Company in 1861, attracted so few buyers that it was only offered for one year.[11] The bottles were placed in a circular wire frame that revolved vertically like a wheel instead of horizontally;

three decades later engineer George Ferris would design an amusement ride for visitors to the Chicago World's Fair based on the same mechanical principles. Although this vertically revolving castor saved much-needed table space, its asymmetrical shape clearly failed to make the same favorable aesthetic impression as the popular and common horizontally revolving castors.

In 1856 inventor and manufacturer Edward Gleason introduced an especially elaborate mechanical castor. Not only did the whole frame revolve horizontally, but the bottles were contained in a tabernaclelike enclosure, with doors that flipped open at the touch of a button (Figure 2). Gleason appropriated the idea from the English firm of Mappin and Webb, who had earlier begun manufacturing boiled egg cruet frames that featured the same mechanism.[12] While the egg cruet made sense — the English liked their boiled eggs served warm, and the enclosure

Figure 2. Edward Gleason's magic castor, ca. 1860.

retained heat — the purpose of Gleason's "magic" castor was theatricality pure and simple; this was a mechanized miniature stage that suggested that its users had reached a higher social plane; a microcosmic version of the dining ritual.

So long as condiments remained among the costliest foods on the dining table, the castor reigned in solitary and inaccessible splendor at the table's center. Over time, it even evolved from a low object, close to the table's surface, to a tall object raised high on a pedestal. But by the third quarter of the century, it was being slowly deposed from its place of honor by the fruit stand, as improved methods of refrigeration and shipping made tropical fruits available to the middle-class diner. By the mid–1880s, pineapples were selling for 25¢; silver-plate companies had cut back on their array of castors, and arbiters of popular taste, such as "Mlle. Bon Ton," writing for *Godey's Ladies' Book*, declared that "castors are going out of date."[13]

The Best Butter

Writing in 1841, Catharine Beecher advised inexperienced hostesses to set the dining table with butter "cooled in cold water if not already hard, and then cut into a smooth regular form."[14] Since butter, like the condiments in the castor set, was costly, and moreover extremely perishable, American inventors looked to create serving dishes that would also serve to preserve it. A little over a decade after Beecher wrote her household manual, a double-walled, ice-chilled metal butter dish began supplanting the simple ceramic and glass butter plates she had been accustomed to.[15] The germ of this invention lay in the double-walled ice cellars built for homes at the beginning of the century, which had in turn been inspired by the construction of ships that transported ice to the tropics.[16] The insulated butter dishes, however, posed a new problem for the mannerly user: where to put the cover when taking butter. Beads of condensed water formed on the rim of the cover, which, if placed on a white damask tablecloth, left a water mark.

Already by 1856, one ingenious inventor, James Stimpson (son of the inventor of the double-walled butter cooler), solved the problem by creating a mechanized butter dish with a base that swiveled out from a stationary high-domed frame when two little doors were opened.[17] The dish remained a cumbersome device. Following the rationale that cold air falls, the ice was contained in the high-domed lid, and as it melted it dripped onto the butter nestled below.

In the 1860s, a more popular solution was offered with the "revolving butter dish."[18] The hemispherical lid of the revolving butter dishes pivoted on two pins at the sides, and slid under the smaller hemisphere of the base

(Figure 3). The ice in revolving butter dishes was held in the base, not the lid, leaving the butter unadulterated. Another popular mechanized butter dish had a lid, which, instead of sliding under the base, slid up the U-shaped handle, to be caught and held from a clasp at the handle's apex. There were other variations: E. G. Webster and Brother Company of Brooklyn sold a butter dish in which the cover was attached to a handle that acted as a lever: the lid was pulled up when the handle was pushed down. They pictured the dish in their 1883 catalog next to a jewel casket that operated the same way, making the comparison between these two prestigious containers visually explicit.

No. 4970. REVOLVING.
With Patent Crystal Drainer.
Chased,   .   .   . $8.50 (ENACT).

Figure 3. Revolving butter dish (1886–87 catalog, Meriden Britannia Company).

Chariots of Mustard

Other minor luxury food items were likewise being housed in objects that spun, snapped open and closed, and raised and lowered themselves. While most served some practical function, there was one very popular but purely ornamental form of mechanization: the wheeled dish. Novelty items of this sort included sardine boxes, preserve dishes, individual salts, napkin rings and mustard pots. They had either two or four wheels, and were cast to appear as wagons or chariots sometimes fancifully drawn by cupids, peacocks, and other creatures. These are such playful objects that it is hard to imagine them in use at a stately formal dinner. Were they pushed across the table to the various diners? For the wheels are usually quite functional.

An equally whimsical object is tantalizingly glimpsed through an 1885 article in *Godey's Lady's Magazine*: "Dishes with concealed music are a novelty. A handsome tureen of beaten silver plays several ravishing airs the moment the cover is removed."[19] As these objects do not appear on the antiques market today, it seems likely that the music-box mechanisms presumably concealed in their lids were removed after the novelty palled.

But by the 1880s, service *à la Russe* had replaced the earlier "old English" style of serving a dinner in fashionable circles: the hosts no longer served their guests from dishes placed upon the table; instead all dishes were placed on the sideboard and served up by waiters in a well-defined series of courses.[20] It seems impossible that so dramatic an object as a singing soup tureen would have languished on the sideboard, to have its tuneful lid lifted out of the sight of guests: it was an object that presumed a scarcity of servants, a less fashionable mode of dining. Indeed, soup tureens were themselves becoming outmoded in the 1880s; by the 1890s they were completely passé since it was considered more elegant to have soup plates filled in the kitchen, out of the sight of guests, and then brought to the table by waiters.[21] For the consumers of these items, members of the lower middle-class, unable to scale the heady heights of fashion, the dining experience may have had a more playful aspect, with a carnival of a table covered with figural napkin rings, a revolving castor, or a musical tureen, and chariots of mustard traversing the stage.

Afternoon Tea

The formal tea was nearly as important a ritual as the formal dinner, and, like dinners, tea parties flourished in Victorian America as socially exclusionary performances.[22] In all levels of society, the hostess, never a servant, poured tea for guests, and so the luxurious appearance of the tea service was of great importance. Despite the fact that tea brewed in ceramic pots tasted better, silver and silver-electroplated pots predominated over ceramics, making a richer display.

The etiquette governing tea drinking was nearly as rigid as that governing dining. "Tea and coffee must be drunk noiselessly, not sucked, from the side of the cup, leaving the spoon in the saucer, and the cup held by the handle," advised etiquette manual author Marion Harland in 1883.[23] The woman who slurped or drank tea from the saucer was clearly no lady.

Many elaborate and remarkable designs for tea dispensers had already evolved in Europe, from the eighteenth through the early part of the nineteenth century. Tea (as well as coffee) urns were the most widespread mechanical objects among these innovations, and they emigrated to the tables of wealthy Americans by the late eighteenth century.[24] Another widespread object of eighteenth-century origin was a tea kettle that rested on a stand over a small heating lamp. Victorians took the design one step further, creating the "swing kettle," which was suspended over the stand by two lugs that fitted into slots on the stand (Figure 4). With this design, tea could be poured as the kettle was swung forward, without its being lifted from its stand, reinforcing the hostess' image as a lady of extreme leisure.

English users often enjoyed swing kettles at gentlemen's suppers, where they were used to serve hot toddy, and no doubt steadied the hand of the host. But most respectable middle-class Americans took temperance seriously,

Figure 4. Tea set with swing kettle (1886–87 catalog, Meriden Britannia Company).

frowning gravely upon alcohol consumption.[25] Indeed, in William Dean Howell's 1885 novel *The Rise of Silas Lapham*, his fictional parvenu is such a complete teetotaler that he lucklessly disgraces himself by getting drunk at the home of the old-moneyed Corey family, never before having been at a dinner where wine was served.[26] The swing *tea* kettle was therefore more popular in America, and in American silverware catalogues, the swing kettle almost invariably appeared as part of a tea set, rather than as an individual item.

The self-pouring "pump kettle" was a more unusual object than the swing kettle; Paine Diehl and Company of Philadelphia held the patent for it and marketed it exclusively.[27] As the hostess depressed the knob on the lid of the kettle, water was pumped through the tea leaves at the base and forced up the S-shaped handle to flow into the waiting cup. As their advertisements boasted, this meant the hostess suffered from "no burnt hands lifting pot, aching arms [or] soiled clothes." She could relax and show herself a lady of perfect grace and poise.[28]

Pure, Healthy Water

The tilting ice water pitcher is an object related to, and perhaps inspired by the swing kettle; as with the swing kettle, the ice water pitcher was suspended from its frame so that the user did not have to lift it. Here, the mechanization served some practical function: the ice water pitcher, when either double-walled or lined with insulating porcelain and filled with water, could weigh anywhere from ten to twenty-five pounds.[29] Nonetheless, silverware catalogues of the period offered as many ordinary ice water pitchers as tilting models, suggesting that the elaboration of the object was as much a matter of heightened presentation as of necessity.

As with the swing tea kettle, the insulated ice water pitcher owed much of its popularity to the American temperance movement.[30] Even before temperance gained ground, middle-class Americans rarely consumed alcohol at formal dinners; as English visitor Frances Trollope noticed in 1830: "Almost everyone drinks water at the table ... the hard drinking, so universally acknowledged, does not take place at jovial dinners."[31] But within a few years of her time of writing, hard-drinking anywhere had become a matter for shame, and by mid-century water had been transformed into what W. J. Rorabaugh calls a "cult beverage," earning it a place of honor in the dining room and a sumptuous container to match its standing.[32]

Insulated ice water pitchers first became popular in American households in the 1850s. The drawback was the vessels' considerable weight, a problem solved in 1869 by professional inventor John Gibson, when he patented the first design for the *tilting* ice water pitcher.[33] Unlike the swing kettle, the tilting ice water pitcher was primarily, if not entirely, an American phenomenon, and one that caught on quickly. In 1873 Meriden Britannia Company offered one tilting pitcher; in 1877, eleven, and by 1886, twenty-three, the most expensive of which featured gold inlay and cost $150. On the other side of the Atlantic, a circa 1882 catalog by the English firm of Elkington Company shows only one pitcher at all, an "iced water pitcher or champagne pitcher, double walls," which is nontilting, and plain in appearance. Similarly, a circa 1883 trade catalog put out by Silber and Fleming of London and Paris advertises only one nontilting pitcher among their wares.[34] Meanwhile, in America, tilting water pitchers grew larger, and their ornamentation ever more frenzied, eclectic and ornate, in a celebration of at least one form of excess (Figure 5).

Tilting pitchers were kept on the sideboard in the dining room, or sometimes on their own table, so that between mealtimes family members and guests could refresh themselves as they wished.[35] There they made an impressive display; they are large objects — about a foot and a half tall — and their mechanization heightens their imposing quality. This stateliness subtly compensated for a common middle-class difficulty: inadequate domestic help. Few middle-class Americans could afford to keep all the servants necessary to support their roles as gentlefolk leading a life of leisure.[36] The tilting pitcher on the sideboard at all times eliminated the need for a servant ready at all times to attend to people entering and leaving the dining room: while a human servant did not pour the water, the user was nonetheless aided by the mechanism.

Figure 5. Elaborately ornamented tilting pitcher (1886–87 catalog, Meriden Britannia Company).

At Beck and Call

Where servants were available, their presence and the distinction between them and their employing family were underscored by the popular call bell. Small handbells used to summon servants had, of course, existed for centuries, but the Victorians superfluously refined the simple trumpet-shaped cup and clapper into a mechanism that operated at the touch of a button. The simple act of ringing a call bell made class hierarchies instantly apparent, and the call bell was an essential item on any dining table. The silver chime of the call bell, like the resounding cathedral bell of old, summoned the humble servant to attendance upon the solemn ceremony of consumption. Combining two or more objects into one was a favorite pastime of Victorian innovators, and the call bell often appeared above a castor, inside a slop bowl, or atop a spoon holder.[37]

The 1858 patent drawing of the first touch-button (or "pressure") bell shows its fairly complex mechanism. The button compressed a spring, pushing the clapper down, and it struck the bell frame as it rebounded upwards. It is similar to the bells that had appeared in clocks for at least a century, but now the human finger, rather than clockworks, triggered the bell's ring. The equally popular revolving call bell, a later innovation, was patented by William H. Nichols of East Hampton, Connecticut. The revolving call bell was a hollow sphere that rotated on a stand, like a miniature globe of the world, while a loosely hinged clapper within struck the frame as the bell was twirled (Figure 6).[38] These mechanical dining objects underscored the power relations at the table: at the touch of a button or by spinning a globe, a servant would silently appear. Silently: for at a formal dinner, speech was only allowed amongst the diners; the hostess would, according to the writers of etiquette manuals "direct the waiters by a look" and "through the meal never speak to

CALL BELLS.

(Half Size, Excepting Nos. 31, 33, 34, 36, 38, 39, and 40, One-Third Size.)

(PRICES PER DOZEN.)

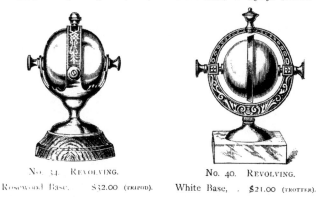

No. 36. Revolving,
Plated Base, . $32.00 (trent).

No. 33. Revolving.
White Base, . $31.50 (triplet).

No. 34. Revolving.
Rosewood Base. $32.00 (tripod).

No. 40. Revolving.
White Base, . $21.00 (trotter).

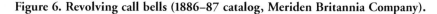

Figure 6. Revolving call bells (1886–87 catalog, Meriden Britannia Company).

servants." The authors of these precepts declared the arts they imparted to be "the machinery of society" that "keeps every cog and wheel in place."[39]

The metaphor of machinery came to permeate nineteenth-century American discourse. Susan Williams asserts that "a popular faith in scientific rationalism" was "one of the most pervasive aspects of American culture. The same scientific principals that had built the foundations of the American factory system during the first half of the century were ... applied to domestic activities during the second fifty years."[40] But in fact, as with the largely afunctional mechanics of dining objects, which indeed betrayed a deep desire to technologize the household, in reality neither machine technology nor scientific management greatly affected the workings of the nineteenth-century home. While an 1852 article in the *New York Times* joyously anticipated the future invention of machines that would perform "nearly all the domestic drudgery now done by hand" in the home, and an 1879 science-fiction story in *Godey's Lady's Book* even envisioned robots that would work as domestic servants at some point in the remote future, few labor-saving machines actually made their way into the home until the twentieth century.[41]

Mechanical dining objects were, at most, minimally utilitarian and labor-saving; their function was tied to elaboration and ceremony, not to efficiency. Yet, for all their futility of design, surely they, too, by their presence on the dining table invoked the utopian dream of mechanized modernity. The nineteenth century was a technological whirlwind, an era that witnessed the arrival of the railroad, had seen it connect the East and the West coasts, had seen the invention of photography, the telegraph and the telephone, indoor plumbing and the home sewing machine, the department store and the skyscraper, among a few thousand other innovations.

Modern Modes

In the end, the modernity that mechanical dining objects heralded killed them by degrees. The foods they exalted, once minor luxuries, became less expensive and more readily available. Owing to mass-production and transportation, by the 1870s the spices and condiments in the castor set had already become commonplace. Inexpensive and readily available good quality butter would soon follow. In 1869 Catharine Beecher and her sister Harriet, writing in *The American Woman's Home* declared, "Americans must have the credit of manufacturing and putting into market more bad butter than all the rest of the world combined."[42] They were referring to the extremely variable hand-churned butter laboriously produced at home by farm wives. The butter that came out of wooden churns sometimes carried unpleasant off-flavors: cheesy, rancid, or even moldy tastes. But by the 1890s, cheaper factory-made butter of uniformly good quality was outselling the homemade competition.[43] The intricate revolving butter dishes of the Victorian era made way for modern butter dishes, simple covered plates to fit over the new bar shape that factory butter was produced in.

New refrigeration methods made the preservation and shipping of all foods easier. By the 1890s numerous refrigerating machines were in commercial use among breweries, meat packers and other food-producing companies.[44] The tilting ice water pitcher lingered into the first decades of the twentieth century, then vanished altogether as refrigerators began to be marketed for household use. And although few householders could afford these refrigerating machines in the nineteen-teens and -twenties, icemen hawked inexpensive manufactured ice through the streets of large cities for use in the old wooden icebox.[45]

New ideas about design also led to the end of mechanized dining objects, along with many other wares on the dining table. The great glory of mechanical dining objects had been their intricacy, their embellishment of the art of living. Victorians viewed elaborate forms and lavish ornamentation as signs of rising fortunes, and delighted in expressing the excesses of their times with their numerous and ornate dining wares. But by the end of the century, design reform was leading to the production of plainer, sleeker objects. Spaciousness and clean design triumphed over opulence. The great de-elaboration of life was beginning, as many heaved a secret sigh of relief at the riddance of clutter and ceremony.

For manners, too, were changing, loosening. In Victorian America, women had been enshrined as the keepers of morality and gentility, the guardians of the home, but the "New Woman" declined the office, declaring herself man's equal, not his conscience. Members of the upper middle-class strove less strenuously to emulate the lifestyles of the truly wealthy, while the younger generation delighted in unceremonious language and behavior. Traditionalists mourned the disintegration of society, lamenting, "Day by day the art of living withers and fades, leaving us to face existence unadorned, in all its nakedness."[46] But by 1929, even such diehards as Emily Post admitted that "no rule of etiquette is of less importance than which fork we use."[47]

By then, revolving castors, tilting water pitchers, swing kettles — all were gone. Only the push-button bell remains in use, although now it summons clerical staff to service desks, not servants to the table. Modern materials, plastics and stainless steel have largely supplanted silver-electroplate as popular mediums; the surface mimicry of a precious metal is no longer all-important. With the passing of the Victorian era, with its passion for the elaborate, its labyrinthine social pathways, and its awe at the then newly unleashed power of technology, mechanical dining objects have fallen by the wayside.

Notes

1. Anthony Trollope, North America (1862; rpt. New York: Alfred A. Knopf, 1951), 120.

2. Brooke Hindle and Steven Lubar, *Engines of Change: The American Industrial Revolution, 1790–1900* (Washington, D.C. and London: Smithsonian Press, 1986), 79; William Ray and Marlys Ray, *The Art of Invention: Patent Models and Their Makers* (Princeton, NJ: Pyne Press, 1971), 8.

3. Leo Marx, *The Machine in the Garden: Technology and the Pastoral Ideal in America* (London, Oxford and New York: Oxford University Press, 1964), 199.

4. Quoted in John Kasson, *Rudeness and Civility: Manners in Nineteenth-Century America* (New York: Hill and Wang, 1990), 60, 200; Charles William Day, *Etiquette; or a Guide to the Usages of Society with a Glance at Bad Habits* (New York: Wilson and Company, 1843), 18.

5. Kasson, *Rudeness and Civility*, 193.

6. Ibid., 207; "Silver and Silver Plate," *Harper's New Monthly Magazine* (September 1869), 434.

7. Susan Williams, *Savory Suppers and Fashionable Feasts: Dining in Victorian America* (New York: Pantheon Books; Rochester, NY: Margaret Woodbury Strong Museum, 1985), 47.

8. Ibid., 120, 126, 139.

9. Dorothy T. Rainwater and Ivan H. Rainwater, *American Silverplate* (Nashville: T. Nelson, 1972), 171.

10. Catharine Beecher, *Domestic Receipt Book: Designed as a Supplement to Her Treatise on Domestic Economy* (1841; rpt. New York: Harper and Brothers, 1846), 236.

11. Rainwater and Rainwater, 172.

12. Ibid., 171.

13. W. J. Rorabaugh, "Beer, Lemonade and Propriety in the Gilded Age," in *Dining in America, 1850–1900*, ed. Kathryn Grover, et al. (Amherst: University of Massachusetts Press; Rochester, NY: Margaret Woodbury Strong Museum, 1987), 35; Mlle Bon Ton, "Hints for the Hostess," *Godey's Lady's Book and Magazine* (March 1885), 349.

14. Beecher, 236.

15. Rainwater and Rainwater, 241.

16. Siegfried Giedion, *Mechanization Takes Command: A Contribution to Anonymous History* (New York: Oxford University Press, 1970), 597.

17. Rainwater and Rainwater, 242.

18. Ibid., 245.

19. Mlle Bon Ton, 349.

20. Kasson, *Rudeness and Civility*, 205–7.

21. Larry Freedman, *Early American Plated Silver* (Watkins Glen, NY: Century House, 1973), 93.

22. Williams, *Savory Suppers*, 126–27.

23. Quoted in Susan Williams, "Introduction," in Grover, *Dining in America*, 4–5.

24. Bernard G. Hughes, *Sheffield Silver Plate* (New York: Praeger, 1970), 141.

25. Mlle Bon Ton, 349; Rorabaugh, 42–45.

26. William Dean Howells, *The Rise of Silas Lapham*, (1885; rpt. New York: Random House, 1951), 169-85.

27. Rainwater and Rainwater, 321.

28. Ibid., 322.

29. Charles L. Venable, "The Silverplated Ice Water Pitcher: An Image of Changing America, 1850–1900," *Material Culture* 19.1 (1987): 41; Barbara McLean Ward and Gerald W. R. Ward, *Silver in American Life* (Boston: David Godline, 1976), 82.

30. Venable, 42.

31. Frances Trollope, *Domestic Manners of the Americans* (1832; rpt. New York: Alfred A Knopf, 1949), 298.

32. Rorabaugh, 42–45.

33. Rainwater and Rainwater, 250. Presumably Gibson was a professional inventor since

he received no fewer than five patents in December 1869. U.S. Patent Office, *Official Gazette* (1869), 764.

34. Meriden Britannia Company, *Appendix to Price List of July 1st, 1871* (Meriden, CT), 30; Meriden Britannia Company, *Illustrated Catalogue and Price List of Electro Silver Plate* (Meriden, CT, 1877), 24–31; Meriden Britannia Company, *Gold and Silver Plate* (Meriden, CT, 1886–7) 260–66, 269, 297; Silber and Fleming of London and Paris, *The Victorian Catalogue of Household Goods: A Complete Compendium of over Five Thousand Items to Furnish and Decorate the Victorian Home* (ca. 1883, rpt. London: Studio Editions Ltd., 1991), 56.

35. Venable, 42; Ethel Spencer also notes that in her 1890s childhood home "a pitcher of pure water always stood on a silver tray at one end of the sideboard ready for the thirsty." Ethel Spencer, *The Spencers of Amberson Avenue: A Turn-of-the-Century Memoir* (Pittsburgh: University of Pittsburgh Press, 1983), 20.

36. Williams, 153.

37. Judy Redfield, "With Bells On!" *Silver Magazine* (September–October 1996): 34–39.

38. U.S. Patent Office, *Official Gazette* (1875), Patent number 162,682, William Nichols, Revolving Chime-Bells.

39. Mrs. L. G. Abell, *Woman in her Various Relations: Containing Practical Rules for American Females* (New York: R. T. Young, 1857): 102; quoted in Kasson, 60.

40. Williams, 95.

41. "Modern Machinery," *New York Times*, November 12, 1852), 6, in ProQuest Historical Newspapers, the *New York Times*; E. T. Corbett, "A Glance into the Future; or, the World in the Twenty-Ninth Century," *Godey's Lady's Book* 97 (March 1879): 262, in Accessible Archives, www.accessible.com/.

42. Catharine Beecher and Harriet Beecher Stowe, *The American Woman's Home* (1869; repr., Hartford, CT: Stowe-Day Foundation, 1985), 117.

43. Paul E. Kindig, *Butter Prints and Molds* (West Chester, PA: Schiffer, 1986), 12.

44. Ruth Schartz Cowan, *More Work for Mother: The Ironies of Household Technology from the Open Hearth to the Microwave* (New York: Basic Books, 1983), 129-30.

45. Ibid., 130.

46. Elizabeth Robins Pennel, "Our Democracy of Bad Manners" (1925), quoted in Arthur M Schlesinger, Jr., *Learning to Behave: A Historical Study of American Etiquette Books* (New York: Macmillan, 1946), 50.

47. Emily Post, "Any Fork Will Do," (1929), quoted in Schlesinger, *Learning to Behave*, 53.

Works Cited

Abell, Mrs. L. G. *Woman in Her Various Relations: Containing Practical Rules for American Females.* New York: R. T. Young, 1857.

Anon. "Modern Machinery." *New York Times,* November 12, 1852, in ProQuest Historical Newspapers, *New York Times.*

Beecher, Catharine. *Domestic Receipt Book: Designed as a Supplement to Her Treatise on Domestic Economy.* 1841. Rpt. New York: Harper and Brothers, 1846.

Beecher, Catharine, and Harriet Beecher Stowe. *The American Woman's Home.* 1869. Reprint. Hartford, CT: Stowe-Day Foundation, 1985.

Bon Ton, Mlle. "Hints for the Hostess." *Godey's Lady's Book and Magazine* (March 1885).

Corbett, E. T. "A Glance into the Future; or, the World in the Twenty-Ninth Century." *Godey's Lady's Book* (March 1879).

Cowan, Ruth Schartz. *More Work for Mother: The Ironies of Household Technology from the Open Hearth to the Microwave.* New York: Basic Books, 1983.

Day, Charles William. *Etiquette; or a Guide to the Usages of Society with a Glance at Bad Habits.* New York: Wilson and Company, 1843.

Freeman, Larry. *Early American Plated Silver.* Watkins Glen, NY: Century House, 1973.

Giedion, Sigfried. *Mechanization Takes Command: A Contribution to Anonymous History*. 1948. Rpt. New York: Oxford University Press, 1970.

Grover, Kathryn, et al. *Dining in America, 1850–1900*. Amherst, MA: University of Massachusetts Press; Rochester, NY: Margaret Woodbury Strong Museum, 1987.

Hindle, Brooke, and Steven Lubar. *Engines of Change: The America Industrial Revolution, 1790–1900*. Washington, D. C. and London: Smithsonian Press, 1986.

Howells, William Dean. *The Rise of Silas Lapham*. 1885. Rpt. New York: Random House, 1951.

Hughes, G. Bernard. *Sheffield Silver Plate*. New York: Praeger, 1970.

Kasson, John F. *Rudeness and Civility: Manners in Nineteenth-Century America*. New York: Hill and Wang, 1990.

Kindig, Paul E. *Butter Prints and Molds*. West Chester, PA: Schiffer, 1986.

Rainwater, Dorothy T., and Ivan H. Rainwater. *American Silverplate*. Nashville: T. Nelson, 1972.

Ray, William, and Marlys Ray. *The Art of Invention: Patent Models and Their Makers*. Princeton, NJ: Pyne Press, 1974.

Redfield, Judy. "With Bells On!" *Silver Magazine* (September–October 1996): 34–40.

Schlesinger, Arthur M, Jr. *Learning How to Behave: A Historical Study of American Etiquette Books*. New York: Macmillan, 1946.

"Silver and Silver Plate." *Harper's New Monthly Magazine* (September 1868).

Spencer, Ethel. *The Spencers of Amberson Avenue: A Turn-of-the-Century Memoir*. Pittsburgh: University of Pittsburgh Press, 1983.

Trollope, Anthony. *North America*. 1862. Rpt. New York: Alfred A. Knopf, 1951.

Trollope, Frances. *Domestic Manners of the Americans*. 1832. Rpt. New York: Alfred A. Knopf, 1949.

U.S. Patent Office. *Official Gazette*. 1850–1900.

Venable, Charles L. "The Silverplated Ice Water Pitcher: An Image of Changing America, 1850–1900." *Material Culture* 19 (1987): 39–48.

Ward, Barbara McLean, and Gerald W. R. Ward, eds. *Silver in American Life*. Boston: David Godline, 1979.

Williams, Susan. *Savory Suppers and Fashionable Feasts: Dining in Victorian America*. New York: Pantheon Books; Rochester, New York: Margaret Woodbury Strong Museum, 1985.

2

Shopping for What Never Was

The Rhetoric of Food, Social Style and Nostalgia

CARLNITA GREENE

From celebrity chefs to specialty stores, over the last decade there has been an explosion of food consciousness within American culture. It is a mainstay of popular media as a focus of local and national news, magazines, books, and even supports a whole network devoted to 24 hours of food for television programming content. Simultaneously, there has been a rise in food studies within the Academy. Although it is not studied very often within the field of communication, I argue that food has rhetorical dimensions. That is to say, food operates as a means by which we "create and manage meanings" in our lives.[1]

Specifically, I assert that while people consume it on a daily basis, food is much more than mere sustenance as it intersects with a whole host of other cultural, social, and political phenomena. It functions symbolically as a communicative and rhetorical practice by which we interact with others, establish relationships, and most importantly it is used in our creations of identity. As such, I propose that today food, and the commodities associated with its production and consumption, are used as conveyors of *social styles* by which we create our identities through rhetorical performances of self. Yet, increasingly in constructing these presentations of self, we also draw upon the past in the form of nostalgia.

To examine how food operates rhetorically in this chapter, I begin with an overview of the methodological framework of social style and how food functions in our creation of identities. Next, I discuss the increasing emergence of nostalgia as a component of our everyday lives. Utilizing rhetorical theory fused with a critical and cultural studies approach, I then analyze the

31

text of Martha Stewart, the multimedia brand, as a case study to illustrate how food functions rhetorically in this manner by asserting that she creates a social style steeped in the nostalgia of an idealized Victorian past. Finally, I conclude by discussing the overall implications of Martha Stewart as a text and the impact that this study has on our understanding of rhetoric, food, identity, and nostalgia.

More Than Mere Sustenance: Social Style, Identity, and Food

In a previous study, I asserted that, due to postmodern conditions, our contemporary identities are more fluid than in the past.[2] As such, I proposed that one of the key ways that we construct our identities today is through the rhetoric of *social styles* to communicate who we are, who we want to become, and how we want to be perceived by others.[3] I further offered that when people utilize social styles to create their identities they construct rhetorical performances of self that are dependent upon the social situations in which they find themselves.[4] Rather than recount the entire study, here I will provide a brief overview of the key components of social style and how food functions in our creations of identities.

The Four Dimensions of Social Style & Rhetorical Homologies

Social style[5] is how we employ a system of signs as a means of creating who we are, who we are becoming, and who we want to be in terms of our identities. It also is a way that we both communicate who we are to others and is a means by which we identify people. This system of signs is comprised of four dimensions which are as follows: 1) performance, 2) use of language, 3) commodities, and 4) aesthetics. Each of these aspects of social style intertwines and overlaps when we communicate our identities, when people identify us, when we identify them, or when social style is used in mass media representations. I recommend that these dimensions are not mutually exclusive as they sometimes overlap, that within given texts we may find one or a combination of these dimensions, and that sometimes one dimension will be more dominant than others.

The first dimension of social style, *performance*, means that in creating our identities we enact certain behaviors and these behaviors are dependent upon the social situations in which we find ourselves.[6] That is to say, we parallel Erving Goffman's work in that we are always already using various performances to communicate our identities to others.[7] In turn, these performances are used rhetorically as a form of influence over others.

The second dimension of social style, *use of language*, means that we use our verbal and nonverbal forms of communication rhetorically.[8] In other words, to communicate our identities to others we employ language strategically such that both our verbal and nonverbal communications act as a means of identifying ourselves to others. We, therefore, will sometimes employ languages that are a reflection of various groups to which we belong, our occupations, our educational levels, and/or as a means of conveying power such as when people sit at the head of the table to assert authority.[9]

The third dimension of social style, *use of commodities*, is perhaps the most dominant means of constructing our social styles and identities today. Several scholars attest that increasingly people employ commodities, such as cars, furniture, clothing, and houses as a means of creating various meanings about their identities. Indeed, one of the key ways that commodities function today is as signs that convey various social meanings. As Jean Baudrillard advocates, commodities as signs have taken over how we view our world to the point that we are obsessed, not with the commodities per se, but what they represent as signs (e.g., wealth, power, youth, and so on).[10] Therefore, people also use commodities rhetorically to communicate their identities.

Finally, the fourth dimension of social style, *aesthetics*, imbues each of the other dimensions in the sense that our uses of performance, language, and commodities often are aesthetic choices. To create their identities through the rhetorical performance of social styles, people use the appeal of various aesthetics in their choices of commodities, use of language, and performances. That is to say, they construct and craft their social styles using particular aesthetics and at the same time, the social styles that they create have an aesthetic appeal. In this sense, we can see how social styles involve an aspect of self–design, or what Celia Lury, in *Consumer Culture*, refers to as a process of "stylization."[11]

Aside from analyzing the four dimensions of social style, to complete as in-depth an exploration into a text as possible, one would want to identify whether a social style appears to be rooted within a particular *homology*, or a similarity underlying objects, actions, and experiences.[12] That is to say, although those experiences, actions and/or objects may appear to be different or unrelated, they match on a *formal* level such that there are "formal parallels among seemingly disparate things or experiences."[13]

In this sense, one would try to determine whether a social style seems to parallel larger cultural, social, or rhetorical phenomena. Again, according to my earlier study, using a combination of social style and rhetorical homology may provide further insight into "how our individual creations of identity are influenced and constrained by larger cultural phenomena such as representations within mass media and/or cultural norms."[14] Yet, I also propose that we can view food as a conveyor of various social styles.

Food as a Conveyor of Social Styles

As stated earlier in this chapter, I believe that one way that we can further understand how food operates is to view its usage as a communicative and rhetorical practice by which we create our identities. As Mary Henderson explains: "Food is a form of communication."[15] That is to say, food operates as a nonverbal means of communication in conjunction with both verbal aspects of dining and our various contexts for eating. As such, each of these discourses combined also may be used to influence others by signifying meanings as a form of rhetoric. Roland Barthes reveals in "Toward a Psychosociology of Contemporary Food Consumption": "Food serves as a sign, not only for themes, but also for situations; and this, all told, means for way of life that is emphasized, much more than expressed by it ... and it is precisely for these reasons that it is a sign."[16] Food participates in multiple symbolic systems in a society, and as such we can discern various meanings from what, when, where and how people consume it.

Moreover, food can be seen as contributing to our personal identities, in our rhetorical performances of social styles, because it is a commodity that involves aspects of performance, creates a language or discourse, and involves aesthetics. Mary Henderson also explains in "Food as Communication in American Culture": "Just as his dress which constitutes another long ignored barometer of a man's [or woman's] attitudes and values, his [or her] choice of food offers similar soundings."[17] Finally, not just our uses of food, but also the associated material goods involved in the preparation and consumption of food, (such as dishes, pots, pans, and stoves), as well as atmospheres for eating (such as dining rooms and kitchens), can be viewed as contributing to our identities as constituted through social styles. Yet another emerging area related to food and culture that I argue also shapes our social styles is nostalgia.

Imbuing Today with Traces of the Past or
the Rise of Nostalgia in Everyday Life

According to Diane Lamude in a "Cultural Model of Nostalgia and Media Use," although historically nostalgia was considered a disease or psychological disorder, today, as scholar Oren Meyers explains, "nostalgia is defined as a longing for the past which was better, simpler, or full of hope."[18] While some scholars assert that there is nostalgia in the sense of a personal longing for the past, more often than not that personal experience is influenced by larger cultural phenomena such that "nostalgic recollections tend to blend the private with the public. Furthermore, people can feel nostalgic not only about historical events in which they personally did not take part, but also about times in which they did not live."[19]

In fact, nostalgia pervades several aspects of American culture ranging from consumer products to mass media; Lamude contends: "In the past 25 years, mass media around the world have derived considerable earnings from a variety of nostalgic products. Television, movies, radio, and magazines have capitalized on rekindling themes, music, and advertising messages from past eras. It is difficult to find a person who has not experienced nostalgia from some media experiences."[20] Furthermore, as Meyers explains: "Nostalgic themes are, indeed abundant in current consumer society."[21] Therefore, this longing for the past pervades popular media and continually is found within advertising for consumer products. Nostalgia even pervades our everyday lives, especially our creations of identity, because: "people are increasingly drawn to nostalgic themes and that nostalgia is used to strengthen people's self identity ... since people can relate nostalgic feelings through objects."[22]

I assert that food also certainly has the potential to function rhetorically in this manner by calling forth a longing for the past. In "Comfort Foods: An Exploration into the Social and Emotional Significance of Foods," Locher and others provide a strong rationale for how and why some foods can be considered nostalgic stating: "food may be used for providing comfort by conjuring up images of a familiar and soothing past way of life.... These images offer us opportunities to experience a nostalgic past through consuming particular food objects."[23] Aside from offering comfort through a visceral experiencing of the past: "The nostalgic longing and consumption of particular food items sustains one's sense of cultural, familial, and self–identity."[24]

Further, since food, social style, and identity intersect in these ways, I assert that we also can examine how nostalgia influences our rhetorical performances of self in the creation of our identities, especially within food preparation and consumption. Now, I turn to the case study of Martha Stewart so that we can better understand how these intertwining facets function.

Postmodernism Meets Mrs. Beeton: Martha Stewart as an Omnimedia Brand

As "perhaps the most famous female brand name in the consumer world,"[25] Martha Stewart is possibly *the* reining domestic goddess in America. Indeed, Martha Stewart, the brand,[26] is one of the most popular and successful ventures today because of its appeal to consumers across a wide range of products such as *Martha Stewart Living* magazine, *The Martha Stewart Show*, and *Martha Stewart Living Radio*.[27] She also sells "mass-market merchandise" in her Martha Stewart Everyday line at K-Mart, has custom-designed KB homes, greeting cards at Kodak.com, and has an upcoming collection of home products that will be sold at Macy's.[28] According to the Web site MarthaStewart.com, one of the key reasons for the brand's success is due to its founder claiming: "Martha's creative vision is the blueprint for Martha Stewart Living Omnimedia and the expansive multimedia portfolio."[29] In fact, according to "Brand Blazers 2006," "Martha and Co. are in a league of their own when it comes to expanding the brand in smart, relevant ways ... [because]... 'They're always thinking about how they can help the consumer enjoy the Martha lifestyle.'"[30] The article further reports that both *Martha Stewart Living* magazine and her daytime television show have an audience of two million.[31] Finally, according to the company's 2006 annual report, "Our revenue rose 36 percent to 288.3 million, our largest growth rate since the company went public in 1999."[32]

As the sheer volume of products and sales attests, Martha Stewart is an extremely popular and lucrative brand. Yet, Martha Stewart as a domestic personality and brand are not without controversy. Several scholars label her as "antifeminist" because she "taps into existing postfeminist sentiments to cultivate and define its audience," without encouraging women to seek political change.[33] Some claim she calls for a return of women to the kitchen and often accuse her of creating unrealistic expectations for consumers in the form of an "upper-class fantasy."[34]

To examine the social style of Martha Stewart Living Omnimeida, I will analyze various aspects of her empire such as *Martha Stewart Living Magazine*, DVDs such as *Martha's Favorite Family Dinners* and *Martha's Holiday Celebrations*, her Web site, as well as Martha Stewart's personality as a part of the brand. To that end, I will draw upon examples from these areas and discuss them as a whole because a key assumption in my approach is that the Martha Stewart brand creates a consistent social style that is constituted through its founder's identity as well as consumer products and media. Therefore, due to the sheer number of ways that one could discuss her social style, I have categorized my analysis according to key themes.

Overall, Martha Stewart's social style seems to parallel that of domestic advice writers of the past. Yet, what is remarkably different about Martha Stewart Living Omnimedia, is that her appeal specifically is one that has been achieved not only through a carefully crafted, consistent brand, but also a social style that is rooted in a perfectionism achieved through today's abundance of aesthetically appealing consumer products. Yet, I will later explain that this perfectionism ultimately is rooted in a nostalgic appeal of an idealized Victorian past. Now, I turn to the first aspect of her social style, performance.

A Performance Rooted in Perfection

One could hardly look at Martha Stewart, the brand, without considering how it is steeped within the performance of perfection. Martha Stewart takes on the role of an expert in matters of domesticity, such as cooking and entertaining, and provides her audience with ways that they also can strive to achieve this perfection. Using a metaphor of sparkling windows to examine Martha Stewart's appeal to her audience, Michael J. Golec, in "Martha Stewart Living and the Marketing of Emersonian Perfection," says that within the pages of her magazine: "The thought that well-being and pride are situated in the home, represented as an ideal place, is the thought that motives *MSL* to take up the project of Emersonian perfection."[35]

For example, over several pages of the magazine, most of the images are presented as still distinction. Everything within the magazine, from cooking supplies to furniture, is placed "thus so." There are no strewn papers or stains on the kitchen counter, flowers are not overgrown in the garden, and no furniture is in disarray. While some would argue that most home magazines operate in this sense, I believe that this seemingly still perfection is a hallmark of *Martha Stewart Living*, especially when combined with her own performances on her television show, DVDs, and Web site.

Through her behavior and performances, Martha Stewart also seems to strive for flawless effort. She is cool, calm, and poised throughout the show and other mediated performances. She undertakes several domestic activities, such as preparing a turkey, creating a holiday flower arrangement, or frying lamb chops.[36] As such, she often presents herself as an expert in matters such as cooking and entertaining. For example, in one episode from *Martha's Thanksgiving Classics* entitled "Turkey, Stuffing, and Gravy 101," her young producer supports this notion by saying that this will be her first Thanksgiving holiday in which she prepares dinner for relatives and her new husband's family. She asks Martha to instruct her in preparing a traditional meal such as a turkey, stuffing, and gravy, claiming that her guests will expect perfection since she works for Martha, whom people identify as the ultimate entertainer."[37]

Although there have always been women who have provided domestic advice, Martha Stewart takes this aspect further through her cross-promotional branding as Cynthia Duquette Smith reveals: "Transforming houses into 'homes' is Stewart's full-time occupation."[38] While she certainly behaves as an expert on all matters domestic, another aspect that compounds this notion of expertise and perfectionism is how she couples her performances with a reliance on experts in various fields. For example, on *Martha's Thanksgiving*

Classics, she has a florist, the Brooklyn-based owner of Rosebud, show her how to make arrangements for the table. On *Martha's Favorite Family Dinners,* the owner of restaurants Miss Mamie's and Miss Maude's demonstrates how to make roast chicken. Finally, in *Martha's Homemade Holidays,* she employs an expert to help her craft fresh holiday wreaths complete with mists of snow.[39] Therefore, this performance of perfection is created through her own performance and those of experts. Yet, through her use of language she seems to suggest that her audiences can also achieve this domestic bliss.

Revealing Household Secrets and the Ease of Domesticity Through Her Use of Language

Through her use of language, Martha Stewart not only tries to position herself as an educated expert, but moreover tries to convey to her audiences that she is an old friend, an aunt, a sister, or a mother who simply is passing on her wisdom to others. For example, as stated earlier in *Martha's Thanksgiving Classics,* she teaches her own producer how to prepare a turkey, and for Christmas she teaches the viewers how to create a traditional Birch De Noel.[40] Further, a key feature throughout her Web site and magazine is the "Ask Martha" column where the audience can ask her for advice about the best way to prepare a meal and/or entertain guests.

Additionally, the advice from experts throughout her multimedia brand operates in this same way. One could even consider Martha as bringing experts to her fans as if these audiences simply were members of her family or friends over for lunch. Of course, she also seems to suggest that the experts would be unknown to viewers if she did not make them aware of her savvy connections as a guru to this world of domestic bliss. Yet, in sharing these secrets, Martha Stewart also reveals one of the most important hidden treasures about cooking and entertaining by suggesting that these activities can be as easy or as difficult as her audience desires.

For example, in the DVDs, on her television show, within the magazine, and on the Web site, she often refers to how "easy" it is to complete a task such as making chicken and dumplings, a crock-pot roast, or pasta.[41] In each aspect of her media content, she also gives audiences stencils for making cookies, provides pictures with step-by-step instructions, and offers video demonstrations. As Ann Mason and Marian Meyers assert in "Living with Martha Stewart Media: Chosen Domesticity in the Experience of Fans," one of the reasons that she is so popular with fans is because her instruction runs the gamut from easy to almost impossible: "Stewart was hailed for covering all the bases — even when the bases seemed unrealistic."[42] Therefore, they acknowledge that she creates both easy and difficult projects for audiences to undertake.[43] Ironically, Martha Stewart, unlike the majority of her viewers, has a whole team to make what she creates look easy. Yet another aspect that contributes to this appearance of ease is the use of commodities.

If You Buy It, You Too Can Achieve It: The Use of Commodities

Perhaps the most prevalent aspect of Martha Stewart's social style is the use of commodities such as food and those products associated with food preparation and consumption. In fact, I assert that a key reason that she has such a strong appeal is because she taps not only into food itself, but also nostalgia linked to food. Throughout her media empire, she continually refers to various brands (e.g., Wedgwood china) or shows product labels in her preparation of foods (e.g., KitchenAid mixers). Not only does she reference other brands, but she continually is self-referential to her own brand, stating that viewers can buy these glasses, linens, or other items at Martha-by-Mail. Additionally, she states that audiences can obtain more information about a product on her Web site or find these products at K-Mart in her Martha Stewart Everyday collection.

Overall, the use and prevalence of commodities seems to suggest that if only consumers buy the same products that Martha Stewart features throughout her Omnimedia brand, then they too can achieve a sublime domestic life rooted in celebrations linking delicious food, family, and friends. Further, Martha Stewart suggests that if audiences buy her books, watch her DVDs, or visit her Web site they will have these commodities on-hand to guide them in their own domestic pursuits. Another area of social style contributing to the brand is the use of aesthetics.

Crisp, Fresh, Pretty, & Tasty Little Things: The Use of Aesthetics

The aesthetic appeal is consistent throughout the Martha Stewart Living Omnimedia brand. She uses clean, straight lines in the magazine, on her DVDs, TV show, and Web site with pastel colors such as pink and yellow. In her kitchen, there is an abundance of white in order to create the appeal of a clean and orderly space. Her dress often parallels these various color schemes, and more often than not she matches the background of her kitchen by wearing white or wears a rich chocolate brown to complement the color of her holiday table.[44] Therefore, she is as polished as the food she presents, which usually appears as fresh, garnished, and professionally prepared.

Overall, her various shows, Web site, and magazine provide a stimulating use of aesthetically pleasing appeals throughout the media content. Furthermore, by using the aesthetics associated with entertainment and eating such as sparking glasses, colorful bowls, shiny equipment, appetizing meals, and rich colors for holiday displays, she creates a classic or traditional aesthetic appeal. Yet, perhaps the *key* way that she utilizes her social style as a whole is by steeping it in nostalgia of an idealized Victorian past.

Returning to the Victorian Past: Martha Stewart's Social Style of Nostalgia

The Victorians are the inventors of several hallmarks of our contemporary society, especially those involving our relationships with consumption and food. For example, they created the dinner party, lunch hour, and made the home a site of public and private entertainments.[45] Yet, as Sally Mitchell says in *Daily Life in Victorian England*, the period that we most often consider and is most idealized as representing the Victorian era actually is from "the years between 1850 and the mid–1870s" and is permeated by middle and upper class notions.[46] I assert that Martha Stewart parallels and draws upon the rhetorical homology of a Victorian past through her creation of social style and identity. Again, I categorize these parallels according to key themes that span both Martha Stewart, as the postmodern Mrs. Beeton, and Victorian times.

The Home as a Site of Domestic Bliss

As Judith Flanders asserts in *Inside the Victorian Home: A Portrait of Domestic Life in Victorian England*, due to the Industrial Revolution and changing working conditions, the Victorian home became viewed as a place of "refuge," simultaneously leading to an increase in the importance of domesticity.[47] In fact, homes became idealized sites that supposedly influenced other aspects of people's identities such that it was a wife's duty to create a well-kept home to instill virtues in her family.[48] To that end, domestic advice manuals also were invented during this period.[49]

As stated earlier, Martha Stewart parallels this precept by privileging the home as a sanctuary. She is a postmodern Mrs. Beeton who guides women in the proper management of "home matters," especially those relating to food preparation and consumption. For example, Sarah Leavitt argues in *Catherine Beecher to Martha Stewart: A Cultural History of Domestic Advice* that Martha often draws upon the historical references of domestic advice manuals: "Stewart displayed a remarkable knowledge of the history of domestic advice. She cited several names of nineteenth-century advisors and noted that she had some works in her office which she referred to from time to time for her magazine ... her assistant ... affirmed that Stewart ... got many of her story ideas from them."[50] In fact, I believe that in several ways Martha crafts traditional holidays, like Christmas, or entertaining, such as a classic family meal, that are rooted in Victorian sentiments.

Dining, Food, and Entertaining as Central Hallmarks of an Idealized Domesticity

According to Judith Flanders, "the dining room was the most public room in the house" in Victorian times.[51] Not only was the dining room central, but it also was where Victorians created various presentations of self through their elaborate dinner parties. As Roy Strong asserts in *Feast: A History of Grand Eating*, "The dining room was a clear symbol of class distinction.... It was a room of display."[52] Further, he suggests that the dinner party

> would be one of the great prestige symbols of the eras, an index of a family's taste, discrimination, bank balance, and connections.... It was an exercise in public relations, an exhibition of a family's degree of refinement and elegance of manners. The décor, the clothes, the number and quality of servants, the decoration of the table, the choice of guests and food, all were indexes of how to impress.[53]

As stated earlier, this impression management steeped in perfection certainly is the social style that Martha Stewart delivers to her audiences through her multimedia brand. In turn, she also tries to inspire her audiences by showing them how to prepare their own means of entertainment with food by recreating an idealized presentation of self that began in the Victorian era.

Consumption as a Public Display to Create Social Prestige

The Victorians' self-presentations were directly linked to their uses of commodities as public displays of their respective social statuses. As Asa Briggs argues in *Victorian Things*: "The Victorians' own consciousness of things, late or early in the reign — and it was not lacking in semiological awareness — was expressed in different ways," such that "food, for example, was considered not just as a subject for cookery books," it was a theme spanning various publications and ways of life.[54] In this sense, Victorians understood how people would be measured socially by what, when, where, and how they ate. Therefore, they went to great lengths to create elaborate menus, table decorations, and various forms of entertainment to augment these auspicious events.[55]

Likewise, commodities within the home and dining rooms themselves were seen to reflect one's identity such as when Sarah Leavitt says: "Ascribing character traits to furniture served to demonstrate that the home could embody values" such that furniture was viewed as a sign of durability.[56] In "Aestheticizing the Home: Textual Strategies of Taste, Self-Identity, and Bourgeois Hegemony in America's 'Gilded Age,'" Reginald Twigg parallels this point by arguing that the use of consumption made people feel that they had stable identities to begin with: "Taste provided the illusion of a stable identity ... taste transformed self–identity by investing it with social distinction."[57]

Certainly, as stated before, Martha Stewart also taps into use of commodities as self–presentations. Again, she seems to suggest it is important to have the "right kinds" of commodities rooted in classic, traditional brand names, own the proper furnishings, and, above all else, present the home as a place of stylized perfection. Yet, by evoking a social style of nostalgia linked to this idealized Victorian past, Martha Stewart encourages audiences to shop for things that never were nor could ever exist as such.

Shopping for What Never Was: Overall Implications of Martha Stewart as a Text

As I alluded to earlier, I propose that a significant reason Martha Stewart Omnimedia brand is so popular with consumers is because it appeals to a mythic past of the Victorian era. Paralleling Oren Meyers' argument, I assert that this brand is appealing because nostalgia allows us to consider a supposedly simpler and better time, whereas increasingly people feel uncertainty due to the influence of the postmodern condition such that they may feel wary about their contemporary lives.

Increasingly, we also are encouraged to create who we are or want to be mainly through the use of commodities as signs. Food augments and multiplies this affect because people can connect with Martha Stewart through her presentations of food and the preparing of recipes. In turn, her role as the consummate host also calls forth a traditional role for women steeped in nostalgia for the mother, aunt, or grandmother who prepared food from scratch with tender love and care. As such, we are encouraged to imagine Martha Stewart in this role of caregiver and confidante. Yet, there are several problems and complications with Martha Stewart as a brand as well as social, rhetorical, and political implications for her audiences.

First, she encourages people to believe in a past that does not exist. This Victorian ideal is a fantasy that we have created and imbued with meanings based upon our own historical period. This vision also certainly is rooted in a white, upper-class ideal of domesticity, which during that time was limited to very small groups of people as the vast majority of women then worked outside of the home. As Sally Mitchell contends, it is a myth that Victorian women did not work.[58] Especially now, most women work outside of the home and do not have the luxury to spend hours creating wonders of domestic delight.

Second, Martha Stewart mainly targets women as the primary caregivers or housekeepers today, which is a role many women do not have the time or inclination to undertake. Ironically, the fantasy she creates is one that she most likely does not participate in outside of the mediated world and certainly is one that upper-class Victorian women in the past would not have engaged in. In fact, rarely were households sites of bliss for the actual people who created and maintained these elaborate affairs such as food preparations, decorating, and cleaning for dinner parties. According to Sally Mitchell, domestic work was hard physical labor and mainly was undertaken by servants.[59] The majority of women in Victorian times also were employed as domestic servants and certainly would not have had the time to manage their own homes in this manner.[60] Although today women have numerous career options, they still do not necessarily have the time to devote to these domestic matters with the same fervor as Martha Stewart.

Finally, the Victorians themselves also were steeped in nostalgia of their own, longing for the past because due to the Industrial Revolution they felt their own identities were unstable.[61] So as *true* postmodern consumers, we are longing for the nostalgia of an already mythologized nostalgia. More importantly, we are drawn in and try to recapture this mythic past that never existed in the first place. As such, we seem to hope that these commodities will imbue us with an element of perfection, style, or prestige.

By using these products, preparing the recipes, or creating artistic food displays, we convey our own social styles and, in turn, our identities to others. These identities, as such, are rooted in nostalgia that attempts to recreate a home life reflecting the ideals of a nonexistent past. Paralleling this point, Ann Mason and Marian Meyers assert several of Martha's fans are proud of the fact that when they entertain they are referred to as trying to be like her.[62] If Martha Stewart roots her social style in nostalgia and her fans try to replicate her when they entertain, then they too are basing their identities on an idealized Victorian past.

I do not believe that this desire or appeal for nostalgia is necessarily a conscious choice on our part as consumers. It could be that in purchasing various products, watching Martha Stewart on TV, or buying her books, we are trying to create our own versions of "the good life" as scholars such as Mark Meister, Pauline Adema, and Cheri Ketchum argue, that food television and lifestyle programming create consumer fantasies and desires for dream lives that only exist in the realms of the small screen, books, and/or magazines.[63] As such, I believe that Martha Stewart as a text demonstrates the power of nostalgic fantasy in contemporary society.

Throughout this chapter, I have suggested that, when combined with nostalgia and food, the rhetoric of social styles has enormous appeal for consumers. Whether we consciously consider it or not, nostalgia is being used within popular cultural texts, like Martha Stewart Living Omnimedia, to call us forth by continually creating desires to imbue our daily lives with a sense of the past. Again, they seem to suggest that we too can capture this supposed quaint, warm, and loving time of domestic bliss if we only add a little pinch of this spice to our pot roasts, decorate our kitchen for the holidays by using a sprig of rosemary, or use one of Martha Stewart's many consumer products. Yet, I hope that this chapter also raises several questions about limitations a social style steeped in nostalgia can create because, as I stated earlier, in a sense we are shopping for what never was. Thus, I believe that increasing nostalgia plays a significant role in how we create and manage our identities through rhetorical performances of social styles today.

Notes

1. Barry Brummett, *Rhetoric of Machine Aesthetics* (Westport, CT: Praeger, 1999), 23.
2. Carlnita Peterson Greene, "Beyond the Binaries to Self-Fashioning: Identity as the Rhetoric of Social Style" (PhD diss., University of Texas at Austin, 2006), 39.
3. Ibid., 3.
4. Ibid., 30.
5. Ibid., 60.
6. Ibid., 61–62.
7. Erving Goffman, *The Presentation of Self in Everyday Life* (New York: Doubleday, 1959), 18–27.
8. Greene, 62–64.
9. Ibid.
10. Jean Baudrillard, "Consumer Society," in *Consumer Society in American History: A Reader*, ed. Lawrence Glickman (Ithaca, NY: Cornell University Press, 1999), 39.
11. Celia Lury, *Consumer Culture* (Oxford: Blackwell, 1996), 4.
12. For more information about rhetorical homologies and the full explanation of my methodological approach, see my previous work, Carlnita Peterson Greene, 84–106.
13. Barry Brummett, "The Homology Hypothesis: Pornography on the VCR," *Critical Studies in Mass Communication* 5 (1988): 202–16.
14. Greene, 94.
15. Mary Henderson, "Food as Communication in American Culture," *Today's Speech* 18 (1979): 3–8.
16. Roland Barthes, "Toward a Psychosociology of Contemporary Food Consumption," in *Food and Culture: A Reader*, ed. Carole Counihan and Penny VanEsterik (New York: Routledge, 1997), 25.
17. Henderson, 3–8.
18. Diane Lamude, "A Cultural Model of Nostalgia," *World Communication* 19 (1990): 38–40; Oren Meyers, "Advertising, Nostalgia and the Construction of Commodities as Realms of Memory," *Proceedings of the International Communication Association Annual Meeting* (New York: International Communication Association, 2005), 6.
19. Meyers, 7.
20. Lamude, "A Cultural Model of Nostalgia," *World Communication* 19 (1990): 37.
21. Meyers, 8.
22. Ibid.
23. Julie L. Locher, "Comfort Foods: An Exploration into the Social and Emotional Significance of Foods," *Food & Foodways* 13 (2005): 278.
24. Ibid.
25. Sarah Leavitt, *Catherine Beecher to Martha Stewart: A Cultural History of Domestic Advice* (Chapel Hill: University of North Carolina Press, 2002), 199.
26. Although Martha Stewart is no longer the CEO of her company due to her somewhat recent financial scandals, according to the annual report on her Web site, she remains "the largest

stockholder" in her company, Martha Stewart Living Omnimedia, Inc. "Investor Relations," Martha Stewart, http://www.marthastewart.com/portal/site/mslo/menuitem.017db2225a7627b 8510467a2b5900aa0/?vgnextoid=0b3ddc2858650110VgnVCM1000003d370a0aRCRD&vgnext fmt=default&rsc=footer (accessed January 3, 2007).

27. Martha Stewart Living Omnimedia, Inc., "About Martha Stewart," http://www. marthastewart.com/portal/site/mslo/menuitem.a869edc68b016ad593598e10d373a0a0/?vgnex toid=d77e95ea62d7f010VgnVCM1000005b09a00aRCRD&vgnextfmt=default&rsc=footer (accessed January 3, 2007).

28. Ibid.

29. Ibid.

30. "Brand Blazers 2006," *Brandweek* (October 23, 2006), SR6.

31. Ibid.

32. Martha Stewart Living Omnimedia, Inc., "Investor Relations," http://www.martha stewart.com/portal/site/mslo/menuitem.017db2225a7627b8510467a2b5900aa0/?vgnextoid=0b 3ddc2858650110VgnVCM1000003d370a0aRCRD&vgnextfmt=default&rsc=footer (accessed January 3, 2007).

33. Cynthia Duquette Smith, "Discipline — It's a 'Good Thing': Rhetorical Constitution and Martha Stewart Living Omnimedia, *Women's Studies in Communication* 23 (2000): 339.

34. Ann Mason and Marian Meyers, "Living with Martha Stewart Media: Chosen Domesticity in the Experience of Fans," *Journal of Communication* 51 (2001): 802.

35. Michael J. Golec, "Martha Stewart Living and the Marketing of Emersonian Perfection," *Home Cultures* (2006): 5–6.

36. Martha Stewart Living Omnimedia, Inc., *Martha's Holiday Celebrations,* DVD (2006); Martha Stewart Living Omnimedia, Inc., *Martha's Favorite Family Dinners,* DVD (2005).

37. Ibid.

38. Cynthia Duquette Smith, "Discipline — It's a 'Good Thing': Rhetorical Constitution and Martha Stewart Living Omnimedia," *Women's Studies in Communication* 23 (2000): 357.

39. *Martha's Holiday Celebrations,* DVD (2006).

40. Ibid.

41. *Martha's Favorite Family Dinners,* DVD (2005).

42. Mason and Meyers, 813.

43. Ibid.

44. *Martha's Holiday Celebrations,* DVD (2006).

45. Roy Strong, *Feast: A History of Grand Eating* (Orlando: Harcourt, 2002), 274–308.

46. Sally Mitchell, *Daily Life in Victorian England* (Westport, CT: Greenwood Press, 1996), 7.

47. Judith Flanders, *Inside the Victorian Home: A Portrait of Domestic Life in Victorian England* (New York: W. W. Norton, 2003), 4–5.

48. Ibid.

49. Leavitt, 9–10.

50. Ibid., 7.

51. Flanders, 255.

52. Strong, 290.

53. Ibid., 293.

54. Asa Briggs, *Victorian Things* (Chicago: University of Chicago Press, 1988). 32.

55. Strong, 274–308.

56. Leavitt, 37.

57. Reginald Twigg, "Aestheticizing the Home: Textual Strategies of Taste, Self-Identity, and Bourgeois Hegemony in America's 'Gilded Age,'" *Text & Performance Quarterly* 12 (1992): 5.

58. Mitchell, 47–48.

59. Ibid., 41–53.

60. Ibid., 50–51.

61. Twigg, 5–7.

62. Mason and Meyers, 813-14.

63. Pauline Adema, "Vicarious Consumption: Food, Television and the Ambiguity of

Modernity," *Journal of American Culture* 23 (2000): 113–23. Mark Meister, "Cultural Feeding, Good Life Science, and the TV Food Network," *Mass Communication and Society* 4 (2001): 165–82; Cheri Ketchum, "The Essence of Food Cooking Shows: How the Food Network Constructs Consumer Fantasies," *Journal of Communication Inquiry* 29 (2005): 217–34.

Works Cited

Adema, Pauline. "Vicarious Consumption: Food, Television and the Ambiguity of Modernity." *Journal of American Culture* 23 (2000): 113–123.

Barthes, Roland. "Toward a Psychosociology of Contemporary Food Consumption." In *Food and Culture: A Reader,* eds. Carole Counihan and Penny VanEsterik, 20–27. New York: Routledge, 1997.

Baudrillard, Jean. "Consumer Society." In *Consumer Society in American History: A Reader,* ed. Lawrence Glickman, 35–36. Ithaca, NY: Cornell University Press, 1999.

"Brand Blazers." *Brandweek*, October 23, 2006, SR6.

Briggs, Asa. *Victorian Things.* Chicago: University of Chicago Press, 1988.

Brummett, Barry. "The Homology Hypothesis: Pornography on the VCR," *Critical Studies in Mass Communication* 5 (1988): 202–16.

_____. *Rhetoric of Machine Aesthetics.* Westport, CT: Praeger, 1999.

Flanders, Judith. *Inside the Victorian Home: A Portrait of Domestic Life in Victorian England.* New York: W. W. Norton, 2003.

Goffman, Erving. *The Presentation of Self in Everyday Life.* New York: Doubleday, 1959.

Golec, Michael J. "Martha Stewart Living and the Marketing of Emersonian Perfection." *Home Cultures* 3 (2006): 1–24.

Greene, Carlnita Peterson. "Beyond the Binaries to Self-Fashioning: Identity as the Rhetoric of Social Style." PhD diss., University of Texas at Austin, 2006.

Henderson, Mary. "Food as Communication in American Culture." *Today's Speech* 18 (1979): 3–8.

Ketchum, Cheri. "The Essence of Food Cooking Shows: How the Food Network Constructs Consumer Fantasies." *Journal of Communication Inquiry* 29 (2005): 217–34.

Lamude, Diane. "A Cultural Model of Nostalgia." *World Communication* 19 (1990): 38–40.

Leavitt, Sarah. *Catherine Beecher to Martha Stewart: A Cultural History of Domestic Advice.* Chapel Hill: University of North Carolina Press, 2002.

Locher, Julie, William C. Yoels, Donna Maurer, and Jillian Van Ells. "Comfort Foods: An Exploration into the Social and Emotional Significance of Foods." *Food & Foodways* 13 (2005): 273–95.

Lury, Celia. *Consumer Culture.* Oxford: Blackwell, 1996.

Martha Stewart Living Omnimedia, Inc. *Martha Stewart Living.* May 2007.

Martha Stewart Living Omnimedia, Inc. *Martha Stewart Outdoor Living.* May 2007.

Martha Stewart Living Omnimedia, Inc. *Martha Stewart Living.* April 2007.

Martha Stewart Living Omnimedia Inc. *Martha's Holiday Celebrations.* DVD. 2006.

Martha Stewart Living Omnimedia, Inc. *Martha's Favorite Family Dinners.* DVD. 2005.

Martha Stewart Living Omnimedia Inc. "Investor Relations," http://www.martha stewart.com/portal/site/mslo/menuitem.017db2225a7627b8510467a2b5900aa0/?vgn extoid=0b3ddc2858650110VgnVCM1000003d370a0aRCRD&vgnextfmt=default&rs c=footer (accessed January 3, 2007).

Martha Stewart Living Omnimedia Inc. "About Martha Stewart." http://www.martha stewart.com/portal/site/mslo/menuitem.a869edc68b016ad593598e10d373a0a0/?vgne xtoid=d77e95ea62d7f010VgnVCM1000005b09a00aRCRD&vgnextfmt=default&rsc =footer (accessed January 3, 2007).

Mason, Ann, and Marian Meyers. "Living with Martha Stewart Media: Chosen Domesticity in the Experience of Fans." *Journal of Communication* 51 (2001): 801–23.

Meister, Mark. "Cultural Feeding, Good Life Science, and the TV Food Network." *Mass Communication and Society* 4 (2001): 165–82.

Meyers, Oren. "Advertising, Nostalgia and the Construction of Commodities as Realms of Memory." *Proceedings of the International Communication Association Annual Meeting*. New York: International Communication Association, 2005.

Mitchell, Sally. *Daily Life in Victorian England*. Westport, CT: Greenwood Press, 1996.

Smith, Cynthia Duquette. "Discipline — It's a 'Good Thing': Rhetorical Constitution and Martha Stewart Living Omnimedia." *Women's Studies in Communication* 23 (2000): 337–65.

Strong, Roy. *Feast: A History of Grand Eating*. Orlando: Harcourt, 2002.

Twigg, Reginald. "Aestheticizing the Home: Textual Strategies of Taste, Self-Identity, and Bourgeois Hegemony in America's 'Gilded Age.'" *Text & Performance Quarterly* 12 (1992): 1–20.

3

All You Can Eat

Sociological Reflections on Food in the Hypermodern Era

SIMON GOTTSCHALK

Strange Brew

Information about food must be gathered wherever it can be found: by direct observations in the economy, in techniques, usages, and advertising; and by indirect observation in the mental life of a given society. (Roland Barthes)[1]

When the editor of this volume e-mailed me about the strange Professional Competitive Eating phenomenon (see Chapter 17), asking me if I would be interested in contributing a chapter to this book, I hesitated a bit. Up until recently, I had rarely been interested in food as a topic of research, theory, or practical activity. However, after thinking about it for a while, I decided to honor his invitation because it seemed that a number of academic and personal interests were leading me in that direction. My recent research on hypermodern society had increasingly forced me to look at food a bit more sociologically; in the last two years, and much to my wife's joy, I had pretty much taken over all activities revolving around food in our house and, until just a few months ago, we had seriously been considering investing money in a small restaurant. The invitation sounded indeed auspicious, and prompted me to develop this chapter.

Before I start, a caveat is in order. In this chapter, I neither review the voluminous literature on the sociology of food, eating and nutrition, nor present findings of a research I have conducted, nor attempt to support, challenge, extend, or produce a theory on the topic. My purpose here is to invite the reader to critically examine the "All You Can Eat" slogan guiding the eating contest, and the two tendencies it articulates: excess and potential. In the following pages, I use the "excessive" meaning as a starting point to (a) discuss the importance of food as a topic of sociological interest, (b) look anew at the McDonaldization thesis, and (c) introduce new arguments positing the rise of hypermodern society. I then turn my attention to the "potential" meaning of "All You Can Eat," the principles of hypermodern eating it articulates, and the alternative approach it promotes.

Feed Your Head

> Food is not only good to eat, but also good to think with. (Claude Levi Strauss)[2]

> Sugar is not just a foodstuff ... it is, if you will, an "attitude." (Roland Barthes)[3]

The "All You Can Eat" logic or promise is especially prominent in Las Vegas, where I live. Since the Las Vegas "experience" and package deal must invariably include gargantuan buffets available at most Strip casino-hotels, this simple, yet puzzling, promise, which appears on countless electronic billboards, is as much part of the Strip mediascape as the omnipresent neon signs boasting "Megabucks." Of course, both are related. I find this "all you can eat" approach to food both disconcerting and symptomatic. Disconcerting, because choosing a restaurant on the basis of sheer quantity, and deciding to stuff oneself literally *ad nauseam* because it is a "good deal" seems to betray a rather disappointing appreciation for the pleasures of food. I anticipate that this remark will immediately brand me as an insufferable European cultural elitist who does not really "get it." Guilty as charged. But — and here is where the "symptomatic" comes in — this approach to food condenses other perplexing trends that characterize the contemporary moment. If Savarin proclaimed "tell me *what* you eat and I'll tell you who you are," one could also suggest "tell me *how* you eat, and I'll tell you who you are."

On a first level, therefore, the "All You Can Eat" slogan seems to encapsulate much broader social trends in the production, consumption, and representations of food in contemporary America. It includes the buffet, but also the simplistic "supersize" option at fast-food outlets, the typically insipid "bottomless cup" at diners, the increasing size of portions at restaurants and supermarkets, and the permanent pounding by commercials urging us to choose from an ever-expanding array of options and promising us huge quantities for "less than five dollars." In brief, this four-word promise or slogan condenses our (typically taken-for-granted) permanent access to immense *quantities* and *varieties* of food, a condition that is unique in human history.[4]

As I discuss below, this promise extends well beyond food, but since it refers primarily to this realm, let us start here.

Food is the stuff of life, literally and metaphorically. Although it is a truism, we might have forgotten that, at a simple biological level, in order to survive, grow and reproduce, every organism must secure continuous access to other organisms that it transforms into food. With rare exceptions, this transformation entails their destruction. As biological organisms *and* meanings-makers, humans have of course bestowed enormous importance on food and the many activities revolving around it. Food does not only deliver nutrients to the body, it also transmits meanings to the mind and feelings to the soul. Accordingly, it is not surprising that it has been the topic of much scholarship in the social sciences and the humanities, the subject of representation and inspiration in the arts,[5] and the source of countless meanings across cultures and historical periods — from the apple in the Garden of Eden through the destruction of a McDonald's in France.[6] From a social constructionist point of view, it is a truism that the meanings people give the food they eat necessarily shape their practices and social relations. But food is also the quintessential infrastructure of other human activities. Since the production, preparation, distribution, and consumption of food have always been central tasks of human life, and since all human activities ultimately depend on, and require their successful accomplishment,[7] it is not surprising that food is both the topic of sociological inquiry and a prism through which we can make sense of other social phenomena. As Beardsworth and Keil note:

> Quite clearly, the act of eating lies at the point of intersection of a whole series of intricate physiological, psychological, ecological, economic, political, social and cultural processes. Such intersections present the human and social sciences with some of their most intriguing questions and challenges.[8]

The very history of the sociological scholarship of food and nutrition illustrates these ideas quite well. Noting that this scholarship is relatively recent, Beardsworth and Keil remark[9] that the long sociological silence on food-related activities is rather curious in light of their obvious importance. For most of human history, hunger was always a risk, contact with the earth and its many species was permanent, and human dependence on food was rarely ignored, as most work consisted of "food work." Of course, multitudes of people still experience food in these ways today. Beardsworth and Keil[10] thus suggest that sociologists' recent interest in food perhaps expresses a reaction to the mounting threats to our food supply that appear daily in the news: Avian flu, mad cow disease, and mercury-laden fish; melamine in pet food and rats at Taco Bell; pesticides in our bloodstream and genetically modified produce between our teeth. We can thus interpret our long silence about, and recent interest in, food-related topics as confirming the quintessential importance of food for all human activities (intellectual ones included). In other words, both silence and interest are, at least partly, motivated by the real or perceived conditions of our food supply. Hence, if it is true that the meanings people give the food they eat shape their practices and social relations, the reverse is also true. The food people eat shapes their meanings, practices, and social relations.

Let me concretize these ideas a bit more. While it seems that a truly rational species witnessing the rapid destruction of its food supplies would logically stop whatever it is doing, and decide that business as usual will have to be postponed until proper measures protecting them from such a daunting risk are implemented, we visibly do not. We seem to react to this news on an ad hoc basis, with submission and resignation. The reasons behind this failure to react appropriately are complex and numerous, but they must include in some fashion the seductive media of mass distraction that obsessively force-feed us particular *representations* of food everywhere we turn and 24/7.[11] At the same time, our silence about the deterioration of our food supply must also be partly explained by the very "nature" of the food we eat and our practices revolving around nutrition.

Soul Kitchen

> To eat is a sacred act. One must be fully conscious of what one is doing. (Rabbi Naham of Brazlaw)[12]

Food is also personal, and in more ways than Savarin probably had in mind. One does not need to be a Freudian to appreciate his idea that our experiences with food start on day one, introduce us to reality, others, and the self, hence shape our consciousness in profound and complex ways, and influence how we experience our lives. Consciously and not. Of course, this influence is not limited to our early years. As Fischler remarks,

> Food is ... central to individual identity, in that any given human individual is constructed, biologically, psychologically and socially by the food he/she chooses to incorporate.[13]

Since food is indeed personal and informs so many other aspects of our lives, a few brief words about some of my own key experiences with food might perhaps be appropriate. After all, and as will become obvious throughout this essay, just like every other aspect of our lives, my/your personal and academic approaches to food are shaped by biography and history.

Spending much time at my grandmother's in Brussels, I grew up amidst the aromas, tastes, sounds and sights of food and the physical activities surrounding its preparation. She seemed to be forever pounding, kneading, peeling, slicing, grinding, frying, boiling, decorating, carrying, and distributing food. My grandparents had many and frequent guests, and their small apartment was the main locale for all family gatherings and religious celebrations. A Jewish immigrant who escaped from Poland during the 1917 pogroms, my grandmother never used canned, frozen, microwaveable, or chemically enhanced food. As a matter of pride and just plain common sense, she only used fresh produce and created most dishes from scratch. Equipped with a small number of simple electric appliances that she used reluctantly, and a stove that would be considered prehistoric by most citizens of contemporary societies, she would still manage to prepare sumptuous meals for the many visiting tribe members. As Holocaust survivors, they assigned enormous importance to food, not as epicureans but as people who had known real hunger, and some even near-starvation in concentration camps. Needless to say that the actual calories released by the dishes we were continuously implored to eat were dwarfed in importance by the symbolic and emotional charges they contained.

Soon after I turned fifteen, I left home and moved to an Israeli kibbutz, where I worked in avocado orchards for a number of years. Call it naïve idealism but, while work was physically demanding, there was something quite rewarding and educational about *collectively* working the land, experiencing through this work a direct relation to the essential activity of food production, and consuming that food together. As 19th-century Zionist-Socialist philosophers understood quite well,[14] Diasporic Jews (and, I suspect, many others as well) can reap many important social, psychological, physical, and even spiritual benefits from working at those activities where the shovel meets the ancestral soil.

As an immigrant to America, my encounter with food was marked by a double culture shock: quantity and taste. Like many immigrants to the U.S., I experienced the "quantity" culture shock the first time I hesitantly stepped through the doors of a supermarket. I had never seen so many brands of the same product, so many products, such gigantic sizes, and such affordability, even on my modest graduate student's salary. The "taste" culture shock took a bit longer. In contrast to the food I grew (up with), the fruits, vegetables and other foodstuff available at typical supermarkets tasted watery, were relatively odorless, and seemed to follow perplexing chemical laws.[15] But while "natural" produce lacked in taste, processed foods had too much of it. The absence of taste in "natural" foods and its overkill in processed ones might partly explain why Americans do not eat enough of the former, but too much of the latter. Moreover, these imbalances amplify each other. The more our taste buds become used to the intensity of processed food, the less flavor we taste in the already compromised natural ones.

However, the increasing replacement of "natural" foods by chemical substitutes has additional consequences that extend beyond just bad nutrition, obesity, and desensitized taste buds. The recent finding that most Americans are one generation removed from real food[16] concretizes Claude Fischler's interesting concept of "gastro-anomie." As he explains:

> food production and processing increasingly take place beyond the view of the average consumer, involving techniques that he or she is vaguely aware of or simply does not understand. Thus, many of the food items routinely purchased may be perceived as having unknown features or unknown ingredients, with a consequent loss of the consumer's confidence. This effect is reinforced by the fact that modern food manufacturing techniques, including the use of synthesized substances and flavourings, can imitate or conceal "natural" textures or tastes, leaving the consumer effectively unable to trust the sensory messages given off by any given food product as a reliable guide to its actual nature.[17]

If ecopsychologists explain the many "mental disorders" we suffer from as resulting from our alienation from the natural environment,[18] gastro-anomie must be associated with particular disorders or dysfunctions as well. Since food is the stuff of life, since food is what we put in our bodies, since food *becomes* our bodies, it does not seem unreasonable to suggest that this growing disconnect from food *naturally* spreads beyond those practical activities that revolve around nutrition. After all, taste does not only mean "to perceive or distinguish the flavor of," but also "to have or get experience; to perceive in any way; to enjoy or appreciate."[19] And since this decreasing familiarity with natural taste and resulting distortion of sensory messages implies *real* biological changes, it must also affect other aspects of the self/mind/body that, at first glance, might appear more "serious" than food. As Fischler puts it: "If one does not know what one is eating, one is liable to lose the awareness of certainty of what one is oneself. How do modern foods transform us from the inside?"[20]

And to elaborate on this question, how does the deterioration *of* natural taste in food then facilitate the deterioration of our natural ability *to* taste — to distinguish between qualities, both in matters of food and others? What other aptitudes are compromised as a result of this deterioration? What other social processes are implicated in gastro-anomie? To provide tentative answers to these questions, we must first make a quick stop at McDonald's.

Them Belly Full

> For lunch we eat hamburgers that taste like they fell off a truck — an entire meal that owes more to the Teamsters, Du Pont, and chemical engineering than it does to, say, earth, soil, or the great chefs of Europe. (Douglas Coupland)[21]

George Ritzer's *McDonaldization of Society* is a landmark in the sociological study of food. Although it has been the topic of many critics,[22] his decision to use the familiar and increasingly global experience of eating at McDonald's to nurture the sociological imagination is original and interesting.[23] As Ritzer emphasizes, McDonaldization is not so much about McDonald's as it is about much broader modern processes (efficiency, calculability, predictability, control) that colonize increasing life spheres. As he documents, institutions such as education, health care, and leisure are increasingly McDonaldized as well, and others are likely to follow suit. Reflecting on these processes, Kellner suggests that McDonaldization articulates both modern and postmodern characteristics.[24] Although there is overlap between these two categories, McDonaldization entails the implementation of mainly *modern* principles to guide the processes of production, preparation, distribution, and consumption, and of mainly *postmodern* ones to guide the process of promotion and advertising. Importantly also, those are two sides of the same coin. In other words, the other side of the commercials showing ecstatic faces, peppy music, the aura of fun, and the promises of postmodern cool, is rationally engineered environmental destruction, cruelty to animals, exploitation of the workforce at home and its repression overseas, cultural imperialism, plain old capitalist greed, and the dehumanization and anonymization of this most human activity that is eating and food preparation. In light of all that we know about the consequences of McDonaldization — and just in the familiar realm of food — it is difficult to argue with the statement that "to eat, and more precisely to choose what we eat can be seen as a political act, a moral or ethical action."[25]

Focusing on the postmodern side of the coin, there are several interesting similarities between McDonaldization principles and the "All You Can Eat" promise, as both promote particular meanings about food. To follow Ritzer's argument, when we go to McDonaldized food outlets, what matters is not *what* we eat, but the experience of efficiency, controllability, predictability, control, and the hype surrounding that sorry excuse for a meal that ultimately appears on the plastic tray. As he notes about this last point:

> Perhaps more important, fast-food restaurants seem to offer ... fun. McDonald's uses a ubiquitous clown Ronald McDonald, an array of cartoon characters, and a colorful décor to remind people that fun awaits them on their next visit.... In essence, many fast-food restaurants are really amusement parks for food.[26]

Thus, the most recent McDonald's Web-commercial slogan ("Havin' Fun") clearly indicates that the main product it sells is indeed an experience. Similarly, its most recent TV commercial slogan ("I'm Lovin' It") cannot reasonably refer to the food being served there. Indeed, the same graphics, visual effects, music, slogans, and smiling faces that appear on McDonald's commercials predictably also appear in commercials promoting other fast-food outlets of the same ilk, and in those advertising vacation cruises, iPods, soft drinks, acne medicine, and clothes. In other words, the quality of the commodity being sold is relatively unimportant in comparison to the promises of fun, abundance, a good deal, immediate access, and near–24/7 availability.

The "All You Can Eat" logic is not that different. Here, what matters is not *what* we eat, but *how much* we manage to swallow for the same low price, with a minimum of effort, in convenient and — judging by ads — generally "fun" locations, that are predictably patronized by a happy, young, attractive and well-dressed clientele. In this case also, the slogan does not promote food as much as experiences, orientations, desires, or as Barthes put it, an *attitude.* Thus, while the "All You Can Eat" logic reproduces its own variation of the McDonaldization principles of efficiency-calculability-predictability-control, it also extols the value of quantity, the desire for more for the sake of more, the logic of excess,[27] a fine example of what Baudrillard calls a "perverse provocation."[28]

The meanings McDonaldization and "All You Can Eat" principles assign to food are also interesting in light of the "omnivore paradox." As Beardsworth and Keil explain, as omnivores, humans confront three key paradoxes when deciding between familiar and unfamiliar foods. The *pleasure/displeasure* paradox refers to the idea that "while food can provide gustatory gratification and a welcome sense of fullness and satisfaction, it can also produce sensations and reactions ranging from mildly unpleasant to severely distressing." The *life/death* paradox "emerges out of the fact that, while the consumption of food is absolutely essential for the maintenance of life, the act of eating usually entails the death and dissolution of other organisms." Finally, the *health/illness* paradox entails the idea that "while food is the source of physical energy and can be conceived of as the foundation of vitality and health, it is also recognized as having the potential to introduce disease-inducing substances or organisms into the body."[29]

McDonaldization solves the pleasure/displeasure paradox by delivering predictability and familiarity: It guarantees that the food will always taste the same. It neutralizes the life/death paradox by completely ignoring it — an easy feat, considering the complete erasure of any possible association between an actual beef, the burger patty, and the complex and increasingly international production networks that transform the former into the latter. The *health/illness* paradox is another matter. Of course, increasingly numerous and mesmerizing commercials successfully persuade us to define a dehumanized eating experience as "fun," to delude ourselves that irradiated food tastes "just like home," and to ignore the sadistic conditions under which the animals we eat are raised and processed. But neither they nor any other "expert system" can compellingly reassure us that the food we eat is safe. On the contrary. As McIntosh notes:

> Critics suggest that food companies have effectively captured the regulatory mechanisms of both the USDA and the FDA, arguing that neither the food supply nor its regulation for safety and quality deserve our trust.[30]

Accordingly, we can also understand the hype in fast-food commercials as strategies that distract us from confronting this most serious paradox. Since McDonaldization cannot guarantee health, it turns up the hype around a new dressing, an extra slice of bacon, more cheese, or plastic action figures. Similarly, it is likely that if we were to witness the objective conditions under which our food is being produced, many of us would probably reconsider our eating practices. But here also the extravagant hype easily persuades us to suppress such distressing realizations. The "All You Can Eat" logic performs the same function. It deflects our latent anxieties about the food we are about to ingest, and conceals both its source and the process of its production by promising us a seemingly advantageous deal: Excess, Profit *and* Fun.

Accordingly, McDonaldization does not solely produce consumer goods, but also good consumers. As Ritzer discusses, the ideal McConsumer is one who behaves as predictably and efficiently as the Mcworkers who cook there, and as the Mcfood they prepare. These consumers know the "code," will be satisfied by the food available, will spend as little time as possible eating, will clean up after themselves, and will come back.[31] Assessing these orientations, Kellner points at a seeming contradiction between a postmodern logic and McDonaldization. He notes: "From a postmodern perspective that valorizes difference, otherness and variety, McDonald's is the paradigm of mass homogeneity, sameness and standardization, which erases individuality, specificity and difference."[32]

But here again, the two are not dichotomous but complicit. In other words, the continuing success of McDonaldization must partly be explained by its ability to envelop a very modern burger in a very postmodern wrapper. Once you remove the slogans of "fun," "happy meals," and "lovin' it," McDonaldization is still about the scientific and precise standardization of food production, preparation, consumption, and taste.[33] Globally. The same obtains with the "All You Can Eat" logic at the buffet. It also produces docile and uncomplicated consumers who will behave as expected, who will not make any demand, and whose relevance is basically calculated in terms of approximate quantity of food ingested during an average time period. In both places, workers, consumers and food move with the implacable logic of the conveyor belt.[34]

In addition to homogenization, standardization, dehumanization, and alienation, McDonaldization and "All You Can Eat" principles also promote the *infantilization* of consumers. They accomplish this by simplifying consumers' experiences with food to its bare essentials, by promising them predictability and immediate satisfaction, by absolving them of all responsibility beyond combining a preset number of items, by emphasizing the "fun" aspects of both their eating experience and the food they eat, by flattering their narcissistic needs, and — characteristic of the infantile mindset — by bragging about quantity and size. Hence, while psychological growth entails increasingly reflexive, responsible, purposeful, creative, and sophisticated relations with world, others, and self (and hence, food), McDonaldization and "All You can Eat" principles invite consumers to occupy a position that is evidently characterized by programmed, obedient, passive, repetitive, and simplistic behaviors. Accordingly, these principles do not only deliver the experiences of efficiency-calculability-predictability-control discussed by Ritzer, but also nurture particular dispositions, expectations, and incompetencies, which we reproduce outside the fast-food outlet and the buffet.

Alice's Restaurant

All excess leads to crime. (Voltaire)[35]

Gluttony is an emotional sign that something is eating us. (Peter Devries)[36]

On a second level, the excessive aspect of the "All You Can Eat" logic is quite in sync with other trends developing in today's society, which a number of French social scientists increasingly describe with the "hyper" prefix. Most prominent among them are Gilles Lipovetsky's *Hypermodern times,* Nicole Aubert's *L'individu hypermdoderne,* Francois Ascher's *La société hypermoderne,* and — more directly relevant to this book — his *Mangeur hypermoderne* (Hypermodern Eater). While the meanings of the *hyper* prefix are varied, these authors still seem to agree about some key definitions. Thus, Aubert distinguishes *hyper*modernity from *post*modernity by emphasizing the experience of intensity, instantaneity, urgency, instant gratification, and excess. As she explains:

By replacing it [*postmodernity*] by the term *hypermodernity*, we emphasize the fact that the society in which contemporary individuals live has changed. We place the accent not on rupture with the foundations of modernity, but on the exacerbation and radicalization of the modern.... The essential mode of hypermodernity is excess, the overabundance of the event in the contemporary world. It is this overabundance rather than the collapse of the idea of progress that is ... at the origin of the difficulty to think the present, because it is overcharged with events that encumber the present as well as the recent past.[37] [my translation]

As Cournut also notes, the hypermodern can be characterized by a

collusion between the temptation toward excess and the means to achieve it. We must acknowledge that if the temptation is this intense, it is surely because our era has provided ample means to achieve it and *actively promotes it*....[38] [my translation, my ellipses]

While I cannot summarize the growing scholarship on hypermodernism in the space allotted here, the idea of excess seems central, and authors have explored it in areas such as pressures, individualism, communication, competition, consumption, information, solicitations, crises, innovations, acceleration,[39] decisions and risks.

As Aubert,[40] De Gaulejac,[41] Enriquez,[42] and others suggest, not only do risks seem to multiply in the hypermodern moment, but we must face them alone, without the help of collectivities, traditions, or stable referents. And to add insult to injury, we are also likely to feel that we bear the sole responsibility when we make the "wrong" choice.[43] Castel suggests that — perhaps as a reaction — contemporary individuals become hyper competitive and hyper individualist:

The hypermodern individual believes himself to be hyper independent to the point of feeling free from all responsibility, to never account for himself to no one for his choices and behaviors ... there is a sort of inflation of individualism, of subjectivity which is difficult to reconcile with the necessity of living a common life, and to take into account collective systems of regulation, which are the essence of life in any society.[44] [my translation]

There are other problems. Exploring the manifestations of hypermodernity at the micro level, De Gaulejac[45] suggests that, while modernity had imposed the self as an individual project, hypermodernity entails an additional dimension:

Individuals are not only expected to be free, responsible, creative, and capable of initiating projects, they must also and simultaneously affirm an irreducible singularity ... they must be similar yet different, affiliated yet unaffiliated. They must be common and uncommon, ordinary and extraordinary.... The more social worlds open up to one another, the more globalization produces de-differentiation, the more cultural models tend to interpenetrate, the more individuals feel the need to distinguish themselves....[46] [my translation]

As Lipovetsky[47] and others document, we seek to produce this significant distinction mainly through our consumption patterns and choices.

Combining those insights, I will suggest that, since we typically eat three times a day, anxieties about food-related risks are perhaps more salient in our everyday experience than the others that increasingly cloud our hypermodern skies. Hence, in light of the current condition of excess, the lack of referents, and solidarity with broader social units, in light of the sense of isolation, individualism, and distrust in "expert systems," and in light of the imperative to "distinction," one possible response is to regain some sense of control over the basic realm of nutrition, and through it, perhaps, over other aspects of one's life as well. Enter the hypermodern eater and the "potential" aspect of the "All You Can Eat" logic.

Bye Bye Miss American Pie

> The fate of nations depends on how they eat. (Savarin)[48]

While on one hand, "All You Can Eat" evokes the idea of irrational excess and the risks it represents, it also refers to new potentials and opportunities at our disposal in the present moment. As Ascher explains:

> The potential choice of food available to the hypermodern individual is obviously increasingly broad, and transforms him into an eclectic eater; the decisions he takes, the comparisons he makes are increasingly differentiated; his meals are decreasingly tied to a specific social habitus.... In contrast, they are increasingly influenced by a series of variables which are not only understandable in terms of his tastes ... they constitute a new context for action and sensation, and entail health, physical fitness, a sense of safety and risk management, physical appearance and the ideal of self-control, collective identities, and ethical and political commitments.[49] [my translation]

To better trace the contours of this "potential" aspect in the realm of food, I compare Ascher's hypermodern nutrition with the McDonaldized one. Contrary to Ritzer's rather pessimistic outlook,[50] food seems to increasingly become one of the media some hypermodern individuals use to resist McDonaldization, to politicize and personalize food, thereby also meeting the imperative to "distinction" emphasized by De Gaulejac. While this approach to food is more visible in the "creative classes,"[51] it is different from — and more individualistic than — Bourdieu's notion of distinction.[52] Nevertheless, it goes without saying that the hypermodern approach I describe here is influenced by class position. To quote Barthes again, hypermodern eating is also an "attitude" that — as the Slow Food Movement, for example attests — can have real economic, political, ecological, cultural, psychological, and physiological consequences.[53] It entails a rejection of the McDonaldized and "All You Can Eat" approaches to food, and the promotion and development of alternative practices, attitudes and choices. Together, they challenge how we currently understand, represent, and enact all food-related activities, from the ecological to the psychological. If, as Ritzer suggests, McDonaldization is grounded in the four modernist principles of efficiency-calculability-predictability-control, the hypermodern approach is informed by the four *other* modernist principles of reflexivity, individuation, social differentiation, and elective association.[54] As a result — and although there are no guarantees — it contains the seeds of more optimistic, ecofriendly, and hence evolved, potentials.

These potentials have emotional and cognitive dimensions. Whereas McDonaldization alienates and infantilizes consumers, the hypermodern approach encourages us to reflect about our eating practices and to make conscious, informed, and ethical choices about what, how, when, where, how much, and in whose company we eat. Whereas McDonaldization thrives on predictability, the hypermodern approach emphasizes unpredictability, creativity, and permanent innovation. Whereas McDonaldization enforces a fixed set of options, the hypermodern approach thrives on constant attempts at new combinations. Whereas McDonaldization aims to accelerate the speed of preparation and consumption, the hypermodern approach is comfortable with a variety of tempos, and, if anything, is more likely to value slowness. Whereas McDonaldization promotes excess, the hypermodern logic values moderation and balance. Whereas McDonaldization aims at the perfect standardization of taste, the hypermodern approach promotes variability and individualized self-expression through the food we prepare and consume.

These potentials have practical and micro-social dimensions. Whereas McDonaldization constantly asks us to surrender the control of food-related activities, promising us efficiency, predictability, speed, "family time," and fun in return, the hypermodern approach insists that we should reclaim them. Not only do these activities produce tangible outcomes (i.e., they produce real meals), but they also open up recurring zones of time/space for collaborative interaction between significant others — a decreasing occurrence in today's society.[55]

These potentials have macro dimensions as well. Whereas McDonaldization seeks to impose the same bland taste on the rest of the planet, the hypermodern logic values and encourages the local, the authentic, and the exotic. Whereas McDonaldization conceals the source of the food it produces and the processes whereby it produces it, the hypermodern logic asks that we familiarize ourselves with the food we eat, and assume its personal, political, ethical, cultural, economic, and ecological dimensions. And while such an approach to food is also predicated on rationality, the difference is that this form of rationality is neither imposed from the central corporate office (à la McDonald's) nor inspired by greed or puerile desires (à la excessive "All You Can Eat").

Tell me what/how you eat, and I will tell who you are. In light of food's multiple dimensions, it does not seem unreasonable to suggest that these radically different practices, attitudes and choices guiding our nutrition can accomplish much more than reduce our gastro-anomie, cholesterol level, and waistline. Having regained more control in the realm of food, we might then look at other areas of our everyday life a little bit more closely, and feel better able to resist playing the obedient consumer favored by our increasingly McDonaldized institutions, and the voracious and profit-driven one hailed by the excessive "All You Can Eat" logic.

Of course, this is not enough, and I do not want to suggest that the extent of one's political activism should start at the Farmers' Market and end at the dinner table. Further, discussing the aesthetic, psychological, individual, and creative uses of food must not obscure the simple fact that food remains a scarce resource for millions of people. It goes without saying that our first concern as sociologists should be to examine, denounce, and propose solutions for the criminal inequalities that characterize the distribution of food across countries and across social classes in our own society. At the same time, it is also clear that these phenomena are related. By producing a disconnect from the food *we* eat, McDonaldization logically also facilitates a disconnect from the food *others cannot eat.* When the meaning of food becomes reduced to a good deal or a medium for corporate-sponsored ideas of fun, it becomes increasingly difficult to recognize its essential biological functions, and its scarcity among less fortunate and exploited others. Accordingly, by challenging McDonaldization and reclaiming nutrition, the hypermodern approach promotes this objective recognition.

The hypermodern approach to eating does not mean that everyone should become vegetarian, that processed food should henceforth be forbidden, or that the vast machinery of postindustrial food production should be dismantled. It is also clear that as Americans are increasingly forced to work more and rest less than most other citizens of the Western world,[56] and have an increasingly difficult time making ends meet, McDonaldized food is incredibly convenient, and saves precious hours of labor and money.[57] Similarly, I do not want to misrepresent myself as a paragon of politically correct eating, for I am not without sin. Still. the hypermodern approach to eating joins the growing chorus of voices that aim to raise our awareness (and memory) of the importance of food, of its multiple dimensions, of its increasing corruption and depletion, of alternatives, and of the benefits inherent in regaining some control over this essential activity. In so doing, it does offer a sort of "recipe for life" by reminding us of the simple lesson that the nutritional is indeed the personal and, hence, the political.[58]

Bon Appétit.

Notes

1. Roland Barthes, "Toward a Psychosociology of Contemporary Food Consumption," in *Food and Culture: A Reader*, ed. Carole M. Counihan and Penny Van Esterik (New York: Routledge, 1997), 20.

2. Jeremy MacClancy, *Consuming Culture: Why You Eat What You Eat* (New York: Henry Holt, 1993), 2.

3. Barthes, 21.

4. This notion of abundance is a bit more complex than sheer quantity because, while we certainly experience an abundance of food in terms of sheer *quantity*, there is a sharp but invisible depletion of species *variety*. This, while it is true that we have constant access to an apparent limitless *quantity* of eggs, milk, beef, and so on ... the species *variety* of these organisms is rapidly decreasing. See especially Carl Honoré (2004), 64–65.

5. Quoting Malraux, Ascher reminds us that "the great contribution of Dutch painting is not to have invented the idea of representing a fish on a plate, but of making it represent much more than the apostles' food" (88).

6. Francois Ascher, *Le mangeur hypermoderne: Une figure de l'individu eclectique* (Paris: Odile-Jacob, 2005).

7. Ibid.

8. Alan Beardsworth and Teresa Keil, *Sociology on the Menu: An Invitation to the Study of Food and Society* (New York: Routledge, 1997), 6.

9. Ibid., 2.

10. Ibid.

11. This general apathy in no way diminishes the sometimes heroic efforts by a variety of groups and organizations that seek to raise our awareness about the cruel treatment of animals, the dishonest, dangerous, and exploitative practices favored by giant food corporations, the hazardous products they sell, the pollution they generate, and the politicians who endorse, support and surrender (us) to them. Many of these organizations establish alternative nutrition-related enterprises, launch legal proceedings, and protest against corporations and other entities whose practices should certainly be labeled as criminal, and prosecuted as such. We all benefit from their actions and should support their efforts.

12. Evène, http://www.evene.fr.

13. Claude Fischler, "Food, Self and Identity," *Social Science Information* 27 (1988): 275.

14. See, for example, David Aaron Gordon.

15. Because of genetic manipulation, pesticides, and so on, many fruits and vegetables will look and stay firm for weeks, but will then unexpectedly shrivel almost overnight.

16. John L. Hess and Karen Hess, "The Taste of Y2K," in *Food in the USA: A Reader,* ed. Carole M. Counihan (London: Routledge, 2002), 15.

17. Claude Fischler, 289.

18. Simon Gottschalk, "The Greening of Identity: Three Environmental Paths," in *Studies in Symbolic Interaction*, ed. Norman K. Denzin (Greenwich, CT: JAI Press, 2001).

19. Dictionary, http://dictionary.reference.com/browse/taste.

20. Claude Fischler, 290.

21. Douglas Coupland, *Shampoo Planet* (New York: Pocket Books, 1992), 221.

22. Barry Smart, ed. *Resisting McDonaldization* (London: Sage, 1999); Mark Alfino, John S. Caputo, and Robin Wynyard, eds., *McDonaldization Revisited: Critical Essays on Consumer Culture* (Westport, CT: Praeger, 1998).

23. Roland Barthes, 20.

24. Douglas Kellner, "Theorizing/Resisting McDonaldization: A Multiperspectivist Approach," in *Resisting McDonaldization*, ed. Barry Smart (London: Sage, 1999), 190–92.

25. Ascher, 192.

26. George Ritzer, *The McDonaldization of Society*, rev. ed. (Thousand Oaks, CA: Pine Forge Press, 2004), 137.

27. This same logic explains the obsessive acceleration of everyday life I have discussed elsewhere. In this logic, faster is *ipso facto* always better.

28. William Alex McIntosh, *Sociologies of Food and Nutrition* (London: Plenum, 1996), 37.

29. Beardsworth and Keil, 152–53.

30. McIntosh, 43.

31. As Ritzer notes, consumers at fast-food restaurant are also put to work in a variety of functions.

32. Kellner, 198–99.

33. Smart, ed., *Resisting McDonaldization*; Alfino, Caputo, and Wynyard, eds., *McDonaldization Revisited*.

34. The "conveyor belt" metaphor is Ritzer's. See also John O'Neill, "Have You Had Your Theory Today?" in *Resisting McDonaldization*, 47.

35. Evène, http://www.evene.fr.

36. World of Quotes, *http://www.worldofquotes.com*.

37. Nicole Aubert, ed. *L'individu hypermoderne* (Paris: Erès, 2005), 14–15.

38. Jean Cournut, "Les défoncés," in *L'individu hypermoderne*, ed. Nicole Aubert (Paris: Erès, 2005), 64.

39. Simon Gottschalk, "Speed Culture: Fast Strategies in TV Commercials," *Qualitative Sociology* 22 (1999): 311–29.

40. Nicole Aubert, "L'intensité de soi," in *L'individu hypermoderne*, ed. Nicole Aubert (Paris: Erès, 2005), 73–87.

41. Vincent De Gaulejac, "Le sujet manqué: L'individu face aux contradictions de l'hypermodernité," in *L'individu hypermoderne*, ed. Nicole Aubert (Paris: Erès, 2005), 129–43.

42. Eugène Enriquez, "L'idéal type de l'individu hypermoderne: L'individu pervers?" in *L'individu hypermoderne*, ed. Nicole Aubert (Paris: Erès, 2005), 38–57.

43. François Ascher, *Le mangeur hypermoderne: Une figure de l'individu eclectique* (Paris: Odile-Jacob, 2005), 246.

44. Robert Castel, "La face cachée de l'individu hypermoderne: L'individu par défaut," in *L'individu hypermoderne*, ed. Nicole Aubert, (Paris: Erès, 2005), 119–28.

45. De Gaulejac, 131.

46. Ibid., 132.

47. Gilles Lipovetsky, *Le bonheur paradoxal: Essai sur la société d'hyperconsommation* (Paris: Gallimard, 2006); *L'ere du vide: Essais sur l'individualisme contemporain* (Paris: Gallimard, 1983); *Hypermodern Times* (Malden, UK: Polity Press, 2005).

48. Evène, *http://www.evene.fr*.

49. Ascher, 242.

50. George Ritzer, ed., *McDonaldization: The Reader* (Thousand Oaks, CA: Pine Forge, 2002), 255–66.

51. Richard L. Florida, *The Rise of the Creative Class and How It's Transforming Work, Leisure, Community, and Everyday Life* (New York: Basic Books, 2002).

52. Pierre Bourdieu, *Distinction: A Social Critique of the Judgment of Taste* (Cambridge, MA: Harvard University Press, 1984).

53. Carlo Petrini, *Slow Food: Collected Thoughts on Taste, Tradition and the Honest Pleasures of Food* (White River Junction, VT: Chelsea Green, 2001); Carl Honoré, *In Praise of Slowness: Challenging the Cult of Speed* (New York: HarperCollins, 2004); Mara Miele and Jonathan Murdoch, "Slow Food," in *McDonaldization: The Reader*, ed. George Ritzer (Thousand Oaks, CA: Pine Forge, 2002), 250–55.

54. Ascher, 241.

55. John de Graaf. ed., *Take Back Your Time: The Official Handbook of the National Movement* (San Francisco: Berrett-Koeler, 2003).

56. Ibid.

57. Current McDonald's Web commercials for the Asian market show that consumers in those societies may find McDonald's helpful for very similar reasons. See http://www.mcdonalds.com.

58. See especially Keith Tester, "The Moral Malaise of McDonaldization: The Values of Vegetarianism," in *Resisting McDonaldization*, 207–21.

Works Cited

Alfino, Mark, John S. Caputo, and Robin Wynyard, eds. *McDonaldization Revisited: Critical Essays on Consumer Culture*. Westport, CT: Praeger, 1998.

Ascher, Francois. *Le mangeur Hypermoderne: Une figure de l'individu eclectique*. Paris: Odile-Jacob, 2005.

Aubert, Nicole, ed. *L'individu hypermoderne*. Paris: Erès, 2005.

_____. "L'intensité de soi." In *L'individu hypermoderne*, edited by Nicole Aubert, 73–87.

Barthes, Roland. "Toward a Psychosociology of Contemporary Food Consumption." In *Food and Culture: A Reader*, ed. Carole M. Counihan and Penny Van Esterik, 20–27. New York: Routledge, 1997.

Beardsworth, Alan, and Teresa Keil. *Sociology on the Menu: An Invitation to the Study of Food and Society*. New York: Routledge, 1997.

Bourdieu, Pierre. *Distinction: A Social Critique of the Judgment of Taste*. Cambridge, MA: Harvard University Press, 1984.

Castel, Robert. "La face cachée de l'individu hypermoderne: L'individu par défaut." In *L'individu hypermoderne*, edited by Nicole Aubert, 19–128. Paris: Erès, 2005.

Coupland, Douglas. *Shampoo Planet*. New York: Pocket Books, 1992.

Cournut, Jean. "Les défoncés." In *L'individu hypermoderne*, edited by Nicole Aubert, 61–71. Paris: Erès, 2005.

de Graaf, John, ed. *Take Back Your Time: The Official Handbook of the National Movement*. San Francisco: Berrett-Koeler, 2003.

De Gaulejac, Vincent. "Le sujet manqué: L'individu face aux contradictions de l'hypermodernité." In *L'individu hypermoderne*, edited by Nicole Aubert, 129–43. Paris: Erès, 2005.

Dictionary.com. http://www.dictionary.references.com (accessed May 1, 2007).

Enriquez, Eugène. "L'idéal type de l'individu hypermoderne: L'individu pervers?" In *L'individu hypermoderne*, edited by Nicole Aubert, 38–57. Paris: Erès, 2005.

Evène. http://evene.fr.

Fischler, Claude. "Food, Self and Identity." *Social Science Information* 27 (1988): 275–92.

Florida, Richard. *The Rise of the Creative Class and How It's Transforming Work, Leisure, Community, and Everyday Life*. New York: Basic Books, 2002.

Gottschalk, Simon. "Speed Culture: Fast Strategies in TV Commercials." *Qualitative Sociology* 22 (1999): 311–29.

_____. "The Greening of Identity: Three Environmental Paths." In *Studies in Symbolic Interaction*, ed. Norman K. Denzin, 245–71. Greenwich, CT: JAI Press, 2001.

Hess, John L, and Karen Hess. "The Taste of Y2K." In *Food in the USA: A Reader*, ed. Carole M. Counihan, 15–21. London: Routledge, 2002.

Honoré, Carl. *In Praise of Slowness: Challenging the Cult of Speed*. New York: Harper-Collins, 2004.

Kellner, Douglas. "Theorizing/Resisting McDonaldization: A Multiperspectivist Approach." In *Resisting McDonaldization*, edited by Barry Smart, 186–206. London: Sage, 1999.

Lipovetsky, Gilles. *Le bonheur paradoxal: Essai sur la société d'hyperconsommation*. Paris: Gallimard, 2006.

_____. *L'ere du vide: Essais sur l'individualisme contemporain*. Paris: Gallimard, 1983.

_____. *Hypermodern Times*. Malden: Polity Press, 2005.

MacClancy, Jeremy. *Consuming Culture: Why You Eat What You Eat*. New York: Henry Holt, 1993.

McIntosh, William Alex. *Sociologies of Food and Nutrition*. London: Plenum, 1996.

Miele, Mara, and Jonathan Murdoch. "Slow Food." In *McDonaldization: The Reader*, edited by George Ritzer, 250–55. Thousand Oaks, CA: Pine Forge, 2002.

O'Neill, John. "Have You Had Your Theory Today?" In *Resisting McDonaldization*, ed. Barry Smart, 41–55. London: Sage, 1999.

Petrini, Carlo. *Slow Food: Collected Thoughts on Taste, Tradition and the Honest Pleasures of Food.* White River Junction, VT: Chelsea Green, 2001.

Ritzer, George. "Some Thoughts on the Future of McDonaldization." In *McDonaldization: The Reader,* edited by George Ritzer, 255–66. Thousand Oaks, CA: Pine Forge, 2002.

_____. *The McDonaldization of Society*, rev. ed. Thousand Oaks, CA: Pine Forge Press, 2004.

Tester, Keith. "The Moral Malaise of McDonaldization: The Values of Vegetarianism." In *Resisting McDonaldization*, ed. Barry Smart, 207–21. London: Sage, 1999.

World of Quote.. http://worldofquotes.com.

4

Raising the Bar

The Complicated Consumption of Chocolate

ELLEN E. MOORE

This essay examines chocolate as a form of unequal exchange that takes place between producers in "developing" nations and "first-world" consumers through an analysis of the way in which chocolate companies represent themselves and their products. Chocolate, a product that is almost wholly grown and harvested overseas for consumption in the U.S. and Europe, is uniquely situated to address a variety of issues including the separation between production and consumption, representation, the articulation of identities through consumption, and the phenomenon of neocolonialism, in which former colonies and "developing" nations remain economically bound to capitalist systems in North America and Europe. Methodology consists of an analysis of websites in the U.S. and the U.K. including more expensive, "luxury" chocolate like Godiva to less expensive, mass-produced chocolate like Cadbury and Hershey. The examination of chocolate companies' advertisements allows a glimpse into how different identities — including gender, ethnic, and national — can be constructed through the consumption of chocolate. The stereotypes presented for the consumer through advertisements serve to reinforce cultural notions of an ethnically homogenous British and U.S. national identity but also have a wider purpose, which is to help conceal the realities of chocolate production in Africa and Central America. The consumption of chocolate is thus almost exclusively associated with whiteness, while production is largely associated with exotic "Others." This paper thus deals with the politics of representation, demonstrating how media analysis of a single cultural object can shed light on the cultural and economic significance of the disconnect between production and consumption.

In a recent article about the relationship between the advertising strategy of Starbucks Coffee Company and the state of disconnect between consumption and production, Charlene Elliot notes that very few communication studies examine global culture using a specific, cultural artifact.[1] This project, which examines chocolate as a form of unequal exchange that takes place between producers in developing nations and U.S. and European consumers, is conducted through an analysis of the way in which chocolate companies represent themselves and their products. Chocolate, a product that is almost wholly grown and harvested overseas for consumption in the U.S. and Europe, is uniquely situated to address a variety of issues, including: the separation between production and consumption (and thus between consumers and producers); representation; the articulation of identities through consumption; and the phenomenon of neocolonialism, in which former colonies and "developing" nations remain economically bound to capitalist systems in North America and Europe.

In particular, this study examines how the residual effects of past empire persist in the portrayal of the "exotic," idealized producer in juxtaposition with white European/U.S. consumers, with analysis drawn primarily from chocolate companies' websites and television advertisements that present subtle stories about race for us to consume along with our chocolate. The stereotypes that are presented for the consumer in the advertisements serve to reinforce cultural notions of an ethnically homogenous British and U.S. national identity, but also have a wider purpose, which is to help conceal the realities of—and the real people involved with—chocolate production in Africa and Central America. This paper thus deals with the politics of representation, demonstrating how media analysis of a single cultural artifact can shed light on issues of cultural and economic hegemony. What becomes clear is that a "memory of empire" influences these practices today or, to use the words of Catherine Hall, "to consume chocolate is to consume history."[2]

The analysis includes an examination of websites from chocolate companies in the U.S. and the U.K., ranging from mass-produced, inexpensive brands like Hershey and Cadbury to "luxury" chocolate like Godiva. Each of these companies uses a particular strategy that falls on a spectrum of representational techniques, depending on the theme or story that is marketed. The examination of chocolate companies' advertisements also allows a glimpse into how different identities — including gender, ethnic, and national — can be constructed through the consumption of chocolate.

What this research shows is that there is an absence of certain information, or "silence," in the advertisements of chocolate companies that communicates just as powerfully as the overt images and texts that are presented.

According to Entman, "frames select and call attention to particular aspects of the reality described, which logically means that frames simultaneously direct attention away from other aspects. Most frames are defined by what they omit as well as include."[3] What follows is an examination of the various discourses of identity as presented by chocolate companies.

The Identity of a Chocolate Consumer

> "Advertisements are selling us something else besides consumer goods: in providing us with a structure in which we, and those goods, are interchangeable, they are selling us ourselves."[4]

According to Sidney Mintz, "Food choices and eating habits reveal distinctions of age, sex, status, culture, and even occupation."[5] From an analysis of chocolate companies' advertisements, it becomes clear that, regardless of the type of chocolate being marketed, chocolate is a gendered product: in most advertisements there is a clearly implied subjectivity of a female consumer. In addition, chocolate companies also include references to the hedonic, "sinful" pleasure associated with chocolate consumption (exemplified in the names of many chocolate desserts, such as "Chocolate Decadence," "Devil's Food Cake," "Chocolate Sin," "Chocolate Orgasm," and many others).

Chocolate companies' ads are thus clearly focused on the pleasurable, gendered aspect of chocolate consumption. But there are also clear ethnic distinctions being made in chocolate companies' advertisements that further constrict and construct the identity of a chocolate consumer as white. This narrow ethnic definition ultimately results in a sharp line being drawn between white consumers from Europe and North America and producers from Africa and Central America. The active construction of an ethnically homogeneous chocolate consumer through the images and text in chocolate companies' advertisements is partly based upon the history of chocolate consumption by the imperial, white European elite, and partly attributable to the current hegemonic relationship between both Europe and the U.S. and the nations that produce chocolate. All of the identities that are suggested by chocolate companies — indulgent pleasure-seeking, white European/American, and female — are explored in the following three sections.

The Chocolate Consumer as Pleasure Seeker

Chocolate has appeared in some form in hundreds of movies, books, songs, and in myriad other forms of mass media, usually as a symbol for love or sex. An indication of chocolate's role in signifying emotions in the U.S. is that chocolate is traditionally given on Valentine's Day as a way to express love or affection. Chocolate companies encourage this and other pleasurable meanings for chocolate through the advertising and packaging of their product, including messages such as Dove's 2003 slogan, "Chocolate is more than a taste: it is a feeling." Through communication like this, chocolate companies attempt to interpolate consumers into the identity of one who not only allows herself these indulgences, but who recognizes that to indulge is a good thing. Illustrating this, Godiva's slogan for its 2003 ad campaign was, "If chocolate is your downfall, you may as well enjoy the ride." In addition, in chocolate advertisements, when people are shown eating chocolate, it is usually in some ethereal, fantasylike setting such as a bath.

Dove Promises™, which are individually wrapped chocolate pieces, contain messages like "Laugh like a child" and "Isn't life sweet?" In this way, the messages in chocolate advertisements play into the growing phenomenon of "self-gifting," in which consumption of a hedonic product is seen as a "reward," and the appeal is to pamper oneself.[6] According to Rita Clifton, head of the marketing agency Interbrand, "This is the ultimate example of taking time out for yourself. OK, I could never quite see the point of eating a (chocolate bar) in the bath — not very practical, but then fantasies aren't meant to be."[7]

Chocolate as a Gendered Product

"Women and chocolate are a dream team and advertisers have cleverly ensured they stay that way."[8]

As evidenced from chocolate companies' marketing strategies, chocolate is a highly gendered product, with advertisements traditionally framed to appeal exclusively to women. Rita Clifton summarizes the gender connection succinctly: "Women are the key to chocolate advertising. They are not only important consumers in their own right but they also act as gatekeepers to the rest of the family. So it's important to get the approach right."[9] The implied female subjectivity in chocolate ads is indicated by several factors, but most overtly by the multiple images of women who are in the process of consuming chocolate in website advertising. The advertisements on Cadbury's website demonstrate the strong association between women and chocolate, especially in the use of the Cadbury "Flake Girl," different women chosen to represent the company during different ad campaigns. Other websites — including Hershey's and Godiva — also are oriented towards women: Hershey's website depicts women cooking chocolate recipes for their children or relaxing at a Hershey World spa, while Godiva (for its most recent ad campaign called "Chocoiste") presents thinner, younger, and more beautiful women.

Regardless of the type of woman represented, these websites make a clear association between women and chocolate consumption. In this sense, the images are telling a story that both creates and reinforces supposedly natural associations (in the sense defined by Goffman[10]) between women and chocolate. Chocolate companies' advertising strategies thus use stereotypical tropes of femininity that seem to indicate that women have a biological "need" for chocolate; what also becomes clear, however, is that the ads also include stereotypical notions regarding the ethnicity of a chocolate consumer.

Ethnic and National Identity: Whiteness and Consumption

According to Alcosta-Alzuru and Kreshel, "Ethnicity is one of the factors that influences the conceptualization ... of what is American."[11] A perusal of mainstream chocolate company websites — including Cadbury, Hershey, and Godiva — tells the story of an ethnically homogenous (i.e., white) chocolate consumer in the U.S. and Europe. In the websites examined for this research, only one (Hershey's) contained a photo of an African American (a child): *none* of the other websites (aside from Fair Trade companies, who normally highlight the African or Central American producers — and not consumers — as a selling point), depicted a person of color as a consumer. The lack of ethnic diversity in chocolate companies' advertisements provides a strong indication that there is a firm line drawn in regard to ethnic boundaries when it comes to chocolate consumption.

According to Molina and Valdivia,[12] the concept of ethnicity is closely tied to the idea of authenticity in national identity, and women's bodies often are used to stand in for national identity. The concept of using the body to represent the qualities of a nation is incorporated into this analysis and extended to chocolate companies' use of the images of white women: just as Latina/o bodies are used to represent the (supposedly homogeneous) Latin American countries and communities, the white women used in the chocolate ads (including Hershey, Godiva and Cadbury) are used to narrowly define U.S. and European identity as white. This homogeneous definition of national identity has several implications: as Sidney Mintz notes in his description of the relationship between colonies and empires, dependent countries (and the people in them) are seen as "remote, poorly known, and imperfect extension(s) of Europe."[13] In this sense, U.S. and European identity is based upon what it is *not*, and people of other ethnicities are depicted in the websites (as producers only) solely to provide a backdrop against which to define European identity.

Mass culture, according to Bell Hooks, is the place that most readily presents the idea of the vicarious enjoyment — and demarcation of — racial difference, which she refers to as the "commodification of Otherness."[14] As other writers have acknowledged, the depiction of race in the media serves to highlight the idea of whiteness.[15, 16] Hooks elaborates upon this idea by describing ethnicity as a "spice, a seasoning that can liven up the dull dish that is mainstream white culture."[17]

According to Goldman and Papson, in order to correctly interpret the stories that advertisements tell, we must discern first how we as the spectator-buyer are positioned, and secondly how the commodity is positioned.[18] In this sense, the images within the Cadbury ads invite us to connect with the story being told about the ethnic identity of a British citizen using idealized, historical images depicting white Europeans. Cadbury's website — like Hershey's, Mars/M&M, and others — provides the company's version of the history of chocolate production, which includes mention of both the original producers of chocolate ("native" peoples of Central America) as well as the shift to consumption by white Europeans in the 17th and 18th centuries. On the Cadbury website, there are multiple depictions of white Europeans enjoying chocolate at parties or while shopping in outdoor markets.

These images in Cadbury's marketing appear to be intended to appeal to the British consumer's familiarity with England's colonial history. Indeed, Cadbury chocolate is so closely tied in to British identity that Catherine Hall notes that for English citizens living in the British colonies "staying English in the Empire could be aided by eating Cadbury's chocolate."[19] This is what Goldman and Papson refer to as a "desirable referent system,"[20] in which the romanticized images of Britain's colonial past — as depicted in Cadbury advertisements — resonate with the consumers of Cadbury chocolate. According to Molina and Valdivia, images in the media are "more than the visuals; instead the images are invitations to sign-on for mainstream narratives,"[21] which, in the case of chocolate companies, are nostalgic themes of an ethnically homogeneous Britain and U.S. Nostalgia-themed advertisements demonstrate how national identities are constructed in the advertising strategies of chocolate companies, but what about the producers of chocolate? As is evident in the website images, chocolate companies maintain a strict control over what information is revealed about the origins of chocolate. This creates a different way to define the "first world" consumer, this time using images of the "Other."

Using the Exotic "Other"

Liebes and Katz describe a process called *cultural flow*, in which media messages about cultural values travel in a one-way kind of flow to developing nations.[22] In a similar form of information control, chocolate companies restrict knowledge that goes *back into* the U.S. about foreign cultures and their values, only allowing their version of the "exotic" into the marketing of the product. This is the case with Starbucks coffee, in which foreign culture is turned into an exotic commodity that people can purchase, a process requiring that the origins of coffee (i.e., the labor practices, the people who harvest the beans, and the economic condition of the region) be obscured except to reveal the appealingly exotic nature of the product.[23] In their analysis of peoples of the Caribbean and Latin America, Molina and Valdivia have recognized this phenomenon, noting that individualism is often obscured by the depiction of a series of tropical, highly sexualized, stereotypes of an exotic "Other."[24]

On Cadbury's website, the section on the history of chocolate includes a series of images that provide a clear depiction of an "exotic" Other in the form of Monteczuma, the Aztec ruler, who is classically orientalized, with brown skin and colorful, ethnic garb, providing an example of what Nakamura refers to as "the familiar iconography of colonialism and its contemporary cousin, tourism."[25] Through images such as these we can take a trip to see through privileged eyes the "unspoiled" natives. He is also depicted in a highly sexualized manner, with his clothing revealing muscular arms and the skin of his stomach. Britain's Cadbury represents the extreme end of this spectrum since, like no other chocolate company, it bases its identity (and that of its consumers) on a romanticized trope of its imperial past.

One particularly telling image on Cadbury's website clearly places the first world viewer/consumer in a position of power over the producer, one who is able to look upon the image from the privileged perspective of a 'first world' gaze. The image is a drawing depicting the value of cacao beans: four beans equal a large squash; 10 beans are equal to a rabbit; and 100 is equivalent to a "native," a man with long dark hair dressed in a loincloth. In theory, Cadbury includes this image to indicate how cacao beans were used as currency in the New World. But it serves another purpose as well: gazing at this illustration, we can see just how many beans we would need to purchase a human being. Hershey's website also provides the counts needed to purchase items using cacao beans but excludes reference to the buying and selling of human beings. However, the site created by Hershey's (www.all chocolate.com) also quite clearly defines producers as exotic people of color and consumers as light-skinned Europeans and Americans.

The Exotic Other and the Disconnect Between Production Versus Consumption

At this juncture, the question must be asked as to who benefits from the perpetuation of these myths. It is clear that the chocolate companies believe that they benefit from the perpetuation of the cultural perception of British and U.S. identity as white, and also from the depiction of "exotic" Otherness. But why is this necessarily the case? There are numerous potential reasons for the state of disconnect between producer and consumer, including the phenomenon of globalization and the many steps between harvesting the raw material, transportation, processing, packaging, and marketing. But what may also play a role is the cultural divide between U.S. and European consumer culture and the producers in poorer countries in Africa and Central America. What is posited here is that there is a connection between the perpetuation of ethnic stereotypes (of both British and U.S. white consumers as well as "third-world" producers) and the effort made by the chocolate companies to hide the realities of chocolate production from the consumer. Specifically, the perpetuation of ethnic stereotypes serves to reinforce the distance (and thus the state of disconnect) between producer and consumer.

Since its creation from the cacao bean, chocolate has been produced and consumed in vastly different geographical locations, with neither the producers nor the consumers having much knowledge of the other. In his discussion of sugar production and consumption, Mintz states that there are two mutually exclusive realities, namely those of producers and of consumers, and as privileged, wealthy consumers we only experience only one reality.[26] Currently, the majority of chocolate that is sold to U.S. and European markets comes from West Africa as an unfinished product;[27] by the time it is refined, virtually no trace of the original African producer is evident. As a result, any information about the producers of chocolate — where and how they live, their socioeconomic status, working conditions, and the like — is easily transformed by the chocolate companies into an exotic trope that is used to sell the product, while concealing the harsher realities of the source. Elliot refers to this process as "conceptual repackaging," which serves to obscure uglier details of the production process that would be incongruous with the pleasure that comes from consuming it.[28] This psychological detachment of the consumer benefits companies that use illegal and injurious human labor to produce their product. What follows is a brief description of the production methods that were used at the inception of European chocolate consumption in the 17th and 18th centuries, how they influenced current labor practices and, ultimately, how Europe's hegemonic relationship with Africa and Central America created the opportunity for using slave labor for chocolate production spanning several centuries and continuing today.

The Chocolate (Dis)connection: "Third-World" Producers Versus "First-World" Consumers

Consumption

Since its creation from the cacao bean by groups in Central America over 2,000 years ago, chocolate has been a product that has used forced labor for consumption by the elite.[29] In Aztec society, chocolate consumption was restricted to the rulers, army warriors, and the *pochteca* (merchants) who carried cocoa beans to the Aztecs in trade.[30, 31] As a result, the consumption of chocolate was used as a signifier of privileged status. This conception — and practice — of chocolate did not change when the first imports of chocolate from Central America arrived in Europe.

From the beginning of the frenzied mass consumption of chocolate, Europeans used slave labor to produce chocolate using intricate and lengthy harvesting and processing methods. Due to the complicated and lengthy process involved in chocolate production (which involves harvesting, fermenting, roasting, hand grinding, and final preparation), as well as the long distance it was transported, the cost of consuming chocolate was prohibitive for the majority of European society; in fact, initially only royalty could afford to consume it.[32, 33, 34] To ensure its elite status, laws were passed in France that no one but the aristocracy could partake of chocolate. In England, however, chocolate followed a different path: there, chocolate houses were opened for anyone who had the money and desire for chocolate, although the cost was initially still prohibitive to the majority of British society.[35] Eventually, however, chocolate houses became so popular in England that they surpassed tea and coffeehouses.[36] During this time, chocolate was still a handmade product; with the advent of the Industrial Revolution and Van Houten's cocoa press, however, chocolate and many other luxury items could be mass-produced (thus with less expense), paving the way for mass consumption.[37]

Mass production and consumption, however, did not change the relationship — or, to use the words of Mintz, the "networks of control and dependence" — between consumer and producer.[38] Today, the definition of "elite" in terms of chocolate consumption has changed: it is not so much a well-defined socioeconomic sector within the U.S. or Europe, but rather the privileged have become the members of wealthy "first world" (the consumers) versus the impoverished, "third world" nations (the producers). Thus, the image of working class, white, British citizens on Cadbury's website who are enjoying chocolate still represents a privilege, one based on membership within white Europe.

Production

Mintz notes that European countries established plantations in the Caribbean, Central America, and elsewhere in the world to produce sugar, coffee, chocolate, and other goods in the 17th and 18th centuries.[39] These plantations used a combination of indigenous labor and African slaves to work the crops. Later, cacao crops were moved to Africa because cacao grew easily there and because there was a ready supply of labor that eliminated the need for slave transport. The Cote d'Ivoire (or Ivory Coast) in West Africa now produces 43 percent of the world's cocoa beans;[40] combined with three other nations — including Cameroon, Ghana and Nigeria — West Africa produces 70 percent of the world's cocoa.[41]

The majority of the children that are involved in the slave trade come from families in impoverished parts of West Africa, like Mali, that desperately need money. Slave traders entice families with promises of relatively large amounts of money for a year's worth of labor from their children. The children are then taken to cacao plantations hundreds of miles away with no communication to their families, and the families do not receive compensation. Untrained and with no access to medical care or adequate nutrition, the children are exposed to the difficult, harmful and sometimes deadly process of harvesting cocoa beans. This labor is made more harmful by the spraying of large amounts of pesticides, exposing the workers to dangerous levels of chemicals.[42] Any government regulations regarding child labor — including the minimum age, the amount of hours to work, how workers are fed and housed — are enforced on an erratic basis only. According to Raghavan and Chatterjee, "Nearly 300,000 children are working on cocoa farms in West Africa in dangerous conditions that endanger their lives," and they estimate that 6,000 children may be enslaved in the Cote d'Ivoire alone.[43]

The chocolate industry appears to be aware of the slavery problems in West Africa: Hershey's site addresses this issue by discussing how it works with African farmers; however, it is unclear how effective their actions are in changing the labor practices. For instance, Godiva chocolate company takes a strong stance against child slavery, with company representatives stating that they receive declarations of fair labor practices from their European cocoa suppliers; however, Godiva's Belgian supplier candidly states that "what we don't control, we can't guarantee."[44] That is, they receive assurances from the Cote d'Ivoire farmers that no unsafe practices are occurring, but they are not there to verify these claims. Within a global economy, and with the multiple subcontracting companies that contribute to a finished product, it is nearly impossible to check out all steps of production involved with different products that are produced on a daily basis. In addition, the problem has not received enough mainstream media attention to warrant dissemination to the majority of consumers of chocolate.

Looking Past Advertising: The Reality of Chocolate Production

The idea put forth in this essay is that the definition of British (and U.S.) nationality by chocolate companies as white serves to complete the disconnect between producer and consumer, which is beneficial to chocolate companies because some of the uglier aspects of production (i.e., the impoverished state of West African countries and the related phenomenon of child slavery) do not "fit" well with chocolate companies' discourse that defines chocolate as a hedonistic, pleasurable product. The ideological, geographical, and socioeconomic rift between producer and consumer is best illustrated through an examination of the messages contained in Dove Chocolate Promises™ (Table 1) and through a comparison of images taken from chocolate companies' websites and those from news reports by Swift[45] and by Raghavan and Chatterjee,[46] whose investigative journalism in West Africa was funded by UNICEF and other international agencies.

Table 1. Differences between Producers and Consumers.

Dove Promise Messages	*Current Working Conditions in the Cote D'Ivoire*
"Work less, sleep more"	Children in the cocoa plantations work as much as 12 hours a day.[20]
"Find your inner child"	Children as young as nine years are forced to apply banned pesticides, use a machete, and haul backbreaking loads on the cocoa plantations.
"Chocolate is not just a taste: it's a feeling"	Children who work on the plantations have never tasted chocolate produced from the beans they harvest year-round.[21]
"The only promise you should break is a Dove Promise™"	Aly Diabate, a young teenage boy from Mali, was promised a new bike and money for his family if he worked for one year. A year and a half later, he told stories of forced labor and being beaten with bicycle chains. His family never received the money promised, and he received no bike.[22]
"Isn't life sweet?"	As a result of the actions of the World Bank in the late 1980s, life in the Cote d'Ivoire has declined from the most prosperous nation in the region to one on the verge of economic collapse.[23]

Utopia Versus Reality

The disconnect between production and consumption is enabled by the fact that most people are not aware of the illegal, injurious labor that is connected with their small moments of chocolate enjoyment. According to Mintz: "When the locus of manufacture and that of use are separated in time and space, when the makers and the users are as little known to each other as are the processes of manufacture and use themselves, the mystery will deepen."[51] However, no amount of marketing by the chocolate companies can completely erase the harsh reality of chocolate production, although chocolate companies appear to try. One example is provided by Cadbury, which, in its section on chocolate production, includes a photo of African cacao

producers. In essence, it is an image of "exotic" Others who represent romanticized, airbrushed tropes of producers that contribute to the story Cadbury
is attempting to tell about the nature of chocolate production and consumption.

In the photo, two people of unspecified African origin stand at the base
of a cacao tree. They gaze up at the tree in an apparent evaluation of the development of the cacao pods, in a manner that implies that they have skill and
knowledge regarding its cultivation. Idealized depictions of life on the plan-
tation are not, of course, new, as Mintz notes in his discussion of 18th-cen-
tury drawings that romanticize the labor performed on colonial sugar
plantations.[52] Mintz states that "The artist's choice of exotic costume was a
common affectation of the time. In fact, cane-cutting gangs worked in rags,
under the direction of a 'driver' who held a whip in his hand."[53]

The Cadbury photo serves to reassure us as the consumer in many ways.
First, their hands are free of machetes and other tools used to harvest cacao,
and their clothes — "traditional" African garb — are clearly visible. As "first-
world" consumers, we can rest assured that that these African producers have
lost nothing in the way of their traditional values in the process of producing chocolate for us. In addition, the clothes are spotless, with the white gar-
ment of the taller individual clearly contrasting with the background. Not
only do cacao producers retain their cultural traditions, but they also possess
a life of relative ease, in which cacao pods mature at a lazy rate, and the har-
vesters are free to participate in other aspects of African cultural life besides
cacao production. Nakamura describes images like these as ones in which
"ethnic difference ... is virtually cleansed of its divisive, problematic, tragic
connotations."[54]

Through these images, Cadbury and other chocolate companies are able
to retain an idea of a not only "exotic," but a happy and contented "Other"
that represents an old trope represented by fictional characters such as Uncle
Tom (the happy slave) and "Sambo." It is very important for Cadbury and
other chocolate companies to present this image because behind it is the harsh
reality of slave labor involving children in West Africa. In a very real way,
then, images of an unproblematic, anachronistic, exotic "Other" provide a
"corrective text" for U.S. and European consumers.[55]

Conclusion

Ultimately, Williamson[56] states that the exchange of meanings between
consumer and product results in a "'vicious circle,' in which we give meaning to ads, and they give meaning to us." As this essay has attempted to
demonstrate, major chocolate companies like Cadbury, Hershey's, and Godiva

enable this process by creating myriad, interconnected discourses that not only identify chocolate as an item of hedonic pleasure that is enjoyed solely by U.S. and European consumers and define U.S. and European consumers — as well as national identity — as white, but the companies also provide idealized, tropicalized images of cacao producers in Africa and Latin America that serve not only to reassure white consumers but also to allow for vicarious consumption of an exotic "Other." Considering the geographical distance between production and consumption sites, as well as a cultural divide created by stereotypes, these discourses contribute in part to the disconnect between producers and consumers. As Sidney Mintz notes, however, although details of the origins may be obscured, it is still true that people who would otherwise be unknown to each other continue to be linked through time and space in a complicated relationship, one that produces separate identities for both producer and consumer.

Notes

1. Charlene Elliot, "Consuming Caffeine: The Discourse of Starbucks and Coffee," *Consumption, Markets and Culture* 4 (2003): 369–82.

2. Catherine Hall, "'Turning a Blind Eye': Memories of Empire," in *Memory*, ed. Patricia Fara and Karalyn Patterson, Darwin College Lecture Series (Cambridge, UK: Cambridge University Press, 1998), 27.

3. Robert Entman, "Framing: Toward Clarification of a Fractured Paradigm," *Journal of Communication* 43 (1993): 54.

4. Judith Williamson, *Decoding Advertisements: Ideology and Meaning in Advertising* (London: Marion Boyers, 1978), 42.

5. Sidney Mintz, *Sweetness and Power: The Place of Sugar in Modern History* (New York: Penguin, 1985), 3.

6. David Glen Mick and Michelle DeMoss, "Self-Gifts: Phenomenological Insights from Four Contexts," *Journal of Consumer Research* 17 (1990): 322–32.

7. Glenda Cooper, "Women and Chocolate: Simply Made for Each Other," *New York Times* March 20, 2004, *http://www.chocolate.org/choclove/wbomen.html* (accessed October 13, 2004).

8. Ibid.

9. Ibid.

10. Erving Goffman, "Introduction to Gender Advertisements," *Studies in the Anthropology of Visual Communication* 3 (1976): 65–68.

11. Carolina Alcosta-Alzuru and Peggy J. Kreshel, "I'm an American Girl... Whatever That Means: Girls Consuming Pleasant Company's American Girl Identity," *Journal of Communication* 52 (2002): 139–61.

12. Isabel Molina and Angharad Valdivia, "Brain, Brow or Bootie: Iconic Latinas in Contemporary Popular Culture," *Communication Review* 7 (2004): 205–21.

13. Sidney Mintz, *Sweetness and Power: The Place of Sugar in Modern History* (New York: Penguin, 1985), xvi.

14. bell hooks, "Eating the Other: Desire and Resistance," in *The New Consumer Society Reader*, ed. Juliet Schor and Douglas B. Holt (New York: New Press, 2000), 343.

15. Rachel Dubrofsky, "The Bachelor: Whiteness in the Harem," *Critical Studies in Media Communication* 23 (2006): 39–56.

16. Kent Ono, "Remembering Spectators: Meditations on Japanese American Cinema,"

in *Countervisions: Asian American Film Criticism,* ed. Darrell Hamamoto and Sandra Liu (Philadelphia: Temple University Press, 2000), 129–49.

17. bell hooks, "Eating the Other: Desire and Resistance," in *The New Consumer Society Reader,* 343.

18. Robert Goldman and Stephen Papson, "Advertising in the Age of Accelerated Meaning," in *The Consumer Society Reader,* ed. Juliet Schor and Douglas B. Holt (New York: New Press, 2000), 81–98.

19. Hall, 38.

20. Goldman and Papson, 81–98.

21. Molina and Valdivia, 210.

22. Tamar Liebes and Elihu Katz, *The Export of Meaning: Cross-Cultural Readings of 'Dallas'"* (Oxford: Polity Press, 1993).

23. Charlene Elliot, "Consuming Caffeine: The Discourse of Starbucks and Coffee," *Consumption, Markets and Culture* 4 (2003): 369–82.

24. Molina and Valdivia, 205–21.

25. Lisa Nakamura, "'Where Do You Want to Go Today?': Cybernetic Tourism, the Internet, and Transnationality," in *Race in Cyberspace,* eds. Beth Kolko and Gilbert Rodman (New York: Routledge, 2002), 98.

26. Mintz, 3.

27. Richard Swift. "The Cocoa Chain," *New Internationalist,* 304 (1998), http://www.newint.org/issue304/introduction.html.

28. Charlene Elliot, 369–82.

29. Sophie D. Coe and Michael D. Coe, *The True History of Chocolate* (London: Thames and Hudson, 1996).

30. Joël Glenn Brenner, *The Emperors of Chocolate: Inside the Secret World of Hershey and Mars* (New York: Random House, 1999).

31. Coe and Coe.

32. Brenner.

33. Swift, "The Cocoa Chain."

34. Coe and Coe.

35. Swift, "The Cocoa Chain."

36. Brenner.

37. Ibid.

38. Mintz, xvi.

39. Ibid.

40. International Cocoa Organization, *Annual Report 2002/03,* http://www.icco.org/anrep/anrep0203english.pdf

41. Sudarsan Raghavan and Sumana Chatterjee, "Youth Sold to Ivory Coast Farmer Killed Trying to Escape," *Kansas City Star,* August 17, 2001.

42. Swift, "The Cocoa Chain."

43. Sumana Chatterjee, "Report: 300,000 West African Children Work in Dangerous Conditions," http://www.globalexchange.org/campaigns/fairtrade/cocoa/323.html (2002).

44. Ibid., 6

45. Swift, "The Cocoa Chain."

46. Chatterjee, "Report."

47. Swift, "The Cocoa Chain."

48. Ibid.

49. Raghavan and Chatterjee.

50. International Labor Rights Foundation, *May 2005 Report— Child Labor in Agriculture: Focus on Child Labor on Cocoa Farms in West Africa and the Chocolate Industry's Initiative to Date,* http://www.laborrights.org/projects/childlab/cocoa_childlabor_update_May05.pdf.

51. Mintz, xxiii.

52. Ibid.

53. Ibid.

54. Nakamura, 94.

55. Ibid, 95.
56. See Williamson, 41.

Works Cited

Acosta-Alzuru, Carolina, and Peggy J. Kreshel. "I'm an American Girl... Whatever That Means: Girls Consuming Pleasant Company's American Girl Identity." *Journal of Communication* 52 (2002): 139–61.

Bordo, Susan. "Hunger as Ideology." In *The Consumer Society*, eds. Juliet Schor and Douglas.B. Holt, 99–116. New York: New Press, 2000.

Brenner, Joël Glenn. *The Emperors of Chocolate: Inside the Secret World of Hershey and Mars.* New York: Random House, 1999.

Chatterjee, Sumana. "Report: 300,000 West African Children Work in Dangerous Conditions." http://www.globalexchange.org/campaigns/fairtrade/cocoa/323.html (2002).

Coe, Sophie D., and Michael D. Coe. *The True History of Chocolate.* London: Thames and Hudson, 1996.

Cooper, Glenda. "Women and Chocolate: Simply Made for Each Other." *New York Times*, March, 13, 2004. http://www.chocolate.org/choclove/women.html.

Dubrofsky, Rachel. "The Bachelor: Whiteness in the Harem." *Critical Studies in Media Communication* 23 (2006): 39–56.

Elliot, Charlene. "Consuming Caffeine: The Discourse of Starbucks and Coffee." *Consumption, Markets and Culture* 4 (2003): 369–82.

Entman, Robert. "Framing: Toward Clarification of a Fractured Paradigm." *Journal of Communication* 43 (1993): 51–58.

Godiva Chocolates. "Company Practice Description." http://www.godiva.com/about/faq.asp.

Goffman, Erving. "Introduction to Gender Advertisements." *Studies in the Anthropology of Visual Communication* 3 (1976): 65–68.

Goldman, Robert, and Stephen Papson. "Advertising in the Age of Accelerated Meaning." In *The Consumer Society Reader*, eds. Juliet. B. Schor and Douglas. B. Holt, 81–98. New York: New Press, 2000.

Hall, Catherine. "'Turning a Blind Eye': Memories of Empire." In *Memory*, eds. Patricia Fara and Karalyn Patterson, 27–46. Darwin College Lecture Series. Cambridge, UK: Cambridge University Press, 1998.

Hooks, Bell. *Black Looks: Race and Representation.* Boston: South End Press, 1992.

International Cocoa Organization, *Annual Report 2002/03.* http://www.icco.org/anrep/anrep0203english.pdf.

Liebes, Tamar, and Elihu Katz. *The Export of Meaning: Cross-Cultural Readings of 'Dallas.'* Oxford: Polity Press, 1993.

Long, Nuala. "The Long Column." Ireland's Marketing Monthly. http://www.marketing.ie/sep03/article3.htm (2003).

Mintz, Sidney. *Sweetness and Power: The Place of Sugar in Modern History.* New York: Penguin, 1985.

Molina Guzmán, Isabel, and Angharad Valdivia. "Brain, Brow or Bootie: Iconic Latinas in Contemporary Popular Culture." *Communication Review* 7 (2004): 205–21.

Nakamura, Lisa. "Where Do You Want to Go Today?: Cybernetic Tourism, the Internet, and Transnationality." In *Race in Cyberspace,* eds. Beth Kolko and Gilbert Rodman, 15–26. New York: Routledge, 2000.

Ono, Kent A. "Remembering Spectators: Meditations on Japanese American Cinema." In *Countervisions: Asian American Film Criticism,* eds. Darrell Hamamoto and Sandra Liu, 129–49. Philadelphia: Temple University Press, 2000.

Raghavan, Sudarsan, and Sumana Chatterjee. *How Your Chocolate May Be Tainted.* http://vision.ucsd.edu/~kbranson/stopchocolateslavery/atasteofslavery.html#part1.

_____. "Youth Sold to Ivory Coast Farmer Killed Trying to Escape." *Kansas City Star,* August 17, 2001.

Redfern, Catherine. "Not for Girls? The Yorkie and Echo Adverts." *The f-word: Contemporary UK Feminism* . http://www.thefword.org.uk/reviews/2002/05/not_for_girls_the_yorkie_and_echo_adverts (May 2002).

Swift, Richard. "The Cocoa Chain." *New Internationalist* 304 (1998). http://www.newint.org/issue304/introduction.html.

Tulley, S. E. "Making Chocolate, Spending Pesos, Consuming Oaxaca: Commercializing a 'Traditional' Food Industry in Southern Mexico." Paper presented at the Annual Meeting of the Society for Applied Anthropology in San Francisco, California, March 24, 2000.

Williamson, Judith. *Decoding Advertisements: Ideology and Meaning in Advertising.* London: Marion Boyars, 1978.

5

The Espresso Revolution

Introducing Coffee-Bar Franchising to Modern China

JACKIE COOK AND ROBERT LEE

Wanchai, January 2007

The self-catering counter in my room at a Chinese business hotel presents me with an interesting snapshot of contemporary hot-beverage tastes. The quick-boil kettle is accompanied by a small stand, with self-serve packages to suit every preference. At the back: sachets of instant coffee. Beside them, powdered milk, labelled "Creamer," in the American way, and refined white sugar. In the front, a choice of tea. Clearly, this is still a tea culture—but a further scan of the labels tells me much, much more....

To the right of the stand is the British choice: an Indian Darjeeling—all six sachets still available. To the left, a traditional Chinese "black tea"—by which is meant a fermented, dark, rich flavoured brew—a Pu-Erh. None of these used, either. In the middle: one remaining Green tea, with jasmine.

It is mid-winter. This high-use of the lighter, hot-weather tea surprises me.

I mention it later to work colleagues. Ms Leung and Ms Cheng laugh. "Fashion!" they say. "Younger Chinese no longer develop the taste for the heavy traditional teas.... They take too long to brew—and in those tiny clay pots.... Who has time for that?"

I watch office workers rushing to the twin cold water/boiled water drink fountain as their meeting takes a break. A quick splash of boiled water into a polystyrene cup—quick swirl of jasmine tea, or instant coffee grains. Ms Leung and Ms Cheng are right: only coffee and the quick-brew lighter teas can produce something drinkable at this pace. Modern Chinese culture is speeding away from its slower, more reflective cultural traditions.[1]

This paper begins a longer, two-year study investigating the cultural politics of the entry of coffee-bar enterprises to the mainland Chinese market. It follows the scoping of a new business opportunity by a Hong Kong financial venturer and a Chinese-Malaysian food-industry manager, as they explore the potential for launching a coffee-bar franchise in Provincial China, outside the major international hub cities.

Cutting in and out of small "snapshots" of the study context such as that outlined above, the chapter tracks three propositions.

Coffee as a Sign of Modernity

Firstly, our evidence suggests that coffee is viewed in China as largely a Western social tradition: a sign of modernity and urban sophistication, likely to achieve its fastest social diffusion through younger city workers. A Western coffee-bar is viewed as a primary sign and validation of economic development in the province. The Chinese view it as a Western brand and as a place that signifies almost a sense of arrival for their local province or their city. In the quest for westernization and modernization, a coffee bar has become the standard in which a city is measured in terms of its economic success.[2]

By examining the locations of existing coffee franchises in the largest mainland Chinese cities, including consideration of their interior design and exterior promotional signage, we are capturing the ways coffee and coffee bars are being presented to urban Chinese workers, and gaining a view of the sorts of demographics most attracted. But coffee bars are not landing in China as if on some *Terra Nullius*,[3] without its own systems of beverage provision and use. Long-established habits of tea-drinking pose complex challenges for the coffee-bar habit.

Chinese Traditions of Teahouse Culture

To establish context, the study is also observing Chinese teahouse traditions, particularly well-preserved in the more distant provinces such as Sichuan. How far have these continued to provide cultural focus and social connection for more remote local communities? Do they parallel coffeehouses in the Islamic world, Europe and the Americas? Can aspects of their role be appropriated into the new coffee-bar culture? Not to displace or replace them, but to help bridge them, too, into the new demands of a rapidly modernizing China.

Coffee-bars as (Small) Hubs in "the Creative City"[4]

Finally, the study takes up the rather more radical possibility introduced within the new "creative industries" or "informational cities" movement. This theorizes that the new data industries, clustered around communication and information services, have been most successful when concentrated into Silicon Valley equivalents, which can link high-intensity research and development institutions, university-based or corporate, with "application and specification" and even "implementation" agents, including venture capital and prototype manufacturing workshops, and even the real estate industries fostering subsequent expansion, whether on undeveloped outer-suburban lands, or redesignated urban industrial space, abandoned by "heavy" manufacturing.[5]

These new, high-intensity creative precincts, now identifiable around the developed world, mark the presence of vibrant digital technologies and communications media connectedness, and have become highly theorized within social planning and economic redevelopment policies at national and regional levels, globally. What this research has noted, however, is the complete absence of any address within this literature or its thinking, of the need to consider precisely what constitutes spaces of human congress: the food outlets and spontaneous meeting spaces through which sociability and ideas exchange enhance creativity. Neither the food-culture movement, nor the now rapidly amassing literature on how to plan and foster the creative city, have linked into entrepreneurship at the level of advising small, local catering businesses on how to set up and succeed in such spaces, despite the fact that coffeehouses in particular, as we shall argue, have so clearly been an originary space for the sorts of freewheeling, cosmopolitan venture capitalism and cooperative "communicative action"[6] human relations behind these new creative industries concepts.

Put simply, we suggest that spaces of social congregation and human servicing, such as coffee bars, are a crucial but to-date disregarded element of the incubator zones of talent-massing and ideas-exchange central to the uptake of Richard Florida's very influential views on creative cities.

"The way I see it, coffee is the energy of the knowledge economy"[7]

Florida's ideas on how to amass creativity in order to jump-start informational industries for the new knowledge economy, adopted widely into economic policy planning for the information era across the Asian region, suggest that of the three key features of the drive towards the new digital informational economy, *reindustrialization, regional development,* and *synergy,* it is the third which is most important. It can be defined as "the generation of new and valuable information through human interaction."[8] This massing of talent, the daily sharing of experiences, trends, early notice of availability and shortages, is common to all flourishing market economies, but not easily enabled by the specialist sequestrations of the modern office, bank and factory, which are thought to have driven the first industrial revolution and its concentration of urban labor and supply servicing. A classic 1890 economic study described the synergy offered by industrialization:

> When an industry has chosen a locality for itself, it is likely to stay there long: so great are the advantages which people following the same skilled trade get from near neighbourhood to one another. The mysteries of the trade become no mysteries; but are as it were in the air, and children learn many of them unconsciously. Good work is rightly appreciated, inventions and improvements in machinery, in processes and the general organisation of the business have their merits promptly discussed: if one man starts a new idea, it is taken up by others and combined with suggestions of their own; and thus it becomes the source of further new ideas....[9]

Within British industrialization, change itself had become "high fashion" by the mid-eighteenth century, as is clear in a satirical representation of the period by Dr. Samuel Johnson:

> The age is running mad after innovation. All the business of the world is to be done in a new way: men are to be hanged in a new way; Tyburn itself is not safe from the fury of innovation.[10]

This frenzy for the new related not to any lust after technology "in the metal"[11] or for the actual machines which change production techniques, but the "soft" technologies of social relations which establish the preconditions for productivity, in the Foucauldian sense.[12] It is these social changes, which so often seem to *result* from the introduction of new technologies, which in fact enable the implementation of the technological breakthrough, bringing the new machines into productivity, and their products to market. A "supervening social necessity" must be present for technical changes to be taken up within either production or consumption: a demand-drive, which moves a good technical idea beyond the bench test and prototype stage.[13] In the mid-eighteenth century, this included for instance the ways in which, after the financial scandals of the South Sea Bubble speculations, "businessmen were actively experimenting with new forms of organisation."[14] The rise of joint-stock associations and fire and marine insurance, systems enabling a marked intensification in otherwise risky international trading, were among the soft or synergistic innovations, influenced by the new forms of social networking:

> Marine insurance, which had been barely distinguishable from frivolous speculation in the early part of the century had become a skilled professional service of some consequence by 1771, when the Society of Underwriters at Lloyd's Coffee House subscribed to build a new Lloyd's Coffee House and to separate itself from the miscellaneous gamblers and brokers of all kinds who frequented the old Coffee House.[15]

This intriguing reminder of the origins of those still-powerful commercial services alerts us to how important it may be to take stock of exactly how, and where, today's business innovators and experimenters actually cluster. Can these sorts of thinking about synergy be used again? Might the original models behind this thinking, coffee- and teahouses introduced into Enlightenment Europe, have one further role to play?

The "Genealogy" of Tea and Coffee Drinkers

One part of the answer lies in the capacity of an entire nation to either change its hot-beverage habits — to exchange tea for coffee — or to assert its own, very powerful, preferences, and so modernize the teahouse. The first relies on a complex question: Can a person's physiological "tastes" change to accommodate fashion? If everyday life regimes such as those which might lead an individual to "the coffee habit" arise within the "habitus"[16] repertoires available inside everyday cultural living, where our identity forms, how difficult is it to achieve such habitus change? In particular, how hard is it to transform at the level of "hexis," or the patterned behaviors of the body? How do tea drinkers become coffee drinkers, and when, and why?

A teahouse/coffee bar ethnography of young Chinese patrons, conducted inside the social rules of relatively informal, sociable "chat," offers insights into this very specific form of identity work. Tea- or coffee-drinking, as some of the anecdotes suggest, is not simply a question of consumer choice. Each in its way establishes a particular palate: a physiologically trained set of very distinctive "tastes," quite literally inscribed onto the body of the drinker, whose taste buds and digestive system must be taught to respond to the altogether unnatural act of swallowing a hot substance, infused with aromatic, but also semi-toxic, herbs.

The body's hexis, or physical responsiveness, forms itself around habitual activities, until it enacts them routinely, as if "natural." Both coffee and tea, with their varying levels of caffeine and tannins, have the known capacity to command hexis formation to levels approaching addiction: to exert consumption desire of irresistible proportions. But this is not an immediate physical response: it cannot be, and is not achieved overnight. Even in major tea and coffee cultures, children, for instance, are largely excluded from full participation — testified to in the introduction of the "babyccino," mostly frothed milk — to coffee-bar culture. At a greater physiological depth hexis helps explain the Hong Kong — and Malaysian — introduction of *yuen yeung:* the evaporated or sweetened-condensed milk-tea habit. It reminds us that China is not, and to some degree cannot be, a milk-drinking culture, not simply because of its relative lack of dairying traditions, a serious supply problem for a short-life product, but because levels of the milk-clotting agents needed to make it a digestible food are low in Chinese populations. To inculcate a milk-product consumption has meant oblique or tangential campaigning: milk introduced through ice cream, and so through sweet-tasting blended drink products such as *yuen yeung*. Evidence of the iced-coffee-with-lemon trend in Hong Kong reinforces the explanation for lemon curdles milk, and allows us to understand that what is meant there by "iced coffee" is not the milkshake derivative of Western cafés, but a drink modeled on iced tea.

Nor do Chinese coffee-bar habitués behave in ways anticipated by Western entrepreneurs.

> In the United States, approximately 80 percent of Starbucks' drinks are ordered "to go," while in China the ratio is inverted, with 80 percent of drinks ordered to be consumed in the store. By better understanding the market and responding to the unique needs of the region, Starbucks is emerging in the minds of Chinese patrons as a destination restaurant and not just an American beverage provider.[17]

Bourdieu's rather broader — and more broadly known — concept of "habitus," or habituated activities, learned within the heavily acculturated social spaces that one "inhabits" with greater or lesser success, helps explain why Chinese coffee-bar clients choose different hours and patterns of service demand. Habitus forms in us and around us, as we adapt to and adopt the behaviors, attitudes and interests of those with whom we share social space. The home, the local community, the wider culture, each contribute to the specifics of habitus, and while it is a dynamic process, open to change, major transformations such as a shift from tea to coffee require the exertion of equally major social, economic and cultural influences.

Coffee-drinking in China is already showing every sign of a strongly entrenched habitus presence, one which is defying expectations from U.S.-based understandings of how coffee drinking is placed within the lives of urban workers. For younger mainland Chinese, like their diasporic cousins across Asia's booming business economies, coffee, and not tea, is associated with the fast pace of modern life, and modernization itself. Having seen cities arise before their eyes, part of urbanization literally from the ground up, they have entered a different world from the public hot-water taps and personal thermos-flasks of their parents' and grandparents' centralized and communal tea-drinking.

Shaanxi Province, North-Central China, 1982

In previous generations of China's modern era, large family-sized flasks, decorated in flashy, high-coloured "good luck" peony or chrysanthemum patterns, were filled with hot water for a day's use, often at the steam-heated brass taps of the commune's bath-house to save lighting a coke stove just to boil water. Then they were carried home by Grandmother or a younger daughter, and tea made straight into the cup. Whether enamelled tin or china, tea-cups came with a lid to conserve the heat, providing a long-term drink through the day, endlessly topped-up with just a little more hot water....

Small portable tea-shops, two panniers on a shoulder yoke, with tea-equipment in one basket and little bamboo chairs for patrons in the other, accompanied citizens everywhere that their mostly female proprietors could reach — and that included onto river ferries, up stepped mountain paths, and into the fields. Train-crew drew hot water from the steam locomotives, and carried it in tin kettles from carriage to carriage, refilling the flasks provided for each berth. Everyone, male or female, had an army water-bottle or a screw-topped glass jar in a beaded carry-net, attached to the belt for easy carriage, and filled and refilled across the day with tea, rather than water.

In the unheated buildings of a North Chinese winter hot tea warmed cold hands, and sent up satisfying small clouds of steam as the lid was removed from the cup, a sign of the restorative powers inside. In the un-air-conditioned heat of the Central or South Chinese summer, tea hot or cold refreshed and slaked thirst. It needed no additives: was entirely itself, and stood without rival as the central medium of every social transaction. Before sunflower or watermelon seeds, before peanuts, before cakes — even before rice — tea would be offered.[18]

The degree to which this diffusion of a single commodity through an entire mass culture went largely unnoticed is, if anything, emphasized by the degree to which that same culture had all but obliterated the more refined traditions of tea as a ceremonial aspect of hospitality, along with its apparatuses of tea-services, tea tastings, the master-crafting of clay pots and china bowls, and the fostering of the personal tea-palate to levels reserved in the West to wine connoisseurs.

By the end of the "proletarianizing" of the Great Cultural Revolution, the central Chinese town of Jingdezhen, scene of three millennia of pottery making, had almost entirely lost the skilled artisans able to make the very finest "four qualities" porcelain ("thin like egg-shell; white like paper; translucent like crystal; rings like a bell") which off set the finest teas. The precious clays of Hangzhou, traditionally reserved to the manufacture of the small, unglazed, black, brown or olive-drab *yixing* teapots said to best infuse the most expensive tea leaves, were reserved to the specialized "Friendship Stores" accessible only to foreign tourists. Those few remaining gourmet tea stores were full of dusty galleries of unlabeled specialist teas, still available for the personal mixes of their mostly elderly patrons, who, like the proprietors, knew already what each tea was, and had no need of any form of promotional or informational cataloguing. It was, in other words, almost impossible to assemble, even in cities with millions of inhabitants, the apparatus needed to develop the palate and the habits of a serious, knowledgeable tea drinker, at least without prior contacts. In "modernizing" China under Mao Zadong and his immediate successors, tea served only the masses, and that in stripped-down, functionalist, standardized ways, which maximized its use by eliminating its infinity of forms.

Only in the more far-flung locations of twentieth-century China did elements of the older traditions of tea-drinking endure. In Chengdu, capital of the mountainous Sichuan province, the wattle-and-beam gabled houses marking local building tradition also maintained working neighborhood teahouses, where patrons came to sample fruit-infused teas as they gossiped, debated politics, played cannon-chess, or listened to traditional storytellers or opera performances. Here, tea remained ceremonial, and retained forms of a traditional etiquette, central to the table, with dishes of dried fruit or herbs progressively offered for steeping. Servers assiduously refilled only those cups whose lids were removed by patrons: the infusion process was not to be disturbed, as individuals calculated the strength and the heat to their own tastes. Accompaniments — nuts, fruit, dumplings, small cakes — were of a flavor and scale not to interfere with the tea, while patrons, unlike those of all other contemporary food or drink providers, could remain hour after hour, in thrall to the long and slow development of their own composition of a perfect tea or tea sequence.

It is this near-lost tradition, tea-drinking at the level of artistic development and aesthetic contemplation, supporting other pastimes which themselves focused sociability — conversation, debate, narrative, and behind them music and song, poetry, and contemplation of nature — which clung on in the tea houses of Chengdu. The habitus it both expressed and sustained, while in marked contrast to that of the dynamic, change-oriented sociability and information exchange of the Western version of the coffeehouse, still focused the particular power of the Chinese tradition: its stability, its capacity to regulate, and, above all, its sense of cultural depth and permanence.

The social uses of space, captured in the design of the built environment, are inevitably constructed around a given set of production-consumption conditions, and equally inevitably reflect relations of social power:

> The urban fabric, with its multiple networks of communication and exchange, is likewise part of the means of production....
> Urban space ... continues to ensure that links are properly maintained between the various flows involved: flows of energy and labor, of commodities and capital. The economy may be defined, practically speaking, as the linkage between flows and networks, a linkage guaranteed in a more or less rational way by institutions and programmed to work within the spatial framework where these institutions exercise operational influence. [19]

What is perhaps less obvious is how both tea- and coffeehouse culture, building themselves into the very foundations of their respective social enterprises, came both to promote and to channel particular forms of social communication. What now remains to be seen is which is better predisposed to support the new communicative flows and "networks" of today. If Habermas is right, and the coffeehouses of Europe became the new *agora* through which economic development was fostered at the level of the sociable exchange of information,[20] then coffee bars — and possibly more modern forms of the teahouse which are already being established — may also prove crucial in the emergence of the super economy that is 21st-century China. But might what results from such a project also, perhaps, come to influence the global culture with which China is now so potently engaged? Is China, like Hong Kong and the active fusion cultures of the Chinese diaspora, already producing new coffeehouse/teahouse "incubators," which analysts are yet to observe?

If it is, then coffee entrepreneurs will need to take account of aspects of a broader set of habitus predispositions than they have so far been prepared for. When, for instance, coffee equals modernity, being seen to be a consumer becomes all- important. To young Chinese consumers, the glass-fronted, café-styled, open-plan coffee bar is itself a space of display: highly lit, glitzy, and entirely continuous with the screened, self-promoting culture of *MySpace* and *YouTube*, across which their own preferred forms of social mobility and information exchange currently work.

Guangzhou, South China, 2007

Ms Li tells me about drinking coffee with her banking colleagues.

It is mid-afternoon, and they are all going to be working late. Several of the younger women decide to take a break in a nearby coffee-bar, to snack before the European market figures come in, since then they will probably miss dinner. They are also going to celebrate a birthday. Ms Li is nervous however about leaving her post, and decides to stay behind.

Suddenly she gets a call on her personal mobile phone. It is the girls from the office — down in the coffee-bar. They have sent her a digital video file: as she holds up her phone they pan across their table, showing each setting with a delicious cake selection....

"Get down here NOW or miss out!" they SMS.

Peer pressure — and the images of a good time — force her downstairs.[21]

Chinese public coffee-drinking, like its tea-drinking and its restaurant traditions, is fundamentally gregarious. It is about sharing: peer relations, building trust. While, like its Western counterparts it is often also about building long-term relations with a local vendor, even in a franchised and so "de-localized" business, clients are likely to arrive in groups, to need substantial seating and tables, and to expect a lengthy stay, and ongoing service.

All of these demands, formed in other aspects of Chinese habitus, change the ways in which any coffee-bar venture will need to approach the Chinese market. How then, do they intersect with the ways in which entrepreneurs in the catering industries approach the development of new business? And are there elements within the almost exclusively informal business-planning processes used in the food industries, which might assist in their adaptation to the Chinese context?

Thought about in such ways, these aspects of mainland Chinese habitus seem interestingly close to the "ideas exchange" public sphere expectations of enterprises setting up within the creative informational hub cities. Is there perhaps a particular synergy available here, intersecting the "fusion" traditions of Asian catering, the "creativity" of Richard Florida's and Manuel Castells' information hubs, and the dynamism and energy associated with Western modernity? What might China be about to add to the coffee-bar culture of the creative city?

The Politics of Guanxi: The Coffee-bar as a Space of Mutual Benefit

Running a successful business venture in China is by now widely known to pose an ongoing challenge for Western entrepreneurs. Commentators within central business studies literature have made it clear that Western ideas do not always prevail in China, where government regulation, staff relations, and ethical foundations are markedly different.[22] Chinese business traditions are strongly enmeshed, self-evidently successful, and absolutely indifferent to Western expectations of change. It is Western entrepreneurs who must adjust to these local unwritten rules if they plan to enter the modern Chinese market. New behaviors — often directly opposed to learned core values — and new contact strategies must be developed.

China is a business culture with traditions millennia old, and where "networking" of the type Marshall identified as crucial to innovation, and which Florida and Castells see as inherent in the creativity of the new information industries and economy, is already central to all business relationships. An unstable policy climate, one subject to personal interventions and unanticipated state decree, means that businesses need protective links and information flow from local bureaucracy. City Party Secretaries, generals in state-owned enterprises, registrants of foreign real estate and directors of foreign investment will all influence a business if they see an interest in the income generated. *Guanxi,* or mutual benefit, introduces a degree of integration into existing business habitus which few Western-trained entrepreneurs could achieve, and yet, perhaps surprisingly, many of the features of this regime mimic those of the family-founded catering businesses central to coffee-bar development. At the same time, the sociability and interpersonal relations achieved within *guanxi* sit comfortably enough with the strongly relational "synergies" model of the creative informational incubator hub to which this study, at least, links the new coffee-bar culture.

For the modern-day coffee-bar entrepreneur seeking start-up status in China, the issues now become clearer. What both the information-hub model and the Chinese cultural tradition seek is an extensible, participatory streaming of ideas and energies, the quality which Castells calls *flow:*

> By milieu of innovation we understand the social, institutional, organisational, economic, and territorial structures that create the conditions for the continuous generation of synergy and its investment in a process of production that results from this very synergistic capacity, both for the units of production that are part of the milieu and for the milieu as a whole.[23]

What Castells and Hall call "the continuous generation of synergy" is precisely what Habermas' isolation of the coffee-house as origin of the modern public sphere identified: a place not simply for congregation, but for *flow* of its collaborative outputs. The Habermasian coffeehouse sought to activate and energize forces inside and outside itself, to pull into its ambit the influential, the dynamic, the creative, and then to have them operate their influence beyond the immediate locale, scoping new business, new ventures, new concepts.

In the work of Manuel Castells, it is this second phase which is crucial: the capacity to pool ideas and to network with contacts in order to arrive at "investment in a process of production," that is, to drive ideas into actual productivity. For Castells, flow is everything. His "space of flows" characterizes the information era, signifying and helping generate and sustain the high-speed informational networks of data — and people — to make enterprises work. The coffeehouse as communications hub and meeting venue can be central to ideas generation.

To get there though will mean an ongoing process of "localizing" adaptation. Since in China the current need is to be *seen* to be a coffee drinker, to be identified with modernity, this may mean taking up the older teahouse tradition of long, settled presence in a given venue, alongside the *guanxi* advantages of being a known and trusted client, able to help build and sustain a protective support group around a business, members of which themselves become clients, and introduce others. The peer-group pressures of Chinese social life, where food consumption involves whole families, or work colleagues, in long-term group formations, introduce and help sustain these "obligation"- and "loyalty"-driven affiliations to spaces of congress, and may mean adapting décor to suit larger groups, longer stays, and different space mixes, such as a return to private rooms for business groups.

At the same time, at an individual level, the relative unfamiliarity with coffee, and especially the lowered capacity for it to be introduced through the milkier varieties, may mean that coffee-drinking in China needs to be diffused through the conventions of tea-tasting, providing for development of the palate. Just as coffee provedores offer advice on the grinding and blending of beans for preparation and serving in the various domestic machines available, so too in coffee-bars, a *barista* may need to be able to advise, reblend, and even offer tastings, to both new and established clients. Such rituals, if introduced, would serve to prolong client presence in the ways Chinese patrons appear to be expecting, and would make the entire coffee-bar experience accessible to more consumers.

In these ways, it seems that China's turn to "modern" coffee-drinking is likely to bring the coffee-bar itself to something very like the incubator status within the creative city, in Florida's terms: to make of it a Castellsian "space of flows" in which "mutual benefit" exchanges of ideas, information, and relationship-building can occur. If it succeeds, it brings the coffee-house back to its originary preeminence, as in itself an incubator of commercialism. Coffee, it seems, as Trang Nguyen suggested, may well be about to provide "the energy" for China's *espresso* revolution.

Notes

1. Quotations from the authors' journals are italicized.

2. See Joseph. A. Michelli, *The Starbucks Experience:— 5 Principles for Turning Ordinary into Extraordinary* (New York: McGraw-Hill, 2007), 121–22; for a *Seattle Times* report by Monica Soto Ouchi, "A U.S. Icon Counts on China to Fill Its Cup," October 9, 2005.

3. *Terra Nullius* is a significant term for Australian researchers, indicating the legal status attributed to the Australian continent by European explorers and subsequently colonists, who failed to acknowledge indigenous culture and ownership, and considered it an "empty" or uninhabited land. Global franchising can be guilty of the same preconceptions.

4. The term is now widely used, but its most popular formulation is in the work of Richard Florida. See especially R. Florida, *The Rise of the Creative Class* (Victoria, Australia: Pluto Press, 2003) and *The Flight of the Creative Class* (New York: Harper Collins, 2005).

5. For a complete account of these changes from manufacturing to information and communication industries and the adaptations they force on urban infrastructure and planning, see especially Manuel Castells and Peter Hall, *Technopoles of the World: The Making of 21st century Industrial Complexes* (London: Routledge, 1994). Also useful is Edward W. Soja, *Postmetropolis: Critical Studies of Cities and Regions* (Oxford: Blackwell, 2000).

6. The concept is part of Jürgen Habermas' theory of communication, in which he posits that a fully democratic "public sphere" communicates through collaborative forms of social congress. See Jürgen Habermas, *The Structural Transformation of the Public Sphere: An Inquiry into a Category of Bourgeois Society* (Cambridge, UK: Polity Press, 1992), and *The Theory of Communicative Action, vol .2: Lifeworld and System: A Critique of Functionalist Reason* (Cambridge, UK: Polity Press, 1987).

7. The quote was recorded in a discussion with Trang Nguyen as Vietnam's principal coffee provedore, discussing how to compete with the Starbuck's franchise, on *CNN Malaysia,* Kuala Lumpur, March 18, 2007.

8. Castells and Hall, 224.

9. Alfred Marshall, "Industrial Organization, Continued. The Concentration of Specialized Industries in Particular Locations," in *Principles of Economics,* Book IV, Chapter 10 (London: McMillan, 1920), 225.

10. Dr. Samuel Johnson, in James Boswell, *Life of Johnson,* Chapter 34. Online: at www.worldwideschool.org/library/books/hist/biography/LifeofJohnson/chap35.html.

11. See especially the work of Brian Winston, *Media Technology and Society: A History from the Telegraph to the Internet* (London: Routledge, 1998).

12. Michel Foucault, "Technologies of the Self," in *Technologies of the Self: A Seminar with Michel Foucault,* ed. Luther H. Martin, H. Gutman, and Patrick H. Hutton (Amherst: University of Massachusetts Press, 1988), 16–49.

13. Winston, *Media Technology and Society.*

14. Phyllis Deane, *The First Industrial Revolution* (Cambridge, UK: Cambridge University Press, 1965), 120.

15. Ibid.

16. The concepts of "habitus" and "hexis" both stem from the work of Pierre Bourdieu. See especially Pierre Bourdieu, *Distinction: A Social Critique of the Judgement of Taste* (London: Routledge and Kegan Paul, 1984), and *Logic of Practice* (Cambridge, UK: Polity Press, 1992).

17. Michelli, 121.

18. From the authors' journals.

19. Henri Lefebvre, *The Production of Space* (Oxford: Blackwell, 1994), 347.

20. See especially Habermas, *The Structural Transformation of the Public Sphere.*

21. From the authors' journals.

22. See in particular works by the following: Carolyn Blackman, *China Business: The Rules of the Game* (Sydney, Australia: Allen and Unwin, 2000); Peter F. Drucker, *Innovation and Entrepreneurship* (New York: Harper Collins, 1985); James McGregor, *One Billion Customers: Lessons from the Front Lines of Doing Business in China* (London: Nicholas Brealey, 2005); Michael E. Porter, *Competitive Advantage: Creating and Sustaining Superior Performance* (New York: Free Press, 1998).

23. Castells and Hall, 9. See also Manuel Castells, *The Network Society* (Oxford: Blackwell, 1996).

Works Cited

Blackman, Carolyn. *China Business: The Rules of the Game.* Sydney, Australia: Allen and Unwin, 2000.

Bourdieu, Pierre. *Distinction: A Social Critique of the Judgement of Taste.* London: Routledge and Kegan Paul, 1984.

_____. *Logic of Practice.* Cambridge, UK: Polity Press, 1992.

Castells, Manuel. *The Network Society.* Oxford: Blackwell, 1996.

Castells, Manuel, and Peter Hall. *Technopoles of the World: The Making of 21st-century Industrial Complexes.* London: Routledge, 1994.

Crombie, Gavin. *The Way of the Dragon.* Queensland, Australia: Wrightbooks, 2005.

Deane, Phyllis. *The First Industrial Revolution.* Cambridge, UK: Cambridge University Press, 1965.

Drucker, Peter. *Innovation and Entrepreneurship.* New York: Harper Collins, 1985.

Florida, Richard. *The Flight of the Creative Class.* New York: HarperCollins, 2005.

_____. *The Rise of the Creative Class.* Victoria, Australia: Pluto Press, 2003.

Foucault, Michel. *The Archaeology of Knowledge.* London: Routledge, 1997.

_____. "Technologies of the Self." In *Technologies of the Self: A Seminar with Michel Foucault,* eds. Luther H. Martin, H. Gutman, and Patrick H. Hutton, 16–49. Amherst: University of Massachusetts Press, 1988.

Habermas, Jürgen. *The Structural Transformation of the Public Sphere: An Inquiry into a Category of Bourgeois Society.* Cambridge, UK: Polity Press, 1992.

Lefebvre, Henri, *The Production of Space*. Oxford: Blackwell, 1994.

McGregor, James. *One Billion Customers: Lessons from the Front Lines of Doing Business in China*. London: Nicholas Brealey, 2005.

Michelli, Joseph. *The Starbucks Experience: 5 Principles for Turning Ordinary into Extraordinary*, New York: McGraw-Hill, 2007.

Porter, Michael. *Competitive Advantage: Creating and Sustaining Superior Performance*. New York: Free Press, 1998.

Soja, Edward. *Postmetropolis: Critical Studies of Cities and Regions*. Oxford: Blackwell, 2000.

Winston, Brian. *Media Technology and Society: A History from the Telegraph to the Internet*. London: Routledge, 1998.

6

Mass Agrarianism

Wal-Mart and Organic Foods

DAWN GILPIN

The organic foods movement came about in part as a reaction against the trend towards industrialized mass production and distribution of processed foods in the United States. Wal-Mart, on the other hand, represents a clear expression of this latter trend. It is the world's largest retailer, and has been a lightning rod for public debate about mass distribution and its effects on the urban landscape, consumer culture, economy, and social justice, among other subjects. Wal-Mart's decision in 2006 to increase its range of organic foods thus represents a cultural conundrum, bringing together two apparently contradictory approaches to food production and distribution. This juxtaposition has forced consumers, policymakers and others to reexamine the notion of "organic," including its economic and cultural significance. The study described in this chapter examined reports from a variety of media sources to explore the social and cultural tensions reflected in competing perceptions of what organic foods represent, and where Wal-Mart fits into the organic landscape.

The World of Organics

From Movement(s) to Industry

The so-called organic movement is far from a unified block of growers, handlers, distributors, and consumers. Its varied landscape is indeed probably one key to its increasingly widespread appeal. The start of the organic farming movement is generally credited to the Englishman Sir Albert Howard, who published several books urging farmers to shun chemicals and focus on enriching the soil through natural means.[1] In the U.S., the Depression and the devastating dust bowl phenomenon spawned a parallel critique of industrialized growing practices.[2] The organic agriculture movement in this country traces its formal lineage to J. I. Rodale, who brought Sir Howard's ideas to the United States.[3] Its continued success has been attributed to the multiple overlapping ideological strands the movement represents: from those concerned with food health and safety to counterculture groups to environmentalists.[4]

Concerns about food safety arose as food production and distribution became increasingly industrialized. The Pure Food and Drug Act was passed in 1906 in response to fears about contamination resulting from unsafe processing and packaging practices.[5] Food safety today is also closely linked to the environmental movement, as one of the reasons most commonly cited by consumers for preferring organic products is the avoidance of pesticides on produce.[6] Since the 1970s, the environmental movement has increasingly emphasized the theme of sustainable development.[7] One key notion of sustainability is "bioregionalism," which suggests that relying on local, seasonal crops and other food products will naturally reduce the need for pesticides, processing, and transport, lessening the impact of food production and distribution on the environment.[8]

The New Left in the 1960s contributed another influence to the organic agriculture movement. This faction of the movement existed in direct opposition to mainstream food production and distribution, seeking to promote alternative modes of land stewardship and ownership. Food production was explicitly linked to issues of social justice, self-actualization through "communing with nature," and anti-establishment sentiment.[9] At another point of the political spectrum, agrarian populism represents the perspective of small, family-owned farms that see agribusiness as a threat to a way of life that is, as Julie Guthman observed, "deeply rooted in U.S. political and cultural history and has emerged repeatedly as a trope of anticorporate sentiment."[10] Given their emphasis on the landowner/farmer, agrarianists do not necessarily espouse the same values of social justice as the counterculturists, and tend to be far more socially and politically conservative than those who come to the organic movement via other routes. Note, however that all of these strands contain underlying critiques of capitalism and industrialization.[11]

Thus, the organic agriculture movement includes a rather motley assortment of bedfellows. As Samuel Fromartz remarked, this diversity of interests leads to sharp conflicts and disagreements concerning the issue of organic foods. The diversity of the movement has also been a strength, "since it increases the pool of potential consumers and prevents any one interest group from controlling its fate."[12] This variety is reflected among consumers of organic foods as well, catering to "a wide base that includes health-and-nutrition devotees, fitness fanatics, foodies, environmentalists and core organic consumers."[13] This broad appeal of organic foods is, of course, precisely what makes it attractive to mass-market food producers and large distribution chains.

The grocery industry has changed considerably since the early '70s, when conventional wisdom said that "nutrition does not sell food."[14] In *The Omnivore's Dilemma*, journalist Michael Pollan wrote that "the inspiration for organic was to find a way to feed ourselves more in keeping with the logic of nature, to build a food system that looked more like an ecosystem that would draw its fertility and energy from the sun."[15] From this perspective, organic foods produced on an industrial scale present some inherent contradictions. And yet, there is no denying that organic foods are a growing economic sector with an increasing industrial component.[16] The organic movement has blurred its edges with industry, becoming an uneasy hybrid of complex cultural values and agricultural practices. What, then, does *organic* mean in practice?

Organic, or What's in a Name?

In the United States today, the term *organic* has a very specific technical meaning. That meaning is constantly shifting; however, as a result of the policymaking process; political writer Alexander Cockburn called it "a word already under very serious stress."[17] Just as the different factions of the organic movement represent different values and understandings of organic, those who participate in shaping policy bring to the table a variegated spectrum of interests and goals. *Organic* is thus a function of its history and the particular configuration of the regulatory bodies and other players responsible for its ongoing construction. A brief overview of the organic policymaking process can offer some insight into how this construction takes place.

The 1990 Farm Bill was the first federal attempt to establish a national scheme for regulating the production, marketing, and labeling of organic foods, known as the Organic Foods Production Act (OFPA).[18] To be classified as organic under the provisions of the OFPA, an agricultural product must be produced and processed without the use of synthetic chemicals, on land to which no such chemicals have been applied for at least three years, and follow an organic plan governing the production and handling processes, created jointly by the producer and/or handler and the accredited certifying agent.[19] Livestock must be fed and raised according to specific criteria, without the use of synthetic hormones or antibiotics, and careful, traceable records must be maintained including information on lineage, feed, and medications administered.[20] It is important to note that the term organic refers solely to how agricultural and other food products are produced and handled, with no implications regarding content, safety, quality, or healthfulness.[21]

The National Organic Program (NOP) provides three categories of labels for organic products. Products produced using only certified organic ingredients and processes may be marked "100 percent Organic," while those containing at least 95 percent organic ingredients and the remainder on the National List of permitted nonorganic inputs may also be labeled "Organic." Both categories are eligible for the official USDA seal. Products containing from 70 percent to 95 percent certified organic agricultural ingredients can be marked as "Made with organic ingredients," but may not bear the USDA seal.[22]

The OFPA also established the National Organic Standards Board (NOSB) to assist in developing standards for organic foods production. Policy recommendations by the NOSB are provisional until accepted by the USDA. The 15 board members are appointed by the secretary and must include four individuals who own or operate organic farming concerns; two who own or operate organic processing firms; one representative from retail; three environmental experts; three representing consumer organizations or other public interest groups; a scientific expert in biochemistry, ecology, or toxicology; and an authorized certifying agent. Members serve staggered 5-year terms.[23]

The composition of the Board is therefore designed to represent the broad spectrum of interests involved in the organic foods issue. It meets at least twice a year, and is open to participation by any citizen who wishes to voice concerns relative to organic foods regulatory policy.[24] However, the structure of the NOSB creates an economic rather than a political model of a regulatory system, in which multiple vested interests negotiate the rules of a circumscribed marketplace.[25] Citizen access to these regulatory bodies is largely symbolic, as people are more likely to become nominal members of various interest groups than participate directly in the policymaking process.[26] The counterculture movement has thus morphed into a form of representative subscription service.

Among those economic interests who come to the organic policymaking table, we now also have the largest company the world has ever known.

Wal-Mart: David, Meet Goliath

When Wal-Mart announced in March 2006 that it would be doubling its offerings of organic products, the response was controversial. This should come as no surprise, since the massive scale of the enterprise and its emphasis on price over quality would seem to place it in direct opposition to the anti-establishment, environmentalist strands of the organic movement.

Wal-Mart's impact on the environment is a controversial issue that has received a fair bit of media attention. Whole ecosystems in distant countries are not immune to the Wal-Mart effect. For example, Charles Fishman reported that salmon prices dropped by about 75 percent from the early 1980s to 2005, thanks to a Chilean salmon farm industry created specifically to serve Wal-Mart customers. This industry is now creating an environmental and public health dilemma for the country due to the poor sanitary conditions of the fisheries, which are kept overstocked to satisfy rising demand by the chain.[27] Increased pressure regarding similar concerns led the company to begin a campaign to improve its "green" reputation in 2006.[28]

The corporate slogan "always low price" is the tip of an organizational iceberg that keeps the company striving to constantly lower costs, and transferring much of that lowered cost to suppliers and consumers. Wal-Mart's cultural values of hard work and frugality, on surface unassailable, have in practice turned back on themselves to represent serious risks due to their unforeseen by-products.[29] A primary cause of this distortion of values and consequences is the company's sheer size. The "rules" and concepts of organizations and our economic, social, and political policies for regulating and dealing with them are based on entities relatively limited in size. Wal-Mart's size puts it in a category by itself, whose long-term effects on the economy are not known and not explained by existing organizational and economic theories.[30] The potential ramifications of scale make the company's foray into the organic foods market worth observing more closely.

The chain's interest in organic foods came about as part of an intersection of two larger campaigns: to improve its sustainability efforts, and to improve its appeal to a more upscale clientele.[31] Given the complex potential for contradictions between these two motivations, and the premise that Wal-Mart and many factions of the organic movement are somewhat uncomfortable bedfellows, mixed reactions in public discourse could only be expected. Those reactions are what the present study set out to explore.

Study

Data for this study were collected from March 2006, when the company made its initial announcement, to February 2007, for a full year of coverage. The system used to collect the data was the Google Alert service, which delivers daily lists of links from media outlets and other dynamic Web sites, based on the search term provided. In this case the term was *organic foods*; all links that mentioned Wal-Mart's involvement in the organic foods sector were then selected for this study, for a total of 93 documents. Google Alerts samples a wide range of information sources, so data for the present study came from food and general interest blogs, organic consumer association Web sites, sites of anti–Wal-Mart groups, small local newspapers from across the United States, mainstream magazines and newspapers such as *Forbes* and the *New York Times*, and others.

The texts were analyzed using a technique known as centering resonance analysis (CRA), which uses theories of language processing and networks to determine which nouns and noun phrases are most influential within the structural logic of a text or set of texts.[32] It can also calculate ties between nonadjacent words, to show pairs and sets that frequently appear in logical proximity, for greater depth of analysis. By not relying on dictionaries or prepared word lists, it reduces the risk of instrumental or researcher bias. At the same time, the computational results alone provide only a starting point for analysis, and the researcher must interpret the output based on context.

Analysis: Crisscrossing Tensions

The themes highlighted by the centering resonance analysis remained remarkably consistent throughout the year, although they varied in intensity at different points in time. Although a detailed discussion of the specific terms that emerged from the CRA and their relative influence at various points in the year is beyond the scope of this chapter, they may be distilled into a series of tension areas, or sites of conflicting perspectives on the situation. We can classify these tensions into five broad categories: individual and environmental health; global versus local orientation; production, distribution and consumption; issues of authenticity; class and access. While these categories are not mutually exclusive, all of these tensions can be seen as sites of conflict within the organic sector in general, and in turn a reflection of larger patterns within contemporary American culture.

Individual and Environmental Health

This category includes terms such as *health, healthy, fat, diet, pesticide, green,* and *sustainable,* and word pairs such as *food-health, organic-benefit, Wal-Mart-sustainable, organic-sustainable,* and *Wal-Mart-green.* Articles that addressed this theme discussed the relative benefits of organic food to human health and the environment, and the potential role of Wal-Mart in enhancing or negating these benefits. For example, a *New York Times* article quoted Wal-Mart representatives, nutritionists and others to discuss the various perceived advantages of organic foods.[33]

Supporters of the move noted that even minor sustainability efforts on the part of the retail colossus could have significant positive impact, and contended that Wal-Mart could contribute to improving the health of Americans by lowering the cost of organic foods and making them accessible to vast numbers of people.[34] One concern expressed in this context, however, was that much of this expansion would take the form of "organic" versions of processed foods, or by importing products labeled as organic from China or other developing countries, where standards may not be as controlled.[35] The implication is that even organic processed foods are not as healthy and environmentally sound as the label would imply. Another facet of this issue is the scope of this impact, which leads to the next set of tensions.

Global Versus Local Orientation

Terms and pairs that focus on the size and scope of the organic market, or Wal-Mart alone, included *large, big, organic-global, big-organic, organic-small, organic-local, food-big, organic-large, Wal-Mart-large, food-local,* and others. The unifying theme is the debate over the relative merits of small farms and crops compared to the massive size of "big organic," with Wal-Mart as potentially the biggest organic of them all. Some expressed fear at this exponential increase in scale, warning, for example, that prices for organic products would fall, small farmers would be squeezed out of business, and imports from cheaper developing countries increased.[36] Still others saw the move as a positive sign that organic foods were finally transitioning from niche to mainstream markets, and pointed out that developing countries might be encouraged to improve their environmental footprint as a result.[37] Another objection to the globalization of organic foods comes from those who argue that the environmental costs of shipping products across the world or even across the country negates any benefits derived from omitting pesticides in production.[38]

Questions of distance are important not only to those concerned with the environmental impact of the food system, but also to people who worry about local businesses, including farmers. While some authors praised Wal-Mart for its efforts to buy local organic produce to reduce food miles,[39] others expressed apprehension about the further impact of big business on what is often seen as an agricultural practice with deep local roots. Small organic farms have a hard time keeping up with the supply and pricing demands of large distribution, especially when unexpected factors such as labor shortages interfere with cultivation and harvesting.[40]

Thus, the underlying source of much of the concern about globalized, mass production has to do with the greater disconnect, whether perceived or in terms of geographical distance, between production, distribution and consumption, the next set of tensions to be addressed.

Production, Distribution and Consumption

From a policy standpoint, *organic* is a term that relates strictly to production. Yet, as the earlier discussion of the organic movement shows, there is more to the broader construct of *organic* than a government labeling scheme: it extends down the supply chain to apply to distributors, such as organic grocers or farmers' markets, and individual or organized consumers as well. Along with these different stages of organic participation, there are different perceptions of what participation means.

A number of the articles examined discussed various aspects of the organic supply chain, and how various individuals and groups believe Wal-Mart's involvement will affect this chain. This category thus includes terms such as *farmer, farm, agriculture, consumer, market, crop, product, shopper, supply, retailer, customer, marketing, production, restaurant*, and pairs such as *farmer-crop, organic-product, Wal-Mart store, organic-store, food-store, organic-farm, organic-farmer, Wal-Mart-market, Wal-Mart-product, food-market, organic-consumer*, and *organic-supplier*. Given the breadth of this subject, the diversity of perspectives is considerable, ranging from the size of organic crops in agrarian or industrial-style production[41] to the competitive landscape of natural foods distribution,[42] from customer opinions to statements by organic consumer and trade associations.[43] These kinds of debates are not limited to the organic foods subject: Wal-Mart is frequently at the center of larger social discussions about its role in shaping the way products are manufactured, imported, distributed, and consumed.[44] The organic foods issue is a microcosm that reflects the larger whole.

In November 2006, the Cornucopia Institute, a group that works to support agricultural policies in favor of small family farms, filed suit against Wal-Mart for allegedly violating organic policy. The Institute made documented claims that the retail chain was shelving uncertified "natural" products alongside their organic offerings without distinguishing between them, thereby making fraudulent claims and potentially confusing shoppers.[45] The incident triggered a reprisal of the debate about potentially loosened standards that might result from Wal-Mart's involvement in the sector.

The case of Wal-Mart's alleged shelving violation is yet another example of how these different categories of tensions are not distinct from one another, but overlapping and constantly shifting as their terms are negotiated. It also illustrates how the question of how and where products are produced, distributed and consumed ties into a larger theme, which we might call "authenticity."

Issues of Authenticity

A series of binary oppositions emerge from the texts that pit what is "natural" and "authentic" against the artificiality of industrialization. The standards themselves are the principle site of conflict here, as different factions bring their values to the negotiating table to argue their positions. In the texts we thus find discussion of *corporate, industry, agricultural, standard, organic-standard, food-standard, Wal-Mart-standard, organic-USDA, organic-natural, food-natural, food-industrial, organic-business, Wal-Mart-corporation, Wal-Mart-farmer.* Note that many of these regard discussion of organic standards, which even as defined are not always strictly enforced. Organic consumer and small-farming associations have been at loggerheads with the USDA for years over the perceived laxity of the federal agency in sanctioning certified industrial producers who fail to uphold the current standards.[46] Some existing standards are vague enough to allow a wide range of interpretations, such as the debate over just how much "access to pasture" is enough to distinguish between organic and factory farming.[47]

Amid these conversations are tongue-in-cheek remarks about organic food losing its "hipness" now that the retailer has moved in, but underneath the cool attitude is a real sense that something has been lost.[48] In some cases, the loss is described in terms of social fabric and social justice, such as claims that the welfare of farm and food factory workers and public health have been sacrificed on the altar of low point-of-purchase costs, due in large part to Wal-Mart, "the biggest purveyor of cheap food in America."[49] Mostly, though, it is the fear that the term *organic* is losing meaning as it becomes available through mass means of production and distribution.[50] The *San Francisco Chronicle* worried about "organic erosion,"[51] and even *Business Week* ran a cover story observing that "as it goes mass market, the organic food business is failing to stay true to its ideals."[52] Even for many outside the movement, *organic* is a term that goes beyond the provisions of the federal labeling scheme to represent a process that must by definition take place on a small scale. This tension represents the heart of the collision between the organic movement and the organic industry.

Is there something inherently better about food produced by a farming family who owns the land on which crops are harvested and does much of the labor by hand, compared to a larger industry that leases its acreage and relies more heavily on mechanical harvesting, if both are held to the same production standards? And will Wal-Mart necessarily favor the latter to the point of putting the livelihood of the former at risk? To answer these questions also necessitates responding to those covered in the final set of tensions addressed here, which essentially ask: Who decides what is "good" — both in absolute terms and for society — and determines who is allowed to have it?

Class and Access

The cultural value of food is long established in disciplines as disparate as sociology, history, and business, given its particular position as "a universal medium that illuminates a wide range of other cultural practices"[53]; this entire volume is a celebration of that cultural connection. If food is culture, then we might view the mass production of food as a form of culture industry. This perspective helps make sense of much of the debate over Wal-Mart's entry into the organic foods sector, as the debates center on the same kinds of conflicts between high and low culture, authenticity and empty reproduction lamented by Matthew Arnold, Walter Benjamin and others for decades.[54] The conflict over organic standards has come to represent a jostling for control of what qualifies as "real" and what is mere imitation, what is good and what is bad — for health, for the economy, for American society and culture.

Organic foods have a complex identity as simple, pure, natural and expensive. Once escaped from the counterculture in mainstream eyes, organics have been considered more of an elitist delicacy, "fixed in the collective imagination as an upper-middle-class luxury, a blue-state affectation as easy to mock as Volvos or lattes."[55] Organic products are often positioned as high-end commodities for yuppies with a conscience.[56] The largest natural-foods supermarket chain in the United States, Whole Foods, is jokingly referred to as "Whole Paycheck" for the cost of its products,[57] and posts profits well above the supermarket industry averages.[58] Organic food has thus come to represent an upscale option that is out of reach for most Americans, and in direct opposition to the inexpensive mass production and distribution of food and other mainstream cultural commodities.

Wal-Mart, of course, embodies the latter. The company's CEO Lee Scott positioned the move into organic foods specifically as a way of breaking down price and class barriers, saying, "We don't think you should have to have a lot of money to feed your family organic foods."[59] The entrance of a megachain like Wal-Mart into the organic arena is seen by many as an indication the movement has become mainstream.[60] The debate centers on whether this trickle-down effect is a positive or negative development. In the texts examined, these tensions are evidenced in words such as *elite, political, price, choice,* and pairs such as *food-cheap, organic-cheap, Wal-Mart-price, organic-price.*

Journalist Michael Pollan has argued that buying directly from local (preferably organic) farmers is actually cheaper, since it takes into account the larger societal costs of damage to the environment and human health.[61] Yet this kind of access and time is undeniably a luxury reserved only for a very few. Indeed, studies have shown that the underprivileged often have limited access even to supermarkets and fresh produce in general.[62] Accordingly, Joseph Rago wrote in the *Wall Street Journal* that "only the reasonably affluent can afford to align their products with their beliefs."[63] The ethics of eating are reserved for the elite.

A similar distinction holds for the phenomenology of grocery shopping. At a chain such as Whole Foods, careful attention is paid to the sensual experience of consumers, who are greeted by an aesthetically appealing setting that contributes to the pleasure of consumption.[64] On the other hand, as Charles Fishman put it, Wal-Mart "isn't really a place to shop, it's a place to buy things."[65] The ultimate goal of the latter remains creating savings for cost-conscious consumers, and comfortable shopping is one way of distinguishing those who must pay more attention to price from those who can afford to embrace other priorities.

Conclusion: A Cultural Conundrum

Wal-Mart's decision to increase its organic foods option sparked wide debate about the social, economic and regulatory implications of the move.[66] Wal-Mart's entrée into the organic food market may thus be seen as the point at which a critical mass of the media and miscellaneous stakeholder groups became aware of the existence of an organic industry: only an industry can supply the kinds of quantities the world's largest retailer demands. But can agrarian ideals and practices be mass-marketed? The concern is that there will be increasing pressure on regulators to loosen standards for organic labeling in order to satisfy this demand.

Supporters of Wal-Mart's decision argue that the retailer will create a larger market for organic products and improve accessibility to healthy, high-quality food to those who were previously unable to afford such products or had no readily available local suppliers.[67] However, the California Institute for Rural Studies recently reported that the increase in consumer demand for organic foods has not led to a parallel increase in organic agriculture.[68] Much of what is sold under the organic rubric is either heavily processed, made using ingredients that meet formal regulatory criteria but do not reflect what many feel to be "organic values." Thus detractors frequently take a critical position against "food in the age of mechanical reproduction," to echo Walter Benjamin, and warn that Wal-Mart's presence in the organic sector poses a threat to currently accepted meanings of the term. Yet these accepted meanings vary significantly across groups of organic stakeholders.

From its beginnings at various fringe points on the social and political spectrum, organic food gradually shifted to become an economic luxury. Wal-Mart, on the other hand, exemplifies the consumption patterns of the lower social and economic classes in this country. Organic foods have become a symbol of a certain type of lifestyle and political orientation, whereas Wal-Mart is a symbol for the opposite.[69] Bringing them together has caused discomfort across the board.

Wal-Mart's size and scale amplify the effects of every action it takes, making noticeable waves where smaller distributors would produce barely a ripple. In the case of the organic foods market, Wal-Mart's entrée has exacerbated a series of existing tensions within the organic foods movement and American culture in general. It raises questions about social justice in terms of access to healthy food by nonelite consumers, conflicting market and political pressures on U.S. agricultural policies, and the relative merits of a globalized and largely centralized industrial food system versus a more varied tapestry of local suppliers. Finally, it highlights the confusion and varied range of perceptions regarding the term *organic* and ongoing debate over the environmental and health benefits of organic foods. The concept is still at the center of a dense web of social, economic and political negotiations nearly a century after the movement first began.

Notes

1. Philip Conford, *The Origins of the Organic Movement* (Edinburgh, Scotland: Floris Books, 2001), 55.

2. Conford, 98–99; Julie Guthman, *Agrarian Dreams: The Paradox of Organic Farming in California* (Berkeley: University of California Press, 2004), 4.

3. Conford, 100–03; Guthman, 4–5. For a negative perspective on the history of the organic movement, see Alex Avery, *The Truth About Organic Foods* (Chesterfield, MO: Henderson Communications LLC, 2006).

4. Guthman, 1–14.

5. Ibid, 5.

6. Samuel Fromartz, *Organic, Inc.* (Orlando: Harcourt, 2006), 240; Guthman, 240.

7. Guthman, 114.

8. Warren Belasco, *Appetite for Change: How the Counterculture Took on the Food Industry* (Ithaca, NY: Cornell University Press, 1993), 247; Conford, 126; Fromartz, 69–74; Guthman, 8, 53–54.

9. Warren Belasco, "Food and the Counterculture: A Story of Bread and Politics," in *The Cultural Politics of Food and Eating: A Reader*, eds. James L. Watson, and Melissa L. Caldwell (Malden, MA: Blackwell, 2005); Guthman, 177–78.

10. Guthman, 10.

11. Fromartz, 18; Guthman, 174–75.

12. Fromartz, 18.

13. Ibid., 241.

14. Harvey Levenstein, *Paradox of Plenty: A Social History of Eating in Modern America* (Berkeley: University of California Press, 2003), 196.

15. Michael Pollan, *The Omnivore's Dilemma: A Natural History of Four Meals* (New York: Penguin, 2006), 183.

16. C. Dimitri and Catherine Greene, *Recent Growth Patterns in the U.S. Organic Foods Market* (Washington, D.C.: United States Department of Agriculture, Economic Research Service, 2003). See also Fromartz.

17. Alexander Cockburn, "Wal-Mart's Coming Lunge Into Organic Food," *Counterpunch Diary* (May 15, 2006). Online at http://www.counterpunch.org/cockburn05152006.html.

18. Kyle W. Lathrop, "Pre-Empting Apples With Oranges: Federal Regulation of Organic Food Labeling," *Journal of Corporation Law* 16, no. 4 (Summer 1991): 885–1031.

19. USDA, Organic Foods Production Act of 1990 [As Amended Through Public Law 109–97] (Nov. 10, 2005): Sec. 2105.

20. Ibid., Sec. 2110.

21. Barbara Robinson, "National Organic Program: Value Through Verification," http://www.ams.usda.gov/NOP/NOPPresentation/home.html(2006).

22. Ibid.

23. USDA, sec. 2119.

24. Agricultural Marketing Service (AMS) USDA, "National Organic Program," 7 CFR Part 205 (2002).

25. G. William Domhoff, "The Power Elite, Public Policy, and Public Opinion," in *Navigating Public Opinion*, ed. Jeff Manza, et al. (New York: Oxford University Press, 2002).

26. Matthew A. Crenson and Benjamin Ginsberg, *Downsizing Democracy: How America Sidelined Its Citizens and Privatized Its Public* (Baltimore: Johns Hopkins University Press, 2002); Domhoff.

27. Charles Fishman, *The Wal-Mart Effect* (New York: Penguin, 2006), 170–74.

28. Mindy Fetterman, "Wal-Mart Grows 'Green' Strategies," *USA Today,* September 25, 2006, 1A.

29. Fishman, 224–29.

30. Ibid., 238.

31. Wal-Mart CEO Lee Scott announced the "Wal-Mart Out in Front" sustainability program at the June shareholders' meeting; see "Lee Scott Speaks at Wal-Mart 2006 Shareholders' Meeting" (June 2, 2006), available at http://www.walmartfacts.com/articles/4406.aspx. The announcement was the culmination of several months of experimentation and planning, with mixed reactions in the media; see Liza Featherstone, "Wal-Mart's Eco–Announcements Generate a Clash Among Activists," *Grist,* November 22, 2005, http://www.grist.org/news/maindish/2005/11/22/featherstone/index.html. For Wal-Mart's attempts to appeal to more upscale consumers, see Melanie Warner, "Wal-Mart Eyes Organic Foods, and Brand Names Get in Line," *New York Times,* May 12, 2006, 1; Tom Van Riper, "Wal-Mart Goes Upscale," *Forbes* 178, no. 4 (September 4, 2006).

32. Steven R. Corman, Timothy Kuhn, Robert D. McPhee, and Kevin J. Dooley, "Studying Complex Discursive Systems: Centering Resonance Analysis of Communication," *Human Communication Research* 28, no. 2 (2002): 157–206. The software used for the analysis was Crawdad, by Crawdad Technologies.

33. Warner, "Wal-Mart Eyes Organic Foods"; Brian White, "Wal-Mart Starting to Offer Waistline Management Food Choices," *AOL Money & Finance: Blogging Stocks,* June 26, 2006, http://www.bloggingstocks.com/2006/06/26/wal-mart-starting-to-offer-waistline-management-food-choices.

34. Ruth Kava, "Organics Business Big and Growing," *HealthFactsandFears.com,* June 8, 2006, *http://www.acsh.org/factsfears/newsID.762/news_detail.asp.*

35. Warner, "Wal-Mart Eyes Organic Foods."

36. Alexander Cockburn, "Wal-Mart's Coming Lunge Into Organic Food," *Counterpunch Diary,* May 15, 2006, http://www.counterpunch.org/cockburn05152006.html.

37. See, for example, industry consultant Harvey Hartman, quoted in Warner, "Wal-Mart Eyes Organic Foods"; also Michael Pollan, "Mass Natural," *New York Times Magazine,* June 18, 2006, 12.

38. Steven Shapin, "Paradise Sold," *Mother Jones* 82, no. 13 (May 15, 2006): 84. For more on the subject of the environmental costs of big organic, also see Fromartz.

39. Marc Gunter, "The Green Machine," *Fortune Magazine* 154, no. 3 (August 7, 2006): 42. More discussion of Wal-Mart's attention to "food miles" can be found in Amanda Griscom Little, "The Writing on the Wal-Mart," *Grist,* July 19, 2006, http://www.grist.org/news/muck/2006/07/19/gore–walmart/index.html.

40. Tom Philpott, "Up Against the Wal-Mart," *Grist,* August 23, 2006, http://www.grist.org/comments/food/2006/08/23/buyers/index.html.

41. Kava, "Organics Business Big and Growing."

42. For example, Nick Eaton, "Grocery Stores Respond to Demand: Organic Food Is a Growth Market," *Seattle Post-Intelligencer* Business, June 7, 2006, D1; David Kaplan, "A Natural in Groceries Finds the Going Tougher: Analysts Say Savvy Competitors and Fast Expansion Have Caused Investors to Turn Away from Whole Foods," *Houston Chronicle* Business & Financial News, January 14, 2007, HO-0114.

43. Organic Consumers Association, "Open Letter to Wal-Mart from the Organic

Consumers Association," July 4, 2006, *http://www.organicconsumers.org/articles/article_1009. cfm.*

44. Examples of some of the discussions referenced in this chapter may be found in David John Farmer, "Wal-Mart: Neo-Feudal (K)Night?," *Administrative Theory & Praxis* 28, no. 1 (2006): 148–61; Charles Fishman, "The Wal-Mart Effect and a Decent Society: Who Knew Shopping Was So Important?" *Academy of Management Perspectives* 20, no. 3 (August 2006): 6–25; R. Edward Freeman, "The Wal-Mart Effect and Business, Ethics, and Society," *Academy of Management Perspectives* 20, no. 3 (August 2006): 38–40; Pankaj Ghemawat, "Business, Society, and the 'Wal-Mart Effect,'" *Academy of Management Perspectives* 20, no. 3 (2006): 41–43; Nelson Lichtenstein, ed., *Wal-Mart: The Face of Twenty-first-century Capitalism* (New York: New Press, 2006); Robert Slater, *The Wal-Mart Decade* (New York: Portfolio, 2003).

45. George Gutowski, "Wal-Mart's Organic Food Initiative: A Case of Hippie Capitalism Gone Awry?" *Seeking Alpha,* November 15, 2006, http://retail.seekingalpha.com/article/20688.

46. Mark percent Kastel, "Organic Watchdog, USDA Headed to Court," *Free Press* February 20, 2007, http://www.freepress.org/departments/display/3/2007/2437.

47. Organic Consumers Association, "Open Letter to Wal-Mart."

48. "Organic Goes Commercial," *Portfolio Weekly* August 29, 2006, http://www.portfolioweekly.com/Pages/InfoPage.php/iID/1888.

49. Pollan, "Mass Natural."

50. One of the harshest critiques in this sense is found in the article, "Wal-Mart: Rotten Ethics, 'Organic' Food," *City on a Hill Press* 40, no. 30 (June 8, 2006), http://chp.ucsc. edu/paper/op/wal_mat_rotten_etheir.txt?40_30. Last accessed on May 11, 2006. Currently unavailable.

51. Jake Whitney, "Organic Erosion: Will the Term *Organic* Still Mean Anything When It's Adopted Whole Hog by Behemoths Such as Wal-Mart?" *San Francisco Chronicle* CM, January 28, 2007, 13.

52. Diane Brady, "The Organic Myth," *Business Week* (October 16, 2006): 50.

53. James L. Watson and Melissa L. Caldwell, "Introduction," in *The Cultural Politics of Food and Eating: A Reader,* eds. James L. Watson and Melissa L. Caldwell (Malden, MA: Blackwell, 2005), 1.

54. See Matthew Arnold, *Culture and Anarchy* (London: Cambridge University Press, 1932); Walter Benjamin, "The Work of Art in the Age of Mechanical Reproduction," in *Illuminations,* ed. Hannah Arendt (New York: Harcourt Brace Jovanovich, 1968); Max Horkheimer and Theodor W. Adorno, "The Culture Industry: Enlightenment as Mass Deception," in *Dialectic of Enlightenment: Philosophical Fragments,* eds. Max Horkheimer, et al. (Stanford: Stanford University Press, 2002).

55. Pollan, "Mass Natural."

56. James H. Joyner, Jr., "Organic Matter," *TCSDaily: Technology,Ccommerce, Society,* June 6, 2006, http://www.tcsdaily.com/article.aspx?id=060606C.

57. Shapin, "Paradise Sold."

58. Christine MacDonald, "As the Popularity of Organics Grows, Wal-Mart Jumps in," *Boston Globe* Food, May 10, 2006, C5.

59. Quoted by Alexander Cockburn.

60. "The Falling Price of Organic Food," *Palm Beach Post* Food, May 4, 2006, 1FN.

61. Michael Pollan, "No Bar Code," *Mother Jones* 31 (May/June 2006): 36–45.

62. Mario Luis Small and Monica McDermott, "The Presence of Organizational Resources in Poor Urban Neighborhoods: An Analysis of Average and Contextual Effects," *Social Forces* 84, no. 3 (March 2006): 1697–724.

63. Joseph Rago, "Conspicuous Virtue and the Sustainable Sofa," *Wall Street Journal,* March 23, 2007, W13.

64. For more discussion of how Whole Foods strategically evokes a comfortable atmosphere for consumers, see Fromartz.

65. Fishman, *The Wal-Mart Effect,* 203.

66. See, for example, Rebekah Denn, "2006 in Food: Politics, Big Business, Consumer Rights and Rachael Ray," *Seattle Post-Intelligencer,* December 27, 2006, 1.

67. See, for example, Kava, "Organics Business Big and Growing"; White, "Wal-Mart Starting to Offer Waistline Management Food Choices".

68. Ron Strochlich and Luis Sierra, *Conventional, Mixed and "Deregistered" Organic Farmers: Entry Barriers and Reasons for Exiting Organic Production in California*, published by California Institute for Rural Studies, February 2007, iii.

69. Pollan, "Mass Natural."

Works Cited

Agricultural Marketing Service (AMS). "National Organic Program." 7 CFR Part 205 (2002).

Arnold, Matthew. *Culture and Anarchy*. London: Cambridge University Press, 1932.

Avery, Alex. *The Truth About Organic Foods*. Chesterfield, MO: Henderson Communications LLC, 2006.

Belasco, Warren. *Appetite for Change: How the Counterculture Took on the Food Industry*. Ithaca, NY: Cornell University Press, 1993.

_____. "Food and the Counterculture: A Story of Bread and Politics." In *The Cultural Politics of Food and Eating: A Reader*, eds. James L. Watson and Melissa L. Caldwell, 217–34. Malden, MA: Blackwell, 2005.

Benjamin, Walter. "The Work of Art in the Age of Mechanical Reproduction." In *Illuminations*, ed. Hannah Arendt, 217–52. New York: Harcourt Brace Jovanovich, 1968.

Brady, Diane. "The Organic Myth." *Business Week*, October 16, 2006.

Conford, Philip. *The Origins of the Organic Movement*. Edinburgh, Scotland: Floris Books, 2001.

Corman, Steven R., Timothy Kuhn, Robert D. McPhee, and Kevin J. Dooley. "Studying Complex Discursive Systems: Centering Resonance Analysis of Communication." *Human Communication Research* 28, no. 2 (2002): 157–206.

Crenson, Matthew A., and Benjamin Ginsberg. *Downsizing Democracy: How America Sidelined Its Citizens and Privatized Its Public*. Baltimore: Johns Hopkins University Press, 2002.

Dimitri, C., and Catherine Greene. *Recent Growth Patterns in the U.S. Organic Foods Market*. Washington, D. C.: U.S. Department of Agriculture, Economic Research Service, 2003.

Domhoff, G. William. "The Power Elite, Public Policy, and Public Opinion." In *Navigating Public Opinion*, eds. Jeff Manza, Fay Lomax Cook, and Benjamin I. Page, 124–37. New York: Oxford University Press, 2002.

Farmer, David John. "Wal-Mart: Neo-Feudal (K)Night?" *Administrative Theory & Praxis* 28, no. 1 (2006): 148–61.

Fishman, Charles. *The Wal-Mart Effect*. New York: Penguin, 2006.

_____. "The Wal-Mart Effect and a Decent Society: Who Knew Shopping Was So Important?" *Academy of Management Perspectives* 20, no. 3 (2006): 6–25.

Freeman, R. Edward. "The Wal-Mart Effect and Business, Ethics, and Society." *Academy of Management Perspectives* 20, no. 3 (2006): 38–40.

Fromartz, Samuel. *Organic, Inc.* Orlando, FL: Harcourt, 2006.

Ghemawat, Pankaj. "Business, Society, and the '"Wal-Mart Effect.'" *Academy of Management Perspectives* 20, no. 3 (2006): 41–43.

Gunter, Marc. "The Green Machine." *Fortune Magazine* (2006), 42.

Guthman, Julie. *Agrarian Dreams: The Paradox of Organic Farming in California*. Berkeley: University of California Press, 2004.

Horkheimer, Max, and Theodor W. Adorno. "The Culture Industry: Enlightenment as Mass Deception." In *Dialectic of Enlightenment: Philosophical Fragments*, eds. Max

Horkheimer, Theodor W. Adorno, and John Cumming, 120–67. Stanford: Stanford University Press, 2002.

Lathrop, Kyle W. "Pre-Empting Apples with Oranges: Federal Regulation of Organic Food Labeling." *Journal of Corporation Law* 16, no. 4 (1991): 885–1031.

Levenstein, Harvey. *Paradox of Plenty: A Social History of Eating in Modern America.* Berkeley: University of California Press, 2003.

Lichtenstein, Nelson, ed. *Wal-Mart: The Face of Twenty-first-century Capitalism.* New York: New Press, 2006.

Pollan, Michael. "Mass Natural." *New York Times Magazine,* June 12, 2006, arts section, 12.

_____. "No Bar Code." *Mother Jones* (2006): 36–45.

_____. *The Omnivore's Dilemma: A Natural History of Four Meals.* New York: Penguin, 2006.

Rago, Joseph. "Conspicuous Virtue and the Sustainable Sofa." *Wall Street Journal,* March 23, 2007.

Robinson, Barbara. "National Organic Program: Value Through Verification." *Agricultural Marketing Service, U.S. Department of Agriculture* (2006). http://www.ams.usda.gov/NOP/NOPPresentation/home.html.

Shapin, Steven. "Paradise Sold." *Mother Jones* 82, no. 13 (2006): 84.

Slater, Robert. *The Wal-Mart Decade.* New York: Portfolio, 2003.

Small, Mario Luis, and Monica McDermott. "The Presence of Organizational Resources in Poor Urban Neighborhoods: An Analysis of Average and Contextual Effects." *Social Forces* 84, no. 3 (2006): 1697–724.

Strochlich, Ron, and Luis Sierra. *Conventional, Mixed and "Deregistered" Organic Farmers: Entry Barriers and Reasons for Exiting Organic Production in California.* Published by the California Institute for Rural Studies, 2007.

USDA. "Organic Foods Production Act of 1990 [As Amended Through Public Law 109–97]." (2005). http://www.ams.usda.gov/nop/NOP/standards.html.

Wargo, John. *Our Children's Toxic Legacy: How Science and the Law Fail to Protect Us from Pesticides.* New Haven: Yale University Press, 1996.

Watson, James L., and Melissa L. Caldwell. "Introduction." In *The Cultural Politics of Food and Eating: A Reader,* eds. James L. Watson, and Melissa L. Caldwell, 1–10. Malden, MA: Blackwell, 2005.

7

"Everybody Eats"

The Food Network and Symbolic Capital

MEGAN MULLEN

Not only do today's media audiences have a growing selection of sophisticated technologies to provide information and entertainment, we also increasingly have the option of accessing our chosen content through more than one media outlet. This is an effect both of media ownership trends, in which an ever-smaller group of media conglomerates strives to achieve "synergy" through cross-promotions, and of audiences' increasing facility with interactive media technologies, particularly the Internet. Marketers of all stripes are quick to jump on the bandwagon in finding ways to address the needs and desires of ever-smaller consumer groups reachable through today's media.

The question needs to be raised, however, as to how much consumers and media users are actually being segregated into isolated media domains, as opposed to being reached through mass media in ways that merely *give the sense of* specialization. After all, the concepts of specialization and niche-based targeting seem antithetical to the goals of a commercially funded mass media, for which the largest possible audiences are sought. Marketing experts, while readily embracing notions of individualization and custom-tailored consumption "experiences," nonetheless acknowledge that any form of specialized targeting is only beneficial to the extent that profits exceed expenditures. Indeed, the present state of consumer or audience targeting is well characterized by the term *mass customization*, in which a variety of standard components are reconfigured in multiple combinations to suit varied needs, interests, and tastes. The short history of specialty cable networks in the United States seems particularly relevant here.

Cable "narrowcasting" was first articulated as an ideal during the late 1960s and early 1970s, when satellite technology stood poised and ready to transform the largely rural retransmission medium of community antenna television (CATV) that was early cable into a "cornucopia" of program diversity.[1] Yet the first wave of satellite cable narrowcasting that took place during the early 1980s proved disappointing.[2] A mass audience accustomed to four decades of the lowest-common-denominator programs supplied by CBS, ABC, and NBC probably was not ready to abandon what has been characterized as a "cultural forum"[3] or "electronic hearth."[4] The audience's intransigence was exacerbated by the inability of fledgling cable ventures to produce specialty programs (or any programs, for that matter) of a quality even remotely approaching that of programs from the "big three." The concept of cable narrowcasting took a brief hiatus as more broadly targeted networks such as HBO, Showtime, TBS, TNT, and USA took off.[5]

Another, more lucrative, wave of specialty cable networks began to appear during the mid–1990s. Some were spin-offs from existing general-interest cable networks. Other specialty programming ventures were launched by corporations with holdings in older media, by this point obviously feeling more optimistic about cable's future. Overall, the success or failure of this wave of networks seemed tied to the preexisting fortunes of their respective genres more than to the success of cable specialty networks as a general phenomenon. Within the more familiar television genres lay a ready supply of off-broadcast syndicated programs, both known to and popular with the television audience.

In this context, the evolution of Food Network provides an interesting and revealing case study. Food Network did not enjoy the same sort of "sheltered launch" as spin-off networks such as History Channel and ESPN2; its backing came from a relatively small newspaper company with no preexisting cable holdings. Instead, Food Network benefited from both a shift in the regulatory environment affecting the cable industry and a founder with keen insight into the public's television programming tastes. Food Network began with a program schedule that likely appealed to a small but predictable collection of cooking and fitness show aficionados, certainly an established television audience. However, its programmers learned quickly that these types of shows, while successful parts of heterogeneous schedules such as those of PBS affiliates, were not sufficient to sustain an entire commercially supported cable network.

Not only has the range of program topics within Food Network's purview expanded since its 1993 launch, the programs themselves now target a broad spectrum of viewers. Rather than emphasize cooking instruction — as in old-style cooking shows such as *The French Chef* or *The Galloping Gourmet* — today's Food Network programs showcase the widest possible range of food-related information and activities, as will be discussed below. Food Network epitomizes the success of cable's ability to offer thematic programming in the early 21st century. It has identified program types that only *seem* narrowly targeted; they satisfy the viewer (or advertiser) looking for a programming niche, but in fact target a very broad slice of the television audience. In order to understand Food Network's success, we must consider how the network has managed to expand the boundaries of preexisting consumer categories and television genres in order to appeal to the greatest possible number of viewers and, hence, to the greatest possible number of commercial sponsors. We must consider, in other words, how it has abandoned the archaic and utopian notion of cable as a niche medium in order to recognize that cable needs to address the same sorts of market constraints that have always shaped television in the United States.

While it is true that commercial media in general have grown more specialized as new technologies have allowed marketers to address potential consumers with increasing sophistication and personalization, cable really holds no special advantages in this environment. To believe otherwise is to privilege its technical advantages over its economic imperatives. Stated simply: to be successful, a specialty cable network must promote a theme that will give it a certain cachet, while nonetheless making every effort to draw the largest possible audience. This is precisely what Food Network does. The innovative cable network manages to strike a balance between elite tastes and popular culture, between snobbism and populism, between cooking and eating, and between work and leisure. As Food Network's visionary founder Reese Schonfeld explained in 1994, Food Network really isn't narrowcast at all, since "everybody eats."[6]

The History of Food Network

Schonfeld first began to develop the Television Food Network (TVFN) concept in 1993, in partnership with the Providence Journal Company. His plans stood in stark contrast to the traditional notion of cable narrowcasting as a collection of small niches to be filled with special-interest programming. He perceived correctly that if narrowcast (or, to use the cable industry's term, *category*) television were to succeed, it would need to draw the largest possible audience. In the early 1980s Schonfeld had been a cofounder of one of the few successful specialty cable ventures of that era, Ted Turner's news network CNN. Not willing to characterize this as narrowcasting, however, Schonfeld attributed the fortunes of CNN to its having translated the front page of a newspaper into audiovisual form. Likewise, when asked about TVFN in 1994, he described it as "transferring another page of the newspaper to TV."[7]

Ultimately, Schonfeld hoped, open architecture technology would allow cable to function as a sort of electronic newsstand, with consumers able to make personal choices from an array of special-topic channels. They would pay for these channels on an à la carte basis. But in the meantime, any niche programming ventures would need to make adjustments to draw a broad enough range of viewers to satisfy advertisers. In addition to amateur chefs, then, Food Network would target women ages 18–35 — women Schonfeld pictured as needing to balance jobs with preparing meals for husbands and children. As many women in this age bracket no longer were stay-at-home mothers, they were no longer a reliable audience for daytime cooking shows on established broadcast stations and networks. According to Schonfeld, a dedicated food channel could reach them during prime time.[8]

The cable programming market had become fairly competitive by the time TVFN was ready to launch, with many new start-up ventures competing for the small amount of "shelf space" left over after local cable operators had filled their lineups with established favorites such as USA, MTV, CNN, and Nickelodeon. In this climate, TVFN benefited from the passage of the 1992 Cable Act and its retransmission consent provisions, mandating that cable systems compensate local broadcast stations — financially or otherwise — for the use of their signals. Schonfeld immediately observed the success with which broadcast networks used their own major-market affiliate stations (O&Os) as leverage in drawing subscribers for their start-up cable ventures (such as FX, America's Talking/MSNBC and ESPN2), and thus formulated a plan to help build TVFN's subscriber base. As explained in his 2001 autobiography, he successfully approached the Chicago Tribune Company, a major television station owner, with an offer of a 20 percent ownership in TVFN in exchange for their retransmission rights — guaranteeing TVFN access to 10 million homes at its start.[9]

Among TVFN's early programs were *Essence of Emeril* with Emeril Lagasse, *Molto Mario* with Mario Batali, *Chillin' and Grillin'* with Bobby Flay, *Too Hot Tamales* with Mary Sue Milliken and Susan Feniger, *Chef du Jour*, featuring a variety of celebrity chefs, *How to Feed Your Family on a Hundred Dollars a Week* with Michelle Urvater, and *Food News & Views* with Donna Hanover and David Rosengarten. This lineup proved solid overall, and several of the personalities from the network's early years continue to populate its schedule.

Still, comparing the early TVFN schedule with that of today's Food Network reveals that quite a few adjustments have been made to steer the network away from the old-style cooking show model that characterized PBS and early syndicated commercial food programming. Part of this might be due to a shift in the network's ownership. Schonfeld's vision certainly suggested an important direction for TVFN; ironically, this vision was not fully realized until after the E. W. Scripps Corporation acquired the controlling interest in the network (subsequently known simply as Food Network) in 1997. TVFN had been quietly sold to Belo Broadcasting in 1995 (Schonfeld retained a 5 percent ownership stake), with virtually no change in programming practices. Then in October 1997, the E. W. Scripps Company took over control of TVFN. Scripps had acquired 56 percent of the network from Belo in exchange for two broadcast stations in San Antonio (Scripps' ownership had increased to 68 percent by the end of 2001). [10]

Scripps was best known for its holdings in newspapers and television stations, but already was a player in cable narrowcasting, having launched Home and Garden Television (HGTV) in 1994. As Food Network was in the process of doing, HGTV had found a niche largely served by PBS — the do-it-yourselfers — and connected it thematically to other niches, including the growing audience for *Lifestyles of the Rich and Famous* and similar celebrity lifestyle shows. Thus, it was able to draw viewers from among those serious about home remodeling as well as those who simply fantasized about unaffordable dream homes. Both categories, and a range in-between, could easily be connected to a variety of consumer products, from home furnishings to power tools to luxury vacations.

Similarly, Food Network's modern-day success lies not simply in changes to the production and marketing of a traditional genre, but more generally in the large-scale infusion of the network schedule with food-themed content addressing a range of lifestyles and interests — not simply those of the amateur chef. Over the years, additions to the schedule have included *Food Finds*, which seeks out unique prepared food products (most available by mail order) from around the continent; *Good Eats*, part instructional cooking show and part science education (in the style of the classic PBS show *Bill Nye, The Science Guy*); and *Cooking School Stories*, a documentary-style chronicle of the lives of students attending well-known culinary institutes.

Imports have also contributed to Food Network's popular programming mix including British shows *Two Fat Ladies* (1997–) and *The Naked Chef* (1999–) and the Japanese cult favorite, *Iron Chef* (1993–present), a stadium-style cooking competition among the nation's top chefs. [11] The imported programs have lent an edgy eclecticism to Food Network's schedule, no doubt redeemable in the coveted viewer "eyeballs." Various observers have likened the eclectic appeal of *Iron Chef* to that of other Japanese imports such as *Pokémon* and the Hello Kitty! line of products. Television writer Sharon Moshavi also points out, however, that *Iron Chef*'s iconoclastic status in Japan gives it ready-made appeal for irreverent American sensibilities.

While it's hard to explain the appeal of "Iron Chef" to the uninitiated, one Tokyo pop culture critic calls it "Julia Child meets the World Cup meets the Metropolitan Opera." In each episode, a challenger chef squares off against one of the champions, the "Iron Chefs." Each has a single hour to make a multicourse meal using the day's secret ingredient, anything from carrots to crab.

"The cooking world has long been conservative in Japan, but the 'Iron Chef' gave us the courage to be adventurous, to enjoy cooking," said Koumei Nakamura, one of the four Iron Chefs.

For decades, Japanese television has brimmed with countless cooking shows, but nothing with the zany intensity of Iron Chef, where cooks, with determination and sweat plastering their faces, compete [12]

Even the traditional instruction-oriented cooking shows have grown more populist on Food Network. A component of the early TVFN schedule was a slot called *Cooking Classics* that showcased rerun programs featuring Julia Child, Graham Kerr, Jacques Pepin and other legendary television chefs. Schonfeld explained that reruns of Child's classic, *The French Chef*, purchased as a package for $500,000, helped to boost TVFN's recognition among the established cooking show audience.[13] Yet comparing this older program to a more recent Food Network instructional cooking program, *The Naked Chef*, starring Jamie Oliver, provides a nice encapsulation of the schedule adjustments that have aided the network's fortunes. It also highlights some critical components of successful specialty cablecasting.

In *The French Chef*, Child is typically positioned behind a kitchen console narrating her way through the preparation of an haute cuisine concoction that is alien to most of the television audience. She is a master chef, but not a performer by U.S. commercial television standards. Oliver, by contrast, is a lively, animated performer who also has facility in the kitchen. His dishes are prepared casually — often chaotically — and the kitchen scenes are interspersed with shots (often edited cinema verité-style) of him romping through the streets of London on foot or motorbike. Where Child is staid and draws a limited audience of connoisseurs, Oliver clearly appeals to amateurs and even non-cooks. Indeed, Oliver has an extraordinarily well-established fan culture — dating back to the debut of his shows on Britain's BBC and his role as a spokesperson for Britain's Sainsbury supermarket chain (a chain that cultivates gourmandism among its clientele through a line of cookbooks, magazines, and recipe cards). Oliver even boasts something of a teen idol status, previously unknown among television chefs. The now-defunct "Unofficial Jamie Oliver" website resembled those of teen music idols, with a biography, gossip, and numerous photos (including some of his baby daughter Poppy in 2002).

Oliver's fan culture came to the U.S. cable network virtually prepackaged. But Food Network built upon it, among other tactics by subsidizing the production of more Jamie Oliver series. It has cultivated the celebrity status of other chefs in similar ways. For example Emeril Lagasse's first show, *The Essence of Emeril*, debuted with the network itself in 1993. It started as a traditional instructional-type cooking show, with its host positioned behind a kitchen console conversing with the camera as audience stand-in. Yet Emeril's boisterous personality and regional, blue-collar inflections set him apart from the foreign accents and formal mannerisms characteristic of his television predecessors, including Julia Child and others. He also presented his specialized culinary knowledge in a self-effacing way, sometimes mispronouncing specialized terms (especially those with foreign origins) or joking about foods (such as escargots) traditionally alien to all but the elite.

Food Network caught on quickly to Emeril's special charm. By late 1995, it was running a promotional spot that featured a group of male sports fans sitting in their living room cheering for the televised Emeril as he prepared a gourmet meal. The program *Emeril Live!*, added to Food Network's schedule at the time of the Scripps acquisition, has built this sensibility. Unlike the earlier show (which is still being rerun on Food Network), *Emeril Live!* features both a studio audience and a house band, much in the style of late-night talk shows.

Emeril Lagasse, Jamie Oliver, and other Food Network celebrities including Rachael Ray and Bobby Flay strike a balance between the culinary expertise that grants legitimacy in a specialized domain and the casual charisma that can draw a very diverse audience, including experts, novices, and even non-cooks. Moreover, these programs manage to flatter any degree of culinary savvy their viewers might possess, while subtly poking fun at the elitism that traditionally has lent legitimacy to that type of knowledge. Food Network's programs also cue its audiences to certain viewing sensibilities and by extension to types of cultural connoisseurship.

Striving for the Middle

Internal audiences, is a term by which television theorist Rick Altman describes any person or people positioned within the television program in a way that allows them to cue home viewers to desired interpretations of the program's content.[14] Traditional studio audiences, such as those on *Emeril Live!*, provide the most obvious example with their laughter and applause. But there are other, more subtle, examples of internal audiences. On *Gordon Elliot's Doorknock Dinners* (1999–2004), an unsuspecting person (nearly always a stay-at-home mother) would be surprised to find Elliot on her doorstep accompanied by a celebrity chef ready to use whatever ingredients she happens to have in the house to prepare a gourmet dinner for her family. Her spontaneous behavior — surprise, embarrassment (over an untidy house, unruly children, etc.), and, ultimately, delight — are intended to mirror the home audience's reactions (as well as spark our fantasies) as we imagine ourselves in a similar situation. Similarly, *Food Fantasy* (2000–2004) would take "ordinary" viewers on a televised journey through some food-related experience of their choosing, allowing them to explain the interests underlying their fantasies, thereby gaining credibility as savvy amateurs and authorizing other viewers to imagine themselves in similar roles.

Food Network, like other effective marketing organizations, reflects the understanding that targeting consumers with varying degrees of economic and cultural capital ultimately is more profitable than targeting only those thought to be the most affluent. The hallmark of 1980s yuppie culture, Barbara Ehrenreich explains, was conspicuous consumption, particularly in the form of luxury versions of everyday necessities. It is not that yuppies represented greater affluence than previous generations of the middle class; in fact their real income actually was lower than that of their middle-class parents. Rather, they perceived (as instructed by marketers) such luxury products as gourmet meals and lavish vacations as compensation for the realities of apartment living and two-income households.[15] Of course, expensive gourmet food products are much easier to market than the more expensive lifestyle choices, such as stay-at-home parenting, of the previous generation. Ehrenreich's argument reinforces the idea that social class is as much about effective consumer targeting as income level itself. While it is true that clusters of affluent consumers are being targeted heavily, especially for luxury goods and services, it is increasingly acknowledged as well that most people are heavy consumers of "everyday" necessities such as food, clothing, and shelter in their many possible manifestations. Perhaps nowhere is this more evident than on Food Network and other specialty cable networks.

In *The Experience Economy*, a book published around the time of Food Network's acquisition by Scripps, marketing experts B. Joseph Pine, II, and James H. Gilmore argue that manufacturers can no longer rely on commodities and goods alone; changes in the conditions of production (including the increased use of offshore sweatshops) have reduced the cost of many products to the point where consumers can purchase them at deep discounts in "superstores" such as Sam's Club and Home Depot.[16] They, like other analysts, point out that the more affluent a consumer is, the more likely that consumer will be extremely busy and willing to pay others to assist with tiresome and time-consuming routine obligations. The most highly valued consumers, in other words, are more willing to pay for personal attention than for tangible objects, hence the rise of personal shoppers, personal trainers, business class air travel, and a range of other forms of aid and comfort for the busy consumer. A logical outgrowth of the service economy is the increased availability of prepackaged experiences marketed to an ever-broader slice of the consumer population. Surely this applies to Food Network.

In particular, Food Network has developed several programs that guide viewers through the experience of "discovering" specialty food products, products that are then offered for sale via the cable network or its website. While programs such as *Cooking Live* and *Emeril Live!* might use their hosts' entertaining and accessible presentation styles to turn non-cooks into amateurs, other programs hold no such aspirations. *Food Finds* (2001–present), for instance, featured host Sandra Pinckney traversing the continent in search of unique, independently produced food items that can be acquired by viewers. While visiting a family-run pierogie business in southwestern Michigan, she chats with the family members. A family-owned candy company in Denver demonstrates how lollipops are made the old-fashioned way. A visit to Texas showcases two candy companies (in Austin and Tyler) and a cheese maker (in Dallas). At the end of every episode (and also on the Food Network website) viewers can find information about how to purchase the featured products by mail order. Interestingly, the 2001 holiday season also witnessed a number of products featured on *Food Finds* in shopping malls and department stores around the country. The program, *The Best of...*, serves as a similar marketing tool for restaurants and specialty food retailers, for example, "The Best of ... Hotel Restaurants."

Taking this experiential concept a step further is the popular and long-running *$40 a Day*, in which host Rachael Ray spends a day at a popular tourist destination with $40 to spend on a day's meals and snacks. The main idea, as articulated by Ray, is to discover off-the-beaten-path restaurants, markets, wineries, and other places that cater to the local more than the tourist population. While audiences (as expressed in the www.foodtv.com chatroom) find the program unrealistic in some respects (for example, the personalized attention a celebrity accompanied by a camera crew receives that the ordinary tourist would not), most seem to agree that its real entertainment value lies in the way it showcases interesting and unusual eating establishments. And of course the notion of tourism on a tight budget cuts across multiple market segments.

Conclusions

The examples of Food Network programs I have given go to show that the television audience itself may well be marketers' best ally in achieving the goals of mass customization. As writers including Joseph Turow[17] and Robert B. Reich[18] have suggested, the rise of niche marketing could portend an end to shared culture. However, this might not be happening as quickly or as completely as they suggest. While the success of Food Network might at first seem to prove that special-interest media are supplanting mass media, Food Network's developmental trajectory has demonstrated the opposite. Although this popular cable network does assert a food-related theme for its program schedule, that theme is so broadly articulated that its appeal is almost as widespread as that of the "big three" broadcast networks during their heyday.

The original goal of specialty cable (at least as it was actually tried in the early 1980s) was to identify special-interest niches, provide programming to serve those interests, and sell commercial time to advertisers wishing to sell related products and services. Those niches were articulated as the ones promising the most affluent potential viewer-consumers. There were significant problems with this, of course, for even the wealthiest consumers are unlikely to spend an inordinate amount on the sorts of products that are advertised on television. Moreover, a steady diet of one category of program (live arts programming in the case of the most prominent early niche-targeting failures) holds little appeal for just about anyone.

Viewed in retrospect, the secret to successful specialization clearly lay in an ability to reach a diverse audience in various and overlapping ways. Not only do viewers of differing backgrounds need to be offered programs that appeal to their tastes, interests, and (above all, perhaps) aspirations, they also need to be flattered for having those tastes, interests, and aspirations in the first place. Thus, the more successful cable specialty networks that began in the mid-to-late 1990s followed a somewhat different model than the one initially envisioned.

Food Network, in spite of lacking a corporate parent with an established place in cable programming, was able to develop a flexible and ultimately profitable program schedule. Food Network has managed to mediate social differences in such a way that its programs address multiple consumer groups. A strong growth rate for its subscribership is one indicator of the network's success, the circulation of its program titles and themes within popular culture perhaps an even more revealing one. While celebrity chefs play a critical role in Food Network's programming, surely the network also owes much of this success to the ways in which it has broadened the appeal of those chefs and other entertainment personalities featured in the programming.

Notes

1. See Thomas Streeter, "The Cable Fable Revisited: Discourse, Policy, and the Making of Cable Television," *Critical Studies in Mass Communication* 4 (1987): 174–200.

2. These included the so-called "culture" networks (ABC-ARTS, Rockefeller Center TV, The Entertainment Channel, and CBS-Cable). Of this wave of specialty channels, only Bravo

survived—through a clever self-transformation into a source of art house movies. ARTS and The Entertainment Channel merged and became A&E, which survived its early years by successfully scheduling off-broadcast detective dramas.

3. Horace Newcomb and Paul M. Hirsch, "Television as a Cultural Forum: Implications for Research," *Quarterly Review of Film Studies* (Summer 1983): 45–55.

4. Cecilia Tichi, *Electronic Hearth: Creating an American Television Culture* (New York: Oxford University Press 1992).

5. Notable exceptions here include CNN and MTV. While, in one sense, these networks represented the vanguard of cable narrowcasting, in another sense each was an exception proving a rule. CNN entered one of the most popular and well-established television genres from throughout television history, and MTV, with its schedule of promotional music video "clips" supplied by recording studios, paid very little for its programming.

6. Reese Schonfeld, personal interview, July 27, 1994, at Schonfeld's office, New York City.

7. Schonfeld interview. Also see Diane Goldner, "Channel Surfers Get a Snack Bar," *New York Times*, January 26, 1994, C1 (retrieved from Lexis-Nexis). Note, however, that in spite of Schonfeld's populist assertions about TVFN's intended audience, it was made clear from the beginning that the primary target would be young to middle-aged women—a market niche considered to be underrepresented on cable.

8. Schonfeld interview.

9. Reese Schonfeld, *Me and Ted Against the World: The Unauthorized Story of the Founding of CNN* (New York: Cliff Street, 2001), 331–39.

10. E. W. Scripps corporate Web site, www.scripps.com, accessed August 2002; also see Mike Farrell, "Scripps Wants to Consume All of Food," *Multichannel News*, Oct. 10, 2003.

11. Note that all dates for Food Network programs are approximations. The network—typical of cable networks generally—sometimes will revive older programs as reruns or, occasionally, as new episodes.

12. Sharon Moshavi, "Skewering Tradition: 'Iron Chef' Stirs Up Japanese Cooking, Draws US Fans," *Boston Globe*, May 3, 2000, A1, retrieved from Lexis-Nexis. For a revealing interpretation of *Iron Chef*, see also Lauri Githens, "Hip, Hip, Soufflé: It's the 'Iron Chef,'" *Buffalo News*, April 23, 2000, retrieved from Lexis-Nexis.

13. Schonfeld, 336.

14. Rick Altman, "Television Sound," in *Television: The Critical View*, ed. Horace Newcomb (New York: Oxford University Press, 1985), 566–84.

15. Barbara Ehrenreich, *Fear of Falling: The Inner Life of the Middle Class* (New York: HarperCollins, 1990); see especially Chapter 5, "The Yuppie Strategy."

16. Pine and Gilmore.

17. Joseph Turow, *Breaking Up America: Advertisers and the New Media World* (Chicago: University of Chicago Press, 1997).

18. Robert B. Reich, *The Future of Success: Working and Living in the New Economy* (New York: Vintage, 2000).

Works Cited

Altman, Rick. "Television Sound." In *Television: The Critical View*, ed. Horace Newcomb, 556–584. New York: Oxford University Press, 1985.

Ehrenreich, Barbara. *Fear of Falling: The Inner Life of the Middle Class*. New York: HarperCollins, 1990.

Farrell, Mike. "Scripps Wants to Consume All of Food." *Multichannel News*, Oct. 10, 2003 (online).

Githens, Lauri. "Hip, Hip, Soufflé: It's the 'Iron Chef.'" *Buffalo News*, April 23, 2000.

Moshavi, Sharon. "Skewering Tradition: 'Iron Chef' Stirs Up Japanese Cooking, Draws US Fans." *Boston Globe*, May 3, 2000, A1.

Newcomb, Horace, and Paul M. Hirsch. "Television as a Cultural Forum: Implications for Research." *Quarterly Review of Film Studies* (Summer 1983).

Reich, Robert B. *The Future of Success: Working and Living in the New Economy.* New York: Vintage, 2000.

Schonfeld, Reese. *Me and Ted Against the World: The Unauthorized Story of the Founding of CNN.* New York: Cliff Street, 2001.

Streeter, Thomas. "The Cable Fable Revisited: Discourse, Policy, and the Making of Cable Television." *Critical Studies in Mass Communication* 4 (1987): 174–200.

Tichi, Cecilia. *Electronic Hearth: Creating an American Television Culture.* New York: Oxford University Press, 1992.

Turow, Joseph. *Breaking Up America: Advertisers and the New Media World.* Chicago: University of Chicago Press, 1997.

8

Semiotic Sound Bites

Toward an Alimentary Analysis of Popular Song

CHRISTOPHER JOSEPH WESTGATE

Maybe you've heard it before in a restaurant, or in your own kitchen, even if it did not spill into your lap: a *musical sound* which surrounded the consumption of a meal. You've heard it here and now, then and there, perhaps as often as you've lent an ear to the latest infomercial. If you think hard, you may remember tasting more than usual in a sonic setting. Even if memory does not serve, you can at least identify the frequent presence of musical sounds in the kitchen, restaurant, dining room, and other culinary contexts.

I cannot help but associate Sicilian musical sounds with the taste of my great-grandmother's gravy. That association is unidirectional: the sound is what conjures the taste. There is a slight sound bias at work here. When I taste gravy today, I do not usually think of my great-grandmother or songs which played during our Sunday meals. Yet if I hear particular songs today which played during our gatherings, I am reminded of her gravy's taste. For years my great-grandmother played Sicilian songs on her small tape deck while our family dined each Sunday. I may not remember which artists played when, but I cannot forget the setting. The select sounds of Sicily were inseparable from the taste of her cooking. Although I'm not a synesthete (one who hears melodic notes of different pitches when consuming different kinds of food), music as a mnemonic trigger for taste is not uncommon in our social lives. The question of *how* the sound of music might trigger the memory of taste motivated the writing of this chapter.

Curiously enough, few media and cultural scholars have explored auditory (sound) and gustatory (taste) convergence, much less how the former might recall the latter. Perhaps it is because this matter is of little consequence in our scholarly lives. Yet let me emphasize that critical-cultural scholars have already established food and music as worthy objects of study[1] *because of* their social implications. We have also recognized the dual benefit of studying individual and collective memory in pluralistic societies such as ours.[2] I aim to explore *how* the sound of music not only connects with the taste of food but in so doing *stands for its memory* with a few examples from our personal and social lives, including but not limited to popular songs. These examples are important beyond their elements of surprise and satisfaction because they appear frequently and widely, often right in front of our nose and within ear shot. But let me first define what I mean by a *sound bite*.

Bites of Sound

As sociologist Todd Gitlin writes, the term *sound bite* transitioned from backstage journalistic jargon to the public lexicon because it became the standard practice of news media producers.[3] The process of editing news footage continues to reflect one expository goal: that of a consistent narrative. The *sound bite* frames a news narrative with a short clip of an informant speaking on point. But the term need not confine itself to the standard practice of journalism. We can translate its meaning from a journalistic to a synesthetic context, from a short-term clip on the media screen to a long-term memory of how sound bites at our thoughts, feelings and actions. The *sound bite* is the way in which the quality of an event (its sound) acts on our present understanding or past memory of that event (its bite).

So it is more than just the sound of certain Sicilian songs priming a memory of how good my great-grandmother's gravy tastes. Although that is part of it, my understanding of a *sound bite* is really about her *quality*— her aura — in a Benjaminian sense.[4] The aura is precisely what grips my auditory and gustatory senses today as I remember how much my great-grandmother loved our family. For Walter Benjamin, an art work's aura was very much here and now in space and time: a unique, singular, authentic existence in a particular place. Benjamin would have agreed human auras resist easy reproduction in others' bodies. In memory, the aura of sound separates its unique texture from other sounds of the same pitch, volume or frequency to compete for storage and retrieval.

We cannot possibly remember every musical sound that accompanies everything we consume. But we can remember those remarkable ones which stand out for reasons we may or may not yet understand. Think of the barrage of musical sounds we process on a daily basis, from others' cell phone ring tones to music interludes on news programs, and how certain ones resonate more than others because of associations they provoke. Sounds invoke sensory memories in many different ways, as Alexander Stein points out:

The kaleidoscope of archaic auditory impressions, perceptions ... and primary relationships, remain audible across the chasms of time and space in the inner ear of imagination and memory, where the internalized voices and sounds of earliest life are permanently ensconced.... They re-sound in dreams, fantasies, and inner speech, ... as well as externalized verbal and linguistic expressions — and, of course, music — symbolically communicating aspects of mental life using sound formations in time.[5]

Stein suggests we are more likely to recall certain sounds because of the pathos behind their verbal or nonverbal expressions. These expressions associate in memory with whatever actions we performed at the time (e.g., cooking, eating, or anything else for that matter). Activated by abstract triggers, our memories catalogue song melodies and lyrics across multiple cognitive pathways.[6] A *sound bite* becomes a useful theoretical framework because it bears on *how* we decide which qualities to recognize or remember from our present or past. Now that we can at least appreciate, if not accept *sound bites*, let's analyze why they are modified by the term *semiotic*.

Signs of Sound Bites

Food involves a structure of idiosyncratic feeling and experience rather than some kind of arbitrary sign language. As Brad Kessler concludes, food is semiotic because it signifies carnality, appetite, desire, and sex inasmuch as eating involves putting things into our bodies.[7] Experiences are fraught with emotions, which are obviously a part of our musical pasts. Food stands for flesh or other human needs just as music stands for food and its taste in memory. Patti Smith's "Summer Cannibals" unwittingly underscores the semiotic relationship between our auditory and gustatory senses; in this song, we are offered a banquet of flesh and bone in the spirit of savagery.

Throughout its verse-chorus-verse structure, the song's lyrics sound off on lean flesh, bubbling cauldrons, and similes between women and piranhas. Carnal flesh is displayed as a sweet sacrifice to the narrative voice. Although the chorus persuades listeners to consume, the dilemma of hunger and human sacrifice is ultimately not resolved by the final verse. What surprises more than the theme's barbarity is the form in which the narrative voice implores listeners to eat: not once or twice, but three times, successively repeated in the imperative mood with frantic tones of desperation. As listeners, we cannot help but feel inquisitive, even if we refuse to obey and eat.[8]

Smith as signifier of musical sound and the cannibal as a signified taster of flesh form a complete sign of how both senses connect. The sound of carnal flesh and its bite are conjured together in our minds as many descriptors (*strange, savage* and so forth) and can no longer be separated. Smith audibly enacts the idea of consuming flesh as effortlessly as language finds itself entangled with performance. The act of eating by summer cannibals allows us to experience the sweetness and leanness of flesh by connecting its quality (essence or aura, if you like) with its real, though more likely, imagined taste.

Sound bites as the quality of the event depend on representational capacities of sensation. We perform a symbol (the act of cooking or listening) according to normative forms (what recipes or sound sources exist) to achieve social ends (a tasty meal or a pleasurable listening experience). We can move one step further, though, and examine the capacity of auditory and gustatory stimuli to create meaning through representation as we perform our daily rituals, in Eric Rothenbuhler's sense of the term:

> Ritual is the voluntary performance of appropriately patterned behavior to symbolically effect or participate in the serious life.... The serious life is a phenomenological category designating those things treated as more important, more morally freighted, and more obligatory than others within any given context.[9]

This definition is elastic enough to apply to the subject at hand. Selecting the right dinner music may not be the most serious of decisions, especially when compared to cooking the right meal with the right ingredients for someone with a fatal food allergy. At the wedding reception, though, who eats what is a serious matter, as serious as who programs what for others to hear. A change in context implies a change in how much weight we assign certain behaviors. Following Rothenbuhler's logic, there are right and wrong ways to listen and to eat, depending on the occasion. Whether we select Bach or Bjork to accompany our wedding reception and its main dish will be understood by others as a *sign* of perfect or poor taste: they will talk about what these signs mean days or years later.

Food and music then are signifiers of performance, or ways of doing. They point to our need to *do* something for others or ourselves, whether that involves cooking, eating, listening or playing a song. We represent this need through the music and food we select for others and for ourselves in specific contexts. Food and music are thus deictic.[10] They are also synesthetic, based in the senses, and often hold some degree of utility in time and space.

Sound and Bite Convergence

Discourse surrounding the sound of music and the taste of food nearly always focuses on sensory textures and how they grab us. When food and music mix in our present or past lives, we taste and hear a *sound bite* in a synesthetic sense. The quality of the event may include specific stimuli, sonic or otherwise, but must signify an earlier memory or present understanding of the event (e.g., a dinner reception or family brunch).

Synesthesia is defined in two ways. Natural scientists have documented a rare condition in which stimulation of one sense produces an involuntary perception in another. Dr. Julia Simner observed ten individuals in Europe and the U.S. with the condition of auditory-gustatory synesthesia.[11] A stimulated region produces one sense (via cognition) while the other emerges from a nonstimulated, separate region (via regulation). The auditory cortex corresponds to the temporal lobe, while olfactory and taste sensations are part of the cerebral cortex.[12] In contrast, scholars in the social sciences and humanities have applied the term to new contexts as a cross-modal trope; I will also take some degree of literary license here because of the term's interpretive fit within my *sound bites* framework.

Consistent with their synesthetic nature, music and food are often interpreted together. The sound of fruit drinks were once called "music to our mouths," just as tortilla chips "screamed with Monterey Jack Cheese flavor" on popular commercials. As one slogan went, it was the "combination that tasted as great as it sounded." In this way, the sense of sound has often correlated with the sense of taste across media studies of advertisements.[13]

However, there are clearly instances when our auditory and gustatory senses must be analyzed separately in order to distinguish one from the other. Produced music *initially sounds the same* each time its studio version is played, even if *interpreted differently*. Contexts change as often as dinner courses. Yet the same song is still played from the same studio recording, excluding "live" renditions or reinterpretations. In contrast, food *does not initially taste the same* each time it is prepared, even if *interpreted similarly*. Tomato sauce may have a touch more basil or garlic than before, or the ingredients may not be as fresh as they once were. Both are "produced," but the song is pre-produced by the same record company while the sauce is produced live, in actuality, by a different cook each time.

Yet rarely do we experience one sense in complete isolation from the other.[14] Even as I write this chapter I am constantly reminded of how my fingers strike the keyboard buttons, both visually as I hunt and peck for certain symbols, and aurally as the keys tap and trigger. The remainder of this chapter will catalogue a few examples of how the sound of music converges with the taste of food, ultimately arguing for one's primacy over the other. Let's first look at our most pressing example of how memory forges a link between sound and taste.

Remembering the Sound of Taste

As Deborah Kapchan writes, we account for the space of performance and the role of the senses in connecting those who perform to a memory of that setting.[15] The quality or strength of the auditory-gustatory link implicates us in reiterative motions of rewind to our past and fast-forward to our present. When heard within an alimentary context, music leaves mnemonic imprints on our minds because the brain stores sound perceptions with emotion and body sensation: smells and tastes are invoked by familiar songs.[16] We may try to remember what we were eating when a particular song played, or why we savored certain flavors more than others.

More importantly, though, food and music are shortcuts to *sound bites*, ways in which certain event qualities impinge on our current understanding or prior recollection of that event, whether the event is a family picnic or a reading respite at the local café. As Jon Holtzman suggests, our reenactment of a previous event allows us to reexperience the emotion behind its temporal and spatial distance from our present circumstance. For example, I might reenact a Sunday dinner with the same set of cassette tapes in order to reexperience the generalized love and devotion my great-grandmother and I felt for each other at that particular time. However, there are also less generalized feelings which were specific to certain Sundays I may choose not to reenact, even if I reexperience or replay them in my mind. It is both the activity of that replay and its outcome, how I feel currently, that matter for future purposes. Above all, I would not want to forget these Sunday dinners, no matter how painful or pleasurable the emotions behind them:

> Personal memory encompasses both the activities and products of remembering. We inscribe experiences in the present to facilitate future recall; such material inscriptions are always filtered through discursive conventions, social and cultural practices, and technological tools.[17]

Thus, to remember the sound of taste we must remember the emotion behind the event's unique quality, or why we felt a certain way at a certain time in a certain place. Food stirs the emotions because of its sensual properties and social meanings, while music stirs food because of its semiotic properties and ritual meanings. These properties and meanings are constituent of our individual and collective identities.[18] In other words, questioning our identities allows us to temporarily escape from the present through emotional release. Food and music do not symbolize social bonds and divisions as much as they allow for a re-creation of those bonds and divisions.

In addition to re-creation, music and food tell stories from our collective pasts. In an intriguing article by Nathan Hill titled "Hot Biscuits, Food as Sexual Metaphor in the Blues," we learn that food, cooking and sexual metaphor have been commonplace in blues lyrics for decades, from Bessie Smith's "Need a Little Sugar in My Bowl" to John Hurt's "Coffee Blues." Blues singers employed metaphorical tools to cover a breadth of meaning which literal language did not permit.

Yet it is not only that food and sex are central to our human existence. It is more important to question why or how they came to be that way. The artist John Mellencamp posed this question with the metaphors of hot dogs and hamburgers, symbols of bodily courtship in the musical story of his encounter with an "Indian" girl. In "Hot Dogs and Hamburgers," Mellencamp travels the countryside with an exotic Other: a different kind of girl, and thus a different kind of sustenance. Bypassing political correctness for colloquiality, the narrative ethos shifts from entitlement to gratitude. The white man realizes how lucky he was to interface with the "Indian" girl, and consequently repents any previous misdeeds. Meanwhile, the listener is treated to an abbreviated oral history on relations between "Indian" nations and the white man. Mellencamp's words echo how an "Indian" girl cannot possibly confide in a white man because of historical conflicts which crush the potential for courtship. As the white man departs, the listener is reminded of the story's arc, from dusk to dawn, and perhaps more banally, that anyone can elect the right or wrong kind of meat.[19]

Mellencamp maintains a critical gaze toward any future relations with the girl not only because of their ethnic differences, but also because he opted for the less exotic Other: he chose to hold on to what he thought was right for him. For Mellencamp, food and music are both storied media. They are forms through which tales are told, corporeal or otherwise. To that extent, food and music enter our bodies through social action. They are products of voluntary choices we make as individuals in society.

Intimate Ingestions of Sound and Taste

Food and music are intimate artifacts that enter our bodies because they are within reach. The decision of what to consume is intensely personal: it may be made for or by us. Whenever we decide to consume a piece of food, we make a voluntary choice, provided we are economically fortunate enough to discern what does from what does not look appetizing.

We voluntarily choose what ingredients to gather, prepare a shopping list, and visit the grocery store to stock up. Or we voluntarily choose the cuisine and restaurant we wish to patronize. The decision of what to prepare or purchase is intimate because we decided to make it or followed another's suggestion. Whether we prepare or purchase, we consume by choice, usually not by force.

In contrast to food consumption, the choice of whether to hear musical sound may not always be ours to make. Indeed, our personal mixes often derive from music we or others we trust select; the order in which songs appear may be random, but their original selection is usually not. We choose to download or listen to certain songs because of the intensely personal meaning those songs have had, do have, or could potentially have. Yet the potential for musical sounds to enter our ears is not always confined to voluntary consumption.

We sometimes cannot choose which type of music we hear. Our exposure to a growing number of sounds from disparate sources is the handiwork of other taste cultures.[20] We encounter these different tastes on a daily basis and they become part and parcel of our rituals. For example, we cannot easily close our ears on an underground train unless we know the route by rote and carry a set of earplugs. Music often bleeds from the "soundproof" headphones of those who have not yet tested the volume before surrounding themselves with music in their own private, bubblelike public space.[21] Such mobile privatization is not soundproof, though, and often bursts for others within listening range.

To that degree, we cannot always control what we hear. As Jacques Attali has shown, it is difficult to tune out a noise we cannot easily escape from.[22] We can conclude that the matter of ingestion is one of kind, not degree: we have more voluntary choice with food than we do with music. Aside from their ability to enter us, food and music also allow us to think of ourselves as refined or sophisticated.

The Sensibility of Sound Bites

Food and music involve matters of taste and sensibility. In other words, they are both pleasurable commodities which reflect how as much as what we choose to consume. Recall that *sound bites* implicate us in quality decisions on which events hold meaning for our lives in the present or past. By the sensibility of sound bites, I mean our capacity to discern *how* we decide which qualities hold meaning. By paying attention, we gradually refine the ingredients we use or the sounds we hear and grow more sophisticated in the choices we make in food and music. These choices are acts of taste: they reflect our talent for discerning what is most appropriate or pleasing from what is not. We usually perform these acts of taste in community, as sociologist Priscilla Ferguson has shown:

> Whereas food calls for eaters, a culinary culture contends with a different sort of consumer, the reader-diners whose consumption of texts rivals their ingestion of food. Reading and evaluating, like eating and cooking, are so many "taste acts" by which individuals "perform" their connections to a taste community. That participation in turn — the culinary practices, norms and values that derive from and support the cuisine in question — sets us in a culinary culture.... Just as the written word fixes speech, so culinary discourse secures the transitory experiences of taste.[23]

Each time we decide which qualities of an event hold meaning for us, we allow those qualities to serve our past or present lives in social ways. In other words, the meaning an event holds is compared to meanings attached to norms, values, or trends from other members of similar taste communities. We reinforce what we decide to hear and taste based on the decisions of others we trust.

How do we know which taste community we belong to? The answer is found in how similarly we perform when "reading" the same text, synonymous with "listening to or eating" the same text. Text is well understood by critical-cultural scholars as anything from a song to a food product. Listening is as much an act of taste as eating because individuals perform their memberships in communities of taste. This idea is not far removed from Stanley Fish's interpretive communities,[24] which argues different readers will perform similarly when reading the same text, while the same reader will perform differently when reading two different texts. We may not have verbal reassurance that we belong to the same community of taste and thus interpret an event's quality in like manner, but every once in a while a wink or some nonverbal cue is communicated to confirm any doubt or disbelief: "You can't wink without knowing what counts as winking."[25]

Through winking or some other nonverbal confirmation, we gradually reinforce our capacity to discern, by sound bites, *how* we decide which qualities hold meaning for our present and past. Culinary culture at large calls for us not only to eat and listen but cook and perform, actively participating in its remaking and refining. Likewise, we only improve the ingredients we select and the way in which we cook, or the songs we choose to sing and the way in which we perform, by paying attention to the way in which we perceive how we and others eat or listen. These acts of sound and taste are ritualistic, voluntary performances of "appropriately patterned behavior [which allow us to] symbolically effect or participate"[26] in culinary culture. In this way, we combine our use of the term *ritual* with all of the overarching concepts and examples presented thus far. In addition to matters of taste and sensibility, the sound of music and the taste of food also rely on careful decisions we make individually and collectively.

These careful decisions are forms of communication we enact to connect with others in the culture at large. We take care in what we decide to hear or eat in several settings: weddings, funerals, ceremonies, office spaces, retail stores, and so forth more than we do when we are alone at home or in transport.

The act of purposeful consumption of just the right sounds and tastes in the restaurant was a careful decision Jimmy Buffett made in "I Wish Lunch Could Last Forever." In this song, the narrative voice reminisces about a local restaurant in which two lovers regularly rendezvous. The man, presumably Buffett or an alter-ego, tastes the smell of seafood in its entirety, and compares its spices to other kinds of sensations one typically experiences while gazing at a lovely woman. Overcome by her beauty and the setting, he decides to order another bottle of wine and drink away ordinary time. The attempt to fictionally extend time on an absent clock becomes a means of converting a fleeting sense of love into an eternal affair, prolonging an otherwise ephemeral meeting into a permanent one with liquor as a lubricant.[27]

The rendezvous is a careful act of volition: Buffett asks for a bottle of wine and consumes the smells of fish as an entrée into the potential timelessness of love. The act of deciding what to ingest is as intimate as the company or setting surrounding the end result. All of these decisions are made in certain orders, at certain times and in certain spaces. The order of events surrounding our ingestion of food and music is carefully orchestrated, usually with a purpose in mind. Food and music can satisfy audiences when their purveyors and performers have good taste. The decisions of when, where and with what music to eat are more imperative in high-pressure settings like funerals and ceremonies than they are in casual dinner gatherings or private picnics. Now that we have analyzed how the sound of music connects with the taste of food through synesthesia, memory, intimacy and sensibility, we can look at *how* one triggers the other.

Priming Taste with Sound

The memory of taste is often primed by sound. According to priming theory, prior presentation of a noise or sound can trigger a memory which makes a concept, such as taste, more accessible.[28]

Philosophers have long argued that taste is a secondary or lower sense which cannot produce art partly because it deals with short-lived stimuli. Instead, sound is much more central to the production of art and its meaning.[29] By deduction, then, our auditory sense, provoked by sound, is a primary sense which precedes taste. Once sound is recognized, taste will often follow. Madalina Diaconu has shown that auditory and gustatory impressions relate to form one sense: "It is true that the synesthetic bias frequently makes it impossible to consider the secondary senses separately; this means only that they require a more complex approach than the usual aesthetic interpretation."[30]

Although we simultaneously input information from many sensory channels, all inputs sum to one output as a single message. These cross-sensory approaches form what David Howes has called "relational intersensoriality."[31] Both senses can only add up to one message, though, provided there are two compatible senses to add. Sound and taste are compatible parts of the materiality of music and food. Yet it is not the materiality of these artifacts which motivates us to think about their relationship. Rather, it is the *immateriality* of the emotions behind these material artifacts which underlies a seemingly simple link between our auditory and gustatory senses.

Singer-songwriter Patti Griffin wrote on the immateriality of a lost love through the material trope of pies. The aura of Griffin in the kitchen transcends her vocal timbre and crumbles any kind of cookie-cutter interpretation. Her unique quality as the singer-songwriter communicates what the feeling behind the sound means in our own presents or pasts. The song's narrative depicts a female who bakes pies to avoid life's tears and trauma. It is not so much the taste of sugar which sweetens the bitter escape, but the physical act of baking the pie. We hear self-doubt, as the narrative voice questions whether she remembered to share a pre-war picture of her lover with an observer. As a resolution, the listener, like the narrative voice, can voluntarily choose to escape any sense of unfulfilled longing by making pies. The gerund *making* reinforces the status of a pie not yet fully baked, a life with all its problems and possibilities in progress.[32]

Whether this song reminds us of how pies taste is not the point. Rather, the song's overall quality (its performer, lyrics, melody, aura, and so forth) represents events for us as listeners with distinct pasts. It is the sound of the music which evokes the taste of our own present or past events, however delightful or disagreeable they are or were.

Digesting Sound Bites

We must now digest this chapter with sound as our solvent. The sound of music explains many things, including but not limited to the taste of food in our present pasts. I combined these temporal frames because I found myself moving frontward and backward between my own memories and modern realities. I discovered it is the essence of sound which mobilizes this niggling movement from past to present.

Thus the question of *how* the sound of music primes the memory of taste is an idiosyncratic one. We find different answers on different days, depending on how we choose to remember intimate details from the past and analyze their resultant emotions in the present. I developed one of many possible theoretical frameworks and provided examples so that we can understand why it is we need to relive emotions behind sensations both as scholars for analytical purposes and as human beings for relational purposes. That is why it is not the materiality of food and music as much as it is the immateriality of the emotions behind these artifacts which matter, emotions which are experienced at the individual and collective level, in scholarly and non-scholarly contexts.

Sound bites are really about *how* the sound of music connects with the taste of food. Sound comes to stand for the memory of taste as it primes our present understanding of an earlier event. I have demonstrated this argument through several examples: first, how food and music create meaning through representation (semiotic); second, how they are often interpreted together (synesthetic); third, how memory forges the link between food and music as storied media in the present (mnemonic); fourth, how their ingestion is usually voluntary, intimate, and motivated by a desire to understand the reasons behind the decisions we make in our social lives (ritualistic).

Future alimentary analyses can take a similar path and analyze the equivalent of popular songs for other senses: sight, smell, and touch, for example, as they interrelate with sound and taste. Even though my great-grandmother is no longer with me in material form, I still recognize her sound and remember her bite.

I would like to thank Dr. Eric Rothenbuhler for his invaluable input on earlier drafts of this chapter. I wrote this in loving memory of Rose Fatta.

Notes

1. Jon Holtzman, "Food and Memory," *Annual Review of Anthropology* 35 (2006): 361–78.

2. James Wertsch, *Voices of Collective Remembering* (New York: Cambridge University Press, 2002), 5–6.

3. Todd Gitlin, *Media Unlimited* (New York: Owl Books, 2002), 96–98, 121–26.

4. Walter Benjamin, *Illuminations* (New York: Schocken, 1969), 217–53.

5. Alexander Stein, "The Sound of Memory: Music and Acoustic Origins," *American Imago* 64 (2007): 59–85.

6. Isabelle Peretz, Monique Radeau, and Martin Arguin, "Two-Way Interactions Between Music and Language: Evidence from Priming Recognition of Tune and Lyrics in Familiar Songs," *Journal of Memory and Cognition* 32 (2004): 142–52.

7. Brad Kessler, "One Reader's Digest: Toward a Gastronomic Theory of Literature," *Kenyon Review* 27 (2005): 1–18.

8. Patti Smith, "Summer Cannibals," *Gone Again* (Arista, 1996).

9. Eric Rothenbuhler, "Communication as Ritual," in *Communication as Perspectives on Theory*, eds. Gregory Shepherd, Jeffrey St. John, and Ted Striphaus (Thousand Oaks, CA: Sage, 2006), 13–21.

10. Roland Barthes, *Empire of Signs* (New York: Hill and Wang, 1983), 11–26.

11. Donald McNeil, "For Rare Few, Taste Is in the Ear of the Beholder," *New York Times*, November 23, 2006, A1.

12. Jean-Pierre Ternaux, "Synesthesia: A Multimodal Combination of Senses," *Leonardo* 36 (2003): 321–22.

13. Michelle Nelson and Jacqueline Hitchon, "Theory of Synesthesia Applied to Persuasion in Print Advertising Headlines," *Journalism and Mass Communication Quarterly* 72 (1995): 346–60.

14. Paul Grainge, "Nostalgia and Style in Retro America: Moods, Modes and Media Recycling," *Journal of American and Comparative Cultures* 23 (2000): 27–34.

15. Deborah Kapchan, "Performance," *Journal of American Folklore* 108 (1995): 479–508.

16. José Van Dijck, "Mediated Memories: Personal Cultural Memory as Object of Cultural Analysis," *Continuum: Journal of Media and Cultural Studies* 18 (2004): 261–77.

17. José Van Dijck, "Record and Hold: Popular Music Between Personal and Collective Memory," *Critical Studies in Media Communication* 23 (2006): 357–74.

18. Deborah Lupton, "Food and Emotion," in *The Taste Culture Reader*, ed. Carolyn Korsmeyer (Oxford: Berg Press, 2005), 317–24.

19. John Mellencamp, "Hotdogs and Hamburgers," *The Lonesome Jubilee* (Island/Mercury, 1987).

20. Herbert Gans, *Popular Culture and High Culture: An Analysis and Evaluation of Taste* (New York: Basic Books, 1999), 6–8, 92–100.

21. Raymond Williams, *Television: Technology and Cultural Form* (New York: Schocken, 1974), 19–21.

22. Jacques Attali, *Noise: The Political Economy of Music* (Minneapolis: University of Minnesota Press, 1985), 3–21.

23. Priscilla Ferguson, *Accounting for Taste: The Triumph of French Cuisine* (Chicago: University of Chicago Press, 2004), 17–18.

24. Stanley Fish, "Interpreting the Valorium," *Critical Inquiry* 2 (1976): 465–86.

25. Clifford Geertz, *The Interpretation of Cultures* (New York: Basic Books, 1973), 12.

26. Eric Rothenbuhler, "Communication as Ritual," in *Communication as Perspectives on Theory*, eds. Gregory Shepherd, Jeffrey St. John, and Ted Striphaus (Thousand Oaks, CA: Sage, 2006), 13–21.

27. Jimmy Buffett, "I Wish Lunch Could Last Forever," *Off to See the Lizard* (MCA, 1989).

28. Roger Ratcliff, "A Retrieval Theory of Priming in Memory," *Psychological Review* 95 (1988): 385–408.

29. Madalina Diaconu, "Reflections on an Aesthetics of Touch, Smell and Taste," *Contemporary Aesthetics* (2006), http://www.contempaesthetics.org/newvolume/pages/article.php?articleID=385.

30. Ibid.

31. David Howes, "Scent, Sound, and Synesthesia," in *Handbook of Material Culture*, eds. Christopher Tilley, Webb Keane, Susanne Kuchler, Mike Rowlands, and Patricia Spyer (Thousand Oaks, CA: Sage, 2006), 161–73.

32. Patty Griffin, "Making Pies," *1,000 Kisses* (ATO, 2001).

Works Cited

Attali, Jacques. *Noise: The Political Economy of Music.* Minneapolis: University of Minnesota Press, 1985.

Barthes, Roland. *Empire of Signs.* New York: Hill and Wang, 1983.

Benjamin, Walter. *Illuminations.* New York: Schocken, 1969.

Bourdieu, Pierre. *Distinction: A Social Critique of the Judgment of Taste.* London: Routledge, 1984.

Buffett, Jimmy. "I Wish Lunch Could Last Forever," *Off to See the Lizard.* MCA, 1989.

Diaconu, Madalina. "Reflections on an Aesthetics of Touch, Smell and Taste." *Contemporary Aesthetics* (2006). http://www.contempaesthetics.org/newvolume/pages/article.php?articleID=385.

Ferguson, Priscilla. *Accounting for Taste: The Triumph of French Cuisine.* Chicago: University of Chicago Press, 2004.

Fish, Stanley. "Interpreting the Valorium." *Critical Inquiry* 2 (1976): 465–86.

Gans, Herbert. *Popular Culture and High Culture: An Analysis and Evaluation of Taste.* New York: Basic Books, 1999.

Geertz, Clifford. *The Interpretation of Cultures.* New York: Basic Books, 1973.

Gitlin, Todd. *Media Unlimited.* New York: Owl Books, 2002.

Grainge, Paul. "Nostalgia and Style in Retro America: Moods, Modes and Media Recycling." *Journal of American and Comparative Cultures* 23 (2000): 27–34.

Griffin, Patty. "Making Pies." *1,000 Kisses*. ATO, 2001.

Hill, Nathan. "Hot Biscuits: Food as Sexual Metaphor in the Blues." *Proteus* 17 (2000): 37–40.

Holtzman, Jon. "Food and Memory." *Annual Review of Anthropology* 35 (2006): 361–78.

Howes, David. "Scent, Sound, and Synesthesia." In *Handbook of Material Culture*, eds. Christopher Tilley, Webb Keane, Susanne Kuchler, Mike Rowlands, and Patricia Spyer, 161–173. Thousand Oaks, CA: Sage, 2006.

Kapchan, Deborah. "Performance." *Journal of American Folklore* 108 (1995): 479–508.

Kessler, Brad. "One Reader's Digest: Toward a Gastronomic Theory of Literature." *Kenyon Review* 27 (2005): 1–18.

Lupton, Deborah. "Food and Emotion." In *The Taste Culture Reader*, ed. Carolyn Korsmeyer, 317–24. Oxford: Berg Press, 2005.

McNeil, Donald. "For Rare Few, Taste Is in the Ear of the Beholder." *New York Times*, November 23, 2006, A1.

Mellencamp, John. "Hotdogs and Hamburgers." *The Lonesome Jubilee*. Island/Mercury, 1987.

Nelson, Michelle, and Jacqueline Hitchon. "Theory of Synesthesia Applied to Persuasion in Print Advertising Headlines." *Journalism and Mass Communication* Quarterly 72 (1995): 346–60.

Peretz, Isabelle, Monique Radeau, and Martin Arguin. "Two-Way Interactions Between Music and Language: Evidence from Priming Recognition of Tune and Lyrics in Familiar Songs." *Journal of Memory and Cognition* 32 (2004): 142–52.

Proust, Marcel. *Remembrance of Things Past*. New York: Random House, 1934.

Ratcliff, Roger. "A Retrieval Theory of Priming in Memory." *Psychological Review* 95 (1988): 385–408.

Rothenbuhler, Eric. "Communication as Ritual." In *Communication as ... Perspectives on Theory*, eds. Gregory Shepherd, Jeffrey St. John, and Ted Striphaus, 13–21. Thousand Oaks, CA: Sage, 2006.

Smith, Patti. "Summer Cannibals." *Gone Again*. Arista, 1996.

Stein, Alexander. "The Sound of Memory: Music and Acoustic Origins." *American Imago* 64 (2007): 59–85.

Ternaux, Jean-Pierre. "Synesthesia: A Multimodal Combination of Senses." *Leonardo* 36 (2003): 321–22.

Van Dijck, José. "Mediated Memories: Personal Cultural Memory as Object of Cultural Analysis." *Continuum: Journal of Media and Cultural Studies* 18 (2004): 261–77.

_____. "Record and Hold: Popular Music between Personal and Collective Memory." *Critical Studies in Media Communication* 23 (2006): 357–74.

Wertsch, James. *Voices of Collective Remembering*. New York: Cambridge University Press, 2002.

Williams, Raymond. *Television: Technology and Cultural Form*. New York: Schocken, 1974.

9

Hunger and Satiety in
Latin American Literature

SANTIAGO DAYDI-TOLSON

After a brief and delightful gastronomical tour of Hungary, Miguel Angel Asturias, the Guatemalan Nobel Prize author, and Pablo Neruda, the author of many odes to food, wrote in collaboration *Comiendo en Hungría* [*Eating in Hungary*], a whimsical book in praise of food and the pleasure of eating.[1] In the introduction to the book Neruda comments how throughout human history nations have marched to the table with "stones and sticks, knifes and scimitars, with fire and drums," that food, in other words, has been the cause for war, conquest, and revolutions. ["Con piedra y palo, cuchillo y cimitarra, con fuego y tambor avanzan los pueblos a la mesa."][2] Since everyone goes to the table, one way or another, the poet calls for humanity to partake in peace of the great supper of human justice: "Sobre la mesa del mundo, con todo el mundo a la mesa, volarán las palomas. Busquemos en el mundo la mesa feliz." [Over the world's table, with the whole world at the table, the doves shall fly. Let us look in the world for the happy table.][3] Food, thus, and in particular the image of the dining table as a place of convivial friendship, becomes an excellent symbol for universal peace and social justice under economic equality.

The suggestive image of the dinner table, with the overt cultural echoes of a Christian symbol ingrained in the Latin American popular mind, appears again in the poem "El gran mantel" [The great table cloth] in which Neruda explicitly applies the image of the banquet to signify social justice in a direct reference to widely spread hunger among peoples living in an economically unequal society. A reference to his duty as a populist poet, provider of words and justice is quite evident in the poem. At lunch time, the poet sets aside his instrument and takes up instead the knife and fork, and the common people come to eat with him at his table.[4]

Towards the end of the poem the poet calls for everyone to sit down soon at the table with all those who have not been able to eat: "Sentémonos pronto a comer/con todos los que no han comido,"[5] and concludes asking only for the justice of lunch: "Por ahora no pido más/que la justicia del almuerzo."[6] Another instance of the same image is found in "Oda a la mesa" [Ode to the table], an homage to the piece of furniture used by the poet both to write his odes and to eat his bread, his wine and meat: "desarrollo mis odas,/despliego el pan, el vino/y el asado.[7] As in the introduction to the book on Hungarian food, in this poem to a simple object Neruda insists on symbolizing the world in the table set for a dinner party to be enjoyed by everyone. The poem concludes with the familiar call to boys and girls: dinner is served! "muchachas y muchachos/a la mesa."[8]

The political implications in the treatment of food as a literary subject acquire even more validity in Neruda's poetic discourse when hunger and food, and the issue of sharing, are seen as recurrent themes in Latin American letters and socioeconomic history. From the first arrival of the Europeans in the new continent, Latin American letters have shown continuous interest in the contrasting forces, natural as well as sociological, represented on one hand by hunger and extreme deprivation, and by the abundance of food and the partaking of it on the other. The exploring, discovery, conquest and settlement of new lands were closely related to the need for daily sustenance and the search for profitable production. Food, and the lack of it, had been a concern for Medieval and Early Renaissance Europe as the unstable availability of alimentary products due to weather, wars and distribution led in many instances to hunger and famine.[9] Spanish literature, as a matter of fact, offers in the picaresque novel of the 16th and 17th centuries a vivid representation of hunger in the period, documenting thus the import poverty and hunger must have had in the enterprise of discovery and colonization of the Indies.

Hunger and Conquest

The need to satisfy the growing European demand for a stable source of nourishment fueled in part the exploration efforts that eventually led to the encounter of the two worlds: the old one, with its growing economies and population, and the new one, destined to become the economic boom of modern European empires as it provided great amounts of natural products, food included, for the satisfaction of an ever more demanding and affluent consumer society. Food, in the form of new crops and of increased production of Old World crops in the New World, was, by all means, one of the most important contributions of the newly conquered lands to the Old World.[10] Soon after the conquest, and as the result of the first writings about the discoveries, the Americas were to be seen by Europe as the geographical materialization of the legendary and mostly utopian Land of Cockaigne, the paradisiacal Garden of Delights that Medieval and Early Renaissance Europe imagined as a consolation for hunger and need.[11] Something of the utopian imagination of the Renaissance was to be attached to the new lands, as might be seen in the missionary and founding work of Vasco de Quiroga in Mexico[12] and the Jesuit order in Paraguay.[13] As in the legendary land of plenty, Europe found in America an abundance of food and riches without precedents. This is confirmed among Spaniards as in their language, enriched by many words from the languages of the conquered peoples, the name of the very real Peruvian valley of Jauja became synonymous with Cockaigne and took over the idealized character of the imaginary.

Reality, though, was more complex than imagined. It presented the conquerors with the common difficulties of finding daily sustenance in an unknown world as they adventured across the ocean and over land with limited and perishable provisions. Innumerable are the tragic stories of wrecks and failed expeditions that ended in death by hunger and thirst. The historian Fernández de Oviedo writes his *Libro último de los infortunios y naufragios* to document many unfortunate cases of hunger and death among the Spanish expeditions. Most first-person accounts of the period deal also with the dire circumstances of explorers lacking the basic necessities of water and food. A most impressive narrative of the daily concern about eating and of the extremes of starvation in a land mistakenly thought to be plentiful is the one written by Alvar Nuñez Cabeza de Vaca after having wandered for a decade, lost and naked, through many and totally alien lands ["en diez años que por muchas y muy extrañas tierras que anduve perdido y en cueros"].[14] His *Naufragios* remain a classic among the numerous true life adventures that documented the extremes of desperation and satiety in the process of conquering the New World.

In some instances hunger was the direct consequence of war and affected equally the invading Spaniards as the native inhabitants. Cortés and his soldiers suffered extreme deprivation when fleeing from the Aztec forces after their defeat of la Noche triste;[15] the conquerors of Chile found a land abandoned by the retreating Indians who, as a means of defense, destroyed all crops, condemning the intruders to starvation.[16] The native peoples were not free from hunger, either. Cabeza de Vaca lived several years in what is today the Southwest of the United States among Indian tribes who fought each other and had great difficulties in getting a stable source of food from the land. The more advanced agricultural societies to the south, which had eradicated hunger through the careful storage and distribution of crops, were faced with starvation as a result of the Spanish invasion and conquest. Their food turned sour in their mouths as their well-organized and prosperous societies collapsed. Hunger established itself in the continent as a leading source of human misery and disgrace and as a recurrent literary motif. An Aztec poem of the conquest laments the loss brought by defeat:

> ¡Oh amigos míos, llorad!
> Sabed que dejamos yerma la nación mexicana.
> Ay, aun el agua está amarga, aún el alimento está amargo.
> [Cry, oh my friends!
> We have made of the Mexican nation a wasteland.
> Alas, even water tastes bitter, even food is bitter.][17]

Related to the ever-present subject of hunger in the early writings is one of the most discussed themes affecting the view Europeans formed of the new continent: anthropophagy, the shocking practice suggestively renamed "cannibalism," in reference to the Caribs, a warlike people who inhabited the islands of the sea also named for them. Although practiced by the conquerors in several occasions of desperate need, cannibalism was a custom mostly attributed to the sinfulness and barbarism of the native populations. A subject too complex to be treated here, the eating of human flesh and the many references to it in the writings of the conquest point to the centrality of hunger and feeding in the conquering and colonizing enterprise.

Satiety in Partaking of a Bountiful Land

In contrast to the narratives of deprivation and suffering, many are the instances when food and satiety speak in literature of abundance and fulfillment. Two main topics appear as central to the treatment of the subject. The most common of these topics is the extolling of the land's fertility and of the variety, novelty and excellence of its fruits; the other is the selfless act of sharing of those fruits as a sign of friendship and appeasement. Both topics point to an optimistic view of the New World and its promising condition as a land of plenty. They support the view of America as the land of opportunity, and to a certain extent they provide an emotive conceptualization of the continent otherwise feared as alien and dangerous. Immigration and settlement depend in part on these literary topics.

Not surprisingly, among the first words Christopher Columbus writes about the newly found territories are the praise of its paradisiacal and promising fertility. In his logbook, in his reports to the Catholic monarchs, and in other writings he expresses repeatedly enthusiastic admiration for what he sees: a very green, flat and very fertile land, he notes in his log entry four days after landing. Such is the excellence of the land that he has no doubt about the natives being able to plant and harvest corn and other crops all year around. ["Ella es isla muy verde y llana y fertilíssima, y no pongo en duda que todo el año siembran panizo y cogen, y así todas otras cosas."][18] He also observes and repeats several times a similar observations in his writings, how a native came to the ships in his canoe bringing the present of his basic staple of cassava bread, the size of a fist, and a gourd of water ["traía un poco de su pan, que sería como el puño y una calabaça de agua"].[19] Conversely, Columbus gives the order to present the native giver with some bread and honey to eat, and something to drink: "y le mandé dar de comer pan y miel y de beber," he writes in his navigation log on October 15, 1492.[20] Cabeza de Vaca, in turn, points to the good grass for raising cattle, seen in a land where he has been starving for month on end ["tiene muy buenos pastos para ganado"],[21] and tells also of the several occasions when the Indians gave the stranded Spaniards some of their meager rations. Bernal Diaz del Castillo, a soldier in Cortés' army, gives detailed information about the lands of Mexico and the fields of corn and other crops maintained by the different tribes; he also writes of the food the invaders were offered by the natives in their advance to Tenochtitlán.

When Hernán Cortés arrives in Mexico he takes careful note of all the riches to be found among the native peoples. Food in its variety and abundance, as seen in the fields and witnessed in the eating habits of Moctezuma's court and in the city markets, merit the admiration of the conqueror, who reports about them in his second letter to Charles V. He writes to the emperor about the abundance of the market products using the classical rhetorical device of enumeration with the anaphoric repetition of the phrase "they sell" at the beginning of several sets of products: "Venden conejos, liebres, venados, y perros pequeños, que crían para comer.... Venden mucho maíz en grano y en pan.... Venden pasteles de aves y empanadas de pescado. Venden huevos de gallinas y de ánsares ... venden tortillas de huevos hechas" [They sell rabbits, hares, venison, and small dogs they raise for eating.... They sell much corn in grain and as bread.... They sell pies of birds and fish turnovers. They sell chicken eggs and duck eggs ... they sell tortillas made of eggs.].[22] Cortés closes the long list of food products by observing that in those markets they sell everything that is produced in the land; so many are the products on display and of such variety that he cannot list them all for lack of space and memory: "Finalmente, que en los dichos mercados se venden todas cuantas cosas se hallan en toda la tierra, que demás de las que he dicho, son tantas y de tantas calidades, que ... no las expreso."[23] The same abundance and variety is served twice daily to Moctezuma by three hundred or four hundred lads who bring him innumerable delights in all kinds of meat and fish dishes as well as all the fruits and herbs that could be found in his dominion: "Venían trescientos o cuatrocientos mancebos con el manjar, que era sin cuento, porque todas las veces que comía o cenaba le traían de todas las maneras de manjares, así de carnes como de pescados y frutas y yerbas que en toda la tierra se podia haber."[24]

As for the topic of the partaking of food by the natives Cortés' letters contain several accounts of his acceptance of the many offers he received as he marched to meet Moctezuma, who, in turn, treated him to splendid meals. Diaz del Castillo remembers how the Aztecs had at their arrival in Tenochtitlán a very sumptuous dinner prepared for them, a well-deserved prize for their successful and daring entrance into the great city: "Y nos tenían aparejada una comida muy suntuosa, a su uso y costumbre, que luego comimos. Y fue esta nuestra venturosa y atrevida entrada en la gran ciudad de Tenustitlan Mexico...."[25]

Satiety in a Settled Land of Plenty

For the explorers, conquerors and settlers, then, writing about food and its abundance became a form of expressing their success and extolling the excellences of the New World. Hunger, on the other hand, represented failure and defeat and soon, after the adventure of discovery and conquest was superseded by colonization and the stability of order and prosperity, it ceased to be of interest as a subject related to America. By the end of the conquest, hunger is no longer a concern for colonial society. The animals, fowl and crops brought from Europe are successfully grown and cultivated, while the native products continue to be an abundant source of nutrition, pleasure and income. Large plantations and ranches provide all the food required by the people in the colonies and satisfy the growing demands of the European markets. America, then, acquired its most salient characteristic: that of a region devoted to the production of natural products for world consumption. The bountiful land and the abundant production of exotic and desirable foods becomes a very early characterization of the region as a world provider. Literature is not oblivious to this fact.

What mattered for the explorer was to find the land of opportunity and open it to exploitation. Once the colonial society established itself as an effective commercial system the focus of interest centered on the successful crops and the enjoyment of abundance. Very early in the process of settlement writers described in detail the natural products and their virtues. The different products new to the European are compared with known staples, suggesting in the colonizer a conflict between praising the new product and recognizing its inferiority with respect to the products they have consumed for generations. Fernández de Oviedo, in his vast history of the discovery and conquest, devotes numerous chapters to describe the crops and products found in the new continent, praising their value as food. The Inca Garcilaso de la Vega includes in his history of Peru several chapters describing and praising the foods the Inca empire had enjoyed for centuries before the arrival of the Spaniards and now available to Europeans. As with other writers of the period, his treatment of the subject leads to a comparison with the Old World products; as a *mestizo*, though, he brings to the comparison a proud sense of ownership, perhaps the first manifestation of an American appreciation of the distinctly American.[26] To prove the superior quality of the American land, the land of his Indian ancestors, he observes how the European agricultural products grown in Peru grew much larger than the ones cultivated in Europe: "En la Ciudad de los Reyes crecieron tanto las primeras escarolas y espinacas que sembraron, que apenas alcanzaba un hombre con la mano los pimpollos de ellas ... la monstruosidad en grandeza y abundancia de algunas legumbres y mieses a los principios sacaron fue increíble."[27] [In the City of the Kings the first endives and spinach that they planted grew so much that a man could barely reach with his hand their new growth ... the monstrous size and abundance of some legumes and grains were incredible at the beginning.]

With time, as *criollo* societies grew more aware of their different identity with respect to Spain, native foods became an even more marked sign of regional pride and differentiation from Europe. The sentimental value of their own food is gracefully shown in a letter written in 1788 to his mother by Manuel Lacunza, a Chilean Jesuit exiled in Italy after the expulsion of the company from the imperial territories. In his letter Lacunza tells her of a dream he had in which he found himself going back to his homeland. The first thing he does in the dream upon arrival in Valparaiso is to eat to his heart's content the sea products native to his land: kingfish, crabs, sea urchins and abalones ["llego a Valparaíso y habiéndome hartado de pejerreyes y jaivas, de erizos y de locos"],[28] and fully satisfied he rides to Santiago to his home. There, in the kitchen, surrounded by the doting servants, he eats all his preferred dishes, specially prepared for him by the cooks: "les como sus pollos, su charquicán y sus cajitas de dulce y también los bizcochuelos y ollitas de Clara y de Rosita" [I eat their chicken, their potato stew and their sweets, and also their cakes and Clara and Rosita's custards.].[29] Having satisfied his nostalgic appetite and with his stomach well filled for the next twenty years, he returns to his exile: "Y habiendo llenado bien mi barriga para otros veinte años, me vuelvo a mi destierro...."[30]

The regional pride in the native fruits is excellently seen also in the neoclassical compositions of two Cuban poets of the late eighteenth century. In "Las frutas de Cuba" [The Fruits from Cuba], Manuel Justo de Rubalcava praises the American fruits as better tasting than the ones from the Old World. The naming of the different fruits and the listing of them and their virtues in the poem are reminiscent of Cortés' admiring description of the Aztec market and of the catalogue of American products offered by Fernández de Oviedo or the Inca Garcilaso de la Vega. All of them are trying to convince the European consumers of the superior quality of the American products. Thus, Rubalcava uses the comparative from the very beginning of his composition: "Más suave que la pera/en Cuba es la gratísima guayaba" [softer than the pear is the Cuban guava].[31] The poet concludes his praise of Cuban fertility with a rhetorical hyperbole:

> No te canses, !oh numen!,
> en alumbrar especies pomonanas,
> pues no tienen resumen
> las del cuerpo floral de las indianas,
> pues a favor producen las Cibeles,
> pan, las raíces, y las cañas, mieles.

[Do not tire yourself, oh deity! in showing the fruit species because the ones in the American flora are innumerable since Cibeles favors their production, making the roots give bread and the reeds produce honey.][32]

Manuel de Zequeira y Arango devotes a whole poem to only one fruit, the most liked pineapple. A classical ode, "A la piña" ["To the Pineapple"], his poem tells the fictional story of the pineapple's arrival on Olympus and of Venus's fascination with its flavor: "La madre Venus cuando al labio rojo/su néctar aplicó, quedó embriagada/de lúbrico placer" [When mother Venus applied the pineapple's nectar to her red lips she was raptured by lascivious pleasure.].[33] Venus, then, orders her nymphs to grow the pineapple in her gardens and to let the balsam of the Cuban fruit overrun her dominions:

> La piña — dijo — la fragante piña,
> en mis pensiles sea cultivada
> por manos de mis ninfas; sí, que corra
> su bálsamo en Idalia.[34]

What better comparison than to make of the American fruit the one preferred by the classical goddess of love?

With the independence and the birth of the new Latin American republics food, as a product of agricultural labor, is seen as a valuable asset for the new economies. Andrés Bello writes an exemplary neoclassical ode to this effect, "Oda a la agricultura de la zona tórrida" ["Ode to the Agriculture of the Torrid Zone"], and a Colombian poet of the second half of the nineteenth century sings in a long bucolic poem, "Memoria sobre el cultivo del maíz en Antioquia" [Memorandum about the cultivation of corn in Antioquia], the national task of growing corn. Both authors view agriculture as a virtuous form of life and as a preferred economic activity for the future success of the new republics. Both write with pride and joy about the fertility of the land and the excellence of its food products.

The naming of the different regional agricultural products by Bello bespeaks a proud and loving view of his land, one that he extols as the paradisiacal New World first admired by Columbus. His ode begins with an enthusiastic and admiring apostrophe to the region:

> ¡Salve, fecunda zona,
> que al sol enamorado circunscribes
> el vago curso, y cuanto a ser se anima
> en cada vario clima,
> acariciada de su luz, concibes!

[Hail, fertile zone, you circumscribe the course of the loving sun, and, caressed by its light, you conceive every being that lives in each varied clime!][35]

Following a long list of fruits and their virtues, not unlike Cortes' catalogue of the offerings in the Mexican markets, or Rubalcalca's comparison of the Cuban fruits, Bello expresses his confidence in a great future for the region based on its fertility and on the work of the younger generations, the free citizens of democratic governments: "1Oh jóvenes naciones...! /Honrad el campo, honrad la simple vida/del labrador y su frugal llaneza" [Oh, young nations.... Honor the field, honor the simple life/of the farmer, and his frugal plainness.].[36] Similarly, Gregorio Gutiérrez González, after a lengthy treatise in verse about the growing of corn, devotes a last section of the poem to the harvest and the workers' celebration of the task done. The poet dwells on the detailed description of different regional foods, their preparation, and their festive consumption, praising the abundance of products and flavors: "¿Quién puede calcular las mil delicias/que proporciona tan sabrosa fiesta?" ["Who can imagine the thousand pleasures that such a delightful festivity provides?].[37]

Hunger and Satiety in Modern Times

Conversely, food production and consumption is related in symbolic ways to political issues of democracy and dictatorship, in the short story "El matadero" [The Slaughterhouse], by the Argentinean romantic writer Echevarría. Hunger reappears as the opposite of satiety and representing social deprivation, in this case the lack of political freedom. Later on in the nineteenth century, when realist, naturalist and *indigenist* novelists focused their attention on social issues, hunger becomes again a recurrent motive in representation of social injustice. The trend continues into the twentieth century with novels centered in political matters, as is the case of Azuela's *Los de abajo* [*The Underdogs*], a narrative of the Mexican revolution whose protagonist begins

as a simple Indian farmer eating corn tortillas with water, becomes a successful popular revolutionary leader who dines and drinks excessively, and concludes suffering hunger and ultimately death as a defeated warrior. Food and
beverages are in this case representative of social and political forces in
conflict.[38] In novels about the Indian life, such as *Los perros hambrientos* [*Hungry Dogs*], by the Peruvian Ciro Alegria, and in many narratives of social strife,
such as Garcia Marquez' *El coronel no tiene quien la escriba* [*No One Writes to
the Colonel*], hunger is shown as a despairing and demeaning injustice. Juan
Rulfo's short stories of *El llano en llamas* [*The Burning Plain*] are exemplary
in their stark, fatalistic treatment of a subject that dominates Latin American society and inspires a literature of deprivation.

Curiously enough, Neruda does not address directly the issue of hunger
in his poetry. When he does it is only to praise the value of simple food in
satisfying the need of the poor. The onion in his "Ode to the Onion" is a
round rose of water on the table of the poor people ["redonda rosa de
agua,/sobre/la mesa/de las pobres gentes"],[39] and as a product of easy reach
to the people of meager recourses, the onion, "moistened with oil, dusted with
a little salt" ["regada con aceite,/espolvoreada/con un poco de sal"], sates deli-
ciously the hunger of the working class.[40]

In his odes to food Neruda does not dwell on references to hunger as
suffering and weakness. On the contrary, as in his book on Hungarian gastronomy, he chooses over the images of hunger the extolling of food and the
joy of satiety. His preference for focusing on appetite and the lively pleasure
of eating has to be seen as an expression of his optimistic view of a world of
natural richness to be enjoyed by everyone. The world envisioned as the great
table, "covered in apples or blood./ The table ready for eating" ["cubierta de
manzanas o de sangre./la mesa preparada"], the table of communal satisfaction and fulfillment.[41]

In his odes to tomatoes and onions, lemons and seafood, artichokes and
tunafish Neruda highlights a subject that has characterized Latin American
as a continent of fecundity and fulfillment. By following the line of praising
food products that characterizes the writings of those who from the days of
the conquest saw in America the rich land of opportunity, he is inserting his
poetry a Latin American discourse of optimism and utopian views. In his
poetic treatment of food Pablo Neruda has brought together the basic elements that have characterized the Latin American fascination with hunger and
food, reaffirming thus the view of the continent as a Land of Jauja, feeder of
the world. The simple, everyday enjoyment of food is the best expression of
a successful life and a just society.

It was in search of success and a new life that the European came to the
Americas, "dreaming of the land of Cockaigne." For Christopher Columbus

and the early explorers the fertile lands they encountered were the promise of a profitable enterprise: consequently they praised to other Europeans the novelty of its fruits, the munificence of its soil. In their search they had to face hunger, as hunger was also the scourge of the conquerors, their followers, and of the native inhabitants who confronted them in war. Hunger was a central subject of their chronicles and narratives of their adventures. Colonial times brought relative peace in submission and prosperity. The promising land gave prodigally its crops and fruits, feeding a world transformed by its fertility. The independent republics, proud of their uniqueness as producers of valuable foods, delighted in the singing of their products; but they had to confront again the injustices of poverty and hunger. Since then the dual motive of hunger and satiety has been present in Latin American letters. Pablo Neruda's writings of the second half of the twentieth century are one of the best examples of how the literary treatment of food has a lasting and significant value in the history of Latin American's cultural self-identification.

Notes

1. In several books of odes to simple things, Neruda includes compositions devoted to food and eating. See Jaime Concha, ed., *Libro de odas, Odas elementales,* 10th ed. (Madrid: Cátedra, 2003), and *Obras completas* (Buenos Aires: Editorial Losada, 1968).

2. Op. cit., II, 933.

3. Ibid.

4. Op. cit., II, 84–86, vv. 40–42.

5. Ibid.

6. Ibid., vv. 48–49.

7. Op. cit., II, 244–246, vv. 1–3.

8. Ibid., vv. 57–58.

9. Fernand Braudel, *The Mediterranean and the Mediterranean World in the Age of Philip II* (New York: Harper & Row, 1972), 734–56; Jack Weatherford, *Indian Givers* (New York: Fawcett Columbine, 1988), 70.

10. Alfred W. Crosby, *Columbian Exchange: Biological and Cultural Consequences of 1492* (Westport, CT: Greenwood, 1972); Weatherford (1988), and *Seeds of Change: A Quincentennial Commemoration,* ed. Herman J. Viola and Carolyn Margolis (Washington, D. C. and London: Smithsonian Institution Press, 1991).

11. For a literary treatment of the Cockaigne see Herman Pleij, *Dreaming of Cockaigne: Medieval Fantasies of the Perfect Life* (New York: Columbia University Press, 2001).

12. Fintan B. Warren, *Vasco de Quiroga and His Pueblo Hospitals of Santa Fe* (Washington, D.C.: Academy of American Franciscan History, 1963).

13. Philip Caraman, *The Lost Paradise: The Jesuit Republic of South America* (New York: Seabury Press, 1976).

14. Alvar Nuñez Cabeza de Vaca. *Naufragios.* Texto restaurado, prologado y anotado por Justo García Morales, ed. Madrid: M. Aguilar (1945), 42. There are many Spanish editions and English translations of this work.

15. Hernán Cortés, *Cartas de relación* (México: Porrúa, 1992), 81–85; Bernal Díaz del Castillo, *Historia verdadera de la conquista de la Nueva España* (México: Porrúa, 1964), 235–42.

16. Pedro Mariño de Lobera, *Crónica del reino de Chile* (Santiago de Chile: Editorial Universitaria, 1970), 42–44.

17. *Poesía indígena de la altiplanicie,* "Canto de Huexotzinco acerca de la conquista," selección, versión, introducción y notas de Angel Ma Garibay K. (México: UNAM, 1962), 40, vv. 29–31.

18. Cristóbal Colón [Christopher Columbus], "Diario del primer viaje," in *Textos y documentos completos. Relaciones de viajes, cartas y memoriales,* prólogo y notas de Consuelo Varela (Madrid: Alianza Editorial, 1982), 36.

19. Ibid., 35.

20. Ibid.

21. *Naufragios* VII, 66.

22. Cortés, 63.

23. Ibid.

24. Ibid., 68.

25. Díaz del Castillo, 150.

26. Daydí-Tolson, "Nostalgia de la comida ...," passim.

27. Garcilaso de la Vega, *Comentarios reales de los incas* (Madrid: Cátedra, 1996), ix, xxix.

28. Juan Luis Espejo, "Cartas del padre Manuel Lacunza," *Revista chilena de historia y geografía* 13 (1914), 213.

29. Ibid.

30. Ibid.

31. Julio Caillet-Bois, *Antología de la poesía hispanoamericana* (Madrid: Aguilar, 1958), 135, vv. 1–2.

32. Ibid., 136, vv. 91–96.

33. Ibid., 119, vv. 41–43.

34. Ibid., 119, vv. 45–48.

35. Bello 201; vv. 1–5.

36. Bello 203; vv. 109, 112–13.

37. Caillet-Bois, 437, vv. 573–74.

38. Daydí-Tolson, "Drinking ...," passim.

39. Neruda, *Odas.* ..., 93, vv. 26–29.

40. Ibid., vv. 44–50.

41. Neruda, "Oda a la mesa," *Obras completas,* II, 244–46, vv. 40–44.

Works Cited

Alegría, Ciro. *Los perros hambrientos.* Santiago de Chile: Zig-Zag, 1939.

Azuela, Mariano. *Los de abajo* (1915). There are many editions of this novel in Spanish and several translations in English including *The Underdogs,* translated by E. Munguía, Jr. New York: Penguin. Signet Classic, 1963.

Braudel, Fernand. *The Mediterranean and the Mediterranean World in the Age of Philip II.* New York: Harper & Row, 1972.

Caillet-Bois, Julio. *Antología de la poesía hispanoamericana.* Madrid: Aguilar, 1958.

Caraman, Philip. *The Lost Paradise: The Jesuit Republic of South America.* New York: Seabury Press, 1976.

Colón, Cristóbal. *Textos y documentos completos: Relaciones de viajes, cartas y memoriales.* Prólogo y notas de Consuelo Varela. Madrid: Alianza Editorial, 1982.

Cortés, Hernán. *Cartas de relación.* México: Porrúa, 1992.

Crosby, Alfred W. *Columbian Exchange: Biological and Cultural Consequences of 1492.* Westport, CT: Greenwood, 1972.

Daydi-Tolson, Santiago. "Drinking: A Narrative Structural Pattern in Mariano Azuela's *Los de abajo,*" *Kentucky Romance Quarterly* 27, 1 (1980): 57–67.

_____. "Nostalgia de la comida en el Inca Gracilazo." In *Jornadas Andinas de Literatura Latinoamericana: Memorias I.* Quito, Ecuador: Publicaciones de la Universidad Andina Simón Bolívar, 2000.

Díaz del Castillo, Bernal. *Historia verdadera de la conquista de la Nueva España*. México: Porrúa, 1964.

Echeverría, Esteban. *Obras completas*. Buenos Aires: Ediciones Antonio Zamora, 1972.

Espejo, Juan Luis. "Cartas del padre Manuel Lacunza." *Revista chilena de historia y geografía* 13 (1914): 200–19.

Fernández de Oviedo, Gonzalo. *Historia general y natural de las Indias*. Edición y estudio preliminar de Juan Pérez de Tudela Bueso. Madrid: Ediciones Atlas, 1959.

_____. *Libro último de los infortunios y naufragios*. Sevilla, Spain: En la impr[n]ta de Iuan Cromberger, 1535. Facsimile edition: http://www.wheatoncollege.edu/Academic/acade micdept/HispanicItalianStudies/ovilibr/.

García Márquez, Gabriel. *El coronel no tiene quien le escriba*. Buenos Aires: Editorial Sudamericana, 1970. Trans. J. S. Berstein in *No One Writes to the Colonel and Other Stories*. New York: Perennial Classics, 2005.

Gracilazo de la Vega, Inca. *Comentarios reales de los incas*. Madrid: Cátedra, 1996.

Mariño de Lobera, Pedro. *Crónica del reino de Chile*. Santiago de Chile: Editorial Universitaria, 1970.

Neruda, Pablo. *Obras completas*. Buenos Aires: Editorial Losada, 1968.

_____. *Odas elementales*, ed. Jaime Concha, 10th ed. Madrid: Cátedra, 2003.

Neruda, Pablo, y Miguel Ángel Asturias. *Comiendo en Hungría*. Barcelona: Ed. Lumen, 1972.

Nuñez Cabeza de Vaca, Alvar. *Naufragios*. Texto restaurado, prologado y anotado por Justo García Morales. Madrid: M. Aguilar, Editor, 1945.

Pleij, Herman. *Dreaming of Cockaigne: Medieval Fantasies of the Perfect Life*. New York: Columbia University Press, 2001.

Poesía indígena de la altiplanicie. Selección, versión, introducción y notas de Angel Ma. Garibay K. México: UNAM, 1962.

Rulfo, Juan. *El llano en llamas* (1953). There are several editions of this novel in Spanish. It has been translated into English by George D. Schade as *The Burning Plane and Other Stories*. Austin: University of Texas Press, 1996.

Viola, Herman J., and Carolyn Margolis, eds. *Seeds of Change: A Quincentennial Commemoration*. Washington, D. C. and London: Smithsonian Institution Press, 1991.

Warren, Fintan B., O.F.M. *Vasco de Quiroga and His Pueblo Hospitals of Santa Fe*. Washington, D. C.: Academy of American Franciscan History, 1963.

Weatherford, Jack. *Indian Givers*. New York: Fawcett Columbine, 1988.

10

Reengineering "Authenticity"

Tourism Encounters with Cuisine in Rural Great Britain

CRAIG WIGHT

Food and eating are firmly established components within the burgeoning mix of new ethical, culturally concerned tourism experiences in the West. Perhaps as much as 25 percent of total UK tourist expenditure is accounted for by food purchases.[1] Cuisine is significantly central to the tourism experience, so much so as to consider food and drink as stand-alone motivations for visitation. There is evidence that demonstrates regional and national culinary tourism products to be widely and successfully promoted in macro destination marketing strategies.[2] However, the UK, in relation to the rest of Europe, is perhaps an anomaly and a culinary silo where food and the sociology of eating are concerned. Most typically in the UK and America, recipe books feature keenly in best-seller lists and celebrity chefs dominate the "A lists"; yet it is most typically in the UK and America that people spend more time watching others prepare fantasy food on television than they spend on experiencing cooking in their own kitchen.[3] In addition, healthy eating advice, safety and the provenance of food dominate popular culture, yet more junk food is consumed in the UK than in the rest of Europe in its entirety.[4] National food is hijacked as regional and what was once local is now national, reflecting some dysfunction in UK culinary identity.

This chapter argues that the language of tourism destination marketing legitimates the myth of the culinary tourism experience providing the increasingly thrill-seeking bourgeoisie tourist with a new type of moral, alternative tourism. It is argued that culinary tourism is part of a wider tourism and leisure trend towards experience and away from materialism (the latter meaning traditionally the pool or the hotel). In an increasingly globally competitive tourism environment, destinations exploit authentic regional culinary strengths to reengineer perceptions of British food. The UK is said to have reached a stage in which society has an awkward relationship with food.[5] If this is so then it is a strand of discourse that is absent from tourism marketing literature yet visible in public culture.

Cuisine Tourism as Alternative, Moral Tourism

There is an axiomatic relationship between food and tourism that is confirmed in almost every personal recall of a vacation experience. Returning travelers systematically tell of new foods eaten and of new food habits learned, and occasionally of a vacation entirely motivated by experiencing food (in the case of, for example, cooking schools or wine tours[6]). Food, in this respect, can be a superficial, if necessary component of travel and tourism. "Culinary tourism," however, is now an established terminology and concept that is increasingly used to describe travel and tourism activity of which food is a much more primary motivation, whether as a prominent component of a wider itinerary or as the sole purpose for visitation. Essential to the success of culinary tourism is finding ways in which to add value to the regular eating experience in order to make it memorable.[7] Food is becoming increasingly distinct and diverse as an aspect of the total tourism experience. Even the operational aspects of food (service and preparation and so forth) are becoming part of the culinary tourism experience. For example, kitchens can be viewed by visitors and waiting staff often sing or provide entertainment.[8]

Culinary tourism has been conceptualized as the exploration of cultures through food and "food ways."[9] It can take place without travel having actually occurred at all, for example when sampling exotic new foods in the home or in local theme restaurants. Culinary tourism activity has been regarded as "traveling *through* food" and eating the food of an other out of curiosity or to encounter a new culture using food as an interpretive vehicle.[10]

The trend towards experience over materialism in tourism means an increasingly central role for food in the pursuit of "experience" as a chief aspect of tourism activity. Culinary tourism has been defined as the exploration of new, exotic, or authentic foods from particular cultures or regions. It can also refer to the exploration of familiar foods in foreign environments that are comforting, consistent and safe to the traveler.[11] All tourism, according to John Urry's theory of the "post tourist,"[12] is about a negotiation of the exotic and the familiar, so tourism encounters must be (to some degree) exotic enough in order to render them interesting or culturally enlightening to tourists.

The emergence of alternative tourism (the pursuit of unusual destinations, experiences and activities) has been noted by a growing number of theorists.[13, 14, 15] The term is increasingly summoned to describe a kind of travel catharsis amongst a Western bourgeoisie who wish to feel more worldly and better about themselves. Alternative tourists will commonly contrast the morality of their travel activity with that of the elusive mass tourist who does not (and cannot) "experience" travel in the way the alternative tourist can.[16] Increasingly, Western tourists turn to memories of experience and authentic tourism encounters as a means to draw distinctions between their Self and its Other (the "mass tourist"). The pursuit of unusual and new culinary experiences is one such element of alternative tourism and is increasingly a vehicle through which to encounter, and interpret, new cultures.

Usually alternative tourism is understood to involve some kind of search for authenticity and there is a growing contentious debate in tourism academia over the extent to which authenticity matters. The authenticity argument is posited quite differently across many schools of thought. It has, for example, been understood in the context of tourism to be an essential competitive marketing skill that is quite necessary to grow the appeal of national and regional tourism products and experiences.[17] In this regard, authenticity is simply a static and representational concept, a way of communicating a romanticized image to niches in order to maximize visitation. It has also been argued that authenticity is a concept originating in the condition of modernity.[18] In this context it is inauthenticity that has come to take on a pejorative meaning and the inauthentic is perceived commonly as a replication (or even an absence) of truth in tourism encounters. As C. Michael Hall muses:

> replication is not intrinsically bad; what is important is the different experiential depth between the original and the replication. Inauthenticity emerges out of the very attempt to retain or regain authenticity. It is more problematic when there is a deliberate attempt to deceive.[19]

If traditions and cultures require to be staged and contrived, then anything truly authentic (in the context of the tourist search for the authentic) is surely lost. Lucy Long suggests that food can be used as a means to sell local histories and to construct marketable and publicly attractive (and thus authentic) identities.[20] Food, and the increasing interest in cuisine as a tourism experience, therefore merits attention as a strand of authenticity discourse. In terms of the search for authentic food, it helps to focus on the language of tourism marketing, particularly of culinary tourism marketing and media representations of national and regional culinary identities. The following paragraphs therefore compare some of the societal discourses inherent in various media in the United Kingdom with the myths of culinary tourism to be found in tourism marketing texts. The term *myth* here is used in a context previously defined by Donald Horne, specifically meaning a belief held in common by a large group of people that gives events and actions a particular meaning.[21]

Myths as defined in this context can be informed by many kinds of media, for example the news and television shows such as soap operas or cooking programs. The term is not essentially concerned with truth.

Towards a Paradigm of Regional Culinary Tourism

Food has become one of the key elements of the tourism product or experience with perhaps as much as 25 percent of total tourist expenditure accounted for by food purchases.[22] Previous empirical research reminds us of the high level of importance tourists attach to food on vacation.[23] Food can be so significantly central to the visitor experience as to be considered as a stand-alone tourism motivation.

The globalization of food production is considered to challenge traditional foods of Western nations and regions. It has been suggested that food can be a historic time machine and a refuge from globalized food.[24] Most destinations now use culinary products to promote tourism and most use tourism to promote gastronomy. Food has become a means for the visitor to arrive at an understanding of national identity so that when the gastronomy of a region is promoted, so too is its culture.

Previous work examines the process of developing regional identity using cuisine as an indicator of success in terms of attracting tourists.[25] The author calls into question the importance of the apparent Western fascination with the nexus between cuisine and traditional or local produce. Tourism has been described as an aesthetic experience based on consumption habits.[26] Food in this context is seen as symbolic of authenticity and regional uniqueness. This symbolism presents in various ways.

• Some foodstuffs form the basis of fantasy through symbolic virtues (for example, bread, wine, cereals, the dark blood in game for hunters).

• Food is a sign of communion (food shared and eaten with others is a fundamental social link in, for example, business lunches, family meals and celebrations).

• Food is a class marker (champagne, caviar, whiskey, wine for everyday consumption.

• Food is an emblem or an icon (of, for example, a given geographical area).[27]

Sweden pioneered attempts to establish regional culinary heritage in Southeast Skåne in 1995.[28] A network consisting of some 20 businesses subsequently grew to around 38 restaurants, farm shops and small-scale food producers. The area was marketed as a culinary tourism destination reflecting a growing cultural interest in "rurality" and locality, engaging visitors in new culinary customs and practices. Culinary tourism probably grew out of a growing interest in the myth of the authentic rural space. As Bessiere ponders:

> tourism in rural areas seems to be influential and idealized today by the myth of nature, the quest for an original "communitas" ... it is often related to the mental perception of the countryside ... (holding) a remarkable appeal in the collective consciousness, After all isn't tourism a quest for identity, a place and other people?[29]

To capitalize upon the imagery of rural tourism marketing in a study of agritourism in Poland,[30] it has been suggested that Polish agritourism is marketed as a way to experience traditional Polish life ("folk traditions are cultivated in every day life") and the natural Polish environment ("peace and quiet and a primeval natural environment await guests at the picturesque Marciniak family farm"). Emphasis, according to the authors, is placed on tasty organic regional home cooking ("meals prepared by Gertruda include Silesian dumplings and apple pie").[31] The authentic rural culinary tourism experience is perpetuated in this way through the language of tourism marketing.

The Language of Tourism Marketing

The rhetoric of tourism marketing is full of the manifestations of the centrality of authenticity.[32] Advertising discourses in tourism typically comprise positive, glowing terminologies and metaphors for the services, attractions and experiences that are being promoted. Yet tourism marketing reneges on a great deal of cultural representation. Entire peoples, places and histories can be misrepresented and can ostensibly be missing altogether from tourism marketing materials. An example is borrowed again from research into Polish agritourism.

> Probably to enhance the image of agritourism holidays, the brochures are almost completely devoid of images of cars, promising walking, cycling and horse riding as the three main modes of transport.[33]

To encounter anything other than these modes of transport during a Polish agritourism vacation may be troublesome or problematic if encountered by the agritourist. Pejorative realities within destinations (unemployment, violence and crime rates and suchlike) are neither displayed on the glossy pages of tourism brochures nor are they visible among the interactive visual wizardry of Internet Web pages. Yet they are realities nonetheless (they simply remain uninterpreted to tourists). Accessing culture and cultural authenticity through tourism can be problematic when realities are less visible (or invisible) in the public cultures of nation states.[34] The tourism reality is often realized by confirming (during a vacation) images that have been constructed through romantic hyperbole that is typical of the language of tourism marketing.

Through static and moving pictures, written texts, audiovisual offerings and other signifiers, the language of tourism, and of tourism marketing, attempts to persuade and seduce, and to construct realities about destinations that can be easily confirmed during the vacation. The argument is illustrated in a study of the conjuring of images associated with Venice in Italy:

> Tourism didn't of course invent the "myth of Venice" but it continues to stage it, because at the heart of the myth is desire and anticipation.[35]

The myth referred to is the image of Gerona, one that is constructed to promise rich visuality, dreams, mystery and magic communicated through tourism marketing literature. Place, in the sense of the destination, is not a material entity that exists autonomously, but is a habit whereby the material place is defined by a series of discourses that have become inseparable from the destination. It is possible to observe manifestations of the postmodern polyglot in cases of the tourism industry (at macro and micro destination levels). Attitudes, interpretation, micro- and macro-management (of attractions and destinations) and performative broadcasting combine to form a postmodern language of and about tourism. Images, symbols, escapism, commentary and narrative can all influence and perpetuate interpretation. Tourism can therefore be considered as prefiguratively postmodern since it is a combination of the visual, the aesthetic, the commercial, and the popular.[36]

The search for authentic, new and exotic foods in tourism is perpetuated in this way through culinary tourism marketing. Indeed, there now exists an International Culinary Tourism Association that provides tips to business owners and Destination Marketing Organizations. For example, visitors to the Website are encouraged to "learn how Culinary Tourism can give your business a unique selling proposition vis-à-vis your competition,"[37] and assured that "*culinary tourism is an interesting, brand new and unique industry. Food is an attraction, just like a museum.*"[38]

Another foodie website promises that

> Here the main course is meaningful conversation in tastes that convey a sense of history from the lands where we originate. The spirit of America is a circle of cultural journeys, sensual exotics from different provinces and languages, yet with like smiles and all under the same sky.[39]

Culinary tourism carries with it an emerging marketing discourse that can be likened to marketing discourses of ecotourism. Ecotourism has been regarded as a mark of moral consumer distinction (and corporate differentiation in terms of the supply of culinary experiences). The concept of ecotourism has been criticized as a "mass exercise in self-deception"[40] that sees organizations simply cashing in on affluent travelers to maximize profits, while ecotourists amass green travel experiences (although many fly to green destinations) as badges of moral distinction and worldliness. Similarly it is not clear if the pronounced trend towards the marketing and consumption of culinary tourism is reflective of a genuine pride in national ingredients and dishes or a spurious marketing strategy intended to strengthen brand by promoting food tourism as moral tourism (perhaps it is a compromise).

This chapter has so far focused on the language of tourism marketing and the culinary tourism paradigm. The following sections discuss food and national identity in the United Kingdom from the point of view of non-tourism discourse in order to comment on the extent to which myths of UK culinary tourism can be confirmed in UK public culture writ large.

Food and UK National Identity

Individual food choices, certainly in the West, are determined by a variety of factors from practical reasons (price and convenience), temporary reasons (mood) and personal ideals such as weight control and the ethics of food choice. Yet mass communications media and strands of popular discourse probably impact consumer culture even more. According to investigative food journalist and author Joanna Blythman, the British live in a fantasy food world, a world of nationalized food tradition that actually hides the diversity in UK food habits.[41] Blythman sees the nationalized UK as a nation of households concealing bookshelves stocked with cookbooks, and television schedules filled with celebrity chef and food programs such as *Ready Steady Cook* and *You Are What You Eat.* There is also what Blythman calls an "obsession with food" spanning issues of provenance, healthiness and food safety.[42] A foodie image is constructed in media (particularly in broadsheet supplements and in some television shows such as *The View from River Cottage*) of a class of gastronomes who (as Blythman rather amusingly summarizes)

> live in lofts and stylish townhouses, or in covetable country houses and holly hocked cottages ... these people are ultra literate in food ... it matters to them that their crème brûlée is correctly caramelized so they give each other blow torches as Christmas presents.[43]

This myth of the bourgeoisie gastronome is perpetuated through many popular UK media, yet such a cadre according to Blythman hardly exists at all in UK public culture. They are instead a construction of how the British like to see themselves. Our diligently prepared diet of "what to eat, where to buy it 'foodie'" lifestyle is engineered and highly accomplished but the edifice is all the more audacious because of the scale of the lie it sells.[44]

There are other individuals according to Blythman who are underrepresented and often absent altogether from UK public culture and tourism marketing texts. These are individuals who are reluctant or unable to cook, who buy ready meals, have no dining table in the home and eat on the go, viewing food as fuel and mealtimes as television time. For such individuals, food is a very different concept about supermarket aisles and branded high street fast-food outlets (not farmyards and herb gardens) and eating is not necessarily synonymous with pleasure. These individuals are not wrong, yet they remain nonetheless unselected to represent UK foodways in tourism marketing texts. The public, and tourists strong among it, continue however to anticipate picturesque "old farming"[45] in artisan, ethereal rural areas.

In the UK, definitions of regional national foods are becoming indistinguishable. Regional iconic foods are becoming nationalized. For example, well-known regional foods such as Cumberland Sausage, York ham and Melton Mowbray pork pie have become representative of national iconic foods.[46] The idea of an unbroken national or regional culinary tradition or collective pattern of consumption is further compromised by other factors such as globalized consumer industries, nationalized regional foods and changing cultural values.[47]

There is however a growing movement in the UK (which includes tourism marketers) that seeks to reauthenticate regional food and position the culture of lost or "forgotten" regional food and foodways more visibly in UK public culture. This movement seeks to combat the loss of culinary authenticity that globalization is perceived to have caused. Regional foods become cultural commodities set against the forces of political and economic change and regional origin is harnessed as a marketing tool for specific forgotten foods. For example, veal and mutton, and beetroot (last year) have all, at the time of writing, undergone a renaissance in popularity with most being reinstated to the in-vogue cookbooks and menus in trendy restaurants.

This forgotten authenticity can appeal to tourists who increasingly seek traditionalism and age to a food experience. As Priscilla Boniface muses in the context here of authentic food events:

> Is it maybe part of the appeal of food and drink occasions their link with a profundity and elementality not much visible in modern life and industrialized, standardized and global processes?[48]

In terms of tourism marketing, the change agents of culinary cultural landscapes (such as tourism marketers) may be struggling to reassert authenticity in culinary (particularly rural) touristic experiences in response to the cloning of towns. Clone towns describe the outcome of the homogenization of towns and individual cultures. The individuality of high streets has been replaced by a monochrome strip of global and national chains. Or as Joanna Blythman puts it:

> Welcome to Asdatown or Tescotown, or Sainsburytown. Make it into the centre of one of these places and you are in Anytown, Anywhere. Or even Clonetown.[49]

By contrast to the clone town, the hometown (the antithesis) has a high street that retains its individual character and is instantly recognizable to those who live there as well as to visitors. Therefore, the more that authenticity can be reengineered in clone towns, the greater the chances are of appealing to the culinary tourist. However, surely tourists should experience cuisine in the UK in all of its cultural forms, rather than through the lens of the authentic hometown. The concept of authenticity surely embraces diversity through communities and it can be just as authentic to visit a supermarket in Asdatown as it is to experience cheesemaking in for example, rural South Lanarkshire (in central Scotland in this example). The postmodern tourist, or post-tourist as defined by John Urry is surely prepared for any touristic encounter, and each is as valuable and as authentic as the last.[50] Indeed it could become difficult to separate "culinary tourism" experiences from national culinary culture as the two become increasingly blurred and indistinct because "those being gazed upon come to construct artificial sites which keep the inquisitive tourist away."[51]

Conclusion

If culinary tourism is the pursuit of authentic cuisine and tourism marketing legitimates the culinary myth, then the culinary tourism experience is merely an experiential cycle for tourists to interpret and confirm marketing texts that perpetuate and confirm the culinary tourism experience. Culinary tourism may be an oversimplification of a more complex and diverse complement of sociocultural groups with varying diets and foodways. Heritage must be legitimized to be genuine[52] and this means providing tourists with a guarantee of historical content, origins and roots which are essential components within a successful heritage market. The extent to which cuisine is perceived as authentic is therefore critical to the culinary tourism experience.

The UK foodie lifestyle is legitimized and continually perpetuated through media discourses and tourism marketing. The less visible strands of culinary discourse in public culture are likely to remain elusive to culinary tourists. Authentic rural cuisine is presented in popular media and by tourism marketers as an alternative to the pejorative globalized food culture. The UK region in culinary terms is imagined through stereotypes of tradition, history and freshness of produce inter alia. It is these pastoral images that are anticipated and confirmed by the culinary tourist. As Tim Edensor puts it:

> The rural is envisaged as the source of varied and distinct products such as cheese and wine and (it) is conceived as producing infinite geographic and gastronomic variety.[53]

The rural imagery of regions in tourism marketing is central to the anticipation of culinary tourism and rurality is sanctified, symbolizing a precious alternative to the homogenous UK clone town that tourism marketers would seek to avoid illuminating through marketing literature. Tourism marketing can legitimate the myth of the rural culinary tourism experience, intimating a form of moral, alterative tourism as part of a Western leisure trend towards experience away from materialism.

Regional identities and discourses of the UK region are ideologically loaded concepts[54] and are constructed through the power of media and power-holding actors. The perpetual reengineering of variously themed culinary regions reflects to a large degree the increasing demand for variety and difference among a growing number of tourists seeking authenticity via tourism encounters. Culture will continue to be heavily mobilized in UK regional destinations and the constructed nostalgia of cuisine interpreted through culinary encounters will mean both culture and region will continue to be engineered, reengineered and challenged.

Notes

1. Lloyd Hudman, "The Travellers' Perception of the Role of Food and Eating in the Tourism Industry," in *The Impact of Catering and Cuisine on Tourism, Proceedings of 36th AIEST Congress,* Montreux, Switzerland, August 31–September 6, 1986, 13–16.

2. Kevin Fields, "Demand for the Gastronomy Tourism Product: Motivational factors," in *Tourism and Gastronomy,* eds. A. Hjalager and G. Richards (London and New York: Routledge, 2002), 36.

3. Joanna Blythman, *Bad Food Britain: How a Nation Ruined Its Appetite* (London: Fourth Estate, 2006), 4.

4. Ibid.

5. Ibid., 5.

6. See http://216.239.59.104/search?q=cache:8KH5tjG5KIgJ:130.91.80.97:591/PDFs/48–1/Chrzan.pdf+why+study+culinary+tourism&hl=en&ct=clnk&cd=1&gl=uk.

7. Greg Richards, "Gastronomy: An Essential Ingredient in Tourism Production and

Consumption," in *Tourism and Gastronomy,* eds. A. Hjalager and G. Richards (London and New York: Routledge, 2002), 11.

8. Ibid.

9. Lucy Long, "Interpreting Food and Culture Through Culinary Tourism," in *Facing Changes and Challenges in Interpretation to Adapt and Grow, Proceedings of Interpreting World Heritage Conference* held in Vancouver, BC, Canada, March 25–29, 2007, 25.

10. Ibid.

11. Long, *Culinary Tourism* (Lexington: University Press of Kentucky, 2003).

12. John Urry, *Consuming Places* (London: Routledge, 1995), 14.

13. Long, *Culinary Tourism.*

14. Anne-Mette Hjalager and Greg Richards, *Tourism and Gastronomy* (London and New York: Routledge, 2002), 224.

15. Fields.

16. Noel Salazar, "Developmental Tourists vs. Developmental Tourism: A Case Study," in *Tourism Behaviour,* ed. Aparna Raj (New Delhi, India: Kanishka Publishers, 2004), 85.

17. Ian Yeoman, Danna Brass, and Una McMahon-Beattie, "Current Issues in Tourism: The Authentic Tourist," *Tourism Management* 28 (2007): 1.

18. C. Michael Hall, *Tourism Management* 28 (2007): 2.

19. Ibid., 1139.

20. Long, *Culinary Tourism.*

21. Donald Horne, *The Public Culture: An Argument with the Future* (London and Boulder, CO: Pluto Press, 1986), 40.

22. Hudman.

23. Andrew Jones and Ian Jenkins, "A Taste of Wales — Blas Ar Gymru: Institutional Malaise in Promoting Welsh Food Tourism Products," in *Tourism and Gastronomy,* ed. A. Hjalager and G. Richards (London and New York: Routledge, 2002), 15.

24. Hjalager and Richards.

25. Jacinthe Bessiere, "Local Development and Heritage: Traditional Food and Cuisine as Tourist Attractions in Rural Areas," *Sociologia Ruralis* 28 (1998): 33.

26. Josef Ploner, "Tourism and the Anesthetization of Backwardness: New Symbolic Orders of Regional Identity in Alpine Austria," in *Proceedings of the Regional Studies Association International Conference on Regional Growth Agendas,* held in the University of Aalborg, Denmark, May 28–31, 2005, 3.

27. Bessiere, 23.

28. Thord Ohlsson, "Regional Culinary Heritage: A European Network for Regional Foods," paper presented at the Local Food and Tourism International Conference, Cyprus, November 9–11, 2000.

29. Bessiere, 22.

30. Adam Jaworski and Sarah Lawson, "Discourses of Polish Agritourism: Global, Local and Pragmatic," in *Discourse, Communication and Tourism,* eds. Adam Jaworski and Annette Pritchard (Clevedon, Buffalo, and Toronto: Channel View Publications, 2005), 128.

31. Ibid.

32. Dean MacCannell, "Staged Authenticity: Arrangements of Social Space in Tourist Settings," *American Journal of Sociology* 79 (1973): 28.

33. Jaworski and Lawson, 128.

34. Horne.

35. See *www.hsc.edu.au/geography/activity/local/tourism/venicep.pdf.*

36. Salazar.

37. See *http://www.culinarytourism.org/.*

38. See *http://www.culinarytourism.org/.*

39. See http://www.main.org/foodways/.

40. See http://www.twnside.org.sg/title/eco15.htm.

41. Blythman.

42. Ibid., 6.

43. Ibid., 2.

44. Ibid., 3.
45. Priscilla Boniface, *Tasting Tourism: Travelling for Food and Drink* (Aldershot, UK and Burlington, VT: Ashgate, 2003), 32.
46. Ibid., 31.
47. Anon., "German Media Nation" (personal communication in possession of the author, 2007).
48. Boniface, 123.
49. Blythman, *Shopped: The Shocking Power of British Supermarkets* (London: Fourth Estate, 2004), 9.
50. Urry, 140.
51. Ibid.
52. Bessiere.
53. Tim Edensor, *National Identity, Popular Culture and Every Day Life* (Oxford and New York: Berg, 2002), 40.
54. Ploner.

Works Cited

Anon. "German Media Nation" (personal communication in possession of the author), 2007.

Bessiere, Jacinthe. "Local Development and Heritage: Traditional Food and Cuisine as Tourist Attractions in Rural Areas." *Sociologia Ruralis* 28 (1998): 21–34.

Blythman, Joanna. *Bad Food Britain: How a Nation Ruined Its Appetite.* London: Fourth Estate, 2006.

_____. *Shopped: The Shocking Power of British Supermarkets.* London: Fourth Estate, 2004.

Boniface, Priscilla. *Tasting Tourism: Travelling for Food and Drink.* Hampshire: Ashgate, 2003.

Chrzan, Janet. "Why Study Culinary Tourism?," Expedition, http://130.91.80.97:591/PDFs/48–1/Chrzan.pdf.

Edensor, Tim. *National Identity, Popular Culture and Every Day Life.* Oxford and New York: Berg, 2002.

Fields, Kevin. "Demand for the Gastronomy Tourism Product: Motivational Factors.," In *Tourism and Gastronomy,* eds. Anne-mette Hjalager and Greg Richards, 36–50. London and New York: Routledge 2002.

Hall, Michael. "The Fakery of the Authentic Tourist." *Tourism Management* 28 (2007):1139–1140.

Hjalager, Anne-Mette, and Greg Richards. *Tourism and Gastronomy.* London and New York: Routledge 2002.

Horne, Donald. *The Public Culture: An Argument with the Future.* London and Boulder, CO: Pluto Press, 1986.

Hudman, Lloyd E. "The Travellers' Perception of the Role of Food and Eating in the Tourism Industry." Paper Presented at The Impact of Catering and Cuisine on Tourism, *Proceedings of 36th AIEST Congress,* Montreux, Switzerland, August 31–September 6, 1986.

Jaworski, Adam, and Sarah Lawson. "Discourses of Polish Agritourism: Global, Local and Pragmatic." In *Discourse, Communication and Tourism,* eds.by Adam Jaworski and Annette Pritchard, 123–149. Clevedon, Buffalo, and Toronto: Channel View Publications, 2005.

Jones, Andrew, and Ian Jenkins. "A Taste of Wales — Blas Ar Gymru: Institutional Malaise in Promoting Welsh Food Tourism Products." In *Tourism and Gastronomy.* eds. Anne-Mette Hjalager and Greg Richards, 115–131. London and New York: Routledge, 2002.

Long, Lucy M. *Culinary Tourism.* Lexington: University Press of Kentucky, 2003.

_____. "Interpreting Food and Culture Through Culinary Tourism." Paper presented at the Second Interpreting World Heritage Conference, Vancouver, BC, Canada, March 25–29, 2007.

MacCannell, Dean. "Staged Authenticity: Arrangements of Social Space in Tourist Settings." *American Journal of Sociology* 79 (1973): 589–603.

Ohlsson, Thord. "Regional Culinary Heritage: A European Network for Regional Foods." Paper presented at the Local Food and Tourism International Conference, Cyprus, November 9–11, 2000.

Ploner, Josef. "Tourism and the Anesthetization of Backwardness: New Symbolic Orders of Regional Identity in Alpine Austria." Paper presented at the Regional Studies Association International Conference on Regional Growth Agendas, University of Aalborg, Denmark, May 28–31, 2005.

Richards, Greg. "Gastronomy: An Essential Ingredient in Tourism Production and Consumption." In *Tourism and Gastronomy,* eds. Anne-Mette Hjalager and Greg Richards, 3–20. London and New York: Routledge, 2002.

Salazar, Noel B. "Developmental Tourists vs. Developmental Tourism: A Case Study." In *Tourism Behaviour: A Psychological Perspective,* ed. Raj Aparna, 85–107. New Delhi, India: Kanishka Publishers, 2004.

Staiff, R. "Contemporary Tourism Issues: Venice: A Case Study." Tourism Geography, http://hsc.csu.edu.au/geography/activity/local/tourism/venicep.pdf.

Urry, John. *Consuming Places.* London: Routledge, 1995.

Yeoman, Ian, Diana Brass, and Una McMahon-Beattie. "Current Issues in Tourism: The Authentic Tourist." *Tourism Management* 28 (2007): 1128–38.

11

Passing Time

The Ironies of Food in Prison Culture

JIM THOMAS

Each agent, wittingly or unwittingly, willy nilly, is a producer and reproducer of objective meaning[1]

If, as they say, "Time is God's way of keeping everything from happening at once," then food becomes a way to fill the existential interstices that time creates. Eating not only sustains us, but it also helps fill the voids in our day, symbolizes our status, identity, and social location, and becomes a focal point for organizing our life. It also functions as a social ritual in communing with others while also providing cultural signposts to negotiate and navigate through our social world.

What we eat, its character and meaning, the function, form, and meaning we attach to it, and our affective or emotional stance toward it, reflect subjective tastes. In "doing food," however, we create, recreate, and act out these subjective predilections to form cultural scripts from which we generate objective cultural "things," such as demonstrable expectations, measurable status symbols, or forms of normative action, such as power, control, or resistance.

There is no shortage of explorations of the importance of food in our culture. There are always new questions to ask and new ways of looking at the questions, as the chapters in this volume illustrate. Changes in culinary trends, diversity of eating habits, the shifting symbolism of food in displaying status and other sociocultural capital, or the mechanics of food as a bonding mechanism permeate media and research. And, of course, the relationships between food and culture periodically urge us to shift our gaze to explore underexamined groups or marginalized cultures. Prisoners are one such culture.

Sometimes, I dine at Charlie Trotters, a high-end, four-star, and rather expensive Chicago restaurant. A dinner for two can easily run $600 with wine and tip. More often, I eat in prison dining rooms. A dinner for two can cost about 58 cents at state expense. No wine, no tip. On occasion, I also eat in prison cells with prisoners who skip the dining hall and prepare meals or snacks themselves. No cost, sometimes wine, and always a big tip: "Watch out for the 'po-lice' [correctional officers]!!" Dollar for dollar, I find food in prisons most interesting. In this chapter, I try to explain why by first providing an overview of the "food thing" and then illustrating the meaning of food in prison culture by drawing from prisoners' experiences.

For people who live in environments where resources are limited and freedom restricted, such as total institutions,[2] food takes on far more meaning than for people in the free world. For prisoners, food is more than nourishment, and meals are more than a taken-for-granted routine. Food symbolizes punishment and powerlessness, becomes a daily reminder of what has been lost because of incarceration, provides a resource for doing time, and offers a way to attain (or lose) status. It also provides a way to resist social control, a way of adapting to prison, and, with luck, can help make a normal day of deprivation just a little less so.

The Background of Food in Prison Culture

In the first U.S. prisons of the early nineteenth century, food was used to reward and punish.[3] In the nineteenth century, prison food was harsh. Incoming prisoners were often served bread and water until they had earned the right for such "luxuries" as meat or cheese. In the Eastern Penitentiary in Philadelphia, breakfasts were sparse and invariant, consisting of coffee, cocoa or green tea, and a mix of bread and Indian mush (cornmeal). The primary midday meal was boiled pork or beef, soup, potatoes or rice, sauerkraut, and tea. Indian mush and tea constituted the evening meal. Although prison fare varied by state, nineteenth-century administrators gradually recognized the importance of proper nutrition in maintaining both discipline and prisoners' health. In addition, prison reformers emphasized dietary improvements on humanistic and ethical grounds, and by the early twentieth century prison diets became more varied, less restrictive, but were still austere.

In the 1960s, a confluence of factors that included the civil rights movement, a growing awareness of prisoners' rights, and awareness of the importance of nutrition on behavior led to gradual changes in prison diets. Since the 1970s, the United States Supreme Court (USSC) has consistently protected the right of prisoners to have an adequate diet that met reasonable standards of quality. But, the meaning of "reasonable standards" may vary, because the quality both of ingredients and preparation swings wildly between states, by security level or size of an institution, and by fiscal resources available to purchase or prepare meals. However, the USSC has consistently ruled that meals must be "nutritious," and that prisoners have a right to a diet consistent with their religion if the diet is reasonable and doesn't subvert the punitive or security goals of the institution.

Under the medical model of rehabilitation emerging after World War II, prison diets reflected the growing scientific research on nutrition. Healthy prisoners presumably would be productive workers, and starchy diets of 5,000 calories or more, coupled with minimal exercise, would produce lethargic prisoners less likely to engage in violence. However, in the past 30 years, most U.S. correctional facilities have followed the prescribed nutritional guidelines of the American Correctional Association, which sets standards with which most prisons comply.[4] This has led to carefully planned diets, attention to preparation processes, posting of the weekly menu so that prisoners may decide whether to eat the scheduled meal, and provide special medical or religious diets. However, the final product may not match the ideal, particularly in prison systems struggling under fiscal constraints or in maximum security prisons, where security needs trump food quality.

Alternatives to the prison diet may be provided by prison commissaries, in which prisoners who can afford it may purchase a limited range of dietary items.[5] Increased protections of religious rights in prison have also become woven into the symbolism of food, as Muslims, Jews, vegans, and other recognized faith-based groups are entitled to a reasonable diet consistent with their beliefs. Although prison administrators generally comply with special diets, many prisoners find it necessary, or at least preferable, to supplement their diet or even prepare their own meals in their cells with commissary items or food purloined from the dining hall. For these prisoners, diet creates a connection to spirituality, which in turn contributes to what some would call a form of rehabilitation and inner growth.[6]

Food culture in prisons falls into two broad categories: Meals delivered on the institution's feeding schedule (breakfast, lunch, dinner), and ad hoc eating outside of the normal routine, in which prisoners creatively devise alternatives to formal prison meals. Unlike the free world, in which we rarely think about our physical safety in a restaurant, mealtime in prisons carries a level of stress because of the potential for violence. Contrary to movie depictions, in which prison dining halls often resemble a gladiator arena, mealtime is generally safe and incident free. But, the infrequency of dining hall violence doesn't desensitize prisoners' awareness that there always remains the potential for volatility. This adds yet another layer of punitive stress: Even when enjoying a dinner, it's necessary to be aware of surroundings and potential cues that signify impending violence. This wariness is reaffirmed by large warning signs on Illinois maximum security prison dining hall walls: "LIE DOWN WHEN SHOTS ARE FIRED!"

Mealtime Dilemmas

Concerns about food are often related to how and when meals are distributed. Serving lines are a constant reminder of the prisoners' vulnerability and their powerlessness over the daily routine. Portions are dolloped on trays as prisoners mechanically move through the serving line. Sanitary standards in kitchens and dining rooms may or may not be rigidly enforced, and on hot days in poorly-ventilated, sweltering preparation areas, the servers' perspiration, mingled with steam from the trays, may drip into the food. The prevalent rumors that some prisoners "sabotage" food with saliva, feces, or other noxious substances perpetuate fears of uncleanliness. Although there are few documented cases of foreign substances such as feces or saliva being placed in meals during preparation, the rumors contribute to lack of confidence in prison sanitation, especially for prisoners isolated in segregation units to whom food is delivered.[7] Prisoners who are constrained from attending the dining hall because of disciplinary or high security restrictions, or who are medically unable to eat with the general population have their meals delivered on food carts, which transport them from the preparation area. Hot food may arrive cold, and cold food warm. The time required to deliver the meals decreases its palatability as it sits on the cart. For these prisoners, who often lack commissary alternatives either because of their reduced privileges in their security status or because of health issues, mealtime is less about food than it provides a signpost of routinization and a break in the boredom of solitary cell life.

Finally, prison food can be repetitive despite variation in menus. This occurs in part because of poor preparation, resulting in meals in which soggy vegetables and overcooked meat are indistinguishable from one meal to the next. Low-security prisoners who have more privileges may have access to hotplates, microwaves, and other items necessary to cook and serve food. Sometimes, sympathetic staff may allow prisoners to prepare food in their cells using illicit "stingers" or other heating devices, or ignore contraband food that prisoners have managed to obtain. The bulk of the population, however, is dependent upon what the institution kitchens produce for everything other than what they may buy at the prison commissary. In combination, these features of prison food provide a dualistic dislike between social control and existential resistance.

Punishment and Control: "Mealtimes? They Ain't No Picnic!"

Once, a prisoner tried to describe her prison experience, and finally broke into gentle tears: "You just can't understand what we go through in here until you understand the food thing." Her point was that food served is a meme, a cultural replicator, of punishment, deprivation, and powerlessness. Eating became more than a pastime; it was a reminder of where she was, meals with her children, and what she had lost. For her and her companions, creative eating was a way to beat the system, resist control, and redefine an abnormal world in a way that allowed emotional and psychological survival. A few examples illustrate the complexity of how, in prison culture, food takes on both symbolic and tangible roles in the dance of punishment, control, resistance, and adaptation.[8] Although editorial parsimony limits these examples, each nonetheless displays the theoretical and conceptual underpinnings that allow us to recognize that food represents more than simply an ingestive act.

In some ways, prison diets reinforce a class-bound, leveling regimen by imposing a standard menu that, while varying in content, reflects what some have described as "plebian fare." That there is a cultural link between culture, class, and food consumption is old news.[9] The variations by which the links play out are more complex. Prisons punish in part by reducing individuality and choice and by reducing status differences among prisoners, relegating all to a subordinate class and social position relative to staff and those in the free world. Imposing class uniformity on a culture, whether with school dress codes or uniforms, acceptable modes of speech, or in other ways that stifle individual expression, is a subtle and noncoercive tool for controlling deviance. Prison food, with its emphasis on Midwestern urban diets of bread and potatoes, basic vegetables and routine cuts of chops, poultry, ground meat, and minimal seasonings, imposes a class-bound diet. Although the menus may be nutritious and seemingly varied, the basic ingredients and style of cooking are far less so. Mushy boiled peas, carrots, or beans remain mushy, boiled, and somewhat indistinguishable on the palate regardless of being served on alternate days. This creates a homogenizing effect and commonality in which all share a minimum common denominator in cuisine and communicates prisoners' lowered status.

That meals are nourishing and resemble those eaten on the streets makes it no less punitive. While many of us may share, even prefer, the basic menu served to prisoners, the difference is that on the streets we have a choice, one which we often exercise, to vary our diet and control the preparation. Prisons restrict this option. The impact can hit with the first meal, which sets the tone for the coming years:

I'll never forget my first meal in an institution. Brutal. I was hungry, man, like stone-ass hungry. I got in the morning after they'd served breakfast. They fed us lunch about 1 o'clock, took us out of single [one-man] cells and lined us up against the wall. Then they marched us down, "No talking!! No talking!!" to the dining hall. They had these little tables that sat about four, but were small, and there were just those tables and the serving line and chairs. They marched us through the line where we picked up those little plastic trays with no compartments to separate the food, at least I don't remember any. I walked through and the servers chucked some watery beans on the tray, and a frankfurter or two. We had Koolade that was mostly sugar, not cool, and needed a lot more aid. Some spinach, and some, oh yeh, they gave us a couple of pieces of wonder bread. No catsup, at least I didn't see any, and no milk or seconds. We picked up a spoon and a fork, they didn't give us knives, and that's how we ate. Man, that was the worst meal I've had in my life. I'd rather eat C-rations. And that meal, that one meal, is how I'll always remember that place. You forget how important a good sandwich or bowl of soup is in your life until you can't get it [fieldnotes, entry from prisoner diary].

Complaining of food quality, either through verbal conflict or by more formal channels such as lawsuits or prison grievance procedures, may be perceived as a futile act that risks repercussions by the administration, which reinforces prisoners' lack of control over their daily lives:

Do you ever eat beef or hotdogs for a month straight? They may put barbecue sauce with it one day, or they may put some noodles with it the next day. Or they just give it to you dry the next day. This is how they do it. And they start all over again. This is how it's been going [since I've been here]. Look. If you challenge it, [you] wind up transferred, they find reasons to transfer you, because they don't have to give no reasons for transfer. They can transfer you to any other institution [interview, Illinois maximum security prisoner].

Attempts to resist control by obtaining extra food in the serving line are common, but discovery carries risks of disciplinary sanctions. A minor offense, such as the following, would likely result in loss of commissary privileges for 30 days:

[Today], Inmate Joe M. was placed on [disciplinary alert] for stealing food in the kitchen. Inmate M. came through line #2 in the kitchen, picked up his tray with his food on it. Inmate M. then grabbed the meat intended for the next person in line, and placed the meat on his tray, hiding the extra meat under his mashed potatoes. I explained to inmate M. the policy and progressive discipline that will occur if this infraction happens again. Inmate M. assured me that he understood the policy, and that it would not happen again. Inmate M. was then taken off [disciplinary alert] status and was free to go [staff disciplinary report, Illinois maximum security prison].

Here, a trivial act of attempting to obtain an extra portion took on more dramatic consequences because the prisoner's attempt to assert some control over his basic existence subverted the punitive and control functions of the institution. This led not only to deprivation of the extra food (and loss of the meal), but the threat of additional loss of privileges for a repeat offense. The message: "You do not control what you eat!"

Mealtimes also function to regiment prisoners. They are short, usually about 20 to 30 minutes from entry to exit. If the lines from the cell into the dining room or through the "chow line" are slow, the time for eating is reduced proportionately. Although variations occur within and across prison systems, mealtimes generally follow a highly structured regimen. Prisoners are taken in groups to the dining hall from their cell blocks or assignments, with one group entering when the previous group exits. Former New York State Chief Judge Sol Wachtler, sentenced to federal prison following a felony conviction, suggested that mealtimes are too short to be a ritual, but the routinization, control, lack of variation, and humiliation rituals imbue them with ritualistic qualities[10] described by one prisoner's experience:

> The eating procedure is, like, you go through a line. They have different letters in the alphabet set up. It is a hassle. Like, you walk down these concrete slabs and they have these half-crescent shapes with seats. And you go in the section where you are pointed out to be by the officer or the sergeant or the lieutenant standing by the door. The letters range from A to M, you dig, and they point out which one you go to, which one your house is eating at on that particular day [fieldnotes, Illinois maximum security prisoner].

The uncertainly of not knowing the ingredients of a dish or of not knowing if foreign substances were maliciously put in the food adds to the uncertainty of meals. Like most urban legends, the "feces in the food" stories possess a long iterative half-life. Just as people are occasionally struck by lightening, sometimes foreign substances are maliciously placed in prison food. Although rare, it nonetheless reinforces powerlessness or feeds paranoia by providing the fodder for persecution fantasies, illustrated by an inmate in segregation who sought my intervention as a prison monitor in protecting him from meals brought to his cell. Although this prisoner's mental health issues might reflect the extreme end of the "paranoia" spectrum, the uncertainty he expressed illustrates the concern:

> Hey, can you do something? They're trying to poison me. I haven't eaten for the last five and a half days since I was transferred up here from [another prison] where I assaulted two guards, you know what I'm saying? The inmates think I'm a snitch, and they're trying to poison me, and I'm dehydrated. I can feel it. I can feel it in my body. I can't shit. The poison is dehydrating me, the guards [at the other institution] assaulted me. It was self–defense, so I stabbed them, and they put me over here. Been here for two weeks, and I won't eat, 'cause they're trying to poison me. They're putting poison in my food. The guards are trying to get

me. They wouldn't give me my [medication] so I had to throw hot water on one of them, and they transferred me up here from [the other prison], and I'm afraid to eat my food. The inmates think I'm a snitch, and I want somebody to know that if I die in here to call the FBI and have them do an investigation [interview, Illinois maximum security segregation prisoner].

The conventional power imbalance between staff and prisoners makes prisoners the supplicants in most interactions. However, food can become a valuable power-mediating currency between prisoners and staff, and hungry officers may become co-conspirators in accommodation rituals, as one prisoner described:

I never sold sandwiches [that I'd ripped off from the kitchen]. We'd just eat, you know what I mean? But we'd give them to the guards that wanted them. If a guard takes a sandwich, that's the best friend you can have, because they've got to take it a second time, you know what I mean? He can't say no. But that's the biggest kind of bribery that I fool with over there, but it ain't bribery. If the guards want to eat, they like to eat, but the other guards can't know about it, because if they do, they'll bust you. If they caught us with the sandwiches taking them out, they'd bust us. The other guards. But the guards that were in on this sandwich thing would watch out for us [interview, federal maximum security prisoner].

The ubiquitousness of food, its importance both as one of life's small luxuries and a survival need, its relative ease of accessibility compared to other illicit resources, and its seemingly benign nature — "who has ever been stabbed with a sandwich?" — disguise both its practical and symbolic dual character as a conveyor of punishment. However, just as food controls, it can also liberate.

Food as Resistance

Even in total institutions, inhabitants attempt to resist constraints and construct a world more to their liking. Ironically, instruments of oppression can also become tools of liberation. The variety of ways by which prisoners attempt to reassert control over their environment may be perceived as maladaptive by administrators and outsiders, but the attempts also function as prisoners' adaptive mechanisms to resist control and to increase a sense of normalcy in an abnormal environment.

Accessibility to ingredients to prepare food and possession of the skills to create alternatives to prison fare become a valuable form of cultural capital that can be parlayed into a way of easing punitive conditions, passing time, bartered for other scarce resources in the prison economy, repaying favors or debts, or enhancing social status in the prisoner hierarchy. Bourdieu argues that cultural capital, like economic and other forms capital, is an asset that comes from possession of valued cultural objects or attributes, such as education, facility with language, or social class.[11] It also comes from knowledge of cultural tools and norms and the ability to manipulate them. Food can be a form of cultural capital in that skills of acquisition, preparation, or distribution can be turned into an investment that reduces the control and punitive aspects of prison and makes "doing time" a bit easier. This occurs when prisoners bypass the sanctioned meal schedule and create their own alternatives.

One way food functions to reassert normalcy is its use in celebrating rituals that might otherwise go unrecognized, such as holidays or ethnic and religious days. Bourdieu observes that one need not master a given skill, such as cooking, for the product to retain its symbolic importance as a ceremony or ritual.[12] For prisoners, the production of a particular type of meal can reaffirm memories of the outside world and better times, the ceremonies of holidays, weddings, cooking for children, or even bonding in gang activities. Christmastime, especially, is a time for loosening restrictions or allowing latitude in what prisoners may eat.[13] The numerous cultural and personal associations attached to food become a useful resource to redefine situations that fail to fit prisoners' fundamental sentiments or to reinforce previous sentiments imported from the free world. Because prison meals tend to be bland and mundane, creative prisoners find ways to reaffirm affective ties to their ethnic or other cultural identities by enhancing their diets with cell cooking. Hispanics, for example, might miss burritos, beans, and rice and rectify the deprivation by making them in their cell. Although cell cooking is generally not allowed, both for punitive reasons and because cell cooking can be considered a fire hazard, prisoners find ways around the restrictions by making snacks or actually preparing meals.

A snack in the cell can be a simple treat, little more than a grilled cheese sandwich made from bread, cold cuts, and cheese pilfered from the dining hall and grilled on makeshift hot plates. Once I saw a prisoner making what appeared to be a doughy ball on a plastic pane. He had a sugary paste in one jar and a jar of mixed fruit from the day's meals in another. He was making a birthday cake for a gang leader, using heat from milk cartons and various contraband items in his cell to make a primitive oven. It was not the quality of the cake, but the meaning behind the ritual of making it that gave it the social significance as a show of respect in honoring the gang leader.

In one female prison, a woman had several prisoners gathered around her in a four-person cell, and the staff were off in another area of the cell block. When asked what she was doing, she explained:

PRISONER: I'm giving my [Mexican] sisters a taste of home; tortillas and beans want some? They're kick-ass great.

JT: Thanks, no, but they smell delicious. How do you make them? How do you keep the guards from busting you?

PRISONER: It's easy. We take the corn chips from commissary and mush up some corn in it from lunch and add some other stuff and make a paste and then fry 'em up like I'm doing.

[JT NOTE: The "fire" was created by flattening wax milk containers and lighting them in a quart can and placing it under a thin sheet of metal made of several metal lids from gallon jars, about one foot square, spread across two plastic milk crates, turning the lids into a makeshift grill.] Then we just add some of the lettuce and tomatoes from [lunch] salad and some chili powder ripped off from the kitchen that we keep. That's the chicken from lunch in that bag over there, and some cheese. We just take what we can from the mess hall when they serve something we can cook later. If they don't serve it, we're fucked, but sometimes we can save it if they give it one day and we use it the next. We get some rice food from the commissary. If they serve beans, we mix up some chicken and beans and rice or pork. We don't do hamburg though, 'cause it's mostly tofu.

JT: How to you keep things from spoiling overnight?

PRISONER: [companions laugh] We wrap it up real good in plastic or maybe even in a plastic bottle or milk carton and tie a string to it and put it in the toilet. Sounds gross, but it works if you wanna eat. Hides it from the guards, too. Most of this is smuggled out from meals and the rest we can get from commissary. All you gotta do is know how.

JT: And the guards?

PRISONER: Sometimes the right ones will join us. The others don't mess with us as long as we're cool [interview with Federal Maximum security prisoner].

Just as many of us feel that no meal is complete without alcohol, neither is commentary on prison food. As in the free world, alcohol is woven into the food culture. Like eating, drinking is often associated with boredom, and boredom is one of the most debilitating aspects of prison life. This leads to creative solutions among prisoners.[14] Although alcohol can be made from any grain or fruit, the easiest and most common way of making it is with fruit juice, either by using yeast as a starter, or by the more difficult way of attempting natural fermentation. Juice or raw fruit can by obtained from sympathetic staff, kitchen personnel, or from the commissary. The concoction is fermented for a few days and then immediately consumed because of the short shelf life. This makes yeast, easily smuggled into prison, a valuable commodity, and high-quality hootch doubly valuable as yeast-based starter for additional batches. This process requires practice and patience to perfect the timing and proportions of ingredients. Once a batch has been made to satisfaction, the starter can be saved for future batches. One of the best sources of making alcohol is from the fruity syrup of canned cherries or berries. The heavy sugar content and fruit residue in the hands of a skilled practitioner provide a flavorful winelike beverage with high alcohol content.

Making alcohol requires skill both in manufacture and concealment. Those who can make it well are able to trade it for other resources or even to staff to obtain favors. On occasion, staff can use it as a control mechanism by gaining compliance or compromise from producers in return for allowing discrete production. When this occurs, there are generally tacit rules that, if violated by prisoners, lead to shakedowns, discipline, and temporary halt of production. The complexity of the functions of alcohol in prison culture can be illustrated by the following experience of a civilian who witnessed a drinking ritual in one maximum security prison.

> I was talking to two prisoners in their cell, and one said "Do you want to try some 'stuff'?" I said sure, and he brought out something [alcoholic] from half-gallon jars, and he said the first bottle was "ready." It was quite nice ... and we finished it. He brought out another half-gallon jug, and we drank that, and got even drunker. A guard walked in and gave [prisoner X] a small can of orange juice while I was there, and [prisoner X] joked that it was a "payoff" [the alcohol was made from orange juice]. I asked what I should do when guards walked by. He said:
>
>> Do whatever you want, just act natural. If they see you in here, they will probably just keep walking, and tell me later, "aha, you're trying to get [the civilian] drunk." If [the guards] walk by, put the glass down. Natural. Everybody knows I make it, the guards know I make it. It's like a trade-off. I violate the formal rules, but the informal rules I get by on, and they know if they bust me when they come by, they won't get a little something when they want it. Guards may come by, and I'll give them some. If I get busted, they know they won't get any more. Just don't make it look like you're challenging them, their authority. [It won't be] a problem for you, probably not even for me. Nobody's going to fuck with me as long as I don't fuck with them [fieldnotes, entry from prisoner's journal].

Ironically, the drinking was an outcome of a set of behavioral give-and-takes in which all participants, including the civilian, became players in a game in which organizational rules were bent to resist the control of prisoners by staff while also allowing staff to better control their charges with a compromise that they could revoke.

In most ways, alternatives to prison food are not just an act of eating, but an act of resistance, of beating the man. As on the streets, "The Man" is the dominant power, the symbol of authority. In prisons, this translates into the control structure, or the organizational equivalent of the alpha male. But, especially in prisons, where power asymmetry gives "The Man" an unequal advantage, "beating the man" brings an extra closeness:

Sneaking food out of the mess hall, a prohibited act, is beating the man. It's done by lining your pocket with a plastic bag, once containing something bought at the commissary. Take out cookies and cake or, if you do a lot of cooking in your unit, take raw vegetables from the salad bar. Or spirit away a baked potato. Food tastes better when taken from the man.[15]

A final point, one that cannot be overemphasized: Sharing food is a bonding mechanism, one that brings prisoners together. It's not always the eating, but the conviviality of "beating the man" and sharing it with others. Failure to share is a serious violation of prisoner norms, as I learned from a social faux pas:

> I was hanging around a cell today. Hot. Must be 90 degrees outside and 10 degrees higher inside. I was chewing a piece of gum, contraband in prisons, that I'd opened about an hour earlier, and CeeTee walked up and said, "Still got that gum, huh?" Seemed an odd way to begin a conversation. He's physically imposing, six-foot four and at least 240 pounds, but he seemed a bit embarrassed, making his size even more impressive. "You popped that gum [into your mouth] in front of a few guys, and I thought I should tell you that it's not cool. Ya see, over here, if ya have something, a cigarette, candy, gum, you should ask others if they want some. I figured you didn't know that, so thought I'd tell ya." He was apologetic and explained, "In the crowd [of prisoners] you're moving with in here, it's one of the small things that separates insiders from outsiders." He laughed and left. About five minutes later he came back with a quart glass of fresh ice tea and handed it to me: "You look hot, brother." He had made his point [fieldnotes, Illinois maximum security prison].

Conclusion

This narrative, of course, isn't really about food in prisons. It's about the human spirit and attempts to reaffirm humanity even among society's outcasts. My introductory claim that I find eating in prisons to be far more interesting than in the free world rests not so much on eating, but on the existential dilemma of expressing our freedom in the face of forces that would restrict it.

Foucault reminds us that in prisons the body becomes an intermediary of punishment in which deprivations of liberties that we normally consider a right or a property are removed and replaced with deprivation. In the free world, we consider the right to obtain food so fundamental that we rarely consider how our world would change if it were forcibly restricted or removed. In prisons, food embodies micro-relations of power in which the subordinate group resists the power of the dominant group. This means that even as food is an instrument and symbol of domination, it reflects a dialectical and ironic potential to become a tool of resistance precisely because prison authorities use it to oppress.

The strategies for obtaining, creating, exchanging, and consuming alternatives to mundane prison cuisine reflect that part of the human spirit that impels us to resist domination, even when deserved for serious social transgressions. The artifices used to create normalcy in abnormal environments are not likely those that appeal to most of us. After all, using toilet bowls as refrigerators, making alcohol from left-over juice from a can of cherries, or baking with ingredients found in junk food are beyond the experiences (or imagination) of most of us. Homemade stoves or ovens fabricated from discarded tinfoil found in the trash, using light bulbs or homemade "stingers" fashioned out of electrical cords or milk cartons as heat units isn't normally how most of us cook.

As make-do symbols of festive occasions, food connects prisoners to the outside world, to their prior biographies, to reminders of family and friends on the outside, and becomes a bonding ritual for new friends on the inside. Food also establishes and reinforces socially valued collective sentiments and sharing it reflects small acts of kindness. And it represents a collective ideology of "sticking it to the man."

The larger issue here isn't about eating. It's about existential rebellion and how food, something we normally take for granted, can become transformed into a cultural symbol of liberation.

Notes

1. Pierre Bourdieu, *Outline of a Theory of Practice* (Cambridge, UK: Cambridge University Press, 1989), 79.

2. A *total institution* refers to organizations guided by numerous rules, the daily life of all participants is highly regulated and regimented, and personal autonomy is dramatically reduced. See Erving Goffman, *Asylums: Essays on the Social Situation of Mental Patients and Other Inmates* (New York: Anchor, 1961), 6.

3. This section draws from and expands on Mary Bosworth and Jim Thomas, "Food," in *Encyclopedia of Prisons and Correctional Facilities,* ed. Mary Bosworth (Thousand Oaks, CA: Sage, 2004), 330–33.

4. American Correctional Association, *Standards for Adult Correctional Institutions* (Lanham, MD: American Correctional Association, 2003), 87–91.

5. For a list of typical items in a commissary, see Barbara Kestler, "A Prison Commissary" (2003). Available at: http://www.prisoners.com/fvclist.html (Accessed April 14, 2007). Generally, commissary food items include "junk food" (candy, chips, crackers), Ramadan noodles, instant foods that can be heated with hot water (usually from the tap) or — for more fortunate prisoners with privileges — in a microwave. Many of these instant foods are identical to those available on the streets, and include "instant meals" that cater to special religious or ethnic preferences. A typical instant meal, such as beef stew or chili con carne, might cost a prisoner between $2.75 and $3.50. For prisoners who make between $15 and $30 a month and who receive no funds from family or friends on the outside, even these low-cost instant meals are a luxury.

6. See Jim Thomas and Barbara H. Zaitzow, "Conning or Conversion? The Role of Religion in Prison Coping," *Prison Journal* 86 (2006): 242–59.

7. Prisoners have little incentive and considerable disincentive to sabotage food. First,

despite public perceptions to the contrary, most prisoners, despite their offense, have a sense of decency. Second, working in a prison kitchen is a privilege because it is considered a valuable job, a job that prisoners would not want to lose. Finally, while a prisoner caught sabotaging food might not fear formal discipline from staff, the "discipline" imposed by other prisoners is far more severe.

    8. These data come from field notes gathered in Illinois prisons between 1980 to the present. They were collected from formal interviews, casual conversations, full-immersion and participation observation, administrative documents, prisoner letters and post–release interviews, and other research on prisons and prisoner culture. The data were gathered as part of my experiences from teaching in prisons, prison monitoring and inspection, and other "inside activity from 1980 to the present."

    9. Bourdieu, *Distinction*, 177. See also Lisbet Oygard, "Studying Food Tastes Among Young Adults Using Bourdieu's Theory," *Journal of Consumer Studies and Home Economics* 24 (2000): 160–69.

    10. Sol Wachtler, *After the Madness: A Judge's Own Prison Memoir* (New York: Random House, 1997), 240.

    11. Pierre Bourdieu, "The Forms of Capital," in *Handbook of Theory and Research for the Sociology of Education*, ed. John Richardson (New York: Greenwood Press, 2006), 241–58.

    12. See especially Pierre Bourdieu, *Distinction: A Social Critique of the Judgment of Taste* (Cambridge, MA: Harvard University Press, 1984), 169–225.

    13. For a richly detailed account of Christmas-as-festival, see especially James W. Marquart and Julian B. Roebuck, "Institutional Control and the Christmas Festival in a Maximum Security Penitentiary," *Urban Life*, January 1987, 449–73.

    14. See Jim Thomas, "Hootch," in *Encyclopedia of Prisons and Correctional Facilities*, ed. M. Bosworth (Thousand Oaks, CA: Sage, 2004), 443–45.

    15. Wachtler, 238–39.

Works Cited

American Correctional Association. *Standards for Adult Correctional Institutions*, Lanham, MD: American Correctional Association, 2003.

Bosworth, Mary and Jim Thomas. "Food." In *Encyclopedia of Prisons and Correctional Facilities*, edited by M. Bosworth, 330-333. Thousand Oaks, CA: Sage, 2004.

Bourdieu, Pierre. *Outline of a Theory of Practice*. Cambridge: UK, 1989.

_____. *Distinction: A Social Critique of the Judgement of Taste*. Cambridge, MA: Harvard University Press, 1984.

_____. "The Forms of Capital." In *Handbook of Theory and Research for the Sociology of Education*, edited by John Richardson, 241-258. New York: Greenwood Press, 1986.

Foucault, Michael. *Discipline and Punish: The Birth of the Prison*. New York: Vintage 1979.

Goffman, Erving. *Asylums: Essays on the Social Situation of Mental Patients and other Inmates*. New York: Anchor, 1961.

Kestler, Barbara. 2003. "A Prison Commisary." Available at: http://www.prisoners.com/ fvclis.html.

Marquart, James W., and Julian B. Roebuck. "Institutional Control and the Christmas Festival in a Maximum Security Penitentiary." *Urban Life*, January 1987.

Oygard, Lisbet. "Studying Food Tastes Among Young Adults Using Bordieu's Theory." *Journal of Consumer Studies and Home Economics* 24 (2000): 160–169.

Thomas, Jim. "Hootch." In *Encyclopedia of Prisons and Correctional Facilities*. Edited by M. Bosworth, 443–445. Thousand Oaks, CA: Sage, 2004.

Thomas, Jim and Barbara H. Zaitzow. "Conning or Conversion? The Role of Religion in Prison Coping." *The Prison Journal* 86 (2006): 242–259.

Wachtler, Sol. *After the Madness: A Judge's Own Prison Memoir*. New York: Random House, 1997.

12

Selfish Consumers

Delmonico's Restaurant and Learning to Satisfy Personal Desire

HEATHER LEE

On February 17, 1873, Edward Luckemeyer threw one of the most original, if not absurd, dinner parties in New York history. Escorted to a private dining room at Delmonico's Restaurant, 74 guests enjoyed 9 courses — one poultry, two fish, and four meat dishes, plus soup and dessert — by chef Charles Ranhofer, and took home gold-embossed menus as souvenirs. Luckemeyer's culinary decadence merely provided the excuse for the main entertainment. In the middle of the table, four live swans graced a scene of mountains, valleys, and one monumental lake, which undulated like the ocean. Violet flowers blanketed hills and dales. Songbirds in gold cages and a 35-piece band serenaded the party. The table-to-ceiling protective gold mesh commissioned from Tiffany's & Co. gave a magical sheen to Luckemeyer's paradise. Dancing followed through midnight.

Despite the skirmishes between ill-tempered swans and the risk of getting wet, neither the guests, society commentators, nor the caterer challenged Luckemeyer's tastes. Rather, the "Swan Dinner" earned Luckemeyer permanent esteem among New York's fickle elite. For half a century, the evening made Luckemeyer and his family famous for their optimism concerning issues facing the reunified nation. Society's self-appointed guardian Ward McAllister applauded Luckemeyer's example: "[A]ll that art could do, all that the cleverest man could devise to spread before his guests, such a feast as the gods should enjoy, and so well done that all present felt, in the way of feasting, that man could do no more!" The event reportedly cost $10,000.[1] While on February 17, 1873, Luckemeyer was indulgent, his business dealings showed another man — one who was calculating and frugal. He had built an importing fortune by finagling customs laws and finessing family connections. Even through retirement, he appeared in court regularly to collect debts, lower customs dues, and avoid taxes. He championed freer trade and supported organizations for liberal regulations. In 1877, Luckemeyer advocated improving customs codes to Congress. Quite predictably, he exercised caution with his investments; he served as a founding director of Germania Life Insurance Company. As a businessman, Luckemeyer hated waste and celebrated accountability.[2]

For Luckemeyer and his ilk, lavish spending and professional shrewdness were not contradictory impulses, but expressions of the same trait: selfishness. They saw the ability to put personal interests above other's a form of masculinity, especially in competitive environments. Successful businessmen of the later nineteenth century competed for trade by exercising to their advantage vagaries in the law and exploiting the general partiality towards laissez-faire politics. The most aggressive were denounced as ruthless capitalists and the socially conscientious were excused as charitable citizens. The spirit of competition carried into their private lives. As men of sport, they appraised masculinity by the ability to outrace, outsmart, and outdo the opponent. Extravagant dinners like Luckemeyer's fit into a culture of displayed prowess. Such events required not only extensive outlays, but also a cleverness and originality that were admired in gaming and business. After all, McAllister remembered the "Swan Dinner" because it raised the ante on grand dinners. Professionally and privately, men competed on their behalf alone and the rigors of contest inured them to think selfishly. Individualism was both a means for survival and a characteristic of victors.

Businessmen practiced selfishness in consumerist contexts like the restaurant. There the customer ruled, and Delmonico's Restaurant famously catered to the whims of those more capricious than Luckemeyer. Satisfying gastronomic desire was the objective of dining out; patrons got whatever they wanted, whenever they wished it. Though the scenario is now pedestrian, such liberties were unusual when Delmonico's opened. In 1827, the brothers John and Peter Delmonico opened a café at 23 William Street, renaming their shop four years later a "restaurant Français." Located on a triangular lot where Beaver Street meets South Williams Street was the "Citadel" (1837) and patrons called it a palace of pleasure. Diarists and memoirists relished the delicate pastries, distinguished wines, and savory sauces. The cuisine, a mix of French, Swiss, and American, was the acme of New York fine dining for some. Many gastronomic histories conclude there, implying that New Yorkers were barbaric eaters until the Delmonicos taught them to dine instead of gorge.[3] While the brothers introduced a few dishes and educated several palates, the explanation is more convenient than accurate, and discounts the

Delmonicos' role in cultivating selfishness. Under their roof, each diner was king and eating was a form of entertainment. The Delmonicos emboldened patrons to order only what pleased their tastes and to consider no one else. In restaurants, New Yorkers had a context for exercising self-interest that eventually evolved into the prerogative of customer tyranny. There the Luckemeyers of the world received attention and service hitherto foreign in the realm of public dining.

Satisfying Desire, Creating Taste

The making of selfish consumers began with the new republic, when aggressiveness at the dinner table was intolerable and when personal tastes were irrelevant. During the early nineteenth century, the concept of hospitality still governed many public tables, and custom required that both guests and hosts fulfill mutual courtesies. While restaurant culture borrowed older forms and symbols, it transformed roles and the relationship of the host and guest. What diners desired became the primary goal of the meal, and the host became the servant. Eating out in restaurants evolved into a form of entertainment that celebrated individual taste. In the restaurant, customers gained a context and language for articulating personal wishes.

By many accounts, the food of early America was embarrassing. At public tables, European travelers to the United States were served profusions of meat, game, seafood, sweetmeats, cakes, pies, and puddings that lacked sophistication. Frenchman Pierre Blot denounced hotel food as inedible: "[H]alf of what is put on the plates is not touched, and, of course, goes to the swills." To compound the problem, Americans ate so quickly and indiscriminately as to appear barbaric in European eyes. Travelers barely had the chance to start before the Americans were finished. During his visit in 1827–1828, Scottish naval captain Basil Hall was insulted by such behavior: "[W]e were baffled by the same cold and civil but very unsociable formality.... It might have been thought that we had assembled rather for the purpose of inhuming the body of some departed friend." Another traveler was kinder and attributed the habit as natural to the accelerated pace of life. The unanimous conclusion was that Americans cared little how or what they ate.[4]

Americans were wounded. They took pride in a plentiful table. In fact, the abundance that Europeans found so vulgar was inextricable from American hospitality, as another British traveler discovered. On October 14, 1810, John Melish rose early to journey from Coshocton, Ohio, to New Philadelphia, Illinois, and wished a quick meal from his innkeeper. Agreeing to oblige, she proceeded to slaughter two chickens. Shocked, Melish restated his order for an egg, bread, and tea, to which the innkeeper added ham, fritters, and butter. She shamed him into accepting more food: "Well, you're the most extraordinary man that I ever saw; but I can't set down a table that way."[5] The conflict arose from differing ideas of breakfast, masculinity, and, most importantly, the obligations of a hostess. Proper behavior on her part required that she serve a generous meal. Accordingly, the innkeeper attempted to coerce Melish by mocking, changing, and refusing his order. Just as crucial, Melish was to allow and eat an acceptable breakfast. Her embarrassment, and ultimately this episode, was over the meaning of a meager meal. In her eyes, an egg, tea, and bread betokened miserliness and would have been an insult. Because Melish was a welcomed guest, the innkeeper reacted bitterly to setting a table that compromised her sense of duty. Such a meal simply could not represent her feelings toward Melish ("I can't set down a table that way"). Ranging between copious and scare, the mealtime spread literalized social relationships between host and guest in a way that linked abundance with hospitality as a display of good will.[6]

Unfortunately the guest's desires often mattered little in how this affection was displayed, as Melish experienced, because the host alone ruled over public tables. European travelers often remarked on their helplessness at getting suitable meals. Fifteen years after Melish passed through America, a similar scenario unfolded in Albany, New York, where Captain Basil Hall and his family stopped for food. The tavern keeper served an "altogether poor dinner" of bread, butter, eggs, and "a miserable bit of hung beef." Hall, however, was more upset to find their driver enjoying "an honest joint" of roast lamb. Apparently, the tavern keeper had already dined on the slab and feared offering paying guests "broken victuals": "They fancied ... that the credit of their house would be hurt by serving you so."[7] Differently from Melish's innkeeper, the Albanian did not consider "abundance" the only expression of hospitality. Offering the best available was just as appropriate. Disharmony again stemmed from conflicting definitions of propriety — the guests demanded what the hosts deemed improper — though hospitality here had a public dimension. The tavern keeper refused to risk his reputation. Desires were met or denied within a cultural matrix that encompassed and extended beyond the host-guest relationship.[8] Ultimately, the Albanian and Melish's innkeeper had a greater obligation to the concept of hospitality than to specific guests. The food, then, was more symbolic than material. The host, not the guest, decided the content and appearance of the meal, a guiding principle that set these public tables apart from the restaurant.

The host's prerogative was coming quickly to an end in cities. New York eating-houses were popular institutions for quick meals instead of hospitality. From the 1820s on, travelers and journalists observed these operations with distressed amusement. Small tables replaced the large, shared table that once represented commensality in taverns and inns. The rearrangement of space was practical and allowed servers to move easily through the dining floor. Waiters and order boys dashed by tables, took orders, and in minutes reappeared with hot plates of meat, bread, boiled vegetables, and beer. George G. Foster, reporter for the *New York Herald*, admired the significance of eating-houses (he estimated 30,000 businessmen lunched in the financial district daily), though he hesitated to consider them proper. Foster objected to the chaos of "clattering plates and clashing knives and forks." Dinner, the important midday meal, was traditionally taken at home among friends and relatives.[9] The communal table signified solidarity and intimacy, a feeling impossible in the eating-house, where strangers gobbled their meals without exchanging words. As for hospitality, their rush prevented diners from playing the thankful guest, while the service structure fragmented the host figure into overly worked servers. No one person's reputation was at stake. Proprietors and patrons oriented their behavior toward one goal: cheap meals. It distressed contemporaries that profane exchanges had displaced community and hospitality. Without behavioral customs, the eating-house had produced an experience as disorderly as its atmosphere.

While dinner was stripped of meaning in the eating-house, it gained importance in the restaurant. Foster was pleased that Delmonico's "aristocratic *restaurant*" led the march toward refined dining. "[I]ts admirable *cuisine*," Foster boosted, "as a work of art, ranks with a picture of Huntington, a poem by Willis, or a statue by Powers." A colleague at the *New York Mirror* simply said there was none other in America.[10] Only with time have those statements proven true. To early devotees, however, Delmonico's raised their culinary awareness. Foster's vocabulary shifted when writing about Delmonico's. *Food* became *cuisine* and *eating-house restaurant*. Diners acquired a new language for eating. By learning to read the menu, which in 1838 listed 371 dishes, diners reconceptualized the meal through French courses —*potages, hors d'oeuvres, entrées, rôts, entremets, entremets sucrés, dessert*.[11] They ordered more, though smaller portioned, dishes, and, if they were like Foster, they slipped in French when describing Delmonico's. For them, eating reached an aesthetic realm that required specialized vocabulary for its description. The point is not that the food was unparalleled, though many claimed so, but that the lexicon of French cooking set the experience apart. Delmonico's differentiated itself from eating-houses and taverns through its vernacular as much as the food, and the distinction was necessary to creating the restaurant's space. The message was that eating was not merely eating, but an art at Delmonico's.

The language of eating was not the only distinguishing characteristic of restaurants. Unlike eating-houses, Delmonico's had a host, but he was radically unlike tavern dictators. Founder John Delmonico recast the host as a paternalist figure who served to entertain. Former New York mayor Philip Hone described John Delmonico as "an amiable man, very obliging in his house." Hone spoke strictly of the restaurant; he never socialized with the Delmonicos privately. The likening of "business" to "house" was crucial to how commercial hosts saw themselves. John Delmonico built rapport with patrons because he was shrewd and ambitious in the catering industry. As in banking and trading, personal feelings strengthened business relations that often lasted lifetimes, and John Delmonico had patrons who felt very personally about him. A regular since his school days, George Templeton Strong invited the Delmonicos to his wedding. New York collectively mourned John Delmonico's death in November 1842. Newspapers and magazines honored his work, and privately his patrons contemplated their loss. "A social host," Abram C. Dayton reminisced, "his ambition was to please the public, and to outstrip competition by a lavish yet judicious expenditure."[12] John Delmonico reinvented the host figure as one who utilized his professional means for the pleasure of customers. Hospitality survived at Delmonco's in the reciprocal relationship between guest and host, and the importance of a single housemaster. John Delmonico's authority, however, was subject to the whims and desires of patrons, and less his sense of pride. The host of tavern days bowed down in the restaurant to the guest.

The shifting of power from host to guest created new opportunities for pleasures. Eating at Delmonico's enabled patrons to escape the rigors of daily life and the dullness of social propriety into carefree entertainment. Dayton remembered his visits as luxuries stolen from routine discipline and frugality. He dined at Delmonico's specifically on weekends, when he had time away from school and other responsibilities. Dayton invested the effort to make eating a leisure pursuit, and his enjoyment was heightened by the solemn activities taking place at home. While his family prepared for the sabbath, Dayton snuck off with friends to Delmonico's. Their disapproval added to his pleasure, and deepened his dedication to finding his own world. Unfortunately for Dayton, little was comparable. A related form of food-based diversion, the dinner party was a social chore. The etiquette of invitations, calling, and receiving made those events complicated and burdensome. The event was often the subject of parody. Writer William Dean Howells observed, "I have by this time become far too well versed in the polite insincerities of the plutocratic world to image, that because she asked me to come to her dinner, very informally, I was not to come in all the state I could put into my dress." His opinion that ceremony prevented everyone's enjoyment was widely shared, and makes the praise for Delmonico's all the more meaningful. For Strong, a frequent dinner-party guest, nothing else compared to Delmonicos, "Dinner at any restaurant is a bore."[13] Delmonico's provided a space to leave behind archaic customs and daily drudgery. Not only in contrast, but unto itself, dinner was transformed into a leisure activity.

The service at Delmonico's complemented the message that eating was entertainment. As ambassadors of restaurant culture, the staff guided diners through the world of Delmonico's dining. "The waiters," Foster wrote, "are always at your elbow at the moment you are beginning to think about wishing for something, and listen to you with grave attention." Compared with Melish's innkeeper or the impersonal eating-house, the service seemed like mind reading, though Foster overcredited the staff. Nonetheless, the attention to customer desire reversed the guest-host relationship and enabled the diner's desires to gain primary importance. Contemporaries were unaccustomed to such treatment. In 1841, the *New Hampshire Patriot* published an anecdote about a customer sending his soup back.[14] The humor commented on the role reversal, notably the brazenness that the customer dared to show. The interactions between employees and customer reinforced the idea that diners had license to desire.

Because taste was in some measure private, Delmonico's took care to protect individual preference. Delmonico's catered to its particular clients with *la carte blanche*, which granted the restaurateurs all means in realizing a customer's culinary vision, including an unlimited budget (Luckemeyer's "Swan Dinner" was one example). Taste was given tyrannical reign over the kitchen, staff, and evening, a privilege that was further entertained in private dining rooms. On the upper floors of "the Citadel" patrons behaved with abandon and feared no consequences — gambling was particularly prevalent. Foster criticized the lawlessness, though he refused to hold the Delmonicos responsible. "[B]ut how is a landlord to know — or how can he possibly interfere with," Foster asked rhetorically, "what is done quietly by his guests in the privacy of their rooms?" In her history of restaurants, Rebecca L. Spang observes that private rooms afforded the privacy that was impossible at home.[15] In the same manner, Foster shrugged his shoulders at what happened. That contemporaries did not interfere shows the extent desire was allowed to rule over the dining room. At Delmonico's, diners had sanction to exercise their tastes without fear of recourse.

As the midday meal took new form in the mid-nineteenth century, so did the public spaces that provided them. The relationship between guest and host transformed along two lines; the eating-house that provided quick, basic meals was the death of hospitality, while the restaurant modernized its function. In the restaurant, public eating was reconceptualized as art with pretensions to the status of paintings and literature. While the elite dined well privately, the restaurant made refined cuisine more widely available. Anyone had access to Delmonico's kitchen, and those unable to pay could participate via the flourishing gastronomy genre. Delmonico's deserves partial credit for raising general awareness about food and dining, the rest belongs to its enthusiastic reviewers and other houses of fine dining. Few proprietors were as famous as John Delmonico during the nascent phase of restaurant culture. Along with successors Peter, Lorenzo, and Charles, John Delmonico engineered a form of desire that was satisfied only in the restaurant. Personal taste found expression in the dining experience. The food fit one's mood, the service matched one's need, and the menu inspired desire. The entire experience was oriented toward creating and cultivating culinary appetite in public spaces. Even private kitchens could not serve 371 dishes on demand. To paraphrase Philip Hone, all else was a bore.

American Gastronomy

As a social practice, dining out got unintended support from discourses on food and health. In the decades preceding and following the Civil War, nutritionists and gastronomists raised awareness about diet through their vigorous attempts to reform it. Gastronomists, who championed the art of eating, in particular led an audience of middling and upper-class Americans to the restaurant. While their suggestions were impractical, their ideas about food and health, however, gave new meaning to dining out. To time-strapped, intellectual workers, restaurants supposedly provided food that suited their bodies. Gastronomy gave meaning to dinner that fit workplace realities.

Food itself became a topic of discussion. In France first, then in England, dining was elevated to an art. European gastronomists during the late eighteenth and early nineteenth centuries stirred public discussions on food, and themselves gained a level of celebrity. Jean Antheleme Brillat-Savarin enjoys credit today for transforming culinary pleasure into a spiritual pursuit.[16] Americans enthusiastically followed suit. Starting in the 1830s, magazines and journals stole essays on gastronomy from Europe, and hired American writers to compose their own, often plagiarized, versions. "History," the Bostonian *Quarterly Review* averred, "affords no materials for filling up the period which intervened between the arrival of Catherine Medicis and the accession of Louis XIV, under whom cookery made prodigious advances." Unfortunately for the *Quarterly Review*, and the New York *Albion*, which reprinted the article, the statement ignored the rich histories produced in Europe at the time. To the writer's benefit, though, "cooking" was extracted during this period from medicine, to which it once belonged, to become a separate discipline. Though the "Gastronomy and Gastronomer" article series failed as a comprehensive history, it shared the growing excitement for food as a topic.[17] Cookery stood on its own as a profession and subject of inquiry.

Food enthusiasts wanted to improve American cuisine. Since the French Revolution, gastronomy has been regarded in Europe and America as an index of a nation's civility, and America, writers felt, could not afford being left behind. Within the same breath of admiration for French cooking American authors defended their national diet.[18] Admitting it was lagging, editors, journalists, and writers confidently believed that the American abundance and ingenuity would put the nation abreast, and took it upon themselves to educate their publics. Newspapers across the nation advised readers on what to eat, and occasionally on how to dine out. Magazines like *Albion, Knickerbocker, Campbell's,* and *Putnam's* regularly ran features on gastronomy.[19] Altogether the genre was amateur until Pierre Blot became its guiding voice. After a decade in America, Blot launched his career with *What to Eat and How to Cook It* (1863) and a school for French cooking. In 1866, he delivered fourteen lectures in Boston that were later published. He wrote columns for *Galaxy* and *Harper's Bazaar* until his death in 1874. "Many intelligent persons ... are exceedingly careless about what concerns their very life," Blot continued, "[b]ut the civilized man, the gastronomer, observes fixed laws in the order of his dishes." [20] Professor Blot crusaded against dietary ignorance like his part-time predecessors, but he had the benefit of a school, lecture tours, books, and several cooperating periodicals. At the outset, Blot's chances at changing American eating seemed fair.

Unfortunately Blot was so overbearing and pedantic that he took the pleasure out of eating. Typical of the times, he believed the nation needed healthier men and he solicited wives to improve domestic cookery. Blot preached seasonability and designed monthly menus for *Galaxy* and *Harper's Bazaar,* though his complicated advice was likely rarely followed. For example, his recipe for January mayonnaise sauce required the room temperature to be neither hot nor cool, or the salad would have a "bad appearance." Blot warned repeatedly that one's health depended on respecting fixed gastronomic laws, which concerned as much the form and aesthetics of the meal as the ingredients and preparation. "'French Cookery' is," reviewed the *New York Times* of Blot's cookbook, "the elegant simplicity of its methods, based on *enlightened experience.*" Few readers honestly had the professional knowledge that Blot demanded. Followers complained that Blot's proposals were impractical for home cooking — their domestics were unable to execute to Blot's designed precisions. Gastronomy would have overtaxed the household economy. Americans suffered chronic shortages in servants, and the extra labor was unaffordable. Housewives soured to suggestions that added burdens to their arduous routines. Interest waned.[21] His basic error was that his cooking requirements were met easily outside the home.

Men had the option of eating out and Blot unintentionally encouraged the practice by persuading America to eat well. He explained that intellectual men required "properly prepared" food. "Let a bookkeeper, or editor, or author, or clerk, etc., adopt a farmer's diet," Blot counseled, "and see how long he will keep in health." He argued that five factors should decide one's diet — "constitutions" and "occupation" headed the list. For desk workers, Blot reasoned that expensive ingredients and elaborate preparations were easily digested and assimilated by their bodies. His affluent audience embraced the license, and found that dining out solved the difficulties posed by his teachings. At Delmonico's, a succession of chefs, including Peter Delmonico, staffed the kitchens, but none was more infamous than Charles Ranhofer. Hired away from their main competitor, Ranhofer catered Delmonico's most important dinners between 1862 and 1896, including Luckemeyer's "Swan Dinner." In 1894, he published a cookbook. Over 1,000 pages long, the *Epicurean* contained season schedules for foods, service timetables, diagrams of obscure instruments, and hundreds of recipes.[22] The book demonstrated that cooking had logic; social laws of propriety and laws of nature governed the length, context, and content of a meal. Like Blot, Ranhofer considered the "gastronomic art" a serious and distinct discipline, and Ranhofer was cautious in what he considered proper for amateurs. The *Epicurean* drove the point that professionals animated their knowledge of science, health, and aesthetics. Though Blot rarely mentioned restaurant dining, his ideas about proper cooking demanded a lifetime's dedication, an opportunity from which celebrity chefs like Ranhofer benefited. It was apparent to many that eating well was accomplished in the restaurants like Delmonico's.

No one said he dined at Delmonico's for health reasons, rather many considered the meal art. For pragmatic reasons at least, eating out was a habit of affluent workingmen who lived far from their offices. George Foster estimated that 30,000 to 50,000 businessmen dined out daily; *Putnam's* wildly guessed New York had double as many eating houses as any city; the *New York Mirror* thought the city needed more. Absurdly high, these estimates nevertheless captured the fact that public dining was significant in their daily lives. Foster recognized that restaurants served necessities in another sense. "[A] look through [Delmonico's] well-filled yet not crowded saloons, and into its admirable *cuisine*, will enable us to pass an hour very profitably," he suggested, "[where] a dinner which is not just a quantity deposited in the stomach, but is in every sense and to all the sense a great work of art." As Foster implied, eating served an aesthetic function. Fine food and a proper setting cultivated character and taste in diners. His portrait of Delmonico's included a courteous son and sagely father pair, a respected journalist, a famous writer, a notable musician, and an eccentric intellectual; men of business were conspicuously missing. Foster acknowledges they comprised Delmonico's most significant patrons, but he was concerned primarily with how Delmonico's elevated the American diet. He named famous individuals because their presence legitimized restaurants. The inarticulate majority also understood dining at Delmonico's as an event. Speaking for the average American, James McCabe wrote, "The house enjoys a large custom, and every visitor to New York who can afford it, takes a meal before leaving the city." McCabe's assertion is corroborated by the multitude of dinner party announcements. In 1873 alone, the year Luckemeyer held his "Swan Dinner," the *New York Times* covered over twenty annual benefit parties.[23] Men patronized Delmonico's because they considered dining there an aesthetic experience.

Despite Blot's effort to improve domestic cookery, his teachings made dining out attractive to men of means. Restaurants practiced similar methods and regulars were already convinced that eating served purposes other than basic necessity. Men who traveled downtown for work ate out for reasons that did not easily yield to Blot's urgings. Restaurant culture by that time had become a part of their world as much as it was a function of necessity. Ultimately the hassle Blot demanded made little sense in the face of easy alternatives. Dining out received an unexpected advocate who presented himself as a competitor to public eating. Blot's ideas melded with existing gourmandism, and even advanced its cause. Because Blot advocated delicate cooking, diners could now eat well for health's sake.

Practiced Masculinity

Restaurants in New York fixed their social meaning in a milieu of transition as a school for masculine education. During the nineteenth century, "space" offered a new vernacular for understanding and affecting the world. Businessmen asserted their sense of independence through architectural grandeur that distinguished them from competitors. Replacing the home-cooked meal, dining out made the same statement about one's autonomy. In the restaurant, young men cultivated a lifestyle of freedom and abandon amongst one another, and came to regard consumerism as means for severing material dependences on the home. Dinner, in other words, became a sport.

Delmonico's appealed to customers who desired their surroundings to proclaim their importance. During the late eighteenth and early nineteenth centuries, middle- and-upper class homes grew in size and became more luxurious. The number of rooms multiplied, each evolving to meet specialized purposes. As the space for ritual unification, the dining room was subject to more decoration fads than any other room. "Cold white walls and ceilings, in a dining-room," *Putnam's* complained, "are enough to destroy a keen appetite."[24] The eating environment mattered in the sense that it could have complemented, or even enhanced, the culinary experience. Recognizing an opportunity, the Delmonicos redesigned their main restaurant. When "the Citadel" opened on September 20, 1837, the Delmonico brothers invited journalists for a preview dinner. Attendees proclaimed the food excellent, though spent more wordage describing the building. In a typical review, the *Albion* noted its convenience from the Merchants' Exchange House, the opulent decor, and the structure's sturdiness, declaring the opening a triumph for both cuisine and architecture.[25] Guests viewed the grand opening through the building as much as the food. As space, Delmonico's provided a dining experience that accommodated aesthetic preferences and their meaning for the meal.

If businessmen articulated their beliefs about the world through spaces, the "character" of a merchant had transformed over the middle decades. His professional education was still rooted in the workplace, where he built relationships and a reputation during his apprenticeship. Differently from men ten or fifteen years his senior, he was also learning a city. New York had transformed from a walking city bordered by wilderness in 1800 to an urban expanse crosshatched by thoroughfares and streetcars by 1850. Young merchants or clerks typically migrated to New York from elsewhere in the United States or from abroad, and stayed in boardinghouses among similar company.[26] Separated from family and friends, young men utilized their anonymity to cultivate a separate culture. They patronized businesses their parents would have disapproved of: gambling houses, taverns, and brothels. Advice manuals warned rural youths of the moral corruption that lay ahead, but they rarely agreed. Banding together, they defended self-indulgence and aggressiveness against moralists. They saw nothing shameful in their leisure activities; in fact, they argued that men had prerogatives that must be exercised to their own and society's benefit. The *New York Herald* concluded that business had "a new code of ethics."[27] Like the new architectural message, young men sought independence from tradition. To them, self-sufficiency meant the ability to exercise one's will and pursue pleasure. Young merchants of the middle decades inhabited a culture that valued selfish freedoms.

Through the power of purchase, customers signaled their autonomy by creating alternative social meanings for dinner. Though boardinghouses supplied food, the residents ate out because their lives revolved around public spaces. Writer Junius Browne fairly stated, "Nowhere else in this country do men live so largely at restaurants as in New York." Since eating establishments clustered in the financial district, most commentators concluded that businessmen were the biggest patrons. According to one contemporary, clerks and merchants expected one another at Delmonico's for noontime drinks; George

Foster added that Delmonico's served mostly merchants.[28] For those without families, dining with peers birthed and reinforced a novel sociability of the table. "Eating in public may beget a certain freedom of manner and *nonchalance*," *Putnam's* cautioned, "but we fear the practice is not calculated to promote the health either of the mind or the body." In other words, "little gentlemen" behaved with abandon towards customs that gave family meals their meaning. But they gained camaraderie. Lobbyist Samuel Ward remembered fondly visiting Delmonico's as a young man:

> I look in vain nowadays for those attractive reflections, enlivened by the rattle of dominoes, and recall the introduction on cold days of a certain hot, rosy, whiskey punch, sweetened with currant jelly and heightened by a dash of peach brandy, which it would be useless for anyone to call for today.[29]

With his wealth and clout, Ward could have ordered the drink at many counters. He preferred instead to preserve his memories of fond times. Ward had found an ersatz home at Delmonico's, and his nostalgia grew from the significance of community. Though he mentions no one by name, the companionship was meaningful: a dominoes opponent or discussion partner. Ward was homesick for those familiar sounds and tastes that comforted during his studies at Columbia College. To regulars, dining out provided the social support to enable emotional independence, and offered in that sense a rite of passage into adulthood. By replacing the functions of home in the commercial realm, young men found means in the urban world for claiming their autonomy.

Through mutual encouragement to act upon desire, male independence became a competition. Originality in what one wished was equated with a man's autonomy. "Sporting men" socialized around gaming activities — horse racing, gambling, cockfighting, and pugilism. Masculine taste gravitated toward cultures of deviance. In that sense, Edward Luckemeyer's "Swan Dinner" and other *la carte blanche* dinners displayed the host's power and achievement by rejecting republican simplicity. It is easy to imagine the oddness of watching creatures that might appear on the menu swim and coo. The Silver, Gold, and Diamond dinners thrown by Leonard Jerome, August Belmont, and William Travers, respectively, were born from the idea of competition — to each outdo another in spending and culinary ingenuity. Quite appropriately, their game was inspired by Jerome Park's failed yacht fest.[30] Throwing dinner parties was no different than horse racing or gambling. Men pinned their reputations and pledged fortunes to beating one another at a game whose only limit was man's creative ability. In other words, food was a measurement of the man. Culinary selfishness linked pleasure and consumption in a way that coded lavish spending with masculinity.

Dining out held social currency that could be parlayed toward other ambitions. From its opening in 1827, Delmonico's was a space for European and American businessmen to convene over food. Deals and plans were discussed and organizations were formed. Luckemeyer's brother-in-law, Hugo Wesendonck, held the future Guardian Life Insurance Company's first meeting at Delmonico's on March 28, 1860. To "young men engaged as clerks," *Dwight's American Magazine* recommended Delmonico's: "[A] valuable introduction to one or more of the languages most important to a merchant."[31] Newcomers noted the importance of food. Businessmen joked that a well-timed meal at Delmonico's turned competitors into partners. According to folklore, one such dinner saved a firm and prevented the Civil War. A New York "sporting man" who loved fast horses discovered his reputation among his southern clients was at stake. To curry favors, he bribed a Southerner with dinner at Delmonico's and riding. "Delmonico did his best," the *Independent* cheered, "[the] Union was saved just seventeen times, and General Washington was pronounced the greatest man that ever lived."[32] A Northern merchant's fantasy when war seemed unavoidable, the story nevertheless speaks to how masculinity was transacted through food. While the Northerner purchased his manliness at Delmonico's, he invited his competitor to share in gastronomic pleasure. Dinner had the appearance of one man extending his friendship, which canceled the potential antagonism between foes. Within a cooperative context, the Southerner did not concede a loss, but did a favor for his friend. The Northerner profited from Delmonico's dual function as a place of business and entertainment by trading a social favor for a professional one.

Young men sought fortunes away from home, and the experience gave them a world to themselves. In commercial spaces of New York, a generation of businessmen learned to behave selfishly in both personal and business matters. Linking masculinity and independence to consumption and pleasure, these men were both agents of and subject to an expanding market of commercial pleasure. Restaurants were spaces for experimenting with and playing out the rules of male competition, which also enabled crafty individuals to parlay social games for professional profit. Differently from their fathers or grandfathers, these young men gained autonomy through consumerist pursuits and cultivated amongst one another a culture that understood displayed wealth as a sign of independence.

Conclusion

The socially and professionally competitive culture of the nineteenth century encouraged young men to equate individualism with masculinity.

Selfishness was useful to men who hoped to reach a measure of success. The ability to consider one's needs above others' marked an ideological break from earlier generations. Young businessmen learned to satisfy their needs in commercial establishments, and to consider their patronage as assertions of independence. Amidst other competitive men, consumerism became an escalating effort to outperform one another. Delmonico's, for its part, provided a context for desire. The menu, culinary vocabulary, and service assisted patrons in articulating their personal tastes. No longer a dull social event, eating became in the restaurant a form of entertainment. Pierre Blot unintentionally helped define eating as a public experience by making gastronomy impossible for the domestic kitchen. While dining out already had many connotations that Blot identified, his health warnings provided additional motivation for seeking well-prepared meals. Even if the nation benefited from able-bodied men, New York's business elite sought mainly to fulfill their self-interests. Their pleasure, their bodies, their needs were the primary concern. The lesson in selfishness translated into professional contexts, where tact, aggressiveness, and ambition were rewarded. Both a social and business space, Delmonico's encouraged individualism in the dual sense. The Delmonico family catered to a generation of diners who were distinguishing culturally from their parents. The Delmonico restaurants, which occupied over nine locations between 1827 and 1925, offered New Yorkers more than food. It cultivated men of the city, aggressive, ambitious, and successful, and displayed for the nation a grittier, more realistic alternative to Horatio Alger's rags to riches morals.

Notes

1. *Duluth Minnesotian*, March 15, 1873; McAllister, *Society as I Have Found It* (1890; rpt. New York: Arno Press, 1975), 233–6, 457; *Galveston (Texas) Daily News*, December 29, 1874; *Milwaukee Journal*, February 7, 1894; Lately Thomas [Robert Steele], *Delmonico's: A Century of Splendor* (Boston: Houghton Mifflin Co., 1967), 148–9; *Lexington (Kentucky) Herald*, January 31, 1909.

2. Chris Walton, "Wagner, Otto and the Three Mathildas: Braut und Schwester bist du dem Bruder," *Musical Times* 143 (2002): 42; *St. Louis Daily Globe-Democrat*, January 20, 1884; *New York Times*, February 19, 1885; *Daily (Chicago) Inter Ocean*, January 6, 1886; *New York Times*, January 7, 1891; *Magone v. Luckemeyer*, 139 US 612 (1891) ; *New York Times*, March 7, 1870; *Daily Arkansas Gazette*, May 25, 1877; *Baltimore Sun*, September 6, 1860.

3. Thomas [Steele], *Delmonico's*, 8–12; Richard J. Hooker, *Food and Drink in America: A History* (Indianapolis: Bobbs-Merrill, 1981), 144; Michael Batterberry and Ariane Batterberry, *On the Town in New York: The Landmark History of Eating, Drinking, and Entertainments from the American Revolution to the Food Revolution* (New York: Routledge, 1999), 71–5; Jay Jacobs, *New York à la Carte* (New York: McGraw-Hill, 1978), 2–11; Peter Andrews, "Delmonico's — The Restaurant Changed the Way We Dined," *American Heritage*, August/September 1980, 96–101; John Mariani, *America Eats Out: An Illustrated History of Restaurants, Taverns, Coffee Shops, Speakeasies, and Other Establishments That Have Fed Us for 350 Years* (New York: William Morrow, 1991), 24–33; Arthur Schwartz, *New York City Food* (New York: Stewart, Tabori, &

Chang, 2004), 47–55; Meryle Evans, "Knickerbocker Hotels and Restaurants 1800–1850," *New York Historical Society Quarterly* 36 (1952): 377–409.

4. Hooker, *Food and Drink in America*, 141–53; Blot, "American Cookery," *The Galaxy*, October 1867, 749; Basil Hall, *Travels in North America, in the Years 1827 and 1828*, vol. 1 (Edinburgh: Cadell & Co., 1829), 10; Fredrick Marryat, *A Diary in America, with Remarks on Its Institutions*, vol. 1 (London: Longman, Orme, Brown, Green, & Longmans, 1839), 18–9; Max Berger, *The British Traveler in North America, 1836–1860* (New York: Columbia University Press, 1943), 25–7.

5. Melish, *Travels in the United States of America, in the Years 1806 & 1807, and 1809, 1810, & 1811*, vol. 2 (Philadelphia: Thomas & George Palmer, 1812), 247–8.

6. Cynthia A. Kierner, "Hospitality, Sociability, and Gender in the Southern Colonies," *Journal of Southern History* 62 (1996): 451–3; Paton Yoder, "Private Hospitality in the South, 1775–1850," *Mississippi Historical Review* 47 (1960): 426–8.

7. Hall, *Travels in North America*, vol. 1, 9, 117–8.

8. Kierner, "Hospitality, Sociability, and Gender," 453–9.

9. [Foster], *New York in Slices: by an Experienced Carver* (New York: W. F. Burgess, 1849), 66–7, 70–1; *New York Literary Gazette*, February 16, 1839; Hall, *Travels in North America*, vol. 1, 31–4; "The American Restaurant," *Scribner's Monthly*, January 1874; Abram C. Dayton, *Last Days of Knickerbocker Life in New York* (New York: George W. Harlan, 1882), 22–3, 42–3, 96–7.

10. [Foster], *New York in Slices*, 69; J. E. F., "Original Sketches of the Metropolis," *New-York Mirror*, August 22, 1840.

11. Thomas [Steele], *Delmonico's*, frontispiece, 176.

12. *The Diary of Philip Hone, 1828–1851*, ed. Allan Nevins (New York: Dodd, Mead & Co., 1936), 631; Strong, *Young Man in New York, 1835–1849*, vol. 1 of *The Diary of George Templeton Strong*, eds. Allan Nevins and Milton Halsey Thomas (New York: Macmillan, 1952), 315; Dayton, *Knickerbocker Life*, 118.

13. Dayton, *Knickerbocker Life*, 115; A. Homos [William Dean Howells], "Letters from an Altrurian Traveller: Dinner, Very Informally," *Cosmopolitan*, June 1894; Strong, *The Civil War, 1860–1865*, vol. 3 of *Diary of George Templeton Strong*, 39.

14. [Foster], *New York in Slices*, 73; *New Hampshire Patriot*, October 21, 1841.

15. Thomas [Steele], *Delmonico's*, 148; J. Cypress, "More Collineomania," *American Turf Register and Sporting Magazine*, October 1839; Foster, *New York in Slices*, 25; Spang, *The Invention of the Restaurant: Paris and Modern Gastronomic Culture* (Cambridge, MA: Harvard University Press, 2000), 208.

16. David S. Shields, "The World I Ate: The Profits of Global Consumption Culture," *Eighteenth-Century Life* 25, no. 2 (2001): 214–22; Stephen Mennell, "Of Gastronomes and Guides," in *The Taste Cultural Reader: Experience Food and Drink*, ed. Carolyn Korsmeyer (Oxford: Berg, 2005); Spang, *Invention of the Restaurant*, 146–58.

17. "Gastronomy and Gastronomer," parts 1–3, *Albion*, August 29, 1835; September 5, 1835; September 12, 1835. See "Royal Gastronomy," *Traveller and Spirit of the Times*, October 6, 1833; "Gastronomy. The Classics of the Table," *Campbell's*, June 16, 1844.

18. In his often quoted "Aphorisms," Brillat-Savarin wrote, "The destiny of nations depends on how they nourish themselves," and, "Tell me what you eat, and I shall tell you what you are." During this writing, the French generally agreed that national standing was gauged through a country's food. Brillat-Savarin, *The Physiology of Taste, or Meditations on Transcendental Gastronomy*, trans. by M. F. K Fisher (New York: Counterpoint, 1999), 3; Spang, *Invention of the Restaurant*, 42–52, 172, 175–9.

19. See S. E., "Tea Table Chat," *Ladies' Companion*, February 1836; *New York Mirror*, May 7, 1836; "A Chapter on Gastronomy," *Albion*, June 27, 1840; "A Chapter on the Art of Eating," *Daguerreotype*, January 8, 1848; C. W. Gesner, "Concerning Restaurants," *Harper's*, April 1866.

20. Blot, "Ancient and Modern Cookery," "A Dinner," *Galaxy*, November 1867; February 1868.

21. Blot, "A Dinner"; Blot, "Market," *Harper's Bazaar*, January 10, 1874; Review of *What*

to Eat and How to Cook It, New York Times, July 14, 1863; Jan Longone, "Professor Blot and the First French Cooking School in New York," parts 1 and 2, *Gastronomica: The Journal of Food and Culture* 1, no. 2 (2001): 65–71; no. 3 (2001): 53–9.

22. Blot, "American Cookery"; Thomas [Steele], *Delmonico's,* 89; Ranhofer, *The Epicurean. A Complete Treatise of Analytical and Practical Studies of the Culinary Art,* vol. 1 (New York: n.p., 1894), 4, 15–20, 169–581 passim; Ranhofer, *The Epicurean,* vol. 2, 583–1029 passim.

23. [Foster], *New York in Slices,* 67, 69, 70; "New York Daguerreotyped," *Putnam's,* April 1853; *New York Mirror,* May 7, 1836; McCabe, *Lights and Shadows of New York Life; Or, the Sights and Sensations of the Great City* (1872; rpt. London: Andre Deutsch, 1971).

24. Richard L. Bushman, *The Refinement of America: Persons, Houses, Cities* (New York: Alfred A. Knopf, 1992), 238–55; Russell Lynes, *The Domesticated Americans* (New York: Harper & Row, 1963), 176–203; "New York Daguerreotyped."

25. "Delmonico's Restaurateur," *Albion,* September 23, 1837.

26. Stuart M. Blumin, "Explaining the New Metropolis: Perception, Depiction, and Analysis in Mid-Nineteenth-Century New York City," *Journal of Urban History* 11 (1984): 9–10, 15; Robert Greenhalgh Albion, *The Rise of New York Port [1815–1860]* (1939; rpt. Newton Abbot, UK: David & Charles, 1970), 235–50; Wendy Gamber, "Tarnished Labor: The Home, the Market, and the Boardinghouse in Antebellum America," *Journal of the Early Republic* 22 (2002): 177–204.

27. Elizabeth Blackmar, *Manhattan for Rent, 1785–1850* (Ithaca, NY: Cornell University Press, 1989), 137–8; Timothy J. Gilfoyle, *City of Eros: New York City, Prostitution, and the Commercialization of Sex, 1790–1920* (New York: W. W. Norton, 1992), 98–104; Karen Halttunen, *Confidence Men and Painted Women: A Study of Middle-Class Culture in American, 1830–1870* (New Haven, CT: Yale University Press, 1982), 1–20; *New York Herald,* 1836, quoted in Gilfoyle, *City of Eros,* 96.

28. Brett Howard, "The Boarding House Reach," *Mankind* 7 (1982): 25–6, 50; Thomas Butler Gunn, *The Physiology of New York Boarding-Houses* (New York: Mason Brothers, 1857), 11, 34–5; Browne, *The Great Metropolis; A Mirror of New York* (San Francisco: H. H. Bancroft, 1869), 261; Walter Barrett [Joseph Alfred Scoville], *The Old Merchants of New York,* 5 vols. (New York: Carleton, 1863), quoted in Albion, *Rise of New York,* 264; [Foster], *New York in Slices,* 72, 75.

29. "New York Daguerreotyped"; Maud Howe Elliot, *Uncle Sam Ward and His Circle* (New York: Macmillan, 1938), 35.

30. Gilfoyle, *City of Eros,* 99; Thomas [Steele], *Delmonico's,* 148; McAllister, *Society,* 183–8.

31. Matthew Hale Smith, *Sunshine and Shadow in New York* (Hartford, CT: J. B. Burr, 1868), 657–8; "Delmonico's Coffee-House," *Dwight's American Magazine,* March 13, 1847; Anita Rapone, *The Guardian Life Insurance Company, 1860–1920: A History of German-American Enterprise* (New York: New York University Press, 1987), 1, 17.

32. "How to Get on the White List," *Independent,* May 24, 1860.

Works Cited

Albion, Robert Greenhalgh. *The Rise of New York Port [1815–1860].* 1939. Rpt. Newton Abbot, UK: David & Charles, 1970.

"The American Restaurant." *Scribner's Monthly,* January 1874.

Baltimore Sun, September 6, 1860.

Barrett, Walter [Joseph Alfred Scoville]. *The Old Merchants of New York.* 5 vols. New York: Carleton, 1863. Quoted in Robert Greenhalgh Albion, *The Rise of New York Port [1815–1860].* Newton Abbot, UK: David & Charles, 1970, 264.

Berger, Max. *The British Traveler in North America, 1836–1860.* New York: Columbia University Press, 1943.

Blackmar, Elizabeth. *Manhattan for Rent, 1785–1850.* Ithaca, NY: Cornell University Press, 1989.

Blot, Pierre. "A Dinner." *Galaxy,* February 1868.

_____. "American Cookery." *Galaxy,* October 1867.

_____. "Ancient and Modern Cookery." *Galaxy,* November 1867.

_____. "Market." *Harper's Bazaar,* January 10, 1874.

Blumin, Stewart M. "Explaining the New Metropolis: Perception, Depiction, and Analysis in Mid-Nineteenth-Century New York City." *Journal of Urban History* 11 (1984): 9–38.

Brillat-Savarin, Jean Anthelme. *The Physiology of Taste, or Meditations on Transcendental Gastronomy.* Translated by M. F. K. Fisher. New York: Counterpoint, 1999.

Browne, Junius Henri. *The Great Metropolis; A Mirror of New York.* San Francisco: H. H. Bancroft, 1869.

Bushman, Richard L. *The Refinement of America: Persons, Houses, Cities.* New York: Alfred A. Knopf, 1992.

Cypress, J. "More Collineomania." *American Turf Register and Sporting Magazine,* October 1839.

Daily Arkansas Gazette, May 25, 1877.

Daily (Chicago) Inter Ocean, January 6, 1886.

Dayton, Abram C. *Last Days of Knickerbocker Life in New York.* New York: George W. Harlan, 1882.

"Delmonico's Restaurateur." *Albion,* September 23, 1837, 303.

Duluth Minnesotian, March 15, 1873.

Dwight's American Magazine, March 13, 1847.

Elliot, Maud Howe. *Uncle Sam Ward and His Circle.* New York: Macmillan, 1938.

[Foster, George]. *New York in Slices: By an Experienced Carver.* New York: W. F. Burgess, 1849.

"Gastronomy and Gastronomer," Part 1. *Albion,* August 29, 1835.

"Gastronomy and Gastronomer," Part 2. *Albion,* September 5, 1835.

"Gastronomy and Gastronomer," Part 3. *Albion,* September 12, 1835.

Galveston (Texas) Daily News, December 29, 1874.

Gamber, Wendy. "Tarnished Labor: The Home, the Market, and the Boardinghouse in Antebellum America." *Journal of the Early Republic* 22 (2002): 177–204.

Gilfoyle, Timothy J. *City of Eros: New York City, Prostitution, and the Commercialization of Sex, 1790–1920.* New York: W. W. Norton, 1992.

Gunn, Thomas Butler *The Physiology of New York Boarding-Houses.* New York: Mason Bros., 1857.

Hale Smith, Matthew. *Sunshine and Shadow in New York.* Hartford, CT: J. B. Burr, 1868.

Hall, Basil. *Travels in North America, in the Years 1827 and 1828,* vol. 1. Edinburgh: Cadell, 1829.

Halttunen, Karen. *Confidence Men and Painted Women: A Study of Middle-Class Culture in America, 1830–1870.* New Haven, CT: Yale University Press, 1982.

Hone, Philip. *The Diary of Philip Hone, 1828–1851.* Edited by Allan Nevins. New York: Dodd, Mead, 1936.

Homos, A. [W. D. Howells]. "Letters from an Altrurian Traveller: Dinner, Very Informally." *Cosmopolitan,* June 1894.

Hooker, Richard J. *Food and Drink in America: A History.* Indianapolis: Bobbs-Merrill, 1981.

Howard, Brett. "The Boarding House Reach." *Mankind* 7 (1982): 25–26, 50.

Independent, May 24, 1860.

Kierner, Cynthia A. "Hospitality, Sociability, and Gender in the Southern Colonies." *Journal of Southern History* 62 (1996): 449–80.

Lexington (Kentucky) *Herald*, January 31, 1909.

Longone, Jan. "Professor Blot and the First French Cooking School in New York." Part 1. *Gastronomica: The Journal of Food and Culture* 1, no. 2 (2001): 65–71.

_____. "Professor Blot and the First French Cooking School in New York." Part 2. *Gastronomica: The Journal of Food and Culture* 1, no. 3 (2001): 53–59.

Lynes, Russell. *The Domesticated Americans*. New York: Harper & Row, 1963.

Magone v. Luckemeyer, 139 US 612 (1891).

Marryat, Fredrick. *A Diary in America, with Remarks on Its Institutions*, vol. 1. London: Longman, Orme, Brown, Green, & Longmans, 1839.

McAllister, Ward. *Society as I Have Found It*. 1890. Rpt. New York: Arno Press, 1975.

McCabe, James D. *Lights and Shadows of New York Life; Or, the Sights and Sensations of the Great City*. 1872. Rpt. London: Andre Deutsch, 1971.

Melish, John. *Travels in the United States of America, in the Years 1806 & 1807, and 1809, 1810, & 1811*, vol. 2. Philadelphia: Thomas & George Palmer, 1812.

Mennell, Stephen. "Of Gastronomes and Guides." In *The Taste Cultural Reader: Experience Food and Drink*, ed. Carolyn Korsmeyer. Oxford: Berg, 2005.

Milwaukee Journal, February 7, 1894.

New Hampshire Patriot, October 21, 1841.

"New York Daguerreotyped." *Putnam's*, April 1853.

New York Literary Gazette, February 16, 1839.

New York Mirror, August 22, 1840.

New York Times, March 7, 1870; February 19, 1885; January 7, 1891; July 14, 1863.

Ranhofer, Charles. *The Epicurean. A Complete Treatise of Analytical and Practical Studies of the Culinary Art*. 2 vols. New York: n.p., 1894.

Rapone, Anita. *The Guardian Life Insurance Company, 1860–1920: A History of German-American Enterprise*. New York: New York University Press, 1987.

St. Louis Daily Globe-Democrat, January 20, 1884.

Shields, David S. "The World I Ate: The Profits of Global Consumption Culture." *Eighteenth-Century Life* 25 (2001): 214–22.

Strong, George Templeton. *The Diary of George Templeton Strong*. Eds. Allan Nevins and Milton Halsey Thomas. 4 vols. New York: Macmillan, 1952.

Spang, Rebecca L. *The Invention of the Restaurant: Paris and Modern Gastronomic Culture* Cambridge, MA: Harvard University Press, 2000.

Thomas, Lately [Robert Steele]. *Delmonico's: A Century of Splendor*. Boston: Houghton Mifflin, 1967.

Walton, Chris. "Wagner, Otto and the Three Mathildas: Braut und Schwester bist du dem Bruder." *Musical Times* 143 (2002): 37–47.

Yoder, Paton. "Private Hospitality in the South, 1775–1850." *Mississippi Historical Review* 47 (1960): 419–33.

13

Is It Really Better to Travel Than to Arrive?

Airline Food as a Reflection of Consumer Anxiety

Guillaume de Syon

The dreariness of today's flying experiences often includes jokes about the food served onboard. Even passengers who have had the opportunity to fly in the rarefied business and first-class sections will usually comment on the leg space, the free drinks, yet rarely will they remember the food. This peculiar attitude is all the more puzzling because in most cultures food is as safe and even fruitful a topic of conversation as the weather. The plot thickens when one considers the financial situation of airline catering (a $40 billion/year operation worldwide), as well as its central role in drawing clients to a specific air carrier. Not only is a considerable amount of money and energy poured into designing and serving passengers, but the attempts to emulate a ground-based eating experience form a little understood aspect of airline travel.

Indeed, the seeming contradiction between airline food jokes and its importance in commercial air transport points to the universal tension about how, not just what, one eats. Studies of our patterns of eating are numerous,[1] and help answer the question as to why passengers generally come away disappointed, but this is only part of the equation: Most passengers surveyed would prefer to eat something (and even look forward to it) than not eat anything at all.[2] Paramount to the issue, airline food is also an intrinsic part of selling a travel seat, in a manner similar to airline advertising, flight attendant uniforms, and praising the latest airplane type acquired. However, whereas all associated forms of selling flight can be successful, this paper argues that food as a central feature of both entertainment and community fails to achieve the same measure of success when associated with flight technology. Several factors, including the tortuous (and tortured) history of airline food, the physical and environmental restrictions on board airplanes, and finally the economics of a globalized airline market all affect what should be an interesting dining experience. Nevertheless, we shall also see that, for all their misgivings about food, passengers expect and even welcome the opportunity to consume, suggesting that while not always enjoyable, the act of eating remains an essential ritual of flying.

To demonstrate these points, it will first be necessary to survey briefly the evolution of in-flight dining, whereby the early propping of one technology (the transport plane) in the 1920s, eventually came to require the devising of new supporting food techniques to make passengers comfortable.

Consuming in Flight

Meals structure our lives, either through their festive nature, or through the everyday expectation of a stable offering.[3] In so doing, they offer a sense of security, because we welcome the event, if only as a routine that divides our day. Where transportation was concerned, the advent of ocean liners and trains in the nineteenth century soon prompted the offering of meals that would serve as a dual mark of routine, and make the act of travel memorable. The menus that have survived confirm this state of affairs.[4]

In light of the already existing tradition of eating in a machine, it followed logically that aircraft would also include such a feature. Pre-war zeppelin flights over Germany were restricted to drinks and crackers, but postwar, the tradition of a picnic on board quickly became a standard feature.[5]

These quick bites were popular with passengers for several reasons. Not only did they take their minds off very bumpy rides, but the association of a sandwich with the more traditional bicycle excursion was not lost on participants. Sharing the scene already, however, was the generous supply of alcohol, both as a source of supplementary income for the airline and as one of comfort for concerned passengers.

British, French and German sources each claim their nations' respective airlines introduced the first full-fledged meals. Regardless of whose claim stands, the description of what it involved suggests how challenging the airplane was as a new consumer technology. For example Air Union (an Air France ancestor), one of the operators of the most profitable Paris-London air link in the interwar years, turned to railway caterer Compagnie International de Wagons-Lits to produce a three-course cold meal, which stewards (as they were then called) were to serve in exactly the same fashion as on board a first-class railcar. This assumed, of course, that none of the passengers fell sick, or that the waiter/flight attendant didn't fall on the floor due to turbulence.[6]

The greatest challenge, ironically, was not getting the food on board, but serving it satisfactorily. Up to World War II, airplanes flew unpressurized at low altitudes, and oil leaks, kerosene smells, deafening noise and serious vibrations were par for the course any passenger chose to fly.[7] All this contributed to a pathology of flying that culminated in the fear of falling or crashing. Thus any occupation that helped keep passengers' mind away from staring at the engines on the wings, for example, was a good thing.

Offering food thus became a central concern of airlines eager to draw passengers away from boats and trains. In April 1929, the same Paris–London airline saw the redesign of an aircraft cabin to accommodate dining tables. The three-course menu this time included freshly cooked food kept warm in covered baskets, but cost as well as security (windshear sent forks, knives and bottles flying in all directions) soon canceled the restaurant service and emulates on other transports.[8] Most airlines proceeded to downgrade to a heavily supplied bar, while some introduced female flight attendants expected to act as nurses administering aspirin and "cordials" to worried passengers.[9]

The only noticeable improvement came with the installation of onboard kitchens that could supply warm meals. Flying boats, the giant aircraft of that time, were the first to make routine use of these, followed by airships. The elite flavor of such dining experiences was often overtaken with wine and fine liquor, however, so the actual quality of the food is hard to gauge from the menu.[10] Nonetheless, the setup of such contraptions, which implied the use of open heating sources and large, hot fluid containers, also showed the importance assigned the role of food in entertaining guests. The way passengers ate, facing each other, also reflected the influence of restaurants on the ground and at sea, and confirmed the basic premise of the meal as a social occasion, where one's conversation partner might matter as much as the dish served. The pictures of the time do indeed contribute to making flying a viable option for businessmen and leisure travelers because they suggest normality, but they also hide the fact that flying remained a bumpy and noisy proposition, with spilled wine and ruined suits a given.

Such a state of affairs did not immediately improve after World War II, though aircraft technology had gotten a considerable boost. To begin, land-based planes had displaced flying boats, and their range now allowed transatlantic crossings in two or three hops. Navigational improvements, the discovery of new wind patterns, and work on pressurizing airliners all suggested a pending air age that would resolve much of the pathology of air travel that had existed earlier. It wasn't so. Whereas as seat comfort did improve the impression of flying on a Pullman coach, noise and vibrations remained a problem for many airlines. Witness, for example, the testimonial of a Ritz chef hired to work for Air France in 1946: "altitude was always [a problem]. Like most passengers, I became ill. While caring for them, I would run to the bathroom and throw up [before going back.]"[11]

Consequently, though flights got longer, airlines still favored feeding their passengers at transit stops. They could eat and especially drink at will, and flight attendants often knew enough to jack up the heat after takeoff to ensure most would doze off.[12] Not only did such landings break the monotony of long journeys, but they resolved the difficulty of making edible food on board. Furthermore, airline seats still did not feature fold-out trays. Passengers on the widely used DC-3 would still use the airline pillow to support their tray on their lap, emulating fast-food experiences of later years.[13] Some airline marketing departments, however, strategized differently about whether food on board was a hindrance or a blessing.

Air France was among the first airlines to decide as a matter of corporate policy that food would be the ideal way for passengers to pass the time, even on short hauls. In an era where flight entertainment was quasi nonexistent (movies did not become universal fare till the early 1970s), this novel concept suggested that, indeed, an airplane seat could double up as a fine dining room experience. Under these circumstances, airline food became a means to compete for passengers among airlines. Air France and BEA (a British Airways predecessor) competed on the Paris-London link to attract wealthy passengers by offering full meals. The French went so far as to call their service "the Epicurean,"[14] and to claim that, like in real French restaurants, "There is no tipping on Air France." As for BEA, its service was considered excellent, and some favored its seat setup, whereby eight seats faced each other over two tables, much in the manner of the formal dining room.[15]

These two details, high-end food and the placement of passengers dining came to form a central element of the golden age of early mass travel, when the seeming routine of a flight masked the adventure associated with a very expensive experience. Just as it did on the ground, food acted as a social marker. Airlines marketed eating as much as they did speed, technology, or the hospitality of their flight attendants. One could expect certain rituals, usually borrowed from hotels and ocean liners, to appear on board, too. Food no longer was about taste alone, but what it looked like and how it was offered.[16] Things might have progressed toward wild excess were it not for two related factors: the dearth of people able to afford the high cost of flying, and the need of airlines to make a profit on the investments they had begun making in new airplanes.

Such concerns about earning returns on brand new technology led to much discussion among airline boards and the International Air Transport Association, a quasi cartel that most air carriers were members of in the times of regulation. The solution IATA came up with was twofold: it recommended the introduction of economy class, but also regulated strictly what passengers might be offered, thus curtailing competition based on gimmicks.[17] This new state of affairs would quickly bring about food fights.

Fearing for their livelihoods, major carriers began gauging what others were offering by way of food to attract passengers. A notorious case in point occurred when Pan Am filed a complaint against Scandinavian Airlines (SAS) on the grounds that the bread it was distributing with meals in its transatlantic tourist class was of far too good a quality for cheaper fares. The "bread war" prompted IATA to appoint a special commission to define how to measure the quality of a sandwich; specifications on what could be served at lunch or dinner also followed.[18] This bizarre state of affairs prompted airlines to find other ways to draw up menus, and place certain foods in the appetizer categories to avoid any challenges had the food in question been a main course.

The design of the food presentation also became paramount in airline marketing departments. When operating its first postwar transatlantic service in 1955, Lufthansa had been forced to rely on paper cups and TWA silverware.[19] What the airline quickly realized by evaluating American as well as European competitors was that the food itself could be branded if served in an attractive, modern manner that doubled as a souvenir for passengers.[20] Design went beyond attractive modernist lines, however, as it was done in response to clear economic and technological imperatives.

The combination of regulatory frenzy with the need for branding in a modernist fashion the all-traditional meal signaled the difficulty of maintaining cost control for the airlines. The advent of the jet age in the late 1950s caused substantial capital increases for carriers wishing to compete efficiently. Standardization of airline operations saw its initial thrust at the time, and ranged from early computer reservations, to code-sharing, to ... tray tables! On the one hand, standardization of dimensions (tray tables began to have the same measurements in economy class as defined by the Boeing 707 and Douglas DC-8) meant a reduction in cost that was much welcome. Approaching famous designers to draw up unique tableware proved more difficult, for the expectation was a design that would be both modern and timeless. Tray ware reminiscent of doll sets would have to go hand in hand with traditionally designed menu cards and heavy foods more conveniently served in chinaware than luran (a kind of plastic).[21] Designer Robin Day, who worked for BOAC, also noted that his was a greatest challenge was logistics: not only did the finished product have to "feel modern," but it needed to fit into tight spaces, weigh little, be easy to grab, be stackable, heat resistant, washable, never lose its color and be reusable many times over.[22] (Raymond Loewy experienced similar challenges when designing Concorde cutlery for Air France.) The logistical nightmare also helps explain why the catering industry began to thrive as it could handle specialty assignments and cut costs. Marriott, for example, began offering meals in the late 1930s, and by the 1960s had broken into the overseas airline market.

Such rebranding also took away from the matter of the food served on board. And with good reason. As pressurization became standard on all aircraft by the late 1950s, no longer could a kitchen offer all amenities of a cooked meal. Airplanes flew at around 35,000 feet, but the inside of the cabin, where air is replenished once every two minutes on average, is pressurized to 8,000 feet or so, not to sea level.[23] The result is that human organs, especially the digestive system, swell, and the ability to taste is limited. As one commentator recently noted, it is hard to appreciate a wine's bouquet or the freshness of a brioche in the literally rarefied atmosphere of an aircraft: nostrils are dry, and associated dehydration prevents taste buds from working properly.[24] Airlines tried many times over to remedy this. BOAC (another British Airways ancestor) had special humidifiers installed on its new 747s when delivered in the 1970s. The heavy weight associated with these contraptions, however, soon ended the experiment.[25] The alternative was to introduce microwavable frozen foods, but the early microwaves were just as heavy and not always reliable, while later ones interfered with flight navigation systems.[26] Finally, one could cheat and add sugar to some beverages to stimulate the palate, or devise new dishes. Eventually, a standard model emerged, still in existence today.

The Sauce Saga

In 1973, as part of a revamping of its image, French airline UTA asked renowned chef Raymond Oliver to suggest sure-fire menu options. Oliver's challenge was substantial in that he needed to offer ideas that could be manufactured easily. His solution consisted of three hearty dishes that most fliers would have experienced at home or in a low-brow restaurant: coq au vin, veal in cream sauce, and beef bourguignon. All three are traditionally heavy items to digest, which would take care of the need to feed passengers again on long flights. Most importantly, when reheated, such dishes lost little of their flavor, and dryness did not affect the meat doused in sauce. This triad came to form the foundation of many airlines' economy menus, and the "chicken or fish" variation is itself based on that approach.[27]

From the 1970s onward then airline catering reached a level of maturity in both the design and the production of airline menus. The preceding examples are but the tip of the iceberg of intricacies involved in bringing food to a passenger table. Other changes that affected such service came later in the consolidation of catering groups, deregulation and the advent of no-frill airlines. Cyclical "bad airline years" such as 1981, 1991 and 2001 also influenced changes in food service. (The latter perhaps had the greatest impact as it banned for good the use of large carving knives in first class, and of metal cutlery in economy.) Regardless of these factors, food remains a central element to airline identity and to convincing a passenger to hop onboard.[28]

Not a week goes by without an airline announcing it has contracted with a famous chef to design onboard meals.[29] Fashion as well as evolving taste allow for such reinvention, especially in the slice of the market most coveted: business-class consumers. Yet any chef's menu, aside from the appetizers, will usually come back to variations on the old standbys Raymond Oliver and others introduced: the food has to be wet, though nowadays it might be Indian rather than French.

The illusion of the proper meal does not end with the technological restrictions an aircraft environment imposes, but with the economics of seating. With the exception of a few airline experiments, seats facing over a table, even in first class, are now a thing of the past. Instead, business-class passengers are treated to exquisitely comfortable seats that face ... the back of another seat.

Breaking Bread

As several food anthropologists have noted, the prestige of a good meal depends as much on the surroundings where food is served as on what appears on the table. In a time of glamour, the illusion might be maintained.[30] Nowadays, it does not match the flying experience, even where business and first-class sections are concerned, and where the food may be rated highly. Indeed, sociological surveys show that to most consumers, including the fortuned ones, eating out means a special setting, a chosen occasion, and the choice of dining companions.[31] The "prawn cocktail" or "steak dinner" rituals identified on either side of the Atlantic do not fit into a winged metal tube. Eating out/in calls for eating in company, which is certainly the case when flying, but it is more akin to the proverbial "bowling alone" experience described elsewhere:[32] the dual veneer of class and community that is seemingly confirmed in the ads for airline service and food eclipses individual preferences thus leaves little space for any experience that might offer a lasting memory. The question remains whether there is indeed a sense of community on board that would allow for a food experience to be successful.

If business travelers are considered the proverbial bulls of the herd, then perhaps community is to be found in the biggest portion of travelers? Some airline surveys suggest this is so, especially because of the presence of organized travel groups. Flight attendants who have written tell-alls offer anecdotes of people rushing to eat their meals because it is both a pass-time as well as a form of restaurant experience. As comedian Shelley Berman once noted, a closer look at what is offered as food suggests that the nature of the food offered matters less than the fact that it is offered at all (as a kind of "freebie").[33] The comedy, however, turns into a bitter farce in the face of airline economics.

Under the economic condition airlines experience, economy-class seats amortize costs, but do not generally provide the sought-after margin. Mass travel here has come to require mass consumerism, and the design of "one kind fits all" meals. Some airlines branded their identity as food connoisseurs, yet in so doing committed themselves to a giant budget. Singapore Airlines, for example, devoted some 6 percent of its yearly budget starting in the 1970s to cabin services alone.[34] Simply put, airlines have had to cut costs in such a way that the very size of portions requires careful technological and business consideration. Two ounces of chopped onions can become three or four in a rich meal, but when 30,000 trays are prepared for transatlantic routes, the cost add-ons can be astronomical. Respected chefs who volunteer recipes for, say, chicken, soon learn that one cannot simply offer a thigh to one passenger and a wing to another: hence the standard breast portion.[35] Guidelines have thus followed, some broadly defined for catering companies, others going so far as to specify which size knife is necessary to prepare a 1.5"-long thin-sliced carrot julienne.[36] Further cost-cutting measures include using established brands to ensure passenger confidence in the meal. In so doing, however, airlines have also assumed the "one size fits all" approach to food: while reducing food costs, it also took away from the identity of food.

We Are Where We Eat— but Where Is That?

In a recent volume on *Consuming Geography*, David Bell and Gill Valentine note the peculiarities of cooking global and eating local in reference to fast-food chains.[37]

The very nature of mass transport reflects in many ways similar issues of food globalization. On the positive side, one can pre-order airline menus varying from Hindu, Kosher, and Muslim to salt-free and vegetarian. While cross-border dietary requirements have become an option for concerned passengers, there is little room for variations on the standard menu, so that disappointment is bound to set in among the economy-class community:[38] a California pizza may shock an Italian salesman, just as Swiss steak (a variation of beef bourguignon) will have any self-respecting Helvetian in stitches (it does not exist in Switzerland). Nobody can be completely pleased. This has not stopped, however, the appearance of an identity associated with airline food, whereby what is served may look like any soft sandwich anywhere, but the surroundings, once again, assume a new importance.

While airline food, first designed to calm fears of flying, in some ways added to the tensions associated with modern flight, it remains a staple of the flight ritual. Passengers look forward to breaking not so much the fear, but the monotony of flying with the pre-meal drinks; and even airlines no longer serving a choice of meals often print a symbolic menu on the back of a postcard or an ad. Even standard health warnings about overeating on board (the air pressure hurts the digestion) do not stop most from inhaling their portions: flight may have become common, yet food retains a certain fascination.[39]

Food, in fact, is expected, regardless of what it consists of. However, the recent trends in airline entertainment reflect a shift away from consuming towards watching TV. Aside from upper-class meals, where airlines continue to emphasize uniqueness of service,[40] replacing food as entertainment, big and small screens now grace passenger seating in a manner reminiscent of the shift in household dining when the television appeared. One may not draw conclusions on the state of the family in an airplane, for the experience is limited in time, but it does suggest that airlines cutting back on their food offerings may in fact be justified: if food as a community experience is in fact impossible on board, then perhaps the individual should be left to his or her own devices to acquire and partake in the food s/he enjoys.

Conclusion

This chapter began with the suggestion that airline food was a doomed experiment, yet one that had become an intrinsic part of the experience of flying: it is both a prop and a hindrance to air transport providers. As historian of technology Melvin Kranzberg once noted somewhat whimsically, yet accurately, invention is the mother of necessity, not the other way around. Airlines first tried to lure elite travelers through features associated with fine dining, like that found aboard ocean liners, but created an illusionary experience, yet one that airline consumers expect: the constant renewal of claims to fine dining has not ceased.

Although airline advertising has suggested for some seventy years that eating would contribute to the uniqueness of flying, the very structure of airliners made it almost impossible to succeed. Most passengers have to face forward and stare at their meals and other seats rather than at their travel partners.

In addition, the air conditioning on board often condemns the best-prepared meals to cool down in seconds, thus further limiting what might be available on board. As comfort seating is further restricted for economic reasons, travelers seek solace in either alcohol or a TV screen, or both. Hence, airline food as part of the adventure of airline travel has also lost its glamour through experience.[41] The ideas that worked in ground transportation do not transpose themselves well 30,000 feet above the ground, and take a second seat to speed, hoped-for efficiency, and the promise of reaching a destination. Yet the nature of the travel experience, and the need to pass time and experience something in common between the ground and the air also means that, for all their misgivings about what will appear in their tray, passengers actually look forward to the dining event. In so doing, they do not confirm Robert Louis Stevenson's assertion that it is better to travel than to arrive, but rather that as a creature of habits, we cling to notions of normality regardless of circumstances.

Notes

Thanks are due Joseph Corn for helpful comments on an earlier version of this chapter presented at the Hagley Fellows Conference in March 2007. Thanks also to my mother Joëlle de Syon and my brother Edouard, who also offered helpful suggestions based on their extensive food and travel experiences.

1. See, for example, the ongoing studies of sociologist Ann Murcott (e.g., *The Nation's Diet: The Social Science of Food Choice* (London: Routledge, 1999); Alan Beardsworth and Teresa Keil, *Sociology on the Menu: An Invitation to the Study of Food and Society* (London: Routledge, 1997); Steven Menell, *All Manners of Food: Eating and Taste in England and France from the Middle Ages to the Present* (London: Blackwell, 1985).

2. Denise Winterman, "The Mile-High Food Fight," *BBC News Magazine* (August 24, 2005), http://news.bbc.co.uk/2/hi/uk_news/magazine/4173640.stm (accessed March 2007).

3. Jeremy McClancy, *Consuming Culture* (New York: Henry Holt, 1992), 52–54.

4. August Menken, *The Railroad Passenger Car* (Baltimore: Johns Hopkins University Press, 2000), 34–37; 176–78.

5. Guillaume de Syon, *Zeppelin: Germany and the Airship, 1900–1939* (Baltimore: Johns Hopkins University Press, 2002), 66.

6. Edmont Petit, *La vie quotidienne dans l'aviation en France au début du XXe siècle* (Paris: Hachette, 1977), 205.

7. Roger Bilstein, "Air Travel and the Traveling Public: The American Experience, 1920–1970," in *From Airships to Airbus: The History of Civil and Commercial Aviation*, vol. 2, ed. William F. Trimble (Washington, D.C.: Smithsonian Institution, 1995), 94.

8. Petit, 206.

9. Joseph Corn, *The Winged Gospel* (New York: Oxford University Press, 1983), 89.

10. University of Texas at Dallas, History of Aviation Archive, papers of Clara Adams, Folders 2, 3, 4; boxes 7, 19.

11. Quoted in Philippe-Michel Thibault, *Mythologies à bord* (Paris: Gallimard, 2005), 110.

12. Hermann Terjung, *Landung im Taifun* (Munich: GeraMond, 2001), 13–15.

13. National Air and Space Museum Archives, Washington, D.C., file FO–09403025, typescript of a speech delivered at the Society of Automotive Engineers in December 1946, complaining of the lack of proper airplane tray supports.

14. George Banks, *Gourmet and Glamour in the Sky* (Peterborough, UK: GMS Enterprises, 2006), 12.
15. Keith Lovegrove, *Airline Identity, Design and Culture* (New York: TeNeues, 2000), 64.
16. E. N. Anderson, *Everyone Eats* (New York: New York University Press, 2005), 124–25.
17. Günther Behrendt, *Die Entwicklung der Marktstruktur im internationalen Luftverkehr* (Berlin: Duncker & Humblot, 1961), 77; Hans-Joachim Burchard, "Preiskartell im internationalen Luftverkehr," *Wirtschaftsdienst* 32, no. 2 (1952): 103–17.
18. Behrendt, 78, n. 24. SAS was eventually fined $20,000 for having served fresh bread.
19. Deutsche Lufthansa archives, Cologne, Germany: "DLH 1955 Eröffnungsflüge LH 401/421," confidential report re FRA-NYC 3/4 June, 6, 1955.
20. Jochen Eisenbrand, "Dining Aloft," in *Airworld,* eds. A. von Vegesack and J. Eisenbrand (Weil am Rhein, Germany: Vitra Design Museum, 2004), 223.
21. Volker Fischer, *The Wings of the Crane* (Stuttgart, Germany: Axel Menges, 2005), 123.
22. Lesely Jackson, *Robin and Lucienne Day* (Princeton, NJ: Princeton Architectural Press, 2001), 136–38.
23. Mark Gottdiener, *Life in the Air* (Lanham, MD: Rowman & Littlefield, 2001), 103–4.
24. Keith Lovegrove, *Airline Identity, Design and* Culture (New York: TeNeues, 2000), 73.
25. *The Air Traveller's Handbook* (New York: Simon & Schuster, 1978), 148.
26. Banks, 103.
27. Banks, 13; for a summary of airline menu recipes in the 1970s and 1980s, see Glenn I. Howe, *Dinner in the Clouds: Great International Airline Recipes* (Corona del Mar, CA: Zeta, 1985), 9–110.
28. Lovegrove, 73, 79.
29. Airline communiqués at major Web sites usually feature the latest food innovations. See also <www.airlinemeals.net>.
30. Gottdiener, 103.
31. Alan Warde and Lydia Martens, "The Prawn Cocktail Ritual," in *Consuming Passions: Food in the Age of Anxiety,* eds. Sian Griffiths and Jennifer Wallace (Manchester, UK: Mandolin, 1998), 118–20.
32. Robert D. Putnam, *Bowling Alone: The Collapse and Revival of American Community* (New York: Simon & Schuster, 2000).
33. Shelley Berman, *Up in the Air* (Los Angeles: Price Stern Sloan, 1986), 66–67.
34. *The Air Traveller's Handbook*, 64.
35. Susan Carey, "Take 2,000 Chicken Thighs, Add 600 Eggs, Stir...," *Wall Street Journal,* August 11, 1997; Sarah Murray, "Haute Cuisine," *Financial Times,* May 29, 2006.
36. Lovegrove, 69.
37. David Bell and Gill Valentine, eds., *Consuming Geographies: We Are Where We Eat* (London: Routledge, 1997), 190.
38. Lovegrove, 69.
39. See, for example, "Dangers of Airline Food," <http://ash.org/airlinefood.html> (accessed April 2007); *Airline Food Report 2003,* <http://www.pcrm.org/health/reports/airline_food_report.html> (accessed April 2007).
40. Kim Severson, "What's Cooking in First Class? Eating and Indulging, You Can Bet It's Not Peanuts," *New York Times,* April 16, 2007.
41. Virginia Postrel, "Up, Up and Away," *Atlantic Monthly,* January 2007, 161.

Works Cited

Anderson, E. N. *Everyone Eats.* New York: New York University Press, 2005.
Banks, George. *Gourmet and Glamour in the Sky.* Peterborough, UK: GMS Enterprises, 2006.

Beardsworth, Alan, and Teresa Keil, eds. *Sociology on the Menu: An Invitation to the Study of Food and Society*. London: Routledge, 1997.

Behrendt, Günther. *Die Entwicklung der Marktstrukture im internationalen Luftverkehr*. Berlin: Duncker & Humblot, 1961.

Bell, David, and Gill Valentine, eds. *Consuming Geographies: We Are Where We Eat*. London: Routledge, 1997.

Berman, Shelley. *Up in the Air*. Los Angeles: Price Stern Sloan, 1986.

Burchard, Hans-Joachim. "Preiskartell im internationalen Luftverkehr." *Wirtschaftsdienst* 32 (1952): 103–117.

Corn, Joseph. *The Winged Gospel*. New York: Oxford University Press, 1983.

de Syon, Guillaume. *Zeppelin: Germany and the Airship, 1900–1939*. Baltimore: Johns Hopkins University Press, 2002.

Fischer, Volker. *The Wings of the Crane*. Stuttgart, Germany: Axel Menges, 2005.

Gottdiener, Mark. *Life in the Air*. Lanham, MD: Rowman & Littlefield, 2001.

Griffiths, Sian, and Jennifer Wallace, eds. *Consuming Passions: Food in the Age of Anxiety*. Manchester, UK: Mandolin, 1998.

Howe, Glenn I. *Dinner in the Clouds: Great International Airline Recipes*. Corona del Mar, CA: Zeta, 1985.

Jackson, Lesely. *Robin and Lucienne Day*. Princeton, NJ: Princeton Architectural Press, 2001.

Lovegrove, Keith. *Airline Identity, Design and Culture*. New York: TeNeues, 2000.

McClancy, Jeremy. *Consuming Culture*. New York: Henry Holt, 1992.

Menell, Steven. *All Manners of Food: Eating and Taste in England and France from the Middle Ages to the Present*. London: Blackwell, 1985.

Menken, August. *The Railroad Passenger Car*. Baltimore: Johns Hopkins University Press, 2000.

Murcott, Ann, ed. *The Nation's Diet: The Social Science of Food Choice*. London: Routledge, 1999.

Petit, Edmond. *La vie quotidienne dans l'aviation en France au début du XXe siècle*. Paris: Hachette, 1977.

Putnam, Robert D. *Bowling Alone: The Collapse and Revival of American Community*. New York: Simon & Schuster, 2000.

Terjung, Hermann. *Landung im Taifun*. Munich, Germany: GeraMond, 2001.

Thibault, Philippe-Michel. *Mythologies à bord*. Paris: Gallimard, 2005.

Trimble, William F., ed. *From Airships to Airbus: The History of Civil and Commercial Aviation*, vol. 2. Washington, D.C.: Smithsonian, 1995.

Varley, Helen. *The Air Traveller's Handbook*. New York: Simon & Schuster, 1978.

Vegesack, Alexander von, and J. Eisenbrand, eds. *Airworld*. Weil am Rhein, Germany: Vitra Design Museum, 2004.

14

Deconstructing the Myth of the Dysfunctional Black Family in the Film *Soul Food*

TINA M. HARRIS

Historically, movie industry moguls have attempted to incite moral responsibility in their filmmakers, but such efforts have not always been successful. In an effort to enlighten the industry on the social significance of cultural sensitivity, whereby the reality of ethnic and cultural diversity is appreciated and not exploited, heavyweights Sergei Eisenstein and Charles Chaplin were morally compelled to address this lack of representation in film. The compelling need for moral initiatives and responsibility in the entertainment industry remains as critical as ever. Aside from racism and prejudice, a frequently cited reason for apathy regarding fair cultural and racial representation is the few non–White writers, producers, and directors creating these cinematic images. Some members of the film industry community have become engaged in this battle by producing, writing, and financing their own cinematic endeavors.

One such film that reflects this vision is *Soul Food*. Using a popular culture approach, this essay uses this film as a narrative text to illustrate the performative function the dinner ritual serves for the on-screen family, the Josephs. Through the Sunday dinner ritual observed in the film, the audience is introduced to the Joseph family and its strong identity, which is challenged when the family is faced with tragedy. Audiences who witness the family engaging in this ritual are able to observe nonstereotypical images of Blackness virtually nonexistent in other mainstreams media. The weekly interaction allows the Josephs to use the dinner as a means for maintaining relational intimacy, connection, and solidarity while instilling values and beliefs only learned through family relationships. The actual dinner scenes are few in the film; however, the importance of maintaining the Joseph family tradition serves as a catalyst for understanding the complex identities of each family member, thereby deconstructing the stereotypical myths historically associated with African Americans. By examining the issues or dialectical tensions that transition the family into a process of redefining itself, this essay will demonstrate how *Soul Food* functions to debunk the myth of the dysfunctional Black family. The film reflects the strength of the Black family and its ability to preserve itself despite the trials and tribulations that come. Through role negotiation and redefinition of the main characters, we observe the dialectical tensions that threaten to tear apart the Joseph family. Ultimately, the family identity, though redefined, simultaneously remains intact and reframes (deconstructs) stereotypic depictions of what it means to be an African American family.

Historical Depictions of African American Identity

In terms of the Black family, stereotypes that attempted to frame this interpersonal network as highly dysfunctional emerged from the historic work of Moynihan[2] in 1965. His interpretation of census data positioned the Black family as a social system innately predisposed to a matriarchal structure, yet failed to take into account the economic and social disparities forced upon African Americans that resulted from slavery and institutional racism. In order to preserve what was left of the African American community because of the slave trade and subsequent dissolution of kin networks, the family was restructured to compensate for its imposed reconstitution. This redefinition called for the female to become the head of household, holding the family together by any means necessary. Comparing this "change" to the White familial (patriarchal) structure, Moynihan attempted to substantiate his claims of the dysfunctional Black family by using census data to support his belief that this "abnormal role reversal" was an innate part of Blackness. Though his assumptions have been widely debated, it remains apparent that a thread of racism continues to frame societal understandings and perceptions of the Black family.

Regarding media and visual images, *The Cosby Show*, however, is one show that attempted to debunk these stereotypes. The show was both praised for communicating a positive image of African American identity and criticized for not being "black" enough. The Huxtable family was an upper-class, financially stable family comprised of a medical doctor father, lawyer mother, and five children. This television family provided a glimpse into the life of a racialized family that overcame societal barriers (i.e., racism) and attained the American Dream; however, the show was heavily criticized for painting a utopian image of Black life in the U.S. In stark contrast to other shows depicting the Black family (*Good Times, The Jeffersons*), *The Cosby Sho*w created the illusion of a race-free zone where issues of race no longer plagued Blacks. The positive image of a family committed to education, hard work, familial love, and community was overshadowed by the show's failure to address the hardships of race that continued to haunt African Americans in the real world.

A Contemporary Depiction of the Black Family

The film *Soul Food* is an excellent example of a visual text that aims to debunk the myth of the dysfunctional Black family. The narratives embedded within the film reveal a family fraught with tension and emotion as it attempts to redefine itself in the midst of tragedy. While their Blackness is an obvious cultural marker to the viewing audience, the centrality and saliency of their identity as a family, a cultural community, take center stage. It is through the stories of the different characters of the Joseph family that we understand the complexities that come with being a family that happens to be Black.

The Dinner Ritual

The dinner ritual is a real-life experience that has become commodified since the 20th century. While the dinner ritual provides families with a sense of unity and connection, it has become a lost art form relegated to holidays and special occasions such as weddings and funerals. As Kennedy and Wolin and Bennett describe it, a ritual has a symbolic function within the communicative process which occurs systematically. More importantly, "eating and its associated activities are embodied, social practices that are meaningful and meaning-making."[1] Similarly, life-altering events such as death, divorce, and remarriage contribute to the demise of this family tradition. Unfortunately, the dinner ritual has lost its cultural significance. This may be attributed to the intense societal and familial pressures placed on family members to de-center the family from Western culture. When a family member becomes more focused on him/herself than their family, a tension emerges that ultimately compromises the family unit and the overall well-being of the family member. In the case of the Joseph family, the Sunday dinner ritual is a private ceremony that provides a discursive space within which the family communicates. This ceremony functions to construct an increased level of relational intimacy among and between family members. The family gathers every Sunday after church at Big Mama's house to partake in the weekly feast. It is in these scenes that we observe the dialectical tension each daughter experiences while dealing with the stress of balancing family life and personal life.

The narrative function of a film is to tell a story through sound and image that is predicated on a climax and resolution that engages its audience in the storytelling process The story told in *Soul Food* is one of solidarity and identity negotiation within the context of a family crisis. Together, these variables structure a complicated story of family communication and discourse transcending racial and cultural differences.

As with other forms of communication, the critical discourse the characters engage in on-screen is a celebration of human events vis-à-vis public dialogue. The viewer is afforded the opportunity to better understand how the communication between family members becomes strained when their familial and individual identities are juxtaposed against each other. It is these images that ultimately function to deconstruct societal notions of and perceptions about the Black family. The trend observed in *Soul Food* is the dinner ritual, which has lost its performative function within the American family. By examining the relational tensions revealed through the performative context of the dinner ritual, we understand how the characters' experiences embrace the very essence of Blackness and humanity in American society as we know it.

Soul Food: Compromising Family and Self

The primary characters of this film experience moral dilemmas that are similar yet uniquely different in their ability to capture this social phenomenon of the lost art of the dinner ritual. The three sisters (Bird, Teri, and Max) are at different stages in their personal and private lives, and it is at this crossroad that they begin to experience frustration with their desires to maintain their individuality within the context of family. As a visual text, *Soul Food* provides a variety of images representing African Americans that challenge those that distort the reality of their existence. It takes to task racial misrepresentations in film and provides an alternative text to the historical definition of the African American family.

In the opening scene of the film, the camera pans an array of family portraits in the Joseph family home. The sound track plays in the background, and the lyrics resound as the singers vocalize the primary theme of the film. The lyrics reflect the symbolism embodied by the dinner feast prepared by Mama: an expression of love that is "like food for the soul." The narrator is grandson Ahmad, who contextualizes for the audience the significance of the Sunday dinner ritual. We learn that the dinner solidifies family ties and provides a time to bond and maintain relational intimacy.

For years, the matriarch, Big Mama, committed herself to preparing a lavish feast for her family every Sunday afternoon after church. Resplendent with a delectable array of vegetables, meats, and desserts, the Sunday dinner ritual provides a context within which the family members share current events as experienced by the entire kin unit. Over time, the dinner ritual became a mainstay for the entire family. In subsequent scenes after the first dinner, the audience is presented with stories and characters that collectively function to debunk the myth of the dysfunctional Black family. Although each character is faced with her own set of issues, we soon learn that they in fact do *not* conform to the aforementioned stereotypes frequently associated with African Americans, specifically African American women. Rather, the sisters face issues that are all too common to women across all racial and ethnic groups who are a part of a familial network. As will be articulated in the following section, the Joseph sisters face internal and external pressures that threaten the very existence of the family as they know it.

Dialectical Tensions: Reframing the Joseph Family

Communication scholar Leslie Baxter posits that personal relationships have dialectics that reflect opposing and continuous tensions. Wood identifies the three types of tensions that plague these interpersonal networks. *Autonomy/connection* refers to an individual's desire to be both separate from and connected to their relational partner(s). This tension occurs when an attempt is made to balance one's competing identities as an individual and a partner. *Novelty/predictability* involves a need for things routine and novel, wherein a person desires a sense of what to expect in the relationship; however, when things are too predictable, s/he may become bored. *Openness/closedness* involves pressure to establish and maintain relational intimacy with one's partner. S/he desires to share intimate details of her/his life with her/his partner, while also reserving a measure of privacy. Responses to these tensions are "consequences" and may result in neutralization (establishing balance), separation (one tension is preferred over another), or segmentation (a demarcation of boundaries for those tensions). Individuals experiencing these tensions ultimately choose strategies that create stability.

The sisters in *Soul Food* are excellent examples of these tensions. Their narratives reveal very complex characters who struggle for normalcy and balance. Initial scenes appear to introduce us to the Jezebel stereotype through Bird and two different versions of the "pseudo-matriarch" in Teri and Max. Recent newlywed Bird is trying to navigate the difficult terrain of married life and life as a Joseph. Despite her new relational status, Bird is observed as a complex character having problems maintaining a healthy balance in her life between these two worlds. She seemingly perpetuates the Jezebel stereotype with her sexual appetite with her husband and use of her feminine wiles with a former boyfriend to secure employment for husband Lemuel.

Teri embodies a contemporary representation of a partial or pseudo-matriarch. She is married, embraces her professional identity (e.g., lawyer), and assumes the masculine gender role in her marriage to Miles. We soon find her to be a controlling woman who is unrelenting in making most, if not all, major marital decisions without input from her husband. Conversely, Max seems to have it all: a loving husband, three children, and a beautiful home. Unlike her siblings, she has successfully managed to become actively engaged in life as a wife/mother and member of the Joseph clan. Max's evolution into the pseudo-matriarch does not occur until Mama Joe becomes ill and no longer occupies the role of matriarch. Although the first dinner scene does not deconstruct the complexities embodied in this sisterhood and family, the dinner ritual itself does provide a context for familial commitment despite the hardships the family faces.

The Dinner Ritual: The Compromise and the Fallout

In the first dinner scene, the Joseph family is enjoying one another's company. The audience is offered a sneak preview of what is to come. Although the sibling rivalry is observed by the audience as the sisters vie for approval from Mama Joe, the tensions that threaten to strain their relationships are subtle, waiting for the precise moment at which to explode. Mama Joe is able to beautifully circumvent all potential outbursts by reminding them of the importance of family and their responsibility to live peaceably with and to love each other like a family should. The thread that holds the family together begins to unravel when Mama Joe becomes gravely ill from her diabetes, slips into a coma, and is admitted into the ICU. In an effort to maintain normalcy, Max proposes the family continue its Sunday dinner ritual despite Mama Joe's hospitalization. Taking extreme offense to Max's perceived insensitivity to Mama Joe's health, Teri questions the absurdity of such a proposal. Max proclaims she will not let Teri "ruin a 40-year family tradition!" Teri responds by staking her claim as the oldest daughter whose professional success, in her eyes, qualifies her to be the matriarch in Big Mama's absence. To circumvent further conflict, Bird suggests they take a vote. The majority vote to have Sunday dinner, which happens to be the next day; however, the façade of familial solidarity and commitment to the ritual dissolves when Bird, her husband, and the church deacon are the only ones who show up.

The volatile exchange between Max and Teri is symptomatic of the rivalry that has been plaguing the family for years. After Big Mama's death, the sisters and the Josephs must deal with their new family identity, which largely remained intact, due in part to the Sunday dinner ritual, a decades-long mainstay. The dinner ritual successfully helped foster a close, intimate bond between the siblings, and its absence and pending demise foreshadowed the internal turmoil plaguing the Joseph sisters. As their narratives unfold, two questions emerge: "What dialectical tensions fracture the remaining threads of the Joseph family dinner ritual?" and "How is the dinner ritual reintroduced after dramatic shifts in their relational landscape?" In the following section, each sister's experience with competing identities and their impact on the family will be briefly described. A discussion will then follow of how these tensions restructured the family's identity and the significance of the Sunday dinner ritual.

LOSING RELATIONAL GROUND: NEGOTIATING TERI

The first sibling to be explored is Teri, the eldest daughter. In terms of dialectical tensions, Teri is observed as dealing with a desire for autonomy/connection, to be separate from yet connected to her family and husband. Her identities as a professional, wife, and sister are in direct competition with each other. She responds to these tensions through separation, whereby her preference for her professional identity over her familial identities becomes apparent. Within the Joseph family, she takes on the role of provider because of her professional success as a lawyer. While this role is optional, Teri uses her wealth to define who she is and how her family should treat her. Additionally, as the eldest, the family appears to expect Teri to take care of them, which she uses to manipulate the family into selling Big Mama's home. Teri argues she is guiding the family toward financial stability. Her efforts to preserve the family's identity are masked by her management of this problem and taking advantage of her role as eldest, both of which lack sincerity. Teri's familial commitment is compromised by her preoccupation with power and status in all areas of her life.

As she and Max struggle over who will assume Big Mama's role as matriarch, Teri repeatedly reminds her siblings of her wealth and attempts to capitalize on this family crisis by underscoring her personal success and rank in the family social order. This approach is patterned after her strategy for meeting her individual identity needs through work, which are grounded in her desire for power and status. Teri defines herself as a career woman first and, as a consequence, her commitment to career is mirrored in her marriage. She appears to want complete control over her own destiny and the destiny of others whom she feels are incapable of making such choices. Throughout the film, Teri uses manipulative power plays to belittle her sisters, particularly Max, and her husband Miles as they each attempt to make decisions directly impacting the family's identity. By referring to herself as "the reliable one" and insulting Max for not finishing college, Teri perpetuates an image of strength and stability she feels others should respect and model. Unfortunately, her efforts backfire and place her in a less powerful position within the family hierarchy and her marriage.

Instead of nurturing her marriage relationship, Teri is more concerned with being a successful lawyer and "committed" family member. It becomes glaringly evident that Teri's attempts to deal with this dialectical tension that emerges in the midst of family crisis are counterintuitive. She blatantly ignores Miles' needs as her husband, which ultimately affects their relational dynamics. Miles still has strong feelings of commitment to his family, but is forced to formally dissolve his stagnant marriage. As her emotionally destructive behaviors suggest, Teri's self-absorption creates a tension regarding how she defines herself within the context of family and career. Unlike her siblings, Teri is more concerned with the control and power afforded her because of her status in the family hierarchy. Teri's persona is one of limited emotional and relational intimacy. Very seldom do we see her share feelings of love, kindness, or closeness with any of her family members. Instead, Teri's familial relationships are treated as power relationships within an "organization" that is being downsized and restructured.

NAVIGATING MARITAL TERRAIN AND INTIMACY: NEGOTIATING BIRD

Youngest sister Robin is affectionately referred to as Bird. Openness/closedness is the dialectical tension experienced by Bird, who feels intense pressure to have relational intimacy with husband (and ex-con) Lem, and rightly so. Unfortunately, relational intimacy and trust are continually compromised, but Bird attempts to respond to these tensions through segmentation (a demarcation of boundaries for those tensions). These boundaries become blurred as she is "forced" to help her husband find steady employment. Bird's experiences as a wife, sister, and businesswoman are most effective in capturing the very nature of the proposed dialectical tension between family and individual identity. Newlywed Bird appears uncertain about her new role as a wife coupled with her identity as a businesswoman. Bird manages and owns a beauty salon financed by Teri, and attempts to create a happy medium between home and work. Unlike her two older sisters, Bird is willing to work towards having both a family life and career without too much compromise.

This dialectical tension becomes apparent as Bird negotiates her new identity as a wife. Thus far, Bird has not gained the financial independence she is aspiring to reach. Unable to absorb the costs of her wedding and new business, Bird remains dependent on Teri to provide the resources for both events. Her financial dependence places her in a position of reliance on family as she attempts to define herself outside of the family unit. Bird's dialectical tension occurs during the sisters' confrontation with Teri over the house. After Teri abruptly leaves the meeting, Bird and Max discuss the state of the family and how important family is in defining who they are. It is in this conversation that Bird reveals how she wants to gain a sense of fulfillment in her familial and individual identities. More importantly, she wants to maintain a healthy balance without giving up her dream of having a career and family of her own. This newfound independence becomes even more significant for Bird upon learning she is pregnant with her first child.

This tension becomes magnified when Lem is unemployed and unable to find a job. In an attempt to demonstrate maturity and support as a wife, she turns to a wealthy ex-boyfriend for help. As a businessman, the ex is able to provide her husband a job in his company. After discovering that his wife has undermined his manhood and ability to support his family, Lem confronts Bird at her beauty salon. In a violent rage, he physically destroys the salon and threatens her with bodily harm. Eventually, Teri becomes involved and rescues her younger sister. Her involvement is because of their sisterhood as well as her financial investment in the salon, which Teri emphasizes is a great sacrifice she has made and is willing to fight for. Teri further complicates matters by hiring men to assault Lem, which is a parole violation and lands him back in jail. After this volatile situation between Lem and Bird calms down, they reconcile and pledge to make their relationship and family work. Bird now realizes what her role as a wife entails. She acknowledges the need for and importance of providing Lem with the emotional support needed to reclaim his role and identity as husband, member of the Joseph family, and soon-to-be father.

Effective Management of Relational Intimacy: Negotiating Max

Unlike Teri, Max is the sister who appears to most effectively deal with the dialectical tensions that she faces. She is able to maintain openness/closedness or relational intimacy with her husband as she maintains her dual family identities. Max's responses to this tension are neutralization, in that she has the skills necessary to establish balance, and segmentation, which involves the ability to create boundaries between these tensions. She enjoys and relishes her multiple roles as wife, mother, and daughter. Instead of pursuing a college degree and professional career, Max elected to be defined primarily by her family identities. As the film progresses, we watch Max gain an increased appreciation for her life and her part in fulfilling the relational needs of her family members. As the middle daughter, Max deviates from the societal expectation that she be the peacemaker and directly challenges her elder sister when necessary. Max is very forthright and vocal in addressing the long-standing conflict between them, regardless of the consequences.

In the first dinner scene, Max and Teri compete over whose culinary skills are better (i.e., who can fix the best cornbread). On the surface, this discourse appears to be about who can cook the best; however, the sisters are using the guise of the dinner ritual to mask their dislike for each other as individuals. The audience soon learns that Teri harbors resentment towards Max because her former high school boyfriend chose Max over her, which resulted in marriage and the happy life she is currently living. This sibling rivalry and relational tension is a foretelling of the relational pattern of communication and intimacy to which they will conform in adulthood.

While Max is content being a mother and wife to her family, it is not until she is belittled by Teri that Max has an increased commitment and appreciation for the life she has chosen. Max's self-sacrificing commitment to family identity becomes more pronounced after Big Mama's death. She becomes increasingly proactive in protecting the family by attacking Teri's attempts to restructure the family hierarchy of power and identity, which is an instinctual response to this perceived threat to family identity. Two critical events that mark this tension are when Teri tries to stop the dinner ritual and when she endeavors to sell the house. Because a large part of Max's identity is largely defined by her multiple roles, dissolution of the family dinner ritual means her roles as provider and matriarch (e.g., cook) are being compromised. Similarly, when Teri aggressively pursues selling the family house, Max, along with Bird, offers a rational argument for preserving this very important part of what remains of the Joseph family heritage. Selling the house would mean the family would no longer have the physical space or context that preserves the sense of family identity.

It is primarily through her interactions/confrontations with Teri and the looming collapse of the Joseph family identity that Max becomes more grounded in who she is. This is evidenced in the scene when she visits the house and stumbles upon their mysterious Uncle Pete. Obviously suffering from Alzheimer's disease, Uncle Pete mistakes Max for his late sister (Big Mama) and reminds her of the importance of cooking those delicious dinners to which he has become accustomed. Opting not to correct him on this mistaken identity, Max interprets his testimonial as an affirmation of her responsibility to preserve the family's identity. Despite their individual differences and shortcomings, Max now feels it is more important for the siblings to compromise as they work towards being a loving, supportive family.

Discussion

It was the purpose of this essay to use the narrative text in *Soul Food* to deconstruct the myth of the dysfunctional Black family by way of the dinner ritual. By exploring the complexities associated with understanding the dialectical tensions faced by the Joseph sisters in this film, we have a better understanding of how the family meal serves the larger purpose of preserving family identity. Using the dinner ritual as a subtext allows the film to reflect the importance of family and the critical role the family dinner plays in maintaining relational intimacy, communication, and a collective identity for the Joseph family. This story of family solidarity is complicated by the difficulties the sisters experience while negotiating their responsibilities to family and self. While the ethnic identity of the family is not addressed as the factor that distinguishes it from other family films, *Soul Food* is a film that challenges existing stereotypes typically associated with African Americans, African American women, and the African American family in particular.

The film captures the intricate nuances of family communication in the 1990s. By using each sister to tell a different story of dialectical tension and identity negotiation, a better understanding of this phenomenon as it relates to the family meal is established. Each of the sisters has a unique situation that challenges her to further understand her identity within the Joseph family. When the very existence of this decades-old family tradition is threatened, Big Mama's untimely death is the catalyst that forces the sisters to renegotiate their roles in the family and/or in their careers. Their realization of the importance of family and its centrality in their lives is crystallized when the dinner ritual is at risk for becoming a thing of the past. The interactions occurring outside of the family dinner create strains and tensions for the relationship that make the family members leery of reconnecting with each as they once had. In the end, the family's temporary decision to avoid the dinner ritual is superseded by their need and desire for commitment, healing, and connection not offered in their other interpersonal relationships.

The dinner ritual and relationship issues the Joseph sisters face are central to the film's ability to deconstruct myths of the dysfunctional African American family. Instead of conforming to the stereotype of the controlling matriarch or sexually promiscuous Jezebel, each sister reflects the complexity of racialized and gendered identities that emerges as the women negotiate the difficulties that come with belonging to a family unit. The dinner is largely symbolic of the need to navigate the difficult terrain that defines family and outlines for its members the implicit commitment that accompanies this identity.

Eldest sister Teri struggles with autonomy/connection with both her family and husband, while also providing the viewer with a complex representation of what it means to be an African American career woman. More pointedly, this character takes to task the matriarch stereotype and shows a character/woman with personal weaknesses that belie her stoic façade. Although Teri initially appears to embody this stereotype, she distances herself from this archetype by acknowledging her need to let go of past relational pains that are preventing her from trusting and loving others. The controlling image that Bird demystifies is that of the Jezebel, or the sexually promiscuous African American woman devoid of morals and values. Bird's youth and naïveté overshadow her need to be a mature, sensitive, and responsible wife for her new husband. Yet, she proves to be a complex character that anxiously learns how to create balance between her familial and individual identities in the midst of change.

Ultimately it is Max who embodies the "true" essence of a woman who is able to effectively manage the joys and stresses of life in the Joseph family. She serves as a model for siblings who ostensibly lack the skills or ability to achieve the same healthy balance in their own lives. The threat to the existence of the dinner ritual catapults the sisters into their evolution into the women and family they desire to be. The final scene in the film recenters the salience of the dinner ritual as the family is gathered at the house for Sunday dinner. They "agree" to accept their differences and newfound roles in the family, agreeing to let bygones be bygones. More importantly, Teri, Max, and Bird have a renewed commitment to their relationship as sisters and demonstrate a willingness to look beyond the idiosyncrasies that threatened the very definition of what it means to be a family.

Conclusion

Although a fictional interpersonal network (i.e., family) was used to offer an alternative text for the historical stereotypical depictions of the African American family, the use of the dinner ritual in the film *Soul Food* is a visual illustration of a lost art form that threatens the very existence of family as we know it. The limited amount of research on the topic of the dinner ritual does not minimize the significance of this communication phenomenon. As illustrated in the film, this communication phenomenon has significant meaning for some families, both fictional and real. *Soul Food* is a symbolic representation of how dialectical tensions (e.g., relational stressors) threaten a family tradition that defines the meaning of family. It is through the dinner ritual, and performance thereof, that we learn how families are able to preserve their collective identity, using dinner as a site for engaging in discourse that fosters relational intimacy and connection.

As noted earlier, it was the goal of industry experts Eisenstein and Chaplin to address the issue of racial, cultural, and ethnic representation in film. This goal, though not completely achieved, has gained some ground through such films as *Soul Food, Like Water for Chocolate,* and *Eat, Drink, Man, Woman,* among others. Individually and collectively they provide positive images of the family meal and the importance of interpersonal connection as it transcends cultural and racial group membership. As a narrative text, *Soul Food* successfully tells a story that reflects the era in which this film was made. Each sister's story illustrates how pressures to conform to gender role expectations to be both mothers/wives and career women make this negotiation process difficult for some and positively challenging for others. The dinner ritual provides a context for discourse to occur among the film's characters. This public dialogue allows the sisters to actively discuss and redefine the importance of family as a result of an unexpected crisis. As with other forms of communication, the critical discourse the characters engage in onscreen is a celebration of human events vis-à-vis public dialogue.

By examining the dialectical tensions that threaten the very existence of the family meal, this essay demonstrates how *Soul Food* functions to debunk the myth of the dysfunctional Black family. The film reflects the strength of the Black family and its ability to preserve itself in spite of the trials and tribulations that come. Through role negotiation and redefinition of the main characters, we observe the dialectical tensions as experienced by the primary characters in *Soul Food,* thus deconstructing negative perceptions typically held of members of the African American community and reframing the importance of the dinner ritual in the African American family.

Notes

1. Deidré D. Matthew, "Towards an Emotional Geography of Eating Practices: An Exploration of the Food Rituals of Women of Colour Working on Farms in the Western Cape," *Gender, Place & Culture: A Journal of Feminist Geography* 11 (2004): 437–43.

2. See http://www.dol.gov/oasam/programs/history/webid-meynihan.htm. For "The Nepro Family: The Case for National Action."

Works Cited

Allen, Jennifer. "The Incredible Healing Power of Family Rituals," *McCall's,* February 1993.

Barr, Terry. "Eating Kosher, Staying Closer." *Journal of Popular Film and Television* 24 (1996): 134–44.

Baxter, Leslie. A. "The Social Side of Personal Relationships: A Dialectical Perspective." In *Understanding Relationship Processes, 3: Social Context and Relationships,* ed. Steve S. Duck, 139–65. Thousand Oaks, CA: Sage, 1993.

Baxter, Leslie, and Catherine Clark. "Perceptions of Family Communication Patterns and the Enactment of Family Rituals." *Western Journal of Communication* 60 (1996): 254–69.

Bria, Gina. "Celebrate Family." *Working Mother,* December 1995.

Burg, Dale. "Dinner-Table Togetherness." *Family Circle,* June 28, 1998.

Collins, Patricia Hill. *Black Feminist Thought: Knowledge, Consciousness and the Politics of Empowerment.* New York: Routledge, 1999.

Dick, Bernard F. *Anatomy of Film.* New York: St. Martin's Press, 1998.

Entman, Robert M. "Representation and Reality in the Portrayal of Blacks on Network Television Shows." *Journalism Quarterly* 71.3 (1994): 509–20.

Gray, Herman. *Watching Race: Television and the Struggle for Blackness.* Minneapolis: University of Minnesota Press, 1996.

Guerrero, Ed. *Framing Blackness: The African American Image in Film.* Philadelphia, PA.: Temple University Press, 1993.

Haggins, Bambi L. "Why 'Beulah' and 'Andy' Still Play Today: Minstrelsy in the New Millennium." *Emergences* 11 (2001): 249–67.

Inniss, Leslie B., and Joe. R. Feagin. "The Cosby Show: The View from the Black Middle Class." *Journal of Black Studies* 25 (1995): 692–711.

Kennedy, M. "Fifteen Ways to Make Family Time Special." *Working Mother,* December 29, 1995.

LaHendro, B., and D. McKayle. *Good Times.* Los Angeles: Bud Yorkin Productions, 1974.

Lally, B., J. Shea, P. Benedict, J. Rich, O. Scott, and A. Smith. *The Jeffersons.* Los Angeles: CBS Television.

Loomis, Christine. "Table Talk." *Parents,* November 1998.

Matthew, Deidré D. "Towards an Emotional Geography of Eating Practices: An Exploration of the Food Rituals of Women of Colour Working on Farms in the Western Cape." *Gender, Place & Culture: A Journal of Feminist Geography* 11 (2004): 437–443.

Means Coleman, Robins. *African American Viewers and the Black Situation Comedy: Situating Racial Humor.* New York: Garland, 2000.

Rosenfield, Lawrence W. "Anatomy of Critical Discourse." *Speech Monographs* 35 (1968): 50–69.

Rosenfield, Lawrence W. "The Experience of Criticism." *Quarterly Journal of Speech* 60 (1974): 489–96.

Rosenfield, Lawrence W. "Rhetorical Criticism and Aristotelian Notion of Process." *Speech Monographs* 33 (March 1966): 1–16.

Rubin, Nancy. "Family Rituals." *Parents Magazine,* March 1998.

Sandrich, J., T. Singletary, C. Lauten, J. Bowab, C. Vinson, R. Life, N. Barnette, M. J. Warner, E. Falcon, and O. Scott. *The Cosby Show.* Atlanta, GA: Bill Cosby Productions.

Shanok, Rebecca Shahmoon. "The Family Funny Bone." *Parents,* March 1990.

Smith, Karen M. "Advertising Discourse and the Marketing of 'I'll Fly Away.'" In *Mediated Messages and African American Culture,* eds. Venise. T. Berry and Carmen. L. Manning-Miller, 172–83. Thousand Oaks, CA: Sage, 1996.

Staples, Robert. *The Black Family: Essays and Studies.* Belmont, CA: Thomson-Wadsworth, 2001.

Swearinger, Richard. "Good-for-the-Soul Food." *Better Homes & Gardens* 75 (March 1997): 242–45.

Tillman, George, Jr. *Soul Food.* DVD. Edmonds Entertainment, 1997.

Whiteside, Mary F. "Family Rituals as a Key to Kinship Connections in Remarried Families." *Family Relations* 38 (1989): 34–39.

Wilson, Clint C., and Felix Gutierrez, eds. *Race, Multiculturalism, and the Media: From Mass to Class Communication.* Thousand Oaks, CA: Sage, 1996.

Wolin, Stephen J., and Linda. A. Bennett. "Family Rituals." *Family Process* 23 (1984): 401–20.

Wood, Julia. *Communication Mosaics: A New Introduction to the Field of Communication.* Belmont, CA: Wadsworth, 1998.

15

Cultural Representation of Taste in Ang Lee's *Eat, Drink, Man, Woman*

MING-YEH T. RAWNSLEY

Food, Culture and Films

As K. C. Chang, author of *Food in Chinese Culture* has observed, Chinese people are very "food oriented."[1] Among all of the human senses, the Chinese privilege "taste" the most. Chinese people believe that a truly fabulous feast should be appealing to most, if not all, the senses: the presentation must be pleasing to the eye ("*se,*" literally meaning "colorful"), the aroma must be enticing to the nose ("*xiang,*" literally "fragrant"), the flavor must be satisfying to the tongue ("*wei,*" that is "tasty"), and the surrounding atmosphere must also contribute to the enjoyment of the experience. Chinese restaurants across the world are usually incredibly noisy because, for the Chinese, noises of human activities ("*re-nao,*" i.e., "hot and noisy") encourage lively and joyous feelings and thus contribute to one's complete enjoyment of the dining experience. Therefore, the focus of this chapter is not on the definition of "taste," but on the experience that the sense of taste constitutes, and its symbolic meanings to us as human beings situated within a particular cultural context.

What do I mean by "symbolic meanings"? Take a common Chinese saying, for example, "Life is a combination of hundreds of tastes that is made of various degrees of sourness, sweetness, bitterness and chili (*suan, tian, ku, la, bai wei ju quan*)." In English, "taste" is also used in many abstract ways, such as taste of "success" or "happiness." Various "taste" words, such as "bitter," "sour," "sweet," are often used to describe an experience or one's personality. Careful attention to cultural references and social behaviors demonstrates how different cultures all use taste, food and drink to translate human emotions, experiences and personalities into something that others can easily identify and relate to. It is no surprise that filmmakers consciously or unconsciously frequently use taste, food and drink as "symbols of life and sensuality"[2] to communicate important aspects of their characters' internal journeys, along with their personal and cultural identities.[3] Food, being such a basic part of everyday life for human beings, becomes an essential element that "the audience experiences rather than understands."[4]

The title of Taiwan director Ang Lee's comedy film, *Eat, Drink, Man, Woman* (1994), is an ancient phrase from one of the Confucian classics, *Record of Rites (Li Ji)*, where one is told that "eat and drink, man and woman — the greatest human desires reside in them (*yin shi nan nü, ren zhi da yu*)." There is also an ancient Chinese saying, "food and sex — the basic nature of human beings (*shi se xing ye*)."[5] Such ancient Chinese commentaries suggest that eating and drinking have not only been an important part of life in Chinese societies, but also Chinese people have discovered great delight in food and drink for well over two thousand years. Through the development and evolution of two millennia, food culture in China has become rich and diverse in taste, ingredients, rituals, varieties of culinary styles and methods of cooking, as well as its cultural representations in literature and art.[6]

From the title of *Eat, Drink, Man, Woman*, even those who have not seen the movie will realize food is a central theme. The story centers on a widower, Mr. Chu, who is the master chef working in one of the top hotels, the Grand Hotel, in modern Taipei, Taiwan. The film recounts the complicated relationships between the chef and each of his three daughters, the daughters' relationships with their boyfriends, and Mr. Chu's relationships with his friends and neighbors. As C. K. Chang has pointed out, Chinese people frequently "use food — of which there are countless variations, many more subtle and more expressive than the tongue can convey — to help speak the language that constitutes a part of every social interaction."[7] This chapter will examine how these relationships are represented by food, cooking and taste in the movie.

Enjoyment of Taste: Chef Chu

We often see on screen that Chef Chu spends his day off on Sundays preparing elaborate dinners for his daughters. It is apparent to the audience that Chef Chu enjoys cooking. It symbolizes both his professional identity and his identity as a father. When we see him, under the urgent request of the hotel manager, rush to the kitchen of Grand Hotel on his day off in order to transform an originally ruined dish of fake shark fins into a magnificent plateful that is served at the wedding banquet for a general's son, we see how much pride, joy and respect he has gained from his skills and knowledge in Chinese kitchens.

However, cooking is different from eating. While Chef Chu has enjoyed cooking for his three grown-up daughters, neither Chu nor any of his children particularly enjoys eating their Sunday feast together as they grow increasingly distant from each other. Chef Chu's taste buds are deteriorating and so he can no longer enjoy foods as much as he is used to. Moreover, each time he wants to convey something important about himself at the dinner table, he is always interrupted by one of his daughters (though not always deliberately) either by complaining about the food or by saying something she considers more important than whatever her father has to say. While the dinners Chef Chu prepares for his family look so delicious on the screen, Chef Chu himself cannot get any pleasure from eating them: he has no sense of taste, and his relationship with his daughters is increasingly bitter.

The first time we see Chef Chu enjoy eating is when he eats and drinks with his old friend, Chef Wen. There is no grand setting; they eat on a worktop in a kitchen; they enjoy no particularly refined menu, just some leftover dishes from the wedding banquet that they just cooked. But Chu and Wen chat nonstop until both are drunk, suggesting this is certainly a much more satisfying meal to Chu than his well-prepared Sunday dinner with daughters.

The second time Chef Chu seems to enjoy a meal is when he tackles a lunch box prepared by his neighbor, Ching-Rong, a divorcee, for her eight-year-old daughter. As a single mother busy with work, Ching-Rong cannot take as good care of her daughter as she would like to. Moreover, she is a lousy cook. Feeling sorry for the child, Chef Chu begins preparing proper (some may say luxurious) lunches for the girl (and later her classmates) and eats the girl's lunch boxes in case her mother finds out and scolds her. But the mother does find out: she tells Chef Chu that the spareribs she cooks are so tough that nobody has ever finished eating them. Hence she becomes suspicious when her daughter brings home a cleared lunch box every day. Chef Chu replies that flavor is not important to him any more as he is losing his sense of taste. He enjoys the lunch boxes because he knows that she spends a lot of effort and pours all her love of the child into preparing them.

In other words, Chef Chu prefers leftover dishes and tough spareribs to his own exquisite creations. Why? As David Knechtges has articulated, one "did not have to eat at a grand banquet to attain satisfaction, and often it was the simplest foods that provided the most pleasure and enjoyment."[8] Similarly, sense of taste is not simply confined to the tongue and the pleasure of eating does not just come from food and drink. This, in fact, is the message that the character, Chef Wen, communicates to the audience several times in the film. For example, he once compares chefs with musicians, saying a good chef (such as Mr. Chu) does not rely on his tongue for cooking because good taste is not in the mouth, just as an excellent musician (such as Beethoven) does not rely on his hearing for composing because good music is not in ears.

Comparable ideas are represented elsewhere. For example, one of the most popular Korean television dramas throughout East and Southeast Asia in recent years, *Dae Jang Geum* (or "The Great Jang Geum," 2003), conveyed almost the same message about taste. The central character, Jang Geum, the royal chef and the only female imperial physician for the Korean emperor in the early 1500s, temporarily damages her taste buds. Only then does she realize that the real sense of taste is not derived from mouth and tongue, but from a variety of sources such as touching, imagining, smelling, feeling and more. Jang Geum, like Chef Chu of *Eat, Drink, Man, Woman,* continues to invent and cook delicious cuisines despite not being able to taste the dishes herself.

Food and Identities: The Three Daughters

In *Eat, Drink, Man, Woman,* Chef Chu's eldest daughter, Chia-Chen, seems to treat "living" purely as a form of "duty." She tried to step into a mother's role when her mother died young. Since then, she begins going through life dutifully without much enjoyment and feels that this is what others expect of her. The audience can reach this conclusion about Chia-Chen's character not only from the dialogue and acting, but also from most of her scenes associated with food as "it is possible to 'say' things with food — resentment, love, compensation, anger, rebellion, withdrawal. This makes it a perfect conveyor of subtexts; messages which are often implicit rather than explicit, but surprisingly varied, strong and sometimes violent or subversive."[9] In Chia-Chen's case, there are few vibrant food scenes devoted to her; she is seen only eating, washing up and dealing with leftover dishes as housekeeping chores. In other words, we see food and drink for her only means mundane matters and she clearly gets increasingly resentful about it.

As Chia-Chen tells her sisters, she thinks she understands her parents, especially her father, more than everybody else simply because she is the eldest. She also thinks she knows what the Sunday gatherings mean to her father and secretly worries about how much longer the family tradition will last. But it turns out that she is so wrapped up in her own internal world that she often misinterprets other people's feelings. The most telling example is when she complains bitterly to her neighbor, Ching-Rong, that she anticipates her father will become her life-long burden, her father is at the same time sighing heavily to his friend, Chef Wen, that Chia-Chen will rely on him for the rest of his life unless he can marry her off. More ironically, after hearing Chia-Chen's complaints, Ching-Rong hints subtly to Chia-Chen that the scenario she imagines for her father and herself is not really what Chef Chu wants. But Chia-Chen ignores Ching-Rong's advice completely until the revelation at the end of the film that Ching-Rong and Chef Chu have in fact developed romantic feelings for each other and plan to set up their own family if their relationship can be accepted by the people they love. Throughout the film, Chia-Chen does not find comfort in ordinary daily routines such as eating and drinking; she seeks spiritual guidance from religion. But eventually she finds liberty and happiness in love.

Chef Chu's youngest daughter, Chia-Ning, is a university student. A rather understated character, she wears plain and simple clothes, eats cheap street food and works part-time in a McDonald's restaurant just as many others in need of part-time jobs have since the late 1980s in Taiwan. The filmmaker did not make the contrast between Western fast food and traditional Chinese cuisine an issue in the movie. The Grand Hotel, traditional family meals, street snack stalls and the McDonald's simply coexist. As Katarzyna Cwiertka of Leiden University has stated, "because dietary patterns and attitudes toward food are integral components of local cultures, introduced foreign foods, catering technologies, and consumption practices tend to become indigenized, resisting the homogenizing power of global forces."[10] The appearance of McDonald's does not seem intrusive in the film. It seems more like a truthful reflection of the major culinary trend of the 1990s in Taiwan and some other regions of Asia.[11]

Since Chia-Ning has been portrayed in the film as such a happy-go-lucky, worry-free, smart and nice girl, it comes as a shock (both to her family and the audience) when she announces out of the blue during one of their Sunday dinners that she is pregnant and plans to move in with her boyfriend, who has not yet met the family. I do not argue that the filmmaker meant to judge the "McDonaldization"[12] of modern courtship, but there is an element of comparison between fast-food restaurants and shotgun weddings because of Chia-Ning's story line. Indeed, fast food and speedy relationships are today prevailing cultural and social phenomena in traditional Confucian societies such as Korea, Hong Kong, Taiwan, and China. Audiences, like the Chu family, may be surprised by the situation at times, but the best strategy, as Director Ang Lee seems to suggest in *Eat, Drink, Man, Woman*, is simply to accept, adapt and move on as McDonald's will continue to coexist with traditional family meals and local restaurants, as well as to influence and be influenced by indigenous cultures, while family structures will continue to evolve into many new forms.[13] In fact, Ang Lee has admitted that the real theme of *Eat, Drink, Man, Woman* is about the transformation of family life in a rapidly modernized world and how family members struggle and learn to adjust to new social structures and personal relationships when old traditions have faced a series of internal and external challenges.[14]

The second daughter, Chia-Chian, is a more complex character than her sisters in the film. On the surface, she enjoys a successful managerial career in an airline and is expected by everyone else to embark on a jet-set lifestyle, all signs of a high achiever. But deep down, her passion is cooking, for which she has received strong discouragement from her father. The audience does not know the reason for his disapproval for sure; perhaps he wants to save her from hardship due to his understanding of the profession, perhaps because he believes that the kitchen is too confined and limited as a career choice for modern women, or perhaps because he thinks only a man can be a distinguished master chef. Dissuaded by her father, Chia-Chian not only stopped pursuing professional cooking, but also ceased cooking at home altogether in order to avoid her father's criticism. Nevertheless, Chia-Chian dreams of cooking freely in her own place one day. When she is promised promotion in the company, she decides to cook a sumptuous spread in her lover's apartment as a way of celebration. It is obvious to the audience that Chia-Chian cooks for her own enjoyment and achievement, but her lover thinks she is actually cooking for him because she loves him and wants to capture his heart by satisfying his stomach.

It seems to me that Ang Lee is pointing out an irony: it is commonly believed that feminism has liberated modern women from the kitchen. Hence if a woman wishes to return to the kitchen, it might be seen as a backwards step as if home cooking can never sit comfortably with a modern woman's ambition and career path. Yet research has shown that "domesticity" and "activism" were not necessarily mutually exclusive even at the end of the 19th century.[15] For example, Janet Theophano has revealed that the founder of the Woman Suffrage Society of Philadelphia, Jane Campbell, wrote many recipes on the backs of her speeches arguing for greater women's rights.[16] In other words, it possible for a woman to enjoy domestic chores while she embraces advanced ideologies and acts on them. There do not have to be contradictions between cooking and progress or women's rights.

Chia-Chian, like her father, is an expert cook. But just as they have different opinions about ways of living their lives, they have different taste in food. They often quarrel and criticize each other's behavior and cooking. However, when they finally reach an understanding and accept their differences, they realize that they are indeed most alike. As it turns out, when the youngest daughter, followed by the eldest daughter, moves out of the family home to set up her own family, it is Chia-Chian, the person that everyone (including the characters in the film and the viewers) thought would have fled the house the earliest, who stays and keeps their father company. More surprisingly, Chef Chu himself finds love and gets remarried. When he decides to sell their old family home in order to move to a modern but smaller flat and establish a new family with his young wife and step-daughter, it is Chia-Chian who buys the old house and holds the whole family together. Chia-Chian's cooking defines her as a perfectionist — she enjoys exquisite taste in food and drink, pursues a successful professional career, searches for true love, and treasures family relationships, even though it means a lot of heartache, hard work and struggle to achieve all of these and she sometimes loses her way.

Filmmaker, Dining Table and Cultural Commentaries

The above discussion has echoed an analysis made by Anne Bower, editor of an excellent book on cinema and food, *Reel Food*. She said, "the consumption of food can stand for consumption of any aspect of culture — whether cultural traditions, cultural hybridity ... or some aspect of gender conflict or definition."[17] Bower went on to argue that "food in films can allow filmmakers to comment on the very role of the filmmaker as a creator of culture," [18] a point with which I agree. Hence this section will explore *Eat, Drink, Man, Woman* further in order to examine how filmmaker Lee's views on cultural formation and transformation have been manifested in the film, even though my reading of the director's cultural commentaries in the movie differ slightly from Bower's interpretations.[19]

As a filmmaker, Ang Lee has a complex and interesting cultural background: his father escaped the Communist mainland to nationalist Taiwan in 1950;[20] Lee was born in Southern Taiwan in 1954 and has been regarded as a "second-generation Mainlander" in Taiwan throughout his life. He went to New York to study theater and cinema at the end of the 1970s and has remained in America as a "Chinese filmmaker working in Hollywood" ever since. Lee's fascination and understanding of Chinese cultural heritage has had a very strong influence on almost all of his films, including apparent Western productions such as *Sense and Sensibility* (1995) and *The Ice Storm* (1997).[21] However, when he travels to mainland China, he has been received as a "Taiwan compatriot."[22] So Lee has experienced the coexistence of multiple identities, many readjustments and perhaps to a certain degree, transformations of fluid cultural identities in relation to the "other," and has witnessed countless local, regional, and global cultural flows, interactions and changes.

Eat, Drink, Man, Woman is Lee's third full-length feature film,[23] made and set in 1994 when Taiwan was facing dramatic cultural, social and political transition and democratic consolidation.[24] As Lee has commented, he wanted to reflect the contradiction and continuity of Chinese traditional culture in modern Taiwan, as well as modern man and woman's constant (re-)negotiation and search for self-identities in an ever changing world. He has been always interested in the gatherings and breakups of human relations and decided to use food and the dining table to symbolize the deconstruction of a family as suggested by a common Chinese saying, "all banquets come to an end."[25] In this regard, Lee's artistic expression and the metaphor he chose to adopt seems to fit Anne Bower's understanding that "movie viewers respond so readily to food imagery because of food's primacy in our lives; it is a primacy that precedes literacy but then becomes part of our symbol-making, symbol-decoding capacity."[26]

Throughout *Eat, Drink, Man, Woman*, Chef Chu and his three daughters cannot enjoy their meals together when they force themselves to stay as a traditional family unit and perform typical family roles that they feel others, but sometimes themselves, imposed on them. While they drift apart, their family is gradually dissolved, a process reflected on the screen: we have never seen a happy scene associated with their family dining table, and have witnessed more and more family members missing from the same table as time passes. Nevertheless Lee is ultimately an optimist. When the Chu family finally accepts the reality and leaves home individually to find their own happiness, they become closer again even though they do not live under the same roof any longer. In other words, although the old family unit breaks up, a new family unit with more members is formed in which each person is allowed to be truthful to their individual desires and to pursue their own new identities.

At the end of the film the second daughter, Chia-Chian, purchases her father's house and becomes the new center of the Chu family. It is a different type of "center" compared to when Chef Chu was in charge not only in terms of gender and generational role, but also in terms of presence. Chia-Chian takes up the job promotion offered by the airline. She has to be stationed in Amsterdam, but she travels back home once very few months and so her presence in the family is more symbolic and casual than her father's used to be. She decides to keep up their Sunday dinner rituals whenever she is in Taipei by taking the trouble to prepare a banquet for every family member. But it seems so apparent to the audience that Chia-Chian does not feel cooking a family meal "trouble" at all because she enjoys it. She does it because she wants to, not because she has to as her father used to feel.

In the final sequences, because of other commitments, none of the family members except Chef Chu can go to the Sunday dinner Chia-Chian prepares. They call Chia-Chian to apologize and have a warm and frank conversation with her instead of forcing themselves to attend the gathering.

Contrasted with the first segments of the film, when all the sisters feel they must rush home for dinner when none of them actually feels like it, the interactions and exchanges between the family members are much more loving and relaxed than before.

Chef Chu comes from his new apartment to the old house. Instead of barging in, he knocks on the door, which shows his respect for Chia-Chian's independence as he knows it is now her house not his. Chia-Chian receives her father and he comes in to sit down next to her in front of the dining table. He tries a spoonful of Chia-Chian's soup, says it is delicious, and then criticizes it for containing too much ginger. While they begin arguing fiercely about cooking and flavoring, it suddenly dawns on Chef Chu that he is actually "tasting" Chia-Chian's dishes! The father and the daughter are both overwhelmed by the sudden realization and become speechless while they hold each other's hands tightly. We do not know if Chef Chu's sense of taste is magically restored temporarily or permanently, perhaps because of Chia-Chian's cooking or due to his ability to be finally rid of unnecessary guilt in order to enjoy a contented life with his young family. But one thing the audience can be certain of is that Chef Chu will definitely enjoy this meal with his daughter because dining is most enjoyable when all the right conditions are in place — delicious food and drink, warm and pleasant company, comfortable settings and eaters themselves being in good health and being in a joyous mood. This is when eating becomes "more than simply a biological or ceremonial function, but rather a source of pleasure that can even be spiritually uplifting."[27]

Ang Lee's representation in *Eat, Drink, Man, Woman* is very much about treasuring traditional family values and honoring Chinese culture as depicted in Chef Chu's beautiful culinary arts. But the film is also very much about breaking cultural stereotypes (for example, Chia-Chen transforms herself from a boring school teacher to a sexy woman; Chia-Ning leaps from a university student to a wife and a mother; Chef Chu stops being simply a tired old father to three grown-up daughters and becomes a husband to a much younger bride pregnant with his baby), facing up to challenges and adapting to changes. In Lee's eyes, new cultural balances and multiple identities are not impossible to achieve as we see Chia-Chian has finally got it all: a career abroad, cooking freely at home, and the respect and love of her extended family. Although the audience is not informed of how long this new-found happiness and family balance will last, just as we are unsure if Chef Chu's sense of taste is completely restored, constant changes of a modern society are implied through long shots of traffic moving through wide streets and busy intersections. Individuals will need to constantly reposition and redefine themselves, just as culture will need to continuously embrace challenges and reformations in order to thrive.[28]

Conclusion

"Food has been part of film since films began, yet only recently have we given extended attention to the many and sometimes startling ways that food functions in movies," said Anne Bower.[29] To summarize, from examining *Eat, Drink, Man, Woman*, we have discovered that food imagery and the sense of taste can be used to perform at least three functions effectively. This symbolic imagery is not unique to film as it is present in other art forms throughout history.[30]

First, food is used to enrich the portrayal of personalities and add depth to characters. A familiar slogan has been invented in recent years, "you are what you eat," in order to alert people to watch their diet. Although the slogan comes from a physical and health point of view, we find food can be used as an effective communicative element in movies to define who the characters are, construct their economic and social aspirations, as well as their cultural and personal identities.

Secondly, activities concerning food, such as eating and cooking, symbolize power relations between characters. For example, when Chef Chu is in the kitchen, we know he is in charge. When the food is brought onto the dining table and his daughters begin talking over him all the time, we know Chef Chu is losing control. When Chia-Chian is cooking in her lover's kitchen, she is happy to be the center of attention. But when her lover sees himself as the focus of the elaborate meal instead of giving Chia-Chian the appreciation and validation of her cooking that she craves, they quarrel bitterly. The viewers are drawn into the subtle changes in relationships between different characters simply by looking at who is cooking and who is eating.

And finally, Ang Lee's treatment of Chinese cookery is a filmmaker's method of glorifying indigenous cultures. From the very long shots of how one meal is prepared — a chicken captured from the back yard, fish caught alive, frogs trying to escape from cooking vessels, display of colorful ingredients and sauces, vegetables, cutlery, and so on — we realize that food on-screen is much more than food. It is traditional Chinese culture itself which has evolved and been evolving for thousands of years that is on display. Even though social and cultural changes are implied through the obstacles presented by modern life, the Chinese love of food will endure.

Notes

1. K. C. Chang, ed., *Food in Chinese Culture* (New Haven, CT, and London: Yale University Press, 1977), 1.

2. Ronald D. LeBlanc, "Love and Death and Food: Woody Allen's Comic Use of Gastronomy," in *Perspectives on Woody Allen,* ed. Renee Curry (New York: G. K. Hall, 1996), 147.

3. Anne L. Bower, ed., *Reel Food: Essays on Food and Film* (New York: Routledge, 2004), 1.

4. Jane F. Ferry, *Food in Film: A Culinary Performance of Communication* (New York: Routledge, 2003), 7.

5. The phrase came from *The Mencius*, chapter of Gaozi. Mencius (c.370–300 B.C.E.), who believed in human potential for goodness, is the first important successor of Confucius (c.551–479 B.C.E.) remembered by history. Gaozi was Mencius' philosophical opponent. He once stressed that human nature is basically about food and sex as his counterargument to Mencius' belief.

6. David R. Knechtges, "Gradually Entering the Realm of Delight: Food and Drink in Early Medieval China," *Journal of the American Oriental Society* 117 (1997): 229–39.

7. Chang, 16.

8. Knechtges, 239.

9. Gaye Poole, *Reel Meals, Set Meals: Food in Film and Theatre* (Sydney, Australia: Currency Press, 1999), 3.

10. Katarzyna Cwiertka and Boudewijn Walraven, eds., *Asian Food: The Global and the Local* (Surrey, UK: Curzon Press, 2002), 2.

11. Ibid., 10.

12. *McDonaldization* means "the process by which the principles of the fast-food restaurant are coming to dominate more and more sectors of ... society." See George Ritzer, *The McDonaldization of Society* (Thousand Oaks, CA: Pine Forge Press, 1991), 1.

13. Anthropologist James L. Watson and his colleagues have provided an illuminating account of how quickly and deeply fast-food chains affected and reflected the lives of people in East Asia, especially in Taipei, Hong Kong, Tokyo, Seoul and Beijing. See James L. Watson, ed., *Golden Arches East: McDonald's in East Asia* (Stanford: Stanford University Press, 1997).

14. Jing-Bei Zhang, *A Cinema Dream of Ten Years: Biography of Ang Lee* (Taipei: China Times Cultural Press, 2002), 127–29.

15. Ellyn Lem, review of *Eat My Words*, by Janet Theophano, *Journal of Popular Culture* 38, no. 4 (2005): 777–79.

16. Janet Theophano, *Eat My Words: Reading Women's Lives Through the Cookbooks They Wrote* (New York: Palgrave/Macmillan, 2002).

17. Bower, 7.

18. Ibid.

19. Ibid., 8. Bower argued that Ang Lee is a traditionalist in this film because she thought the second daughter, Chia-Chian, due to filial loyalty to her father, turned down a job promotion that would have taken her out of the country. This is a misunderstanding of the film plot as Chia-Chian did take the promotion and moved to Amsterdam at the end of the film. The move was revealed in the telephone conversation between Chia-Chian and her brother-in-law in the final sequences of the film. Bower's misunderstanding may have affected her consequent interpretations of Lee's views on traditional cultural values.

20. Taiwan was colonized by Japan in 1895, and was returned by the Allies to the Republic of China, under the Nationalist Government, in 1945. But the civil war soon broke out between the Nationalists and the Communists on the Chinese mainland. The Communists defeated the Nationalists and the latter fled to the island of Taiwan in 1949. Taiwan, or the Republic of China, was under the rule of the Nationalist government until 2000, when the leader of the main opposition party won the national election and became president. There is a wealth of English literature on Taiwan's political and social transition to democracy. See Gary Rawnsley and Ming-Yeh Rawnsley, *Critical Security, Democratisation and Television in Taiwan* (London: Ashgate Press, 2001) and Gary Rawnsley and Ming-Yeh Rawnsley, eds., *Political Communications in Greater China: The Construction and Reflection of Identity* (London: Routledge/Curzon, 2003).

21. As revealed in his biography, Lee described how he tried to use traditional Chinese imagery to describe the relationship between nature and humans in *Sense and Sensibility* and *The Ice Storm* in order to portray and emphasize subtle emotions and fragile relationships. See Zhang, 154–229.

22. Ibid.

23. The first one is *Pushing Hand* (1991) and the second *The Wedding Banquet* (1993).

24. The process of democratization officially began in Taiwan when martial law was lifted in 1987. The most notable change that subsequently occurred, which fundamentally transformed the society on every level, was the rapid proliferation of legal media. See Gary Rawnsley and Ming-Yeh Rawnsley, "The Media in Taiwan: Change and Continuity," in *What Has Changed? Taiwan Before and After the Change in Ruling Parties*, eds. Dafydd Fell, Kloter Henning, and Bi-yu Chang (Wiesbaden, Germany: Harrassowitz, 2006).

25. Zhang, 135–38.

26. Bower, 10.

27. Knechtges, 239.

28. Zhang, 126–51.

29. Bower, 3.

30. Pi-Li Hsiao, "Food Imagery in Amy Tan's *The Joy Luck Club* and *The Kitchen God's Wife*," *Feng Chia Journal of Humanities and Social Sciences* 1 (2000): 205–27.

Works Cited

Bower, Anne L., ed. *Reel Food: Essays on Food and Film*. New York: Routledge, 2004.

Chang, K. C., ed. *Food in Chinese Culture*. New Haven, CT, and London: Yale University Press, 1977.

Cwiertka, Katarzyna, and Boudewijn Walraven, eds. *Asian Food: The Global and the Local*. Surrey, UK: Curzon Press, 2002.

Fell, Dafydd, Klotter Henning and Bi-yu Chang, eds. *What Has Changed? Taiwan Before and After the Change in Ruling Parties*. Wiesbaden, Germany: Harrassowitz, 2006.

Ferry, Jane F. *Food in Film: A Culinary Performance of Communication*. New York: Routledge, 2003.

Hsiao, Pi-Li. "Food Imagery in Amy Tan's *The Joy Luck Club* and *The Kitchen God's Wife*." *Feng Chia Journal of Humanities and Social Sciences* 1 (2000): 205–27.

Knechtges, David R. "Gradually Entering the Realm of Delight: Food and Drink in Early Medieval China." *Journal of the American Oriental Society* 117 (1997): 229–39.

LeBlanc, Ronald D. "Love and Death and Food: Woody Allen's Comic Use of Gastronomy." In *Perspectives on Woody Allen*, ed. Renee Curry, 146–57. New York: G. K. Hall, 1996.

Lem, Ellyn. Review of *Eat My Words: Reading Women's Lives Through the Cookbooks They Wrote*, by Janet Theophano. *Journal of Popular Culture* 38, no. 4 (2005): 777–79.

Poole, Gaye. *Reel Meals, Set Meals: Food in Film and Theatre*. Sydney, Australia: Currency Press, 1999.

Rawnsley, Gary, and Ming-Yeh Rawnsley. *Critical Security, Democratisation and Television in Taiwan*. London: Ashgate Press, 2001.

_____, eds. *Political Communications in Greater China: The Construction and Reflection of Identity*. London: Routledge/Curzon, 2003.

Ritzer, George. *The McDonaldization of Society*. Thousand Oaks, CA: Pine Forge Press, 1991.

Theophano, Janet. *Eat My Words: Reading Women's Lives Through the Cookbooks They Wrote*. New York: Palgrave/Macmillan, 2002.

Watson, James L., ed. *Golden Arches East: McDonald's in East Asia*. Stanford: Stanford University Press, 1997.

Zhang, Jing-Bei. *A Cinema Dream of Ten Years: Biography of Ang Lee*. Taipei, Taiwan: China Times Cultural Press, 2002.

16

Snacking as Ritual

Eating Behavior in Public Places

PHILLIP VANNINI

Full of enthusiasm, hope, and hungry for a life change, I migrated from Italy to the United States when I was twenty-three years old. My first few weeks in my promised land of milk and honey proved to be challenging in a great number of ways, as any outrageously spoiled only child who was about to live on his own for the first time should have expected. My sudden difficulties with eating, however, surfaced as a complete surprise. The problem did not lie in food preparation per se — after all even I, characteristically endowed with a dangerous amount of self-confidence, had predicted the inevitability of climbing that steep learning curve — but in what felt like the need for an actual adult culinary resocialization.

It all began the first day I went grocery-shopping at the Safeway® on Roosevelt and N.E. 50th Street, just a few blocks north of the University of Washington. Not only was I grocery shopping for myself, alone without the directions and counsel of my mother — who had bought and prepared my food all my life — but I was shopping for foods in a language that was still very much foreign to me. Learning a new culinary vocabulary, I discovered, had to go well beyond learning the English equivalents for the various staples of Italian cuisine such as *pasta* (pasta), *pizza* (pizza), *pane* (bread), *mozzarella* (mozzarella), and the few other words that even the most advanced language reference book would provide the overseas reader. Learning a new culinary vocabulary meant learning a vocabulary of idioms, practices, and social situations that would make eating sufficiently elaborate not only to fill my stomach, but also to fulfill the prescriptions of food-consummation rituals of American culture. This process unfolded in all but an expedient fashion, and not without a great amount of embarrassment and frustration.

Coming from an alimentary conservative popular culture — rural Tuscany — meant having to abandon all reserve and taste inhibitions as well as needing to closely observe those around me to absorb clues on what, how, and where to eat in American everyday life. My first meals were deviant, even unashamedly so at times. I would eat tofu (for which I had no readily available Italian translation and thus no knowledge of its identity) just like cheese: by cutting symmetric slices of it and accompanying it with untoasted bread. I would scoop up sour cream with a teaspoon and eat it like yogurt (after all, I thought, is yogurt not some kind of sour cream?). And I would pig out on English muffins like I would do with *focaccia* bread: by toasting them and spreading on them simple (but alas, novel to me) condiments like Dijon mustard, horseradish, and Worcestershire sauce. Needless to say it wasn't long before my roommates — much better versed in all local manners of gustatory propriety than I — would find my meals a circuslike spectacle worth momentarily abandoning their preferred television entertainment for. Having a regular audience, who even at the highest peaks of their folksiness certainly weren't laughing *with* me, prompted me to seriously consider investing time in understanding food consumption as a more or less sacred ritual and enacting it, pronto. After all, years of jeering in Florentine restaurants at unwitting American tourists who routinely ask for ketchup or soy sauce to garnish their spaghetti should have taught me that eating in public is indeed a social drama, one that is carefully scripted and enacted before a vigilant audience who demands respect toward the profound moral and aesthetic significance of the role played by food in everyday life.

My intent in this chapter is to focus on the popular culture aspects of a particular type of food-consummation ritual: the consumption of snacks. The topic seems esoteric enough to demand both qualification and accounting. First the qualification: it is not toward all types of snacks that I direct my attention, but only to those that are most often and typically consumed when other people are present. Thus, crunching on a candy bar while driving does not concern me here, whereas eating a hot dog at the ballpark does. The reason why I choose to write about this is both analytical and personal: from an analytical perspective it seems apropos to write about a topic around which no academic knowledge has yet been developed, and from a personal perspective I cannot but confess my utmost fascination with the deep symbolic significance of snack foods, as well as with the long-established rituals typical of its conditions of consumption. I take the first bite out of this chapter by introducing the idea of food consumption as ritual and drama.

The Ritual of Eating

The fact that eating is a multidimensional social ritual, rich with cultural significance and global variations has certainly not escaped anthropologists.[1] Ethnographers have observed how food is connected to rituals and belief systems through the reenactment of venerated stories[2] and how it works as a binding tie between different generations and their respective collective memories,[3] and between people and supernatural deities.[4] Ritual meals strengthen relationships with co-present others[5] and can reinforce ethnic and religious group identities and inter-group boundaries.[6]

Several studies have shed light on how food consumption structures ritual performances. A typical example is that of table etiquette.[7] Anderson's[8] study of the etiquette of the Japanese tea ceremony and Curran's[9] ethnographic work on the ritual performance of bodily discipline amongst American nuns describe well how ritual meals construct a shared sense of commonality with both present others and past traditions. The historical rootedness of ritual meals has also been examined, amongst others, by Brandes,[10] who looked at the significance of sugar in the Mexican ritual of the Day of the Dead and questioned its continuity with Aztec practices, and Weismantel,[11] who studied the present cultural heritage of Inca traditions within Andean Indian practices of food and drink consumption during religious festivals.

Typical of the eating-as-ritual literature is the theoretical concern with the role of commensality in cementing bonds and social solidarity. For example Voss[12] has viewed ritual food consumption as a functional mechanism for maintaining social-ecological balance through the distribution and redistribution of food, whereas Lindenbaum[13] has expressed the opposite position by showing how unequal access to food as material goods highlights hierarchical power relations.

In the present writing, eating rituals are seen through a communicative rather than a functionalist lens. I understand food to be a medium of communication through which social dramas, narratives, and cultural performances are practiced. Food consumption, as medium and material technology, is neither a function for the creation of a common culture's collective consciousness nor a product of its primordial existence, but instead a process "thoroughly cultural from the outset: an expression and creation of the very outlooks and aspirations we pretend it merely demonstrates."[14] From this perspective, the ritual of eating is thus to be viewed not as a means to an end or as an end in itself, but as participation, as communion, and as communication manifesting "an ongoing and fragile social process."[15] The public ritual of eating is thus here understood as a social drama inviting or denying our participation, and requiring symbolic actions through which multiple symbolic realities are achieved.

I embrace the idea that the public consumption of food is equivalent to the performance of a ritual because I believe that the social circumstances in which food is publicly consumed are best examined from the metaphorical perspective of social life as drama.[16] Eating in the presence of others is marked by the presence of a "limited time span, a beginning and an end, an organized program of activity, a set of performers, an audience, and a place and occasion."[17] Cultural conventions frame the ritual of snacking as interaction and alert co-present participants to the generation of a shared reality by way of an "embodied action that produces a heightened moment of communication."[18] Public snacking can thus be understood as a social drama or social performance.

Social performances are everyday interactions amongst individuals who exercise their conduct by negotiating and enacting cultural scripts. Individuals are hardly aware that their performances are scripted and faithfully enacted, that their roles are more or less closely prescribed, that certain ways of managing fronts are consistently structured, and that fellow interactants constitute an audience for our actions. Yet we all play along in synchrony, attempting to rescue others when their lines or conduct is jeopardized by incidents, or when expectations are breached by unexpected nonconformities.

Social dramas also have the unique characteristic of rising out of the ever-shifting social process of movement between structure and antistructure. Structure is order within a system whereas antistructure is the "dissolution of normative social structure, with its role-sets, statuses, jural rights, and duties."[19] Antistructure is the seedbed of relentless creativity, growth, and change.

I posit the ritual and social drama of snacking in public as a *liminoid* phenomenon: a state of being between and betwixt two alternate structures and situations. According to Turner, the liminoid is the threshold between alternate systems, between the structure and antistructure typical of post-industrial societies. The liminoid is predominantly an individual or small group ritual, yet one which often takes place in the presence of many others. The liminoid is also a form of ambiguity; it is a way of being neither inside nor outside a structure. During such liminoid moments as preparing camping foods or eating hot dogs at a ballpark, we merge into a fleeting unity in spontaneous *communitas*[20] in which hierarchies and differences momentarily fade and all individuals become actors in the same drama. Spontaneous communitas never lasts too long; status, order, and privilege can never be fully eliminated. Yet, for as long as they last they have something magical about them.[21] Foods consumed in liminoid circumstances are essential actors in the performance of communitas. To their consideration in some detail I now turn.

By the Campfire

It was two years after my very first experiment with tofu and sour cream that I lost my camping virginity. My new American friends were hell-bent on giving me the real American camping experience: "Forget campsites and all the shower booths and frills," they insisted, "for your first camping trip you *have* to do wild camping!" I was sold on the idea without much additional propaganda. I soon began fantasizing hiking down to a deserted river bank, fishing for river trout, opening cans of beans with a jackknife, snacking on pemmican, and sitting by the fire listening to my friend's harmonica tunes while staring at the flames and the summer sky.

Instead, once again, the dream all began and ended at Safeway®. It took us about two hours to stock up: sunflower seeds, marshmallows, zesty tortilla chips with a hint of lime, pepperoni sticks, industrial amounts of beer in both cans and bottles, three different types of frankfurters, hamburger meat, three different types of barbecue sauce, six different condiments, five different types of soda pop, and on and on. Throughout the shopping trip I was once again useless. This time I knew all the linguistic (and by now even brand) labels, but I was for the most part paralyzed: nonplussed at the need for such alimentary bonanza for an overnight trip.

"How are we going to carry all this stuff in our backpacks?" I timidly asked before handing my friends my share of the cash.

"Uh, what backpacks?"

Good answer. After *driving* down a steep quarter-of-a-mile unpaved road off the main thoroughfare we snugly parked our two-too-many cars in such a way that each car's rear would face the others, as if to form a triangle. Just enough space was left in the middle for our three tents and the campfire. If no exercise came from trekking away from the cars, it sure came from unloading them. As I helped build the campfire, heavy coolers filled with food and drinks began to flood out of trunks and pickup truck beds. We were snacking in no time. Kielbasa dogs, beer, trail-mix nuts, beer, beef and salmon jerky, then more beer. Everything was either ready straight out of the bag or meticulously prepared by us using utensils, appliances, and accessories, half of which I did not even have in my apartment. Mostly everything (with the obvious exception of the various ales consumed) was just "camping-right": foods that were either exclusively consumed on a camping trip, or foods that "tasted better" when eaten on a camping trip. Some products were even sized and packaged with camping in the marketing mind.

Among the first rounds of after-dinner snacks was this sticky, overly rich dessert that I learned was called "s'mores." "What? You never had s'mores before?" asked Bill, both incredulous and eager to colonize my still-much-too-foreign palate, "let me show you, dude: you grab a wood stick like that one over there, you poke it through a marshmallow puff, and you roast the puff on the fire. Once it's done just right you jam it between two graham crackers and a piece of chocolate and shove it in your mouth. Try..."

Uh! I had no idea they had bought chocolate and graham crackers too. Who knows what else was in the two coolers that were still in the back of our cars. Breakfast, perhaps? All that, in a way, kind of explained the amount of that Safeway bill, though.

"So, what do you think Phillip, would you like s'ome mores?" giggled Bill, as I was still negotiating my first s'more in my mouth.

"It's pretty good stuff, dude, but can I ask you guys a question? What exactly makes this here *wild* camping?" I ventured to ask.

Brief silence met my question. Then, as he laid down his dish still heaped with potato salad, Bill replied: "Well, you know that *wood stick* you roasted the marshmallow with...?"

"Good point, man!" replied William as he violently spat a sunflower seed shell, missing the aimed-for fire pit and helplessly witnessing it land instead on the half-cut watermelon.

Wild. Indeed.

* * *

Camping, no matter *where* one camps, is a strange world. The experience of camping feels as if one is suspended between two opposite worlds that have little in common with one another. One world is the cosmos of work life, of mundane routines, of structure. The other world is that of *true* wilderness: the world of rough survival, of unexpected encounters, of improvisation, and antistructure. Camping, in this post-industrial day and age, is truly neither pure routine nor antistructure. It is almost as if, however, it carried the genes of both. Camping evokes ancient ways of creating a proto-cultural structure in an unpredictable world of natural elements; camping brings forth improvised rituals of survival and tales of human adaptation. Through the symbolic action of camping, we can express collective memory and historical patterns of a bygone mode of living: "the crystallized secretion of once living human experience."[22] Caught in the middle of structure and anti-structure, camping is thus but a form of play: a ritual expression which provides us with brief moments of self-reflection about both natural and cultural possibilities.

Camping foods have a critical role in this experience. Being neither direct replicas of everyday foods, nor radical alterations of them, camping foods are symbolic expressions that exaggerate the routine social dramas of adaptation — adaptation in both the worlds of structured work and antistructural wilderness. In order for their unique role within ritual to work, that is, for their role in constituting something different from both routine and unpredictability, camping foods must work as symbolic *separations* from mundane existence and structure. True camping foods, in other words, must have an aura of specialness; something that is not consumed regularly. Separation allows for a *transition* into the symbolic form of the ritual event.[23] Yet the ritual event is hardly a radical *new* world; within ritual there is but *reaggregation* into common elements of secular life. That is why camping foods are never revolutionary departures from routine diets. While camping people play with each other and their foods, with their material and symbolic expressions of home, of work, and of alimentary subsistence. Campsite eating is thus ritual play that defamiliarizes the familiar ritual that gives rise to a sense of novelty that is not revolutionary but the outcome of recombination. That is why camping food, even when made with common ingredients, never tastes the same at home.

Co-participating in the production of food, often with the aide of ingenious technologies, gathering up by the fire, and eating together in a group was once a daily routine. Today the form of food preparation and consumption typical of camping is clearly a separation from the everyday post-industrial routine of consuming ready-made or semi-prepared foods, often in isolation from family and friends, or perhaps within a mass-mediated situation whereby dinner television programming has replaced the campfire. Within such a cultural climate, play and work are clearly separate activities; camping is always vacation, i.e., departure from structure. In such a post-industrial world ritual is always liminoid: "an independent domain of creative activity" which has the potential to shape "a plurality of alternative models for living."[24] And indeed camping does shape a momentary "*communitas*": a "way by which persons see, understand, and act towards one another," in a setting marked by "a direct, immediate and total confrontation of human identities."[25] Yet the creativity and spontaneity of camping is always compromised. The roasting of s'mores may be a creative activity, but its independence is compromised by the necessity of purchasing the appropriate consumer goods. Spitting sunflower seeds may be a departure from table etiquette but Spitz® too must come from Safeway® shelves.

The consumption of camping foods is thus a meaningful ritual; a way of performing a momentary *communitas* with friends and family, a way of bridging ways of the past and routines of the present time, a dialectic practice shaping our relation with both the natural world of antistructure and the urban realm of work and everyday structure. Camping is not a unique ritual in our society. A similar symbolic expression takes place daily in movie theaters and ballparks across the continent. These rituals too express liminoid play, albeit with a slightly different flavor. To the consumption of snack foods in such halls of play I now turn.

Snacking and Vicarious Action

"Everybody listen! We've got to put a barrier between us and the snakes," screams the cop-turned-airplane savior in a sudden burst of energy fraught with both teleological insight and clinical wisdom.

"Good thinking, Sherlock," I murmur to my buddies as I reach for a handful of popcorn from Frank's bag.

"What are you doing, man? You *hate* popcorn!?"

"I gotta do something with my time in here," I think to myself as I shrug off Frank's question. "I wonder what brings people to a theater for a movie like this," my mind drifts off, "must be the added artificial smell of extra butter. Or maybe it's the ten-dollar-a-pound jelly beans. Nah, I'm just being negative. Not everybody is as cynical as me. People do like action movies...."

"All right, well, I know what I've got to do," Rick shouts from the silver screen, interrupting my reflection. He continues: "We're in a two-hundred foot aluminium tube and we're thirty thousand feet in the air, and any one of those slimy little pieces of shit can trip a circuit or a relay or a hydraulic and this bird goes down faster than a Thai hooker."

...That artificial butter is dangerous stuff.

* * *

Action movies portray..., well, action. But in general, *all* movies are a form of action, regardless of their genre. *Going out* to the movies is also a form of action. Comedian Jerry Seinfeld perhaps puts it best when he remarks on the contemporary urge that people have to go out of their homes, to do something, to have fun, to meet and greet people, or perhaps just to watch others from a distance. "Look at the people around you," urges Seinfeld in one of his routines, "these are the people who are *out*. This is it; this is what we've all been looking forward to. Your phone at home is ringing and no one is answering, and the caller is thinking 'where did they go? Where could they possibly be? They must be *out*. What are they doing *out?*' Well, this is it, folks: we've made it, we are *out!*"

Erving Goffman had a different type of action in mind when he defined it as consequential, fateful, and problematic chance-taking typical of risk-taking, dangerous activities, and practical gambling.[26] Yet Goffman was too insightful to confine his observations to such a narrow niche of social interaction. Action, of the extraordinarily exciting kind, may not be found easily during weekday routines on the job or at home, yet even the average citizen can find opportunities for some vicarious action in commercialized competitive sports, nonspectator risky sports, entertainment venues, and all sites offering the chance for "fancy milling" with other people.[27] "This is the action of consumption," observed Goffman.[28] By going out, by engaging in routinized, organized, commercial, vicarious action the individual gets a taste of the real action without the risk: he "brings into himself the role of performer and the role of spectator; he is the one who engages in the action, yet he is the one who is unlikely to be affected by it."[29] Action, whether full of dramatic risk or carefully scripted as a more organized replica of it, is performance: a social ritual whereby characters are shaped and the meanings of symbolic activities generated and exchanged.

In today's world of going out, commercialized action is almost synonymous with liminoid eating/snacking. To *go out* means to dine out, to go for a treat. A date is hardly a date without restaurant dining. A movie at the theater is hardly a cinematic experience without popcorn. A day at the beach is not summer fun without ice cream. A day at the county fair is not the same without kettle corn or cotton candy. A picnic needs watermelon. A baseball game is not worth a seventh inning stretch without hot dogs, peanuts, and Cracker-jacks™. And try and convince the kids that today there will be no Slurpie™ after the game. To go out, to have fun, to get some action in between one's daily routines means to experience the ritual of play as a departure from structure. And to depart from that structure, to perform that departure, one needs to practice liminoid rituals such as snacking. Snacking turns food from a functional duty of self-sustenance into a temporal and spatial interface marked by moderate subversion. By snacking in public and as part of public rituals of action, we create and re-create momentary inversions of cultural structures: we step out of normative and mundane existence and create the very conditions whereby experiences of relative novelty are possible. Snacking is thus not a functional necessity of a preexistent ritual but a communicative and generative ritual in and of itself: "an expression and creation of the very outlooks and aspirations we pretend it merely demonstrates," in the words of Carey.[30]

Eating is a powerful social drama because it is central to life itself: both to biological regeneration and to cultural reproduction. A diet — intended not as slimming practice but as a pattern of eating foods whose material and symbolic properties are rich in significance within the culture in which they are prepared and consumed — is among the most elementary expressions of social organization. To radically alter a diet, as I did when I moved to North America, is a way to alter self and social identity. To refuse to eat is to sever oneself from common human biological needs and from social contractual needs of integration; it is no accident that a hunger strike conveys the message that one's place in the social order is imperiled by lack of humanity and observance of elementary social values. But to play with the interstices present within a socially shared diet is to find temporary shelter from the demands of routine and revolution. To snack is to create that liminoid space, to architect a spontaneous, fleeting *communitas* that is neither bent on liberating human volition from the shackles of routine nor preoccupied with maintaining the culinary status quo. After all, to snack one needs neither a table nor much etiquette. A wood stick picked from the bush is wild enough. Yet be careful, for too much ice cream will ruin your dinner.

Notes

1. Sidney Mintz and Christine DuBois, "The Anthropology of Food and Eating," *Annual Review of Anthropology* 31 (2002): 103.

2. See Andrew Brisebarre, *La fête du mouton: Un sacrifice Musulman dans l'espace urbain* (Paris: Ed. CNRS, 1998), and Paul Bonte, Andrew Brisebarre, and Anne Gokalp, *Sacrifices en Islam: Espaces et temps d'un rituel* (Paris: Ed. CNRS, 1999), 11–14.

3. See David Sutton, *Remembrance of Repasts: An Anthropology of Food and Memory* (Oxford: Berg, 2001), 109, and Gerry Feeley-Hamik, "Religion and Food: An Anthropological Perspective," *American Academy of Religion* 63, no. 3 (1995): 565–82.

4. See Kyle Brown, "Serving the Spirits: The Ritual Economy of Haitian Vodou," in *Sacred Arts of Haitian Vodou,* ed. Darren Cosentino (Los Angeles: UCLA Fowler Museum of Cultural History, 1995), 205–23.

5. See Michael Buitellar, *Fasting and Feasting in Morocco: Women's Participation in Ramadan* (Oxford: Berg, 1993), 3.

6. See Fabre-Vassas Calle, *The Singular Beast: Jews, Christians, and the Pig* (New York: Columbia University Press, 1997), 2.

7. See Elizabeth Cooper, "Chinese Table Manners: You Are *How* You Eat," *Human Organization* 45, no. 2 (1986): 179–84.

8. See Jennifer L. Anderson, *An Introduction to Japanese Tea Ritual* (Albany: SUNY Press, 1991), 179–84.

9. See Paula Curran, *Grace Before Meals: Food Ritual and Body Discipline in Convent Culture* (Urbana: University of Illinois Press, 1989), 23.

10. See Stephen Brandes, "Sugar, Colonialism, and Death: On the Origins of Mexico's Day of the Dead," *Comparative Studies in Social History* 39, no. 2 (1997): 270–99.

11. See Mike Weismantel, *Food, Gender, and Poverty in the Ecuadorian Andes* (Philadelphia: University of Pennsylvania Press, 1988), 19.

12. See Jim Voss, "The Politics of Pork and the Rituals of Rice: Redistributive Feasting and Commodity Circulation in Northem Luzon, Philippines," *Beyond the New Economic Anthropology,* ed. John Slammer (New York: Macmillan, 1987), 121–41.

13. See Stephen Lindenbaum, "Rice and Wheat: The Meaning of Food in Bangladesh," *Food, Society, and Culture,* eds. Abraham Khare and Mihn Rao (Raleigh: Carolina Academic Press, 1986), 253–76.

14. James Carey, *Communication as Culture* (New York: Routledge, 1989), 9.

15. Ibid., 19.

16. Dennis Brissett and Charles Edgley, eds., *Life as Theater: A Dramaturgical Sourcebook* (Chicago: Aldine, 1975), 19.

17. Milton Singer, *Man's Glossy Essence: Explorations in Semiotic Anthropology* (Bloomington: Indiana University Press, 1984), 12.

18. Soyini Madison, *Critical Ethnography: Method, Ethics, and Performance* (Thousand Oaks, CA: Sage, 2005), 154.

19. Victor Turner, *From Ritual to Theater: The Human Seriousness of Play* (New York: Paj Publications, 1992), 28.

20. Ibid., 13.

21. Ibid.

22. Ibid., 18.

23. Ibid., 26.

24. Ibid., 33.

25. Ibid., 46–47.
26. See Erving Goffman, *Interaction Ritual: Essays on Face-to-Face Behavior* (New York: Pantheon, 1967), 141.
27. Ibid., 194–97.
28. Ibid., 197.
29. Ibid., 198.
30. Carey, 9.

Works Cited

Anderson, Jennifer L. *An Introduction to Japanese Tea Ritual.* Albany: SUNY Press, 1991.
Bonte Paul, Andrew Brisebarre, and Anne Gokalp, eds. *Sacrifices en Islam: Espaces et temps d'un rituel.* Paris: Ed. CNRS, 1999.
Brandes, Stephen. "Sugar, Colonialism, and Death: On the Origins of Mexico's Day of the Dead." *Comparative Studies in Social History* 39, no. 2 (1997): 270–99.
Brisebarre, Andrew, ed. *La fête du mouton: Un sacrifice Musulman dans l'espace urbain.* Paris: Ed. CNRS, 1998.
Brissett, Dennis, and Charles Edgley, eds. *Life as Theater: A Dramaturgical Sourcebook.* Chicago: Aldine, 1975.
Brown, Kyle. "Serving the Spirits: The Ritual Economy of Haitian Vodou." In *Sacred Arts of Haitian Vodou,* ed. Darren Cosentino, 205–23. Los Angeles: UCLA Fowler Museum of Cultural History, 1995.
Buitellar, Michael. *Fasting and Feasting in Morocco: Women's Participation in Ramadan.* Oxford: Berg, 1993.
Carey, James. *Communication as Culture.* New York: Routledge, 1989.
Cooper, Elizabeth. "Chinese Table Manners: You Are *How* You Eat." *Human Organization* 45. 2 (1986): 179–84.
Curran, Paula. *Grace Before Meals: Food Ritual and Body Discipline in Convent Culture.* Urbana: University of Illinois Press, 1989.
Fabre-Vassas, Calle. *The Singular Beast: Jews, Christians, and the Pig.* New York: Columbia University Press, 1997.
Feeley-Hamik, Gerry. "Religion and Food: An Anthropological Perspective." *American Academy of Religion* 63 (1995): 565–82.
Goffman, Erving. *Interaction Ritual: Essays on Face-to-Face Behavior.* New York: Pantheon Books, 1967.
Lindenbaum, Stephen. "Rice and Wheat: The Meaning of Food in Bangladesh." *Food, Society, and Culture,* eds. Abraham Khare and Mihn Rao, 253–76. Raleigh: Carolina Academic Press, 1986.
Madison, D. Soyini. *Critical Ethnography: Method, Ethics, and Performance.* Thousand Oaks, CA: Sage, 2005.
Mintz, Sydney, and Christine Du Bois. "The Anthropology of Food and Eating." *Annual Review of Anthropology* 31, no. 1 (2002): 99–119.
Singer, Milton. *Man's Glossy Essence: Explorations in Semiotic Anthropology.* Bloomington: Indiana University Press, 1984.
Sutton, David. *Remembrance of Repasts: An Anthropology of Food and Memory.* Oxford: Berg, 2001.
Turner, Victor. *From Ritual to Theater: The Human Seriousness of Play.* New York: Paj Publications, 1992.
Voss, Jim. "The Politics of Pork and the Rituals of Rice: Redistributive Feasting and Commodity Circulation in Northern Luzon, Philippines." In *Beyond the New Economic Anthropology,* ed. John Slammer, 121–41. New York: Macmillan, 1987.
Weismantel, Mike. *Food, Gender, and Poverty in the Ecuadorian Andes.* Philadelphia: University of Pennsylvania Press, 1988.

17

Beyond Bread and Circuses

Professional Competitive Eating

LAWRENCE C. RUBIN

In Voro, Veritas
— IFOCE Motto[1]

Faster than a drive-thru snacker, more powerful than a buffet gorger, able to clear vast platefuls in a single swallow. Look, up at the table; it's an athlete, it's a spectacle ... it's a gurgitator![2] Yes, it's a gurgitator. Strange visitor from another dimension, who came to television with eating powers and entertaining abilities far beyond those of mortal eaters. A gurgitator; who can change the course of mighty franchises, bend imagination in his bare teeth. And who, disguised as average Joe(sephine), mild-mannered citizen of the great metropolitan centers, fights a never-ending battle for hot dogs, cannoli, and the gluttonist way.

Why begin an essay on a novel and recent phenomenon that is considered by some to be little more than circus and which is limited to a small number of wealthy industrialized nations,[3] with a tribute to yet another vestige of popular culture — the 1950s *Adventures of Superman* television program?[4] Is not professional competitive eating simply the latest hairball coughed up by the insensibilities of popular culture? Is not professional competitive eating simply one more expression of rampant and vulgar conspicuous consumption, and a hubristic display of the corrupting influence of power and wealth? Is not professional competitive eating an arrogant snub to the hungry of the world and to those who have watched the agricultural legacy of their families and the nation succumb to the machinations of big business, government control and political agenda? Is not professional competitive eating, along with corporate debauchery, congressional gerrymandering and deferred prosecution of corporate raiders one of the sure signs of societal decay and cultural Armageddon?[5] If professional competitive eating is as its promoters would lead us to believe, not just a carnival spectacle, but a serious and powerful sociocultural phenomenon with historical roots and significance, then why is the lion's share of its publicity limited to tabloid journalism rather than the serious gaze of academics and scholars?

In order to answer all these questions, it will be necessary to understand professional competitive eating in a slightly less sensationalistic manner than was offered in the opening of this essay. Consider instead the following....

Faster than political scandal, more powerful than global warming, able to attract vast audiences in a single broadcast. Look, up on the stage; it's nostalgia, it's ritual ... it's professional competitive eating. Yes, it's professional competitive eating. Strange spectacle from another time in history, that came into consciousness with compelling allure and profound implicit meaning, far beyond that of mere carnival sideshow. Professional competitive eating, which can change the course of our cultural identity, bend accepted wisdoms in its bare hands. And what, disguised as ludicrous mockery, mild-mannered and passing fad, fights a never-ending battle for validation, meaning and the American way.

The following discussion of professional competitive eating will be divided into two main sections, roughly corresponding to a structural/functional dichotomy often evoked in other fields of study including biology, psychology, anthropology and sociology. In the first, the structure of professional competitive eating will be addressed, followed by a series of theoretical speculations on the possible functions of the phenomenon for the participant, the spectators and the broader culture.

Welcome to the Midway

For the purpose of this discussion, a distinction must be made between eating contests, eating stunts and competitive eating; and in the case of the latter, the relatively recent phenomenon of "professional competitive eating." I define an eating contest as a highly localized and informal stakes-based challenge between opponents who are known to each other through family and/or community ties. While eating battles and contests tied to land ownership and dominance date to antiquity,[6] the more recent and uniquely American pie-eating contests at town, county, state and regional fairs are classic contemporary examples of such an event. They are typically done in good spirit, and tied to the agricultural legacy of the fair.[7] Such fairs have been in continuous existence in the United States since Elkanah Watson, commonly regarded as the father of the county fair, brought the tradition from England to Pittsfield, Massachusetts, in 1810.[8] The food consumed is usually accepted as a regular component of the local diet and the contestants are typically ordinary citizens or, perhaps, those known for their consummatory prowess. Probably, the most renowned example of the pie-eating contest was a scene from the film *Stand By Me*[9] in which a robust teen, who went by the unflattering name of Lardass, devoured the competition and all of the pies, but experienced a reversal of fortune, all over the audience! There are other examples of eating contests throughout American popular culture.

Eating stunts, in contrast, are performed in response to a monetary or pride-based challenge to consume items not typically part of the human diet, such as live (small) animals[10] and parts of dead animals.[11]

I define *competitive eating* as engaging in a contest of skill, in this case eating voluminously and/or rapidly for remuneration, which may or may not be monetary, and includes, but is not limited to money, material objects, visibility and fame. In the United States, this phenomenon traces most directly to New York's Nathan's Famous Hot Dog stand at Coney Island in Brooklyn, which was established by Nathan Handwerker in 1916. The first competition reportedly occurred two years later as a promotional stunt and has been a July 4th mainstay ever since.[12] The concept of "professional competitive eating," on the other hand requires further consideration. The term *professional*[13] implies that the individual is skilled, if not expert, remunerated, learned, and performing within promulgated guidelines. This brings us to the modern era, and the International Federation of Competitive Eaters (IFOCE). While certainly not alone in the field, which it shares with the Association of Independent Competitive Eaters (AICE),[14] and the efforts of numerous organizations and entities including restaurants, malls, civic and religious organizations, the IFOCE appears to be the most highly articulated of the professional eating organizations, and therefore will be used as the gold standard, so to speak. Like other professional sport organizations, the IFOCE collaborates with and advertises through sponsors, promulgates guidelines and rules for its contests, establishes venues for the competitions, glorifies the records established by its contenders and has a formal ranking system. While professional competitive eating has gained recognition and market share in Canada, England, Japan (where it is regularly televised), Germany, Thailand, Russia and Scotland, this discussion will focus on the United States.

If the medium is truly the message,[15] then professional competitive eating has gained an enormous foothold in the American cultural scene over the last ten years, since the inception of the IFOCE. With the more recent advent of AICE, professional eating competitions have received attention in countless local, state and international newspapers and magazines; scientific theories have been espoused in mainstream periodicals;[16] photographs of the contests and contestants are regularly broadcast over the Internet (thanks to the AP and UP), and there has even been a documentary film entitled *Crazy Legs Conti: Zen and the Art of Competitive Eating*.[17] In addition, two books have been written on the subject,[18] there have been television documentaries on professional competitive eating on major television and cable networks, including MTV, the Discovery channel and NBC,[19] and plot lines centering on eating contests and competitions have found their way onto popular prime-time television shows for both children and adults.[20]

And then there is the food, the glorious food, the staple, if you will, of professional competitive eating. Contenders may be either specialists or generalists, focusing on one or a number of food categories in which to compete. And the range of food is indeed impressive. It includes pizza, asparagus, baked beans, sausage, beef tongue, birthday cake, bologna, brats (bratwurst), buffet, burritos, butter, cabbage, candy bars, cannoli, cheesecake, chicken nuggets, chicken wings, chili, chocolate, conch fritters, corn dogs, corned beef hash, cow brains, crab cakes, crawfish, okra, donuts, dumplings, eggs, French fries, fruit cake, jello, grapes, green beans, grilled cheese sandwiches, gyoza, sliced ham, hamburger, hot dogs, huevos rancheros, ice cream, jalapeños, jambalaya, lobster, matzo balls, mayonnaise, meatballs, native American fry bread, onions, oysters, pancakes, pasta, peas, pickles, pies (strawberry, key lime, pumpkin, shoofly, meat, mince, rhubarb and apple), pomme frits, pork ribs, posole, quesadillas, rice balls, shrimp, spam, sweet corn, sweet potatoes, tacos, tamales, Tex-Mex rolls, tiramisu, ravioli, turducken (a chicken stuffed inside a duck stuffed inside a turkey), waffles, watermelon, and whole turkey.

To date, the IFOCE posts ratings of the top 50 contenders. At the time of this writing, the most respected of the gurgitators were Takeru Kobayashi, whose records include 53 ¾ hot dogs (with buns) in 12 minutes and 97 Krystal burgers in 8 minutes; Joey Chestnut, whose records include 173 chicken wings in 30 minutes and 47 grilled cheese sandwiches in 10 minutes; Sonya Thomas, whose records include 11 pounds of cheesecake in 9 minutes and 80 chicken nuggets in 5 minutes; Tim Janus (Eater 'X') whose records include 26 cannoli in 6 minutes and 51 tamales in 12 minutes; and Dale Boone (purported descendant of Daniel), whose records include 28 reindeer sausage in 10 minutes and 274 dumplings in 6 minutes.

These gurgitators move up the rankings by competing in small venues, where they gain attention and recognition, before being invited to compete in larger venues for more lucrative prizes. Competitions are held at restaurants, malls, amphitheaters, state and county fairs and on cruise ships, with the number of events sanctioned by the IFOCE alone growing to over 75 per year. Attendance at these events ranges from hundreds to thousands, as in the case of the Annual 4th of July Hot Dog Eating Contest at Nathans' in Brooklyn. This litany doesn't even begin to scratch at the surface of the number of annual eating competitions which are far less formal, televised or attended, let alone sanctioned by either the IFOCE or AICE.

Loose from Its Moorings

In the previous section, I explored the structure of competitive eating, addressing the "what" of the phenomenon. However, in order to answer some of the deeper questions posed at the outset of this discussion, those that seek to address the "why" of professional competitive eating, we must move beyond the simple outward trappings of the sport to the rich and complex cultural and historical tapestry within which it is woven. In order to do so, I will invoke both Manning's notion of the "cultural production"[21] and Aristotle's related observations on drama/tragedy.[22]

A cultural production is a dramatic presentation comprised of several elements including a model, or embodied ideal, an influence, a medium, an audience and a producer. In anthropology, cultural productions would include, but are not limited to, sports spectacles, fairs, celebrations and ceremonies. Each of these forms are signifiers or narrative texts which are "vivid aesthetic creations that reflexively depict, interpret and inform the social context."[23] In the case of professional competitive eating, the model or ideal would be immoderate consumption, the influence would be the norms for eating in the particular society, the medium of communication would be the public gathering at which it occurs (fairs, restaurant promotions, carnivals and sporting events), the audience would be those witnessing the event, either by reading about it in newspapers and magazines, watching it on television or attending it in person; and the producer would be the emcee of the event. Reframing eating competition thusly allows us to look beyond the hot dogs, hoopla and hype to what the spectacle tells us about ourselves as a society.

In his *Poetics*,[24] Aristotle considered drama and dramatic poetry to be an imitation of action, designed to arouse the imagination and emotion of an audience. The actions he referred to were the frequent and often unpredictable painful circumstances of life (loss, harm, reversal of fortune) that befell people, both ordinary and elevated. Aristotle believed that through the dramatic depiction, the poet spoke from his imagination to that of the audience with the intention of arousing pity, evoking fear and providing catharsis. All of these consequences connected the audience to the double-sided richness of the human experience while also offering relief through purgation once they left the theater. He saw the power of theater as addictive, offering a venue for both the experience and relief of intense feeling. Reframing competitive eating as modern-day drama, in addition to cultural production, allows us to consider even more deeply the relationship between the eater, audience and culture who share in the feast we call professional competitive eating.

The Gurgitators: Fifteen Minutes of Fame

I believe, as did Aristotle, that the actor in the drama, although he moves and speaks (and eats, in our case), is simply the vehicle through which the poet shares his imagination in order to provoke the audience to heights of emotion to be both experienced and purged. Similarly, I believe that the professional competitive eater, while obviously essential, is little more than foreground in the unfolding drama on the stage, which is a dynamic microcosm given meaning and energy through the audience, which revels and reviles, and the society which sanctions it.

With this said, and before moving on to the macrocosm that includes the audience and society, some reflections on the gurgitator are warranted. Andy Warhol is credited with the notion of "15 minutes of fame," which in its original form was "in the future, everyone will be world-famous for 15 minutes."[25] If fame is a function of name recognition, money earnings, "world records" and/or media exposure, then Dale Boon, Coon-Dog O'Karma, Joey Chestnut, Eater 'X,' Sonya Thomas, Crazy Legs Conti and Takeru Kobayashi have earned their 15 minutes. Not only the reputed (and ranked) as the best eaters on the professional circuit, they are also the most colorful, spirited and competitive, typifying the drama in a most Aristotelian fashion. Each of these individuals has a story, some more colorful than the next, and each has a *raison d'être*, which may or may not be directly connected to professional competitive eating.[26]

While it is appealing to psychoanalyze these competitors who consume prodigious and seemingly self-destructive quantities of food that wreak havoc on their gastrointestinal, cardiovascular and physiological well-being, I will leave this bit of pathography[27] to others. Similarly, it would be seductive to consider these competitors as actors in a socially sanctioned gorge fest which represents the "expression of the social body to establish equilibrium [and] to break free of restraints,"[28] just as private eating disorders reflect failed attempts of the individual to regulate him- or herself. And, finally, it might be fascinating to consider the public gluttony of professional competitive eaters as a form of self-debasement designed as purgation.

On the other hand, and perhaps, from a more benign perspective, professional competitive eating represents the fruits, so to speak, of the democratization of professional competitive sport. It provides anyone with the opportunity to compete, gain fame — albeit for 15 minutes — and fortune. Such was the case of an enthusiastic young man who recently volunteered at the last minute to participate in a soft-pretzel eating competition sponsored by the IFOCE in Miami, Florida. While he could certainly not hold his own with the likes of Joey Chestnut, who consumed 21 pretzels, or Eater X, who ate only four less, he was nevertheless being cheered on by hundreds of enthusiastic spectators. Sadly, he did not fare well.

Stories like this abound, and will no doubt someday rise to the level of urban legend. The association between professional sport and professional eating, as well as that between professional athletes and gurgitators, will continue to be vociferously argued from both sides of the table. In the end, it will be up to history to record the role and value of the professional competitive eater. Long may he gorge! I now turn to the audience in order to understand the deeper significance of professional competitive eating.

The Audience: The Faithful Followers

Beyond this brief discussion of the role of the contestant in the professional eating competition, it is appealing to consider the food, and in doing so, its anthropological significance as a "functional unit of a system of communication."[29] However, I believe that the true narrative drama of the event is captured in the interplay between the eater and the audience. Specifically, I posit that in an archetypical sense, the gorger is us, and we are the gorger; he is but a shadowy reflection of our primitive insatiability. Drawn from the ranks of the everyday man (and woman), rather from a rarified farm system that grooms the professional athlete from early life for high stakes and high publicity, it is, as in the case of the hapless volunteer in the pretzel contest mentioned above, ourselves who are up on the stage. Without the audience cheering and jeering, these competitors are little more than aberrant, albeit spectacular gluttons who choose to perform their gluttony in public. What, then, can we learn about ourselves by considering the audience?

In order to understand the audience, I have chosen to focus on the "omnivore's dilemma."[30] Simply stated, this notion suggests that, because humans have evolved to be able to eat anything, they do so at the cost of heightened vigilance for harmful food. Unlike the koala bear, whose foraging range is limited to eucalyptus trees and their sustenance to its leaves, we are capable of consuming the flora and fauna of all places, and must be ever careful of eating the wrong mushroom, the diseased animal, or ingesting the wrong bacterium. With the advent and complexity of the industrial food chain, which adds the potential dangers of additives, preservatives, fertilizers, pesticides, bacteria, viruses and parasites, not to mention the toxic wastes of the manufacturing process, the perils to the omnivore multiply exponentially. This expansion in the range of potential dangers in everything we eat, either natural or manufactured, contributes to the fact that "we humans have to rely on culture to remember and keep it all straight. So we codify the rules of wise eating in an elaborate structure of taboos, rituals, manners and culinary traditions covering everything from the proper size of portions to the order in which food should be consumed to the kind of animals that it is not OK to eat."[31] This dilemma, and its accompanying anxiety about eating, may very well account in large part for what has been termed our *national eating disorder,* or "tendency to reinvent the American way of eating every generation in great paroxysms of neophilia and neophobia."[32]

Why, then, would crowds rush to professional eating competitions to watch others ingest foods that are considered by science and common sense to be the unhealthiest — French fries, chicken wings, cannoli, mayonnaise, hot dogs, candy bars, birthday cake, ice cream and chicken nuggets, to name a few? Anthropology tells us that "throughout history, there have been many stringent taboos on watching other people eat in the presence of others."[33] And since these particular foods are considered to be the most taboo, given our current state of nutritional science, perhaps the act of watching these spectacles functions as a reversal ritual of sorts, allowing the audience to vicariously consume these forbidden foodstuffs. This hypothesis is given further credence in the observation that at the end of many of these competitions the audience rushes the stage to consume the uneaten and partially eaten leftovers. This group ritual around the frenzied ingestion of taboo (or polluting) foods may function to impose system [and order] on an inherently untidy experience,"[34] which eating has become in our society. It may even be argued that this mass ritual of the ingestion of taboo food, both during and after the formal competition, is a rich and textured social narrative befitting our *fast-food nation*[35] in which "the process of ingestion portrays political absorption ... in which bodily orifices seem to represent points of entry or exit to social units."[36] In the case of this frenzied ingestion, the social unit would be the consumer, both competitor and audience of the mass-produced food, who are rising up, rebelling perhaps against the anxiety inherent in the omnivore's dilemma.

Along similar lines, we might consider that the audience, by both watching and participating, albeit after the fact, is engaging in counterphobic behavior, or watching/engaging in feared behavior as a means of compensating for or overcoming the fear. This is consistent with what has been termed the *American Paradox,*[37] or Americans' tendency to associate food most with health, and least with pleasure, and in spite of preoccupation with the fruits of medical and nutritional science, to be among the unhealthiest and nutritionally unfit among industrialized nations. In an Aristotelian sense, the audience experiences catharsis by watching (and partaking) in the unfolding drama onstage.

Lastly, the motivation of the audience may be understood within the context of the *gustatory abject.*[38] As the audience cheers on the contestants, who ingest prodigious amounts of taboo food and who teeter precipitously on the verge of regurgitation (called euphemistically *reversal of fortune*), they experience both fascination and revulsion. Both reactions are related to the notion of *food loathing*,[39] which is experienced by seeing a detested food or watching someone consume it. The food becomes abject, or detestable, by virtue of its inherent unpleasantness or the way in which it is consumed, in our case rapidly and voluminously. By witnessing this gustatory abject, the audience may either vicariously or directly experience the pleasure of (over)eating or watching someone defy the limits of their bodies,[40] and in so doing overcome their own food loathing by participating vicariously. For the audience, the sacredness of food and the profanity[41] of its abject consumption merge in the shared experience of the eating competition. The end result is a projection of the spectators into the body of the competitors, and that of the competition, to vanquish the ravages of the omnivore's dilemma. This is not entirely dissimilar to watching a reality TV show[42] on which the contestants engage in disgusting and/or humiliating food-based contests while millions sit transfixed in a voyeuristic admixture of horror, fascination, disgust and relief. Like reality TV, professional competitive eating may in the most fundamental way be "prompting us to explore our own taboos in an uninhibited fashion."[43]

Society

In the above, it was argued that the professional competitive eater gives voice to and assists the audience in moderating the impact of the omnivore's dilemma. The eater and the audience are one! In a parallel vein, it will now be posited that the stage upon which the professional eating contest is enacted is a microcosm for the larger issues confronted by our society, particularly those that came with the industrialization of the food chain and the growing distance from our agricultural tradition. As opposed to simply being the next big thing in an already saturated, sports-driven and media-frenzied marketplace, professional competitive eating may function as a powerful and multitextured societal ritual.

Ritual

Numerous in form, and multifunctional, rituals in an Aristotelian sense are enacted dramas that reveal, inform and shape culture. Whether to assist a group or society in self-definition,[44] to ensure balance between the sacred (mortal) and profane (transcendent),[45] or to provide the opportunity for the release and reintegration of societal tensions,[46] rituals like mythology "impose an order, account for the origins and nature of that order, and shape people's dispositions to experience order in the world around them."[47] Further, while there have historically been a wide variety of rituals[48] including, but not limited to rites of passage (births, deaths, marriages), calendrical celebrations (of the seasons or harvest), rites of exchange (offerings and sacrifices), rites of affliction (purification and purgation) and rites of reversal (festivals and carnivals), each to a greater or lesser extent contains a form, tradition, symbolism and drama. Professional competitive eating is, with its invariant structure and sequence, props (including T-shirts, trophies, the emcee and elevated stage), in every way a ritual, dating back nearly a century to the Nathan's 4th of July hot dog–eating contest. However, and more significantly, beyond its ancestral link to Coney Island, professional competitive eating is the stage upon which the battle between the sacred act of self-denial battles with the profanity and sinfulness of gluttony, providing both participants and audience with the opportunity for freedom from the constraints of the omnivore's dilemma. And in its controlled and contrived structure, professional competitive eating provides an outlet for, and thus a sense of control over, the ravages of our national eating disorder.

From a historical perspective, the ingestion of the most common foods in our society (oftentimes junk food) have compelling dramaturgical and symbolic ties to celebrations of the bounty of the harvest that date to antiquity and which may celebrate both our dominance over nature and the plenty of food which is the legacy of industrial food production. The adversarial nature of these competitions traces its lineage to the eating displays and contests (including pie-eating competitions) traditional to the municipal, county, state and regional fairs of the last two centuries in America, and long before that in Europe, which can be construed as societal bonding mechanisms. And in the spirit of the Egyptian celebrations of Osiris, and the Greco–Roman Bacchanalia,[49] professional competitive eating is, in its unrestrained nature, similar to the liberating rites of reversal[50] still in existence today, the most notable of which are Bike Week in Daytona and the Mardi Gras in New Orleans.

One other ritual that warrants consideration is the *feast,* which, unlike the everyday domestic meal, is "constituted by [copious and conspicuous] communal consumption of food and/or drink"[51] with dramaturgical effects that mark social transition, strengthen group solidarity, display financial wealth and political power, and express either thanks for the bounty or the subordination of the fickle and often cruel vicissitudes of nature. Records of feasting in the context of military victory, imperial display, and placation of the gods date to antiquity,[52] and wind their way through medieval celebrations of the harvest[53] to the royal and presidential pomp of the 19th and 20th centuries.

While the legacy of the great feast continues to find expression in modern-day state banquets, in lavish holiday home gatherings and both secular and religious rites of passage, they are but a vestige of their ancestral origins. In this context, "the demise of formal prescribed feasting rituals ... is probably directly related to industrialization and the advent of mass-produced consumer goods in late 19th and 20th century America."[54] With the mechanization of the kitchen manifested in the refrigerator, microwave, mass production, preservation technology and rapid global food transport, the feast has been replaced with snacking, grazing, fast and instant food, and dining out. Professional competitive eating, or sanctioned high-speed feasting, although an ostensibly banal, if not perverse, popular culture phenomenon, may represent an attempt to reintegrate feasting into culture, and culture into history.

Nostalgia and Fairs

The earliest rituals and rites, both secular and religious (although often both), were agricultural, "performed upon the body of the mother earth to unleash the sacred powers of vegetation and to appease and control death forces that are part of the life cycle."[55] Fairs and festivals have historically been the venue within which these have taken place, and, as such, have been the stages upon which societies have remained connected to the earth. References to fairs and festivals, both commercial and religious, can be found in both the Old and New Testaments, and the art and literature of both the Old and New World[56] are replete with these gatherings during which people came together to display, trade, share and sell commodities, both hand-made and grown. The European fair traveled to North America in the late 18th century, settling in Nova Scotia, moving south to northern New York State, and settling in Pittsfield, Massachusetts, thanks to the efforts of Elkana Watson, who staged the 1810 Berkshire Cattle Show.

Historically, county, state, regional and even world's fairs and expositions have been showplaces for domestic handiwork, animal husbandry and agriculture. In the modern era, less than 3 percent of Americans are engaged in farming due to industrial food production, and homemade handicrafts have given way to mass production, both here and abroad.[57] While there are still an estimated 3,200 fairs annually in the United States, "they have become big business, with high-paid country acts and hi-tech rides pushing aside the real reason fairs were born ... to be annual reminders of the nation's agricultural heritage."[58] Along with our growing disconnection from the land, the replacement of agriculture with technology at the fairs has been considered a threat to our national heritage and a nostalgic breach.

Eating contests still occur at fairs and festivals; however, their numbers are relatively small.[59] Further, while the presence of eating competitions, both informal and those sanctioned by both the International Federation of

Competitive Eaters and the Association of Independent Competitive Eaters, have grown steadily in the last several years,[60] the number of these events is also still miniscule, and insufficient to resuscitate our dying ties to the land. In contrast, eating competitions, both sanctioned and non, outside of fairs and festivals, have proliferated, thanks largely to the media. These competitions have become mainstays at malls, restaurants and carnivals, and, as was mentioned earlier, in the plotlines of television shows, movies and documentaries. It is therefore fair to speculate that the proliferation of competitive eating, both professional and amateur, is our society's attempt to nostalgically reconnect to our agricultural heritage. Food, whether homegrown or industrially wrought, and its consumption, whether private or public, moderate or gluttonous, remains the constant, and these competitions provide a societal outlet or stage for this constancy.

Conclusion

We are a competitive, achievement-oriented society, if not species. We compete for everything and with everyone, both here and abroad, both alive and dead, both present and past. We compete in sports, in school, in the marketplace and in politics, for prizes that range from self-esteem to global domination. We compete with ourselves, with family members, with friends, strangers and people across the street, the nation and the globe. At the time of this writing, religions and cultures were competing for their fair share of eternity, politicians were competing for their party's presidential nomination, industrial giants and emerging nations were competing for nuclear domination, pharmaceutical megalopolies were competing for the cures to cancer and AIDS, children were competing with each other on playgrounds and in the classroom, and America sat nervously on the verge of Super Bowl LXI, the Roman denotation for which bespeaks its identification with the great competitive spectacles and rituals of antiquity.

At the very same time, Las Vegas, the showdown capital of the world, rippled in anticipation of the First International Best (grocery) Bagging Championship. The WCW (World Championship Wrestling) universe readied for the much heralded Nitro Trading Card Game Championship. The North American Tiddlywinks Association prepared its upcoming series of mind-bending events. Players around the world were donning their dark glasses and game faces for the National Heads-up Poker Championship. And in a little office in New York City, plans were afoot for the Wienerschnitzel World Chili Cheese Fries Eating Championship on the Queen Mary, where contestants would vie for their share of ten thousand dollars and fifteen minutes of fame.

What dichotomy shall we use to compare and contrast these competitions? Sacred and profane? Significant and trivial? Informed and ignorant? Mainstream and marginal? Perhaps it is not quite as important to reconcile these dichotomies as it is to ask what each of them tells us about who we are, where we have come from, and where it is we might be going. Thoughts to consider, as we sit back, munch on our next soft pretzel, slice of cheesecake, hard-boiled egg or hot dog, join friends in friendly competition, and wash it down with our favorite blend of discourse.

Notes

1. Translated as "In Gorging, Truth," this is the official motto of the International Federation of Competitive Eaters (IFOCE), which can be found on the coat of arms of the organization (www.ifoce.com) directly below two griffins eating a hot dog from opposite ends, with their respective talons grasping mustard and ketchup bottles.

2. The name given to contestants at professional (and amateur) eating competitions.

3. According to the IFOCE, professional competitive eating has been embraced in Canada, Germany, Thailand, England, Russia, Japan and Scotland.

4. "Look, up in the sky!" is part of the opening voice-over narrative to the television show starring George Reeves (*The Adventures of Superman*, dir. Thomas Carr, Motion Pictures for Television, Inc., 1952–1958).

5. Ralph Nader, *The Nader Page,* October 24, 2003, http://www.nader.org/interest/102403.html (accessed December 14, 2006).

6. See Jason Fagone, *Horsemen of the Esophagus: Competitive Eating and the Big Fat American Dream* (New York: Crown, 2006).

7. According to Lindsey Becker (personal communication, January 22, 2007) of the International Association of Fairs and Expositions (www.iafe.com), pie-eating contests are still to be found at state and regional fairs.

8. International Association of Fairs and Expos, *History of Fairs January 2007, http://www.fairsandexpos.com/about/historyfairs.aspx,* (accessed January 10, 2007).

9. *Stand By Me*, videocassette, directed by Rob Reiner (Columbia Pictures, 1986).

10. See Nat Eastman, "Deadly Sin for Fun and Profit," *Verb* 3 (2005), for an interesting discussion of some rather bizarre eating challenges taken up during the 18th and 19th centuries in England.

11. The most well-known examples of stunt eating can be found on the "reality" cable television show *Fear Factor* (Randall Einhorrn and J. Rupert Thomason, Directors. NBC, 2001), on which contestants eat live worms, spiders, intestines, eyeballs and gonads.

12. See http://www.ifoce.com/about–history.php.

13. The term *professional* is defined at Dictionary.com. *The American Heritage(r) Dictionary of the English Language*, 4th ed. (Boston: Houghton Mifflin, 2004). *http://dictionary.reference.com/browse/professional* (accessed January 23, 2007).

14. See *http://www.competitiveeaters.com.*

15. See Marshall McLuhan, *Understanding Media: The Extensions of Man* (New York: McGraw-Hill, 1963), vii.

16. See Ariana Green, "Why a 145-pound Man Can Outeat a Former Defensive Tackle Nick-named 'The Frige,'" *Popular Science,* November 2003, 120–21.

17. *Crazy Legs Conti: Zen and the Art of Competitive Eating,* videocassette, directed by Danielle Franco and Christopher Kenneally (Oyster Productions, 2004).

18. See Fagone, *Horsemen of the Esophagus: Competitive Eating and the Big Fat American Dream* and Ryan Nerz, *Eat This Book: A Year of Gorging and Glory on the Competitive Eating Circuit* (New York: St. Martin's Griffin, 2006).

19. These include *Gut Busters* on the Discovery Channel in 2002, *The Big Eat* on NBC in 2005, and *True Life: I'm a Competitive Eater* on MTV in 2006.

20. Some of these include *The Simpsons, King of the Hill, Hey Arnold* and *Hi Hi Puffy Ami Yumi.*

21. See Frank Manning, *The Celebration of Society: Perspectives on Contemporary Cultural Performance* (Bowling Green, OH: Bowling Green University Popular Press, 1983).

22. Aristotle, *Poetics, http://www.iep.utm.edu/a/aris-poe.htm* (accessed January 25,2007).

23. Manning, 6.

24. Aristotle, *Poetics,* trans. Gerald Else (Ann Arbor: University of Michigan Press, 1967).

25. *15 Minutes of Fame,* http://en.wikipedia.org/wiki/15_minutes_of_fame (accessed January 25, 2007).

26. For information about a number of these competitors, see *http://www.ifoce.com/ eaters.php,* as well as Fagone, *Horsemen of the Esophagus* and Ryan Nerz, *Eat This Book.*

27. The term *pathography* refers to a biographical narrative focusing on disability or a negative feature of the subject. See *pathography* at Dictionary.com. *The American Heritage(r) Dictionary of the English Language,* 4th ed. (Boston: Houghton Mifflin, 2004). On-line: *http://dictionary.reference.com/browse/pathography* (accessed January 25, 2007).

28. In Emile Durkheim, "Anomie and the Moral Structure of Industry," in *Emile Durkheim: Selected Writings,* ed. and trans. Anthony Giddens (London: Cambridge University Press, 1972), 73–88. Durkheim addresses the inevitable tension in both the individual and society as they struggle to simultaneously express and contain their consumptive needs.

29. See Roland Barthes, "Toward a Psychosociology of Contemporary Food Consumption," in *Food and Culture: A Reader,* eds. Carole Counihan and Penny Van Esterik (New York: Routledge, 1997), 21, for a full discussion of the functional significance of food in society.

30. Although first offered by Claude Fischler (see Claude Fischler, *L'Homnivore* [Paris: Odile Jacob, 1990]), the concept is fully explicated in Michael Pollan, *The Omnivore's Dilemma* (New York: Penguin, 2006).

31. Pollan, 296.

32. Pollan, 299.

33. See Margaret Mead, "The Changing Significance of Food," in *Food and Culture: A Reader,* eds. Carole Counihan and Penny Van Esterik (New York: Routledge, 1997).

34. Mary Douglas, *Purity and Danger: An Analysis of the Concepts of Pollution and Taboo* (New York: Ark Paperbacks, 1988), 4.

35. See Eric Schlosser, *Fast-Food Nation: The Dark Side of the All-American Meal* (Boston: Houghton Mifflin, 2001).

36. Douglas, 4.

37. See P. Rozin, C. Fischler, S. Imada, A. Sarubin, and A. Wrezeesniewski, "Attitudes to Food and the Role of Food in Life in the U.S.A., Japan, Flemish Belgium and France: Implications for the Diet-Health Debate," *Appetite* 33 (1999): 163–80. This research presents a multination survey of food attitudes and eating habits.

38. See Vivian Halloran, "Biting Reality: Extreme Eating and the Fascination with the Gustatory Abject," *Iowa Journal of Cultural Studies* 4 (2004): 27–42.

39. For a complete discussion of food loathing and the gustatory abject, see Julia Kristeva, *Powers of Horror: An Essay on Abjection,* trans. Leon S. Roudiez (New York: Columbia University Press, 1982).

40. See Halloran, 27–42. She discusses the gustatory abject in the context of professional competitive eating, reality TV eating stunts, and *Fat Memoirs.*

41. For a complete discussion of the sacred and profane symbol, see Emile Durkheim, "Religion and Ritual," in *Emile Durkheim: Selected Writings,* ed. and trans. Anthony Giddens (London: Cambridge University Press, 1972), 219–38.

42. See Steven Johnson, *Everything Bad Is Good for You: Why Popular Culture Is Making Us Smarter* (London: Penguin, 2005), for a discussion of how reality television provides a powerful vicarious experience that simultaneously attracts and repels viewers.

43. Nerz, 144.

44. See Victor Turner, ed., *Celebration: Studies in Festivity and Ritual* (Washington, D.C.: Smithsonian Institution Press, 1982).

45. Durkheim, "Religion and Ritual."

46. Alan Pratt, "Modern America and Its Discontents: The Ride-Hard, Die-Free Fantasy of Bike Week," *Americana: The Journal of American Popular Culture* 1 (2002).

47. Catherine Bell, *Ritual: Perspectives and Dimensions* (Oxford: Oxford University Press, 1997), 21.

48. Catherine Bell offers an impressive classification of the numerous rites and rituals dating to antiquity.

49. Pratt.

50. A "rite of reversal" is a staged and tolerated event during which revelers — members of society who are seen as repressed, constrained or ostracized — have free rein in wild celebrations of mock defiance of the status quo and the ruling or in-power class. They are similar in tone and expression to an orgy, a temporary return to primitive chaos. See Mircea Eliade, *Patterns in Comparative Religion,* trans. Rosemary Sheed (New York: Meridian Press, 1966).

51. Michael Deiter and Bryan Hayden, "Digesting the Feast: Good to Eat, Good to Drink, Good to Think: An Introduction to Feasts," in *Feasts: Archaeological and Ethnographic Perspectives on Food, Politics and Power,* eds. Michael Deiter and Bryan Hayden (Washington, D.C.: Smithsonian Institution Press, 2001), 4.

52. See Roy Strong, *Feast, A History of Grand Eating* (New York: Harcourt, 2002).

53. See Robert Lacey and Danny Danziger, *The Year 1000: What Life Was Like at the Turn of the First Millennium* (New York: Little, Brown, 1999).

54. Douglas Wilson and William Rathje, "Garbage and the Modern American Feast," in *Feasts: Archaeological and Ethnographic Perspectives on Food, Politics and Power,* eds. Michael Deiter and Bryan Hayden (Washington, D.C.: Smithsonian Institution Press, 2001), 416.

55. Mircea Eliade, *Patterns in Comparative Religion*, trans. Rosemary Sheed (New York: Meridian Press, 1966), 332.

56. International Association of Fairs and Expos, *History of Fairs January 2007.* Online at http://www.fairsandexpos.com/about/historyfairs.aspx (accessed January 10, 2007).

57. John McCarry and Randy Olson, "County Fairs," *National Geographic* (October 1997), 32–36.

58. See Daniel Wood, "The Great State Fair Conundrum," *Christian Science Monitor* 90 (1998): 1.

59. Personal communication with Jim Tucker of the International Federation of Fairs and Expositions. On-line: http://www.iafe.com (accessed January 1, 2007).

60. Personal communication with Matthew Rizzetta of the International Federation of Competitive Eaters.

Works Cited

Aristotle. *Poetics.* Translated by Gerald Else. Ann Arbor: University of Michigan Press, 1967.

Barthes, Roland. "Toward a Psychosociology of Contemporary Food Consumption." In *Food and Culture: A Reader,* eds. Carole Counihan and Penny Van Esterik, 20–27. New York: Routledge, 1997.

Bell, Catherine. *Ritual: Perspectives and Dimensions.* Oxford: Oxford University Press, 1997.

Crazy Legs Conti: Zen and the Art of Competitive Eating. Videocassette. Directed by Danielle Franco and Christopher Kenneally. Oyster Productions, 2004.

Deiter, Michael, and Bryan Hayden. "Digesting the Feast: Good to Eat, Good to Drink, Good to Think: An Introduction to Feasts." In *Feasts: Archaeological and Ethnographic Perspectives on Food, Politics and Power,* eds. Michael Deiter and Bryan Hayden, 1–20. Washington, D.C.: Smithsonian Institution Press, 2001.

Douglas, Mary. *Purity and Danger: An Analysis of the Concepts of Pollution and Taboo.* New York: Ark Paperbacks, 1988.

Durkheim, Emile. "Anomie and the Moral Structure of Industry." In *Emile Durkheim: Selected Writings,* ed. and trans. Anthony Giddens, 239–252. London: Cambridge University Press, 1972.

_____. "Religion and Ritual." In *Emile Durkheim: Selected Writings,* ed. and trans. Anthony Giddens, 219–238. London: Cambridge University Press, 1972.

Eastman, Nat. "Deadly Sin for Fun and Profit." *Verb* 3 (2005).

Eliade, Mircea. *Patterns in Comparative Religion.* Translated by Rosemary Sheed. New York: Meridian Press, 1966.

Fagone, Jason. *Horsemen of the Esophagus: Competitive Eating and the Big Fat American Dream.* New York: Crown, 2006.

Fear Factor. Directed by Randall Einhornn and J. Rupert Thomason. NBC, 2001.

Green, Ariana. "Why a 145-pound Man Can Outeat a Former Defensive Tackle Nicknamed 'The Frige,'" *Popular Science,* November, 2003.

Halloran, Vivian. "Biting Reality: Extreme Eating and the Fascination with the Gustatory Abject." *Iowa Journal of Cultural Studies* 4 (2004): 24–42.

Johnson, Steven. *Everything Bad Is Good for You: Why Popular Culture Is Making Us Smarter.* London: Penguin, 2005.

Kristeva, Julia. *Powers of Horror: An Essay on Abjection.* Trans. Leon S. Roudiez. New York: Columbia University Press, 1982.

Lacey, Robert, and Danny Danziger. *The Year 1000: What Life Was Like at the Turn of the First Millennium.* New York: Little, Brown, 1999.

Manning, Frank. *The Celebration of Society: Perspectives on Contemporary Cultural Performance.* Bowling Green, OH: Bowling Green University Popular Press, 1983.

McCarry, John, and Randy Olson. "County Fairs," *National Geographic,* October 1997.

McLuhan, Marshall. *Understanding Media: The Extensions of Man.* New York: McGraw-Hill, 1963.

Mead, Margaret. "The Changing Significance of Food." In *Food and Culture: A Reader,* eds. Carole Counihan and Penny Van Esterik, 11–19. New York: Routledge, 1997.

Nerz, Ryan. *Eat This Book: A Year of Gorging and Glory on the Competitive Eating Circuit.* New York: St. Martin's Griffin, 2006.

Pollan, Michael. *The Omnivore's Dilemma.* New York: Penguin, 2006.

Pratt, Alan. "Modern America and Its Discontents: The Ride-Hard, Die-Free Fantasy of Bike Week." *Americana: The Journal of American Popular Culture 1900 to Present* 1, no. 1 (2002). On-line at http://www.americanpopularculture.com/journal/articles/spring_2002/pratt.htm.

Rozin, P., C. Fischler, S. Imada, A. Sarubin, and A. Wrezeesniewski. "Attitudes to Food and the Role of Food in Life in the U.S.A., Japan, Flemish Belgium and France: Implications for the Diet-Health Debate." *Appetite* 33 (1999): 163–80.

Schlosser, Eric. *Fast-Food Nation: The Dark Side of the All-American Meal.* Boston: Houghton Mifflin, 2001.

Stand By Me. Videocassette. Directed by Rob Reiner. Columbia Pictures, 1986.

Strong, Roy. *Feast: A History of Grand Eating.* New York: Harcourt, 2002.

Turner, Victor, ed. *Celebration: Studies in Festivity and Ritual.* Washington, DC: Smithsonian Institution Press, 1982.

Wilson, Douglas, and William Rathje. "Garbage and the Modern American Feast." In *Feasts: Archaeological and Ethnographic Perspectives on Food, Politics and Power,* eds. Michael Deiter and Bryan Hayden, 404–21. Washington D.C.: Smithsonian Institution Press, 2001.

Wood, Daniel. "The Great State Fair Conundrum." *Christian Science Monitor* 90 (1998): 1–4.

18

"Gourmandizing," Gluttony and Oral Fixations

Perspectives on Overeating in the American Journal of Psychiatry, *1844 to the Present*

DR. MALLAY OCCHIOGROSSO

The meaning of "overeating," which I will loosely define as eating more than a "normal" person, or more than what is purportedly "good for you," has varied since the inception of academic psychiatry in the middle of the nineteenth century. Although there exist useful accounts of the histories of the two other main eating-related psychiatric disorders, anorexia and bulimia nervosa, the subject of overeating has never been studied in a systematic and comprehensive fashion by the discipline.

As an abnormal type of feeding behavior, overeating, or *bulimia* (the term comes from the word for "ox-like hunger"), has been observed and reported in documents as far back as the medical texts of the Ancient Greeks[1] and the Babylonian Talmud,[2] as an entry in compendiums of human behavioral aberrations, as well as anecdotally, as a kind of medico-psychological curiosity. In academic psychiatric accounts, overeating was until recently almost always treated as an epiphenomenon, with an unclear claim to being a discrete behavioral or psychological entity. It would be disinguous to proceed simply with a "history" of overeating without acknowledging that from the perspective of many of my colleagues in the field, this is a behavior that is too protean and heterogeneous to offer any hope of meaningful integration and representation over time. So why try? For two main reasons!

First of all, overeating, in the form of "binge-eating disorder," has recently garnered the "distinction" of being proposed as an official psychiatric disorder. This is in the context of an explosion in psychiatric research on various feeding behaviors in the past three decades. For example, in the database that this writer compiled in the course of preparing this essay, the number of studies of overeating alone tripled in the 1980s and 1990s (and it would have multiplied wildly had studies of anorexia nervosa and bulimia nervosa been included). Notwithstanding the amount of attention it has garnered, the binge-eating disorder diagnosis has been viewed by many within the field as provisional and controversial. However, a drastic shift in the amount of attention given to a topic often indicates that something noteworthy is afoot within a given scientific culture, from the perspective of both its internal dynamics and the broader culture within which it resides.

Observers of this explosive interest in overeating who also study the history and anthropology of contemporary psychiatry have taken a variety of different views of it. Some have viewed it as frankly suspect, either as part of the broader trend of casting as deviant those who overeat, or as another example of our attempt to sanitize certain behaviors by "medicalizing" them — a kind of special pleading on the part of a culture devoted to excess and self-indulgence.

That leads me to my second point. It is not within the scope of this chapter to summarize the work of the many writers who would criticize everything from contemporary notions of drug addiction as an illness to legal uses of psychiatric arguments to exculpate certain crimes (e.g., the "Twinkie Defense") as just so much psychiatric rhetoric. Nor do I have the space to review what seems to me the often overly reductionist views of the diagnosis as simply another reflection of the imperialist efforts of a pernicious, profit-seeking medico-pharmaceutical industrial complex.

However, the thoughtful and spirited work produced by recent writers such as Marilyn Wann, Paul Campos, Kathleen LeBesco and Richard Klein, and by scholars working in the Fat Studies field generally, has more convincingly questioned medicine's, and by implication psychiatry's, unreflectively critical stance toward overeating and fatness. From studies of popular culture, they note that the surge in medical interest in overeating has occurred in the context of the dramatic increase in media coverage of weight issues, and ever thinner standards of physical beauty. This, in turn, has led some theorists, particularly those affiliated with the fat-acceptance movement, to accuse doctors of trying to pathologize a condition that, they argue, is, in fact, actually a complex cosmetic and social issue. From reviews of the scientific literature, they point out the controversy over the links among health, overeating, and fatness, and the numerous studies linking dieting and increased overweight. They also note the low success rates of most modes of weight reduction.

It is the work of these various observers and critics that emboldened me to tackle what has at times seemed a quixotic endeavor. For when, in the course of summarizing the literature linking overeating with attempts to diet, Klein writes, "Obesity may [actually] be an iatric [sic] disease — that is, one caused by doctors, nutritionists, and health and beauty therapists,"[3] it seems time for psychiatrists to take notice.

Could Klein's statement possibly be true? We will never find a way to definitively prove or disprove it. However, why not make a start, at least, of reviewing our ways of reporting on and conceptualizing overeating, as they have (or have not) changed over time? Certainly, "ideas" about overeating are not the same thing as "facts" about overeating, and more quantitatively minded colleagues will be skeptical that a longitudinal study of our attitudes could bear much relevance to our understanding and treatment of the condition. I would disagree. In an era where the psychiatric and medical facts about overeating and its treatment are still very much in flux, I would argue that attitudes are the bulk of what we "have." This is with all due respect to colleagues who toil in the vineyards of eating disorders research — I also think their work is crucially important, since there is real information to be gathered and we must advance on both fronts at once, and I by no means wish to imply otherwise.

To help me manage what would otherwise be an overly scattered and far-ranging data set, as a preliminary approach to answering my question, I embarked on a study of the "text" surrounding overeating found in the *American Journal of Psychiatry* (*AJP*). This is the journal of record of the American Psychiatric Association, the most prominent and established official psychiatric organization in America, and, for most of its history, the most mainstream. The *AJP*, initially published under the title *The American Journal of Insanity*, was founded in 1844 and has been published continuously since, and maintains an online database of its articles, which can be searched by key word. I developed a list of 71 key words related to overeating and overweight and used the search engine to identify articles containing one or more of these key words, of which over 10,000 were found. Many of these were duplicate findings or were not relevant to my investigation, and so could be eliminated.

What follows is a preliminary summary of my review of the contents of the articles that remained. In my selection, I was interested as much in the casual remark as the "comprehensive study," for it is in the off-the-cuff comments that a culture's most unquestioned assumptions may sometimes be found. Despite my limited field of inquiry, the material I uncovered was still sufficiently varied that I cannot in any way do justice to its nuances, but must content myself with outlining its broad themes.

Starving

The earliest psychiatrists were asylum superintendents. Their main concern was not the fatness of their patients, but simply having enough money to feed them. They mainly communicated with each other via "asylum reports," which were replete with boasts of the abundant, healthy food at *their* institution, compared to others,' where inmates starved or were fed poor, non-nutritious diets.

These superintendents also repeatedly came up against the food refusal that accompanies many altered mental states, and, in their published writing, would share tips on methods for circumventing it — including, if need be, force-feeding patients — or note, with relief, when such undereating stopped or was cured. "March 3d. — Improving; has developed a large appetite, and is gaining in weight," reads a typical report, an account of the successful treatment (with thyroid gland) of a 34-year-old woman admitted with a case of "puerperal melancholia, with stupor."[4] The journal went so far as to devote a full 42 pages of its July 1859 issue to a printed version of a talk given before the Association of Medical Superintendents of American Institutions for the Insane on the causes and treatment of the condition, termed "sitomania"; the lengthy discussion that followed the talk was also reprinted. Noted one participant: "There is, perhaps, no class of cases so troublesome and attended with such great anxiety of mind as those who obstinately persist in refusing food...."[5]

These superintendents apparently enjoyed the occasional good meal themselves. In reports of their annual conventions, following painstakingly detailed accounts of the scientific programs, they write of adjourning to delightful, abundant, and refreshing repasts.

"Gormandizing," Gluttony, and the Criminal Mind

In contrast to the above, accounts of overeating in the psychiatrically disturbed do surface in these early reports as well. These references mainly fall into two general categories. The first type is what was termed *gormandizing* [sic] or *gluttony* (the former term carrying more of an implication of sensual pleasure than the latter), and in accounts it is usually described with a tone of moral censure.

Take, for example, the case of "Madame Zelia," a "privileged" 23-year-old treated in England. "By her beauty, her wit, her various talents, she exercised an irresistible influence: she could converse readily in three languages. Yet she was a creature of the worst instincts, given up to the pleasures of sense. From her earliest years she showed herself a gourmand, was slovenly, deceitful, disorderly, lazy, excessively inclined to sexual pleasures." Mme. Z. was held in an asylum for six months, given an unspecified "uterine" treatment for her nymphomania, and finally discharged back to the care of her family.[6] The author states that she typifies a case of one of those "vicious, unhealthy organizations" who (among other signs of psychopathology) "abandon themselves to sensual excesses."[7]

Another observer, in 1855, described a gourmand as someone "whose 'god was in his belly,' and who thought of little else during life than how to satisfy its morbid cravings."[8] Here, overtones of a Protestant ethic that found excessive indulgence of fleshly appetites sinful seem audible — or is the author being more arch, or even tongue-in-cheek, than a reader at a remove is able to discern? Over a century later, an anonymous editor at the journal would insert into the blank space following a journal article, presumably as a simple space filler, the following bit of waggery from Ambrose Bierce: "GLUTTON, n. A person who escapes the evils of moderation by committing dyspepsia."[9]

It was commonplace in that era to regard temperance in diet as a crucial foundation to good mental health. Some psychiatrists went so far as to link habitual overindulgence in food and drink to the development of criminality. In the *AJP*, we find this sentiment reflected in the records of an 1862 debate over the insanity plea at a superintendents' conference, where one participant, a Dr. Alex Stevens, said that he agreed with the sentiment that some classes of insanity "are voluntarily brought out by the indulgence of evil passions." As a logical extension of this belief, "if we would rescue from punishment those who have voluntarily brought insanity upon themselves, we must keep a strict guard over all the vices, the practice of which leads to such a result."

Rebutted the next speaker: "It seems to me that if we are compelled to decide, in the eyes of the law, the innocence or guilt of the party on the ground taken by Dr. Stevens, no one would escape punishment. How common is it to indulge in too much eating, drinking, and in various other acts which are known as the causes of insanity...?"[10] Possibly he had that evening's banquet already in mind.

The other type of overeating described in this era was that which was observed in patients who suffered from some type of frank brain pathology, such as in "imbeciles" and "idiots," victims of "dementia praecox" (what we today call schizophrenia), or the encephalitic. The comments in this context tend to be more reportorial in tone. Notwithstanding, the authors make clear the belief of the time that inculcating more temperate and restrained eating habits in these patients would be equivalent to advancing them morally.

Sick: Psychiatric Illness Makes You Overeat

The gluttons and gourmands of the nineteenth century made way for new kinds of patients in the twentieth, and the number of psychiatric and medical diagnoses associated with disorders of consumption expanded. The presence of food-related symptoms also starts to be recorded and reported with more frequency in the journal. Illnesses in which patients were noted to overeat, either episodically or chronically, ranged from the biological (neurosyphilis, brain tumors, brain aneurysms, Alzheimer's disease, Huntington's disease, drug withdrawal, hypopituitarism, catatonia, "macropsia") to the psychiatric and psychological (schizophrenia, atypical depression, stress caused by space travel [!], neurosis and "excessive orality").

Beginning in the 1940s, when insulin shock therapy was supplanted by electroconvulsive therapy and lithium salts in the 1950s, and then into our current era of psychotropic medications, psychiatric treatments were noted to cause overeating. Numerous articles appear in the *AJP* that are devoted to studying and treating the associated weight gain.

While the frank moral censure of the nineteenth century of overeating faded from these accounts, the activity was not viewed with particular kindness or sympathy. Nor did plain old good food or its enjoyment fare particularly well. In a 1933 article criticizing psychoanalysis, the author accused analysts of labeling those who simply "enjoy a good meal" as having an "oral character."[11] Whether this writer was simply setting up a straw man in psychoanalysts is unclear, but the unease at being possibly associated with gourmandism was not. A 1942 report on the course of 22 patients who had undergone frontal lobotomy found that "enormous increases in appetite" occurred in four patients, and one manifested "a rather vulgar enjoyment of food." In general, the article noted with evident regret, the patients lost interest in the more "sophisticated" "intellectual and artistic pursuits" and were contented with simpler things like "an ice-cream cone."[12] A 1966 review of a book of collected essays on the subject of family therapy stated that "the reader will come up with the sensation that follows eating a frothy, rich dessert — a sort of empty satiation."[13]

In subsequent writings dedicated to advancing "mental hygiene" in the worried well, as well as in the psychiatrically ill, criminality and overindulgence in food are no longer linked. But overeating is still viewed as one of the stones that paves the way to chronic unhappiness and maladjustment. A writer in 2003, reviewing what he considered to be the five main models of mental health, stated that "experts" should not always be permitted to have the last word in what constituted true happiness, because there was also a role for an individual's subjective sense of fulfillment. However, this subjective happiness was not always so trustworthy, and the author used overeating as an example: "Examples of maladaptive 'happiness' include the ... short-lived satisfaction from binge eating, tantrums, promiscuity, and revenge."[14] (At least it is in good company.)

This is not the place to review Western culture's perennial love-hate relationship with tasty treats; for a readable and succinct contemporary account, the reader is referred to Francine Prose's *Gluttony*. Nor is it within the scope of this discussion to summarize the elegant work done by Elizabeth Lunbeck and Georges Canguilhem in delineating the complex role played by both patients and psychiatrists in extending the domain of the discipline from warehousing of the chronically psychotic or mentally handicapped into the realm of both defining and upholding as a treatment ideal the "normal." Suffice it to say that this historical trend encompasses the psychiatric community's willingness to take under its purview issues of weight and eating, and its sense of prerogative in passing judgment on those who deviate from its standards.

Ego Lesions and Excessive Orality

In 1943, the first article in the *AJP* devoted to overeating and overweight per se appears: Hilde Bruch's "Psychiatric Aspects of Obesity in Children." This article opens with a brisk refutation of the then-popular theory that obesity in children was always caused by "glandular disorder," and then reviews the behavioral and psychological factors that Bruch had observed in her clinical practice. As elsewhere in her writing, Bruch describes overeating as having certain protective aspects: "[The obese child] uses excessive eating [...] to alleviate his feelings of insecurity and insignificance. [...] Though in a distorted form, he does give expression to his creative striving in this static form of bodily largeness."[15]

Bruch aside, psychoanalysts in the *AJP* generally had nothing positive to say about overeating. They painted a dismal picture of overeating in adults as a behavior indicative of a flawed, inadequate personality structure, one with "oral conflicts" or excessive oral needs. One of the most pessimistic personality assessments came from psychologist Alexander Guiora, writing in 1967, who proposed that bulimia was actually one end of a spectrum of disordered eating, whose other "pole" was anorexia nervosa. He proposed to call this type of eating "dysorexia," and the six cases he had observed were all of young women with striking reports of extremely disordered eating patterns, from massive episodic binges to starvation. Of these women he wrote: "They [...] express an insatiable emotional hunger, manifest egocentricity and infantile behavior, and experience difficulties in sexual identification and doubts as to their heterosexual status." He viewed the root cause of their eating difficulties as a severe "ego lesion" with an exceedingly poor prognosis.[16]

The one exception to this general tone of gravity, or even alarm, among the psychodynamically informed observers merits note. A 1960 article by a doctor who studied the psychological effects of working for lengthy periods of time on a scientific research crew in the Antarctic documents striking appetite increases among the men. The author writes, "'oral' needs were enhanced, presumably because of tensions that could not be readily expressed, and because of the absence of other basic gratifications. Appetite and consumption were enormous, and weight gains of 20 or 30 pounds during the year were not unusual. When the cook was adequate to the challenge, his prestige was of course enormous."[17] *Of course!*

It is fascinating to speculate why massive weight gain among young men in the pursuit of science is treated as droll, whereas in young women it is inevitably treated as cause for alarm. This writer cannot help but wonder if it reflects the difference in the wider cultural meaning in being overweight for the two genders, and the presumed divergent levels of distress that such a weight gain would cause. As Canguilhelm has pointed out, many maladies seen in medicine are "created" by patients, i.e., they became disorders not so much because of any evident pathology but because the patients feel themselves to be abnormal. Some feminist theory-informed thinkers, on the other hand, might argue that the impetus to this dichotomous treatment is a patriarchal scientific culture's embrace of conventional beauty and behavior standards for women.

A New Era: The "Discovery" of Binge Eating and Bulimia

The 1967 Guiora article dedicated to the syndrome of "dysorexia" was the bellwether for a new trend in describing overeating that would emerge in the 1970s and 1980s in a flood of new research and articles. This was to associate overeating with diagnoses of binge-eating disorder (and its less-discussed variant, night-eating syndrome) and bulimia, which, in turn, occurred in the broader context of the crystallization of eating disorders nosology within the psychiatric community of that era. This trend would be canonized in the formation of a separate "eating disorders" section in the *Diagnostic and Statistical Manual of Mental Disorders,* which in that era also rose to prominence itself as the era's diagnostic bible.

To consider these entities as discrete syndromes in themselves was a watershed in the psychiatric conceptualizations of overeating. It should be noted here that the "syndromization" of overeating in this era was not unique to it; the era was one that witnessed an unprecedented mushrooming of and splintering of psychiatric diagnostic categories. Concomitantly, there was a similar preoccupation with eating disorders in the media, for example, *Newsweek* dubbed 1981 the "year of the binge-purge syndrome."[18] A full discussion of this cultural phenomenon and its possible link with trends in psychiatric research is unfortunately beyond the scope of this paper.

The literature on binge eating and bulimia from this era was not particularly concerned with character structure and personality traits. Rather, its focus was on population studies, in concordance with the general rise to prominence in that era of the "neo–Kraepelinian" approach of both eschewing psychoanalytic, personality function-based diagnoses and of parsing nosological, treatment and epidemiological nuances using ever larger empirical samples.

The existence of a binge-eating disorder was first proposed in another journal by prominent obesity researcher Albert Stunkard in 1959. In 1961, in his article "Hunger and Satiety," Stunkard used the term *binge* in connection with eating in the *AJP* (prior to that, it occurs only in the context of drug and alcohol ingestion),[19] and ten years after that, first use of the term in conjunction with a clinical case is found.[20]

The bulimia diagnosis was not merely one of overeating. While the details varied, and were the subject of much controversy, it was generally agreed that the overeating had to occur in discrete episodes which some now termed "binges," accompanied by distress, and a feeling of shame following the episode. Whether it had to be followed by a "compensatory activity" such as self-induced vomiting, strenuous exercising, or purging such as with laxatives, was initially a matter of debate.

Within the articles in the *AJP*, the themes that emerge in discussions of bulimia are twofold. The first is an emphasis on the disease's demographics. Bulimia is often presented, frequently in the article's opening sentences, as an unexpectedly prevalent condition, but within a particular population — America's young (white) women. Other ethnicities were studied as well, but less prominently. While the tone is customarily neutral, the positioning of such rather provocative demographic data front and center in the articles suggests concern and urgency. Second, the young women so affected usually also are noted to be quite troubled in their "life adaptation," like Guiora's dysorectics, and to be more vulnerable to mood and anxiety problems and excessive preoccupations with their weight and appearance.

The publication of the 1987 edition of the *DSM* formally changed the official definition of *bulimia nervosa* to include vomiting or some other form of purging. In the wake of this, research attention on "pure" overeating shifted to the binge-eating disorder. Again, the criteria varied, though researchers agreed that it had to be accompanied by significant distress — either gastric or emotional — and occur on some kind of regular basis to qualify as a "real" psychiatric condition.

Demographically, the emphasis in the binge-eating disorder literature was less on college girls than on the obese, who were seen as particularly vulnerable to it in some studies and not in others. As with bulimia nervosa, researchers conscientiously combed through massive amounts of data to attempt to characterize the activity in a meaningful and consistent way. What *exactly* was a binge? How often did you have to binge to suffer from binge-eating syndrome? Were people who had binge-eating syndrome, assuming such a phenomenon did, in fact, exist, crazier than the rest of us?

Conclusion

Indulgent at times, censorious at others, blandly "diagnostic" or nosologically curious, psychiatrists' attitudes towards and perspectives on overeating as revealed in their most mainstream academic journal over the past 150 years have varied widely. The pioneering and fiercely independent-minded obesity researcher Hilde Bruch, in her 1957 study of fatness, *The Importance of Overweight*, noted that researchers in her era had vastly more questions than answers where overweight, obesity, and overeating were concerned. She did feel that one thing, however, was clear — that these represented the end result of a protective psychic mechanism that psychiatrists should only try to "fix" once they and the patient had replaced it, through psychotherapy, with other, "more adaptive," defenses.

Fifty years later, psychiatrists and the medical community at large are not much closer to definitive answers about the biological and psychological underpinnings of overeating, but it is not for lack of trying. The past two decades have seen an explosion of research on the subject, and a shift from the previous scattershot accounts to a conceptualization of certain forms of overeating as a discrete psychiatric syndrome. This research has not followed Bruch's lead in the regard that it frankly treats any degree of overweight as something to be cured and fatness as something to be overcome, even in the absence of clear data regarding health risks, and the presence of extremely uneven treatment results. The reasons for this divergence remain speculative. Taking the long view over the last 150 years, however, it is precisely this lack of agnosticism that stands out with regard to perspectives on overeating in the field, as well as a continual strand of puritanical attitudes toward food. Suspiciously similar to broader cultural messages about overeating? Certainly. So which came first, the disapproving social or scientific attitudes? We will never know for sure, but the finding is tantalizingly suggestive of how profoundly embedded a putatitively objective scientific culture is in its broader social context.

Notes

1. Albert J. Stunkard, "A History of Binge Eating," in *Binge Eating: Nature, Assessment, and Treatment,* eds. by Christopher G. Fairburn and Terence G. Wilson (New York: Guildford Press, 1993), 15.

2. Allan S. Kaplan and Paul E. Garfinkel, "Bulimia in the Talmud," *American Journal of Psychiatry* 141 (1984): 721.

3. Richard Klein, *Eat Fat* (New York: Vintage, 1998), 13.

4. C. R. Clarke, "Thyroid Feeding in Some Forms of Mental Trouble," *American Journal of Insanity* 52 (1895): 226.

5. Dr. T. R. H. Smith, cited in *Proceedings of the Fourteenth Annual Meeting of the Association of Medical Superintendents of American Institutions for the Insane, American Journal of Insanity* 16 (1859): 69.

6. A. Bierre de Boismont, "The Criminal Insane of England: A Medico-Psychological and Legal Study," *American Journal of Insanity* 27 (1871): 303.

7. De Boismont, 300.

8. A. O. Kellogg, "Considerations on the Reciprocal Influence of the Physical Organization and Mental Manifestations," *American Journal of Insanity* 12 (1855): 32.

9. *American Journal of Psychiatry* 126 (1969): 304.

10. Dr. Alex H. Stevens and Dr. Percy, cited in "Remarks Upon Dr. Parigot's Paper, 'On Moral Insanity in Relation to Criminal Acts,' Before the New York Academy of Medicine," *American Journal of Insanity* 18 (1862): 412.

11. Bernard Sachs, "The False Claims of the Psychoanalyst: A Review and a Protest," *American Journal of Psychiatry* (1933): 745.

12. Edward A. Strecker, Harold D. Palmer, and Francis C. Grant, "A Study of Frontal Lobotomy: Neurosurgical and Psychiatric Features and Results in 22 Cases with a Detailed Report on 5 Chronic Schizophrenics," *American Journal of Psychiatry* 98 (1942): 525.

13. Don D. Jackson, review of *Intensive Family Therapy,* by Ivan Boszormeny-Nagy and James L. Framo, *American Journal of Psychiatry* 122 (1966): 1320.

14. George E. Vaillant, "Mental Health," *American Journal of Psychiatry* 160 (2003): 1380.

15. Hilde Bruch, "Psychiatric Aspects of Obesity in Children," *American Journal of Psychiatry* 99 (1943): 756.

16. Alexander Z. Guiora, "Dysorexia: A Psychopathological Study of Anorexia Nervosa and Bulimia," *American Journal of Psychiatry* 124 (1967): 391.

17. Charles S. Mullin, "Some Psychological Aspects of Isolated Antarctic Living," *American Journal of Psychiatry* 117 (1960): 325.

18. Jerry Adler, "Looking Back at '81," *Newsweek,* January 4, 1982, 29.

19. Albert Stunkard, "Hunger and Satiety," *American Journal of Psychiatry* 118 (1961): 217.

20. Gene M. Abroms, Carl H. Fellner, and Carl A. Whitaker, "The Family Enters the Hospital," *American Journal of Psychiatry* 127 (1971): 1368.

Works Cited

Abroms, Gene M., Carl H. Fellner, and Carl A. Whitaker. "The Family Enters the Hospital." *American Journal of Psychiatry* 127 (1971): 1363–70.

Anonymous. "Proceedings of the Fourteenth Annual Meeting of the Association of Medical Superintendents of American Institutions for the Insane." *American Journal of Insanity* 16 (1859): 42–96.

Bruch, Hilde. *The Importance of Overweight.* New York: W. W. Norton, 1957.

_____. "Psychiatric Aspects of Obesity in Children." *American Journal of Psychiatry* 99 (1943): 752–57.

Campos, Paul. *The Obesity Myth: Why America's Obsession with Weight Is Hazardous to Your Health.* New York: Gotham Books, 2004.

Canguilhem, Georges. *The Normal and the Pathological.* New York: Zone Books, 1991.

Chipley, William S. "Sitomania: Its Causes and Treatment." *American Journal of Insanity* 16 (1859): 1–42.

Clarke, C. R. "Thyroid Feeding in Some Forms of Mental Trouble." *American Journal of Insanity* 52 (1895): 218–27.

De Boismont, A. Bierre. "The Criminal Insane of England: A Medico-Psychological and Legal Study." *American Journal of Insanity* 27 (1871): 278–308.

Guiora, Alexander Z. "Dysorexia: A Psychopathological Study of Anorexia Nervosa and Bulimia." *American Journal of Psychiatry* 124 (1967): 391–93.

Jackson, Don D. Review of *Intensive Family Therapy,* by Ivan Boszormeny-Nagy and James L. Framo. *American Journal of Psychiatry* 122 (1966): 1320–22.

Kaplan, Allan S., and Paul E. Garfinkel. "Bulimia in the Talmud." *American Journal of Psychiatry* 141 (1984): 721.

Kellogg, A. O. "Considerations on the Reciprocal Influence of the Physical Organization and Mental Manifestations." *American Journal of Insanity* 12 (1855): 30–38.

Klein, Richard. *Eat Fat.* New York: Vintage, 1998.

LeBesco, Kathleen. *Revolting Bodies? The Struggle to Redefine Fat Identity.* Amherst and Boston: University of Massachusetts Press, 2004.

Lunbeck, Elizabeth. *The Psychiatric Persuasion: Knowledge, Gender, and Power in Modern America.* Princeton, NJ: Princeton University Press, 1994.

Mullin, Charles S. "Some Psychological Aspects of Isolated Antarctic Living." *American Journal of Psychiatry* 117 (1960): 323–25.

Peterson, Frederick. "The Psychology of the Idiot." *American Journal of Insanity* 53 (1896): 1–25.

Prose, Francine. *Gluttony.* New York: Oxford University Press, 2003.

"Remarks Upon Dr. Parigot's Paper, 'On Moral Insanity in Relation to Criminal Acts,' Before the New York Academy of Medicine." *American Journal of Insanity* 18 (1862): 404–21.

Sachs, Bernard. "The False Claims of the Psychoanalyst: A Review and a Protest." *American Journal of Psychiatry* 89 (1933): 725–49.

Strecker, Edward A., Harold D. Palmer, and Francis C. Grant. "A Study of Frontal Lobotomy: Neurosurgical and Psychiatric Features and Results in 22 Cases with a Detailed Report on 5 Chronic Schizophrenics." *American Journal of Psychiatry* 98 (1942): 524–32.

Stunkard, Albert J. "Eating Patterns and Obesity." *Psychiatric Quarterly* 33 (1959): 284–95.

_____. "A History of Binge Eating." In *Binge Eating: Nature, Assessment, and Treatment,* eds. Christopher G. Fairburn and Terence G. Wilson, 15–34. New York: Guildford Press, 1993.

_____. "Hunger and Satiety." *American Journal of Psychiatry* 118 (1961): 212–17.

Vaillant, George E. "Mental Health." *American Journal of Psychiatry* 160 (2003): 1373–84.

Wann, Marilyn. *Fat! So? Because You Don't Have to Apologize for Your Size!* Berkeley: 10 Speed Press, 1998.

19

Having It His Way

The Construction of Masculinity in Fast-Food TV Advertising

Carrie Packwood Freeman
and Debra Merskin

An attractive twenty-something guy buying organic tofu and produce at a grocery checkout counter looks sheepishly at the man behind him who is buying about half a pig's worth of ribs. The healthy shopper's masculinity is in question when he looks over his choice of wimpy health food. Not to worry. Help is on the way when he spies a Hummer ad in the magazine rack. It is clear what he must do in order to restore his manhood; he leaves the produce and buys the SUV.

Why does this humorous Hummer TV advertisement about meat and masculinity make sense to American viewers? Clearly, advertisers trust we believe that a traditional American male does not eat organic, plant-based proteins — he primarily eats meat, which would also explain the prominence of masculine themes in advertisements for meat products, like burgers and subs.

Anthropologists have documented the historical connection between males and domination of nature and other animals, such as evidenced by humans' traditional role as animal hunters.[1] These historical relations contribute to food remaining a highly gendered cultural object in America today, particularly the gendering of meat as masculine food. Even though most women also eat meat, females are more closely associated with cultivation and consumption of plant-based foods, whereas males are more heavily associated with the killing, grilling, and consuming of animals.[2]

Ecofeminism has critiqued this patriarchal domination of animals and nature as being linked to sexist oppression of women, contributing to a larger

277

environmental and animal rights discourse that seeks to reduce humanity's role in the destruction of other species. Yet, despite these critiques, the masculine identity of man as defined by meat-eating is still celebrated by media in the twenty-first century, particularly in fast-food advertisements. To examine how this identity is often reinforced instead of challenged in American culture, this study conducts a semiotic analysis of representations of masculinity in a small selection of television advertisements for various fast-food restaurants in 2006–2007.

Advertising doesn't just sell things, it articulates values and builds meaning, sometimes through constructing stereotypes that simplify a complex trait such as gender.[3] If largely unchallenged, these carefully cultivated constructions of gender become normalized as a "regime of truth" in the American popular imagination. This analysis of American television fast-food advertising critically explores the techniques used by advertisers to exploit and perpetuate a perceived connection between masculinity and meat. We unpack the connotative messages within these commercials in order to read what they tell us about masculine identity and values in America. As we evaluate what this means for society in the twenty-first century, our analysis is influenced by our roles as feminists, vegetarians, and environmentalists. Thus, we argue that the heteronormative, sex-role stereotypes promoted in fast-food commercials are as unhealthy as the fast food itself.

To begin, we contextualize social problems surrounding the promotion of both masculinity and meat by expanding on: man's anthropological association with meat, ecofeminist perspectives on patriarchy and meat, issues with the fast-food and meat industries, and the construction of masculinity in advertising.

Human Anthropological Connections with Eating Meat

In *An Unnatural Order*, Mason explains that the human practices of killing and eating animals are "virtual sacraments in our culture" because many theories have promoted the belief that humans have been natural hunters throughout our entire evolution.[4] But new evidence suggests that, for millions of years of evolution, we humans were largely vegetarian.[5] Organized hunting of large animals, primarily by men, did not begin until approximately 20,000 years ago. Multiple anthropologists theorize that men created rituals around hunting, most of which excluded women, to gain status for themselves, as previously women had been the more revered sex for their roles as food-gatherers and procreators. As the primary foragers, women likely invented plant agriculture, which accounts for women's association with plant food as well as their importance in early agrarian societies, where many gods were female.

The domestication of animals about 11,000 years ago created a transition for many human societies to a more sedentary, agricultural way of life that included surpluses and a division of wealth. In order to protect this wealth, patriarchal warrior cultures developed, creating oppressive systems of control labor such as slavery and imperialism. Herdsmen of larger, fast-moving animals like cows had to be most warlike herders, which accounts for the later masculine mystique around cowboys and beef. According to Mason, while forager societies often viewed other animals with wonder, respect, and partnership, herder/agrarian societies disempowered animals in order to control and demystify them.[6] Thus, many human groups came to view domesticated animals as commodities and wild animals as competition and pests. Religion was often used to justify this newfound domination over nature.

In the book *Beyond Beef,* Rifkin traces the connection between meat, masculinity, and religion to ancient Egypt, where the first universal religion was bull worship, based on the bull god, Apis, who represented strength, virility and a masculine passion for war and subjugation. To mark the year's end, the Apis bull would be ritually sacrificed and fed to the king so he could incorporate the bull's fierce strength and power. More recently, in American culture, cowboys tamed the "Wild West" (and all its inhabitants), reducing millions of acres to a vast cattle grazing area, forever associating red meat with this supposedly brave and tough category of American men. Meat is further linked to masculinity by its historic association with war and male aggression, as in the practice of reserving meat for warriors.[7] In fact, the Vedic word for "war" means "desire for cows," and the Sanskrit word for "battle," *gavisti,* means "desire for cattle."

Ecofeminist Perspectives on Meat and Patriarchy

In *The Sexual Politics of Meat,* Adams promotes an ecofeminist-vegetarian theory, asserting that "women and animals are similarly positioned in a patriarchal world, as objects rather than subjects,"[8] both enduring a "cycle of objectification, fragmentation, and consumption."[9] This actuality is reinforced through media images where men "consume" women and other animals like pieces of meat. She concludes that "eating animals acts as a mirror and representation of patriarchal values. Meat-eating is the reinscription of male power at every meal."[10]

Adams highlights men's historical role in hunting animals and its perceived high social value in many cultures. "Meat was a valuable economic commodity; those who controlled this commodity achieved power."[11] Sanday found that when economies relied on plant food women held more status, and the society tended to be egalitarian, while meat-based cultures were more patriarchal.[12] Leakey and Lewin similarly found "women's social standing is roughly equal to men's only when society itself is not formalized around roles for distributing meat."[13]

Because of this history of men as meat-eaters, the men of today who eschew meat often face the stigmatization of being labeled effeminate. Adams cites nutritionist Jean Mayer, who believes that in modern society "the more men sit at their desks all day, the more they want to be reassured about their maleness in eating those large slabs of bleeding meat which are the last symbols of machismo."[14]

There is a gendered dichotomy in America's association with certain types of food for men versus women. Adams describes this dichotomy:

> Meat is king: this noun describing meat is a noun denoting male power. Vegetables ... have become as associated with women as meat is with men, recalling on a subconscious level the days of Woman the Gatherer. Since women have been made subsidiary in a male-dominated, meat-eating world, so has our food.[15]

Furthermore, nutritional scientist Sobal found this gendering of food persists in modern marriages, "men and women 'do gender' by consuming gender appropriate foods. Men emphasize meat."[16]

Issues with the Meat and Fast-Food Industries

Popular media such as *Fast Food Nation* and *Super Size Me* call attention to problems with the fast-food industry, such as low pay for workers, marketing to children, and unhealthy, and sometimes unsafe, food.[17] Many of their menu items are low in fiber and high in fat, sodium, cholesterol and simple carbohydrates, which can contribute to obesity and disease, especially when consumed in the extra-large portion sizes that are common.[18] Also, fast-food companies are the chief financial supporter of the meat industry, a problematic industry which is associated with labor exploitation (especially of immigrants),[19] mass animal cruelty and death,[20] and environmental destruction, including being a leading cause of global warming.[21] In addition, people who consume large amounts of animal products, and less whole grains and produce, may be at increased risk of contracting diseases like cancer, heart disease, and diabetes, as animal products are devoid of fiber yet contain cholesterol and saturated fat.[22] This is why the American Dietetic Association (ADA) suggests a plant-based diet prevents disease.

But since only 2.5 percent of Americans claim to be vegetarian, the average American is consuming meat, approximately 211 pounds of animal flesh a year, half of which is red meat.[23] While census data on meat consumption are not segmented by gender, at least one study proves the common belief that men tend to eat more meat than women.[24] Also, physician Emily Senay contends that despite the health risks red meat remains a staple of the masculine diet: "If they had their druthers, many men would eat a big steak and a baked potato every night for dinner."[25]

Constructions of Masculinity in Advertising

Script theory helps explain manly characters in media stories.[26] The "macho personality constellation" is comprised of three behavioral dispositions: entitlement to callous sex, propensity toward violence, and danger as exciting. When it comes to advertising specifically, research conducted in the 1970s, which has yet to be rebuked, described the basic aspects and attributes of men.[27] In relation to women, men are shown as more autonomous, employed in more occupations, used more often than women as voices of authority in voice-overs, and more often located in the public sphere (offices and outdoors).

Katz claims that today's advertisers are challenged to maintain historical heteronormative gender differences in a more progressive era "characterized by a loosening of rigid gender distinctions," so advertising masculinity must be constructed in direct opposition to femininity.[28] One way modern advertisers accomplish this is to "equate masculinity with violence, power, and control (and femininity with passivity)."[29]

Beer advertising is one genre that clearly demonstrates heteronormative male behaviors, attitudes, and beliefs. Strate's study of beer commercials found men seek acceptance among their male peers and use beer as a reward that "functions as a symbol of initiation and group membership."[30] Generally, men monopolize activity in beer commercials, although occasionally women enter the story, typically as decorative objects or as the symbolic "other woman."

The marketing of meat also often relies on gender. As there is a dearth of literature specifically addressing meat and masculinity in advertising, Adams' *Pornography of Meat* stands out. Her analysis shows how animals are feminized and women are animalized and both are often sexualized, to their ultimate detriment. The provocative title is an accusation that the dominant perspective of our advertising culture is the "pleasurable consumption of consumable beings," where Adams explains "how someone becomes a piece of meat."[31] She claims male dominance over women and all other animals virtually "disappears as a privilege and is experienced as 'desire,' as 'appetite,' as 'pleasure.'"[32]

Meating Men

To examine meat's association with masculinity in male-targeted fast-food television advertisements, we conducted an interpretive textual analysis of approximately 17 ads, using Hall's theory of representation and Barthes' method of semiotic analysis. In selecting texts, we sought fast-food television commercials that appeared to be targeted to males. The following types of codes indicated a male focus: men had the lead parts and did most of the talking, women were used primarily as objects of the male gaze, men hung out with other men and outnumbered women, and/or the narrator mentioned men specifically. In addition, while we cannot prove that other fast-food ads do not associate meat with *femininity*, a rudimentary perusal of most fast-food ads fails to suggest that the industry is constructing an association between meat and women as specifically and frequently as it is between meat and men

We included ads from Burger King, Carl's Jr., Jack in the Box, Arby's, Quizno's, and Subway. Marketing experts confirm the Burger King and Carl's Jr. campaigns are specifically targeted toward young men.[33] We initially included Subway's 2006 diet campaign with Jared as a counterexample of a more positive and less hypermasculinized approach than that used by Carl's Jr. or Burger King; however, in 2007, even Subway began to exemplify masculinity by using athletes to emphasize the meatiness of its subs.

To analyze the texts, we watched the advertisements multiple times while taking detailed notes. We then analyzed each according to common semiotic signifier including: location, music, slogans, narration, colors, gender roles, gender relations, demographics, bodily appearance, power level by gender, violent acts, food types and descriptions, relationship between food and gender, and values. Taking all the ads into consideration, we looked for themes, patterns, and anomalies across all these signifying elements.

The following are brief descriptions of the ads we included in our analysis, all of which appeared on television in the Pacific Northwest in 2006 and early 2007.

Burger King (slogan "Have It Your Way")

BK Manthem (Texas Double Whopper) — A man inspires a crowd of men to march in the streets to reclaim their right to eat meat instead of "chick food." The narrative follows an over-the-top, male-themed remake of Helen Reddy's feminist song, "I Am Woman Hear me Roar." Tagline "Eat like a man, man."

BK Stacker Construction (Double, Triple or Quadruple "Stacker" Burgers) — A boss on a mock burger construction site angrily instructs another worker, both played by little people, not to include any veggies on the stacker, as it only contains meat and cheese. He sexually harasses a full-size female employee who flicks him into a bulldozer. Tagline "Stack it high, tough guy."

Hootie Country Song (Tender Crisp Bacon Cheddar Ranch) — The lead singer from the rock group Hootie and the Blowfish sings a country song about a male fantasy land set around the sandwich. It is located on a colorful, theatrical, Western-themed set with cheerful cowboys and sexualized cowgirls — including Dallas Cowboy Cheerleaders.

Whopper Senior and Junior — A series of humorous commercials where a dad, wearing a large whopper costume, tries to teach life lessons to his rebellious teenage son, wearing the whopper junior costume. It is set in the home with female relatives playing non-burger background characters. Tagline "Whopper Jr. for a buck."

Carl's Jr

Wings (Buffalo Chicken Sandwich) — A young man chomping on chicken wings stares at a voluptuous, flirty, blond waitress. Then we see his girlfriend giving him a reproachful look, as he innocently asks "What?" The announcer tells us it is more fun to eat wings when out with the guys.

Series of at least four commercials featuring a young woman acting seductively while eating a juicy burger. 1. Paris Hilton wears a leather bathing suit while washing a luxury car, 2. Woman rides a mechanical bull in a warehouse, 3. Woman models lingerie, and 4. Woman in an office almost drips sauce on her white suit while her male coworkers watch from afar. The latter is the only ad in this series in which men appear. None of the women have speaking roles, as male narrators inform us about the sandwiches.

Jack in the Box

Test Marketing (Diner Melt Combo). Jack (company spokesman) and another executive stand behind a two-way mirror watching a group of male test subjects prove men prefer fast food over other variables meant to capture their attention, such as a motorcycle, a keg of beer, TV with sports, and women having a pillow fight. The executive informs Jack that with these findings they can rule the world. Tagline "Indulge."

Arby's

Construction Workers (Reuben sandwich) — Three male construction workers on a break stare silently at two attractive women walking by. They only start catcalling when a balding man in a suit walks by carrying an Arby's bag. Guitar music and slow motion lead the viewer to see the man in the unexpected role of a sex object. Tagline "I'm thinking Arby's."

Quizno's

Testimonials (Submarine sandwiches) — A man displaying a sub next to a Quizno's sub interviews at least seven men on the street who all testify that the Quizno's subs are better because they are meatier. No females are interviewed in this version.

Subway (slogan "Eat Fresh")

Low-Fat Subs — Jared, a male spokesman who is known for losing lots of weight on a diet of low-fat Subway sandwiches, informs us that Subway has eight sandwiches with six grams of fat or less (a veggie sub is seen as one of them but is farthest from the camera). He compares this to the BK Stacker that has 54 grams of fat, saying, "That's more fat than in all eight of these subway sandwiches combined."

Athletes say "More Meat" (Foot-long Subway Club) — A series of at least three ads featuring Jared continuing in his role of promoting the low-fat benefit of the subs while a professional athlete promotes its meatiness. The athletes include a large male football player, a large male wrestler, and a petite female ice-skater. Jared proclaims, "A foot-long subway club is half the fat of a McDonald's Big Mac but twice the meat." Reminiscent of the old Miller Lite commercials, the athletes repeat "more meat" while Jared repeats "less fat" until Jared gives in to the athlete's side of the debate. The males use a more bullying approach to convince Jared to agree with their "more meat" argument, while the female uses a coy and sweet approach.

Coding Masculinity

This section begins with a description of the codes used to signify masculinity in these advertisements, followed by a discussion of the major themes uncovered regarding meat's role in representing freedom from constraints and loyalty to the heterosexual male group identity.

The commercials analyzed for this study illustrate a strong connection between meat and masculinity. These fast-food ads share basic gendered codes that reinforce lessons of heterosexual male socialization. For example, all of the voice-overs and the lead actors with speaking roles are men. In fact, in all but a few ads women are presented as silent and willing objects of the male gaze. Rather than the pastel tones of female targeted advertising, the colors in these ads are grays, neutrals, with some bright primary colors. When music is used, it is either sung by a male lead or is a growling rock guitar riff meant to emphasize a female character's sexuality. While most slogans are gender neutral, Burger King specifically targets men with instructions to "stack it high, tough guy," and "eat like a man, man."

In addition, action in the commercials takes place in groups of men in the public sphere such as outdoors on city streets, reinforcing the traditional locations most advertising situates males instead of female.[34] Only a few scenes take place inside an office, demonstrating a general sense of freedom from responsibility at home or at work. An exception is Burger King, which uses home and family as a setting to emphasize the father/son relationship of its Whopper Senior and Junior.

Of Mosher and Anderson's three macho personality character traits, sex is emphasized more explicitly than are violence and danger in these food ads.[35] Most ads avoid denotatively demonstrating *violent* acts, with the exception of the BK Manthem's humorous scenes of property destruction and fighting. However, connotatively, violence is implied because animals are killed to produce the meat used in the sandwiches. Whether stated outright or implied, all of the male characters implicitly seek meat sandwiches as prey, and the hunting ground is fast-food restaurants. Third, the only aspect of *danger* demonstrated in these ads is men's overall disregard of health, as the food's unhealthy nutritional content goes unmentioned by all companies except Subway, and no company overtly promotes any vegetarian sandwiches.

The following section provides a discussion of the primary themes found in the ads where men's consumption of meat, and often women, enable them to (1) seek freedom from personal and social constraints and (2) remain loyal to the (heterosexual) male group.

Freedom via Food: Having It His Way

Consistent with Burger King's mandate to "Have It Your Way," fast-food ads promote a narcissistic focus on fulfilling individual short-term desires free from concerns over the consequences to oneself or society. Subway is the only advertiser who raises a rational concern, in this case health, by using Jared to promote low-fat sandwich choices. But most fast-food commercials show a general irreverence to long-term health issues, favoring immediate gratification instead, such as is indicated by Jack in the Box's tagline "indulge." Food becomes just a tool for satisfying desires, even gluttonous ones. Thus size does matter in the burger battles, as Subway brags its sandwiches have twice the meat of burgers, while Quizno's brags its subs are even meatier than Subway's. And Burger King's slogan instructs men to "stack it high, tough guy," emphasizing how customers can choose three or four layers of beef and cheese. Commercials create a sense of plenty by constructing sandwiches that bulge and overflow with condiments literally dripping onto tables and fingers.

Plentitude is part of the male fantasyland that Burger King creates in its Hootie ad, where a guy can get anything he wants, as much as he wants, and when he wants it. In this ad, meat grows on trees, ranch dressing overflows the maidens' buckets, and the streets are paved with cheese. While the basis for this fantasy is abundance of fast food, one also sees an abundance of sexually available females — attractive, young, Daisy Duke "country" women wear low-cut tops and/or short skirts and dance happily around the Western-themed set. The ad demonstrates how men's "wildest fantasies" come true by having Dallas Cowboys cheerleaders shave them.

Hootie's lyrics also list several kinds of freedoms found in its fantasy land — financial freedom ("all the lotto tickets pay") and freedom from work and obligation (being able to "veg all day"). In this paradise, guys "never get in trouble, never need an excuse" and "no one tells you to behave." Most fast-food commercials do not show men on the job or dressed for work, preferring to emphasize leisure.

Ads also imply freedom from another constraint, women: nagging wives, girlfriends, and mothers. The annoyance of obligation to women is avoided, as committed or familial relationships between men and women are rarely shown. In fact, besides the Burger King Whopper Senior/Junior commercials showing a wife and daughter in the background, only two other commercials feature a man in a committed relationship with a woman. In both cases, the girlfriends are portrayed as restricting a man's freedom. First, a Carl's Jr. buffalo wing commercial reveals a woman giving her boyfriend a disdainful and accusing look after catching him staring at an attractive waitress. The announcer emphasizes that men should only go out with other guys to eat wings if they want to have any fun. Second, the BK Manthem singer walks out on his sophisticated girlfriend because he is sick of her dictating that he eat small-portioned gourmet meals that appear more leafy than meaty.

The Manthem ad states men have been so nutritionally constrained and emasculated by the modern woman, that guys should unite in revolution to regain control over their ability to eat meat. It openly mocks the women's rights movement by satirizing Helen Reddy's feminist song "I am woman hear me roar" and showing men burning their underwear in the streets to make fun of alleged "bra burnings" by feminist activists in the 1960s. Similarly, many ads show a preference for disempowered women by either symbolically annihilating them or concentrating on sexualized female body parts instead of female partnership, intelligence, speech, or social contributions. By disempowering women in these commercials, men gain more freedom and control to have it their way.

Loyalty to Male Group: Bonding over Beef and Babes

While the first theme of freedom may seem contradictory to the second theme of group loyalty, they are actually complementary as being "one of the guys" is made to seem effortless and natural. Two commercials in particular strongly emphasize stereotypes of straight, meat-eating men as if they are a homogenous group with a pack mentality. The first is the Jack in the Box ad demonstrating guys being drawn in packs to a combo meal more so than to other stereotypical male temptations such as motorcycles, kegs of beer, televised sports, and young women pillow-fighting. Second, in the BK Man-them, men's fervor over their right to eat meat causes them to act out "typical" male exploits, such as flexing muscles, punching each other, chopping cement blocks, destroying property, and playing with big machinery.

In many ways, fast-food commercials stereotype men most according to their gender, rather than by other human characteristics such age, race, body type, or class. For example, although white is the most common race, the men in these ads are often shown in racially mixed groups, are a wide range of ages, and have a variety of body types. Class, however, is a category where there is some stereotyping, as working- and middle-class men are more common than upper-class, yet when jobs are shown we see both blue and white collar represented. But what most commonly unites all these men in fast-food commercials is their gender identity as heterosexual males who share a desire to communally consume animal meat and symbolically consume the "flesh" of sexualized and objectified women.

Objectification of Women

Commercials sometimes show the meat becoming conflated with the flesh of women as mutual objects of male desire. Burger King's male fantasy commercial, staring Hootie, refers to products on the sandwich while showing related parts of female actresses. For example, chicken breasts equate with breasts of a woman and ranch dressing overflows like milk from a woman's breast. Burger King's stacker commercial has a guy implying that a woman's rear end is a "bun." The Carl's Jr. plastic surgeon commercial equates naturally large chicken breasts with women wanting breast augmentation. In addition, in the series of Carl's Jr. commercials that focus on a lone, sexualized woman doing something seductive while also eating a burger, the flesh of both humans and nonhumans become objects of the camera's implied heterosexual male gaze.

Meat as the Supreme Male Identity Trait

As the Jack in the Box commercial indicated, a desire for meat is the quintessential factor defining a homogeneous male identity, even more so than other temptations, like women. For example, Arby's assumes it is humorous, yet believable, that construction workers would get more excited by a Reuben sandwich, even when carried by a man, than they would by attractive women.

And Burger King's Manthem considers red meat's allure so powerful that it can serve as the sole motivating factor inspiring hundreds of men to unite into a spontaneous men's movement. This ad constructs red meat as distinctly male, in direct opposition to "chick food," such as tofu and quiche. In fact, the lyrics "I will eat this meat, until my innie turns into an outie" tells men that if they have become sissies by giving in to women and eating too many vegetables, meat can literally transform them back into a man. Men must stand up in defiance, presumably against women, for their right to "eat like a man" and have meat.

Guys are the presumed experts when it comes to finding meat, as demonstrated by Quizno's *man*-on-the-street testimonials asking only men about the meatiness of subs. This mirrors most commercials, where meat is a man's food and women need not be consulted.[36] So, perhaps it is no surprise when Burger King went looking for people to portray its Whoppers in costume, who seemed more natural to personify its burgers than guys?

Conclusion

In this chapter we have identified some recent commercials which illustrate the American fast-food industry's propensity for equating meat with heterosexual masculinity. Many common elements reveal the presumed target audience to be straight males, in accordance with male advertising stereotypes: male characters dominate and do all the speaking; locations are in the public and avoid the domestic sphere; and the male gaze objectifies women, who are relegated to secondary, often mute, status. The ads connote meat is used by men to both experience freedom from constraints and remain loyal to their group identity as heterosexual males.

Despite their health benefits, plant foods are derided as feminine and not as satisfying as meat. The ads suggest men should seek immediate gratification of their hunger by eating meat, often in large quantities, without being hindered by notions of social responsibility, sustainability or health, as may be dictated by women. Even Subway, which shows some respect for women and health, still reinforces some male stereotypes by associating muscular athletes with meat and using Jared, a wimpier "smart" guy, to represent the more feminine concern of dieting; Cebrzynski observed that, in all its ads, Subway uses only Jared to promote health while it uses other men, both athletes and comedians, to promote other food traits. Subway's use of a football player and a pro wrestler to emphasize the meatiness of low-fat subs bolsters Katz' contention that advertising uses "violent male athletes to help sell products... that have historically been gendered female."[37] Fast food is part of a hedonistic male fantasy where men have plenty of meat, women, money, and leisure time and are free from responsibility. Men are stereotyped as a homogeneous group whose most central feature is a shared desire for the consumption of meat, including that of women as silent sexual objects. In cases where human and animal flesh are conflated, as in "breast" meat, it bolsters Adams' contention that advertising often sexualizes animals and animalizes females. In some cases, men's temptations for both kinds of flesh can be enjoyed simultaneously, as in the Carl's Jr. assertion that guys go out to eat wings together so they can ogle waitresses. In other cases (Arby's and Jack in the Box), meat consumption is privileged as being even more tempting to men than looking at women's bodies.

While aspects of these advertisements seem like harmless commercial entertainment, we suggest a concern that the overall message of hedonism is detrimental to social justice (for human and nonhuman animals) and ecological sustainability. To the extent that it perpetuates stereotypes of men in one-dimensional terms as self-indulgent, womanizing carnivores, fast-food advertising lowers society's expectations for the positive contributions men should be and often are making to promoting equality and social responsibility. Many of these commercials urge men to behave in self-interested ways that disregard the social consequences of their actions and prioritize an individualistic sense of *taking* over a more community-oriented sense of *giving*.

Another disturbing outcome of using gender stereotypes to sell fast food is the resulting reinforcement of the male/female dichotomy that has been the basis for patriarchal oppression. The ads construct the ideal woman as a silent, passive, meat-eating, agreeable stranger who is young, pretty, thin, and fair-skinned with long hair and a voluptuous body willingly put on display for the male viewer. The objectification of women in many of these commercials may in fact be a backlash against the empowerment American women have achieved in the centuries' old struggle for women's rights. And, while we admit that it is challenging to market products which are not particularly socially responsible, we hope that it could be done in a way that does not continue to sacrifice the rights of traditionally oppressed groups in order to further empower a dominant social group such as heterosexual American men. When fast-food companies insist on telling men to "have it your way" in the twenty-first century, they might as well be telling them to turn back the clock on social progress.

Drawing on Strate's study of beer commercials, "the myth of masculinity does have a number of redeeming features (facing challenges and taking risks are valuable activities in many contexts), but the unrelenting one-dimensionality of masculinity as presented by," in this case fast-food commercials, "is clearly anachronistic, possibly laughable, but without a doubt," too filling.[38]

Notes

1. See Jim Mason, *An Unnatural Order: Why We Are Destroying the Planet and Each Other* (New York: Continuum, 1993), and Jeremy Rifkin, *Beyond Beef* (New York: Plume, 1992).

2. See Carol Adams, *The Pornography of Meat* (New York: Continuum, 2003), and Carol Adams, *The Sexual Politics of Meat: A Feminist-Vegetarian Critical Theory* (New York: Continuum, 1990).

3. See Stuart Hall, *Representation: Cultural Representations and Signifying Practices* (London: Sage, 1997); Stuart Hall, "Introduction," in *Paper Voices: The Popular Press and Social Change, 1935–1965*, ed. Anthony Charles Smith (London: Chatto & Windus, 1975), 11–24; Judith Williamson, *Decoding Advertisements: Ideology and Meaning in Advertising* (New York: Marion Boyars, 1978).

4. Mason, 81.

5. Ibid.

6. Ibid.

7. See Carol Adams, *Sexual Politics.*

8. Adams, *Sexual Politics*, 168.

9. Ibid.

10. Ibid., 187.

11. Ibid., 34.

12. See Peggy Sanday, *Female Power and Male Dominance: On the Origins of Sexual Inequality* (Cambridge and New York: Cambridge University Press, 1981).

13. Richard E. Leakey and Roger Lewin, *People of the Lake: Mankind and Its Beginnings* (New York: Doubleday, 1978), x.

14. Adams, *Sexual Politics*, 34.

15. Ibid., 33.

16. Jeffery Sobal, "Men, Meat, and Marriage: Models of Masculinity," *Food & Foodways* 13 (2005): 135.

17. See Eric Schlosser, *Fast-Food Nation: The Dark Side of the All-American Meal* (New York: Harper Collins, 2002), and Morgan Spurlock (Prod., Dir., and Writer), *Super Size Me.* Film. (Culver City, CA: Columbia TriStar Home Entertainment, 2004).

18. See also Alex Jamieson, *The Great American Detox Diet: Feel Better, Look Better, and Lose Weight by Cleaning up Your Diet* (New York: Rodale, 2005).

19. Schlosser.

20. See also David Fraser, "Farm Animal Production: Changing Agriculture in a Changing Culture," *Journal of Applied Animal Welfare Science* 4 (2001): 3, and Peter Singer and Jim Mason, *The Way We Eat: Why Our Food Choices Matter* (New York: Rodale, 2006).

21. Kathy Freston, "Vegetarian Is the New Prius," *Common Dreams*, January 20, 2007. Online: http://www.commondreams.org/views07/0120–20.htm (accessed March 31, 2007), and Sierra Club, (2006), "Clean Water and Factory Farms. Report and Fact Sheets from the Sierra Club. Online: http://www.sierraclub.org/factoryfarms/factsheets/ (accessed April 1, 2007).

22. See also Neal Barnard, *Food for Life: How the New Four Food Groups Can Save Your Life* (New York: Three Rivers Press, 1993), and Howard Lyman, *No More Bull! The Mad Cowboy Targets America's Worst Enemy: Our Diet* (New York: Scribner, 2005).

23. See also Katrina Arabe, "Eat, Drink, Man, Woman," February, 2003. Thomasnet. Online: http://news.thomasnet.com/IMT/archives/2003/02/eat_drink_man_w.html (accessed March 29, 2007).

24. Alison McCook, "Men: I'll Take Meat and Hold the Veggies, Starch," *Reuter's Health.* Online: http://preventdisease.com/news/articles/men_take_meat.shtml (accessed March 29, 2007).

25. Emily Senay and Rob Waters, *From Boys to Men: A Woman's Guide to the Health of Husbands, Partners, Sons, Fathers, and Brothers* (New York: Simon & Schuster, 2004), 297.

26. See Donald L. Mosher, and Ronald D. Anderson, "Macho Personality, Sexual Aggression, and Reactions to Guided Imagery of Realistic Rape," *Journal of Research in Personality* 18 (1986): 150–63.

27. Joseph R. Dominick and Gail E. Rauch, "The Image of Women in Network TV Commercials," *Journal of Broadcasting* 16 (1972): 259–65; Kenneth Schneider and Sharon Schneider, "Trends in Sex Roles in Television Commercials," *Journal of Marketing* 43 (1979): 79–84.

28. Jackson Katz, "Advertising and the Construction of Violent White Masculinity," in *Gender, Race, and Class in Media,* ed. Gail Dines and J. Humez (Thousand Oaks, CA: Sage, 2003), 351.

29. Ibid., 352.

30. Lance Strate, "Beer Commercials: A Manual on Masculinity," in *Men, Masculinity, and the Media,* ed. Steve Craig (Newbury Park, CA: Sage, 1992), 85.

31. Adams, *The Pornography of Meat,* 13.

32. Ibid., 171.

33. See also Gregg Cebrzynski, "Please rise — if you're a guy — for singing of national 'Manthem,'" *Nation's Restaurant News* 40, no. 21(2006a): 18, available Online at: Business Source Premier database (accessed March 31, 2007); Gregg Cebrzynski, "Creepy King, 'Whopperheads' Give BK Ads an Edge They Never Had," *Nation's Restaurant News* 38 (2004): 14, available Online at: Business Source Premier database (accessed March 30, 2007); Marianne Paskowski, "Paris Hilton to the Rescue," *Multichannel News* 26, no. 22: 50, available Online at: Business Source Premier database (accessed March 30, 2007); Randi Schmelzer and Axel Koester, "Raunchy Ranch," *Adweek* 46, no. 7 (2005): 24, available Online at: Business Source Premier database (accessed March 30, 2007).

34. See Dominick and Rauch; Schneider and Schneider.

35. See Mosher and Anderson.

36. With the lone exception of Subway's use of a female athlete.

37. See Katz, 356.

38. See Strate, 92.

Works Cited

Adams, Carol. *The Pornography of Meat.* New York: Continuum, 2003.

_____. *The Sexual Politics of Meat: A Feminist-Vegetarian Critical Theory.* New York: Continuum, 1990.

American Dietetic Association. "Position Paper on Vegetarianism," available online at http://www.eatright.org/cps/rde/xchg/ada/hs.xsl/advocacy_933_ENU_HTML.htm (accessed March 31, 2007).

_____. "Research Says Fast Food Intake May Affect Children's Nutrition," available online at http://www.eatright.org/cps/rde/xchg/ada/hs.xsl/home_4400_ENU_HTML.htm (accessed March 31, 2007).

Arabe, Katrina. "Eat, Drink, Man, Woman." February, 2003. Available online at Thomasnet. http://news.thomasnet.com/IMT/archives/2003/02/eat_drink_man_w.html (accessed March 29, 2007).

Barnard, Neal. *Food for Life: How the New Four Food Groups Can Save Your Life.* New York: Three Rivers Press, 1993.

Barthes, Roland. *Mythologies.* New York: Hill and Wang, 1972.

Bussey, Kay, and Albert Bandura. "Social Cognitive Theory of Gender Development and Differentiation." *Psychological Review* 106 (1999): 676–713.

Cebrzynski, Gregg. "Creepy King, 'Whopperheads' Give BK Ads an Edge They Never Had." *Nation's Restaurant News* 38 (2004): 14–30.

_____. "Jared Fogle Goes on the Attack for Subway's Low-Fat Sandwiches." *Nation's Restaurant News* 40 (2006): 16–31.

_____. "Please rise — if you're a guy — for singing of national 'Manthem.'" *Nation's Restaurant News* 40 (2006): 18.

Coombes, Rosemary J. *The Cultural Life of Intellectual Properties: Authorship, Appropriation, and the Law.* Durham: Duke University Press, 1998.

Craig, Steve. "Considering Men and the Media." In *Men, Masculinity, and the Media,* ed. S. Craig, 1–7. Newbury Park, CA: Sage, 1992.

DeFleur, Melvin L., and Everette E. Dennis. *Understanding Mass Communication.* Boston: Houghton Mifflin, 1998.

Dominick, Joseph R., and G. E. Rauch. "The Image of Women in Network TV Commercials." *Journal of Broadcasting* 16 (1972): 259–65.

Fraser, David. "Farm Animal Production: Changing Agriculture in a Changing Culture." *Journal of Applied Animal Welfare Science* 4 (2001): 3.

Freston, Kathy. "Vegetarian Is the New Prius." *Common Dreams,* January 20, 2007. Available online at http://www.commondreams.org/views07/0120-20.htm (accessed March 31, 2007).

Hall, Stuart. Introduction. In *Paper Voices: The Popular Press and Social Change, 1935–1965,* ed. Anthony Charles Smith, 11–24. London: Chatto & Windus, 1975.

_____. *Representation: Cultural Representations and Signifying Practices.* London: Sage, 1997.

Jamieson, Alex. *The Great American Detox Diet: Feel Better, Look Better, and Lose Weight by Cleaning up Your Diet.* New York: Rodale, 2005.

Katz, Jackson. "Advertising and the Construction of Violent White Masculinity." In *Gender, Race, and Class in Media,* edited by G. Dines and J. Humez, 349–58. Thousand Oaks, CA: Sage, 2003.

Leakey, Richard E., and Roger Lewin. *People of the Lake: Mankind and Its Beginnings.* New York: Doubleday, 1978.

Lyman, Howard. *No More Bull! The Mad Cowboy Targets America's Worst Enemy: Our Diet.* New York: Scribner, 2005.

Mason, Jim. *An Unnatural Order: Why We Are Destroying the Planet and Each Other.* New York: Continuum, 1993.

McCook, Alison. "Men: I'll Take Meat and Hold the Veggies, Starch." *Reuter's Health.* Available online at http://preventdisease.com/news/articles/men_take_meat.shtml (accessed March 29, 2007).

Mosher, Donald L., and Ronald D. Anderson. "Macho Personality, Sexual Aggression, and Reactions to Guided Imagery of Realistic Rape." *Journal of Research in Personality* 18 (1986): 150–63.

Parasecoli, Fabio. "Feeding Hard Bodies: Food and Masculinities in Men's Fitness Magazines." *Food & Foodways* 13 (2005): 17–37.

Paskowski, Marianne. "Paris Hilton to the Rescue." *Multichannel News* 26, no. 22 (2005): 50. Available online at Business Source Premier database (accessed March 30, 2007).

Rifkin, Jeremy. *Beyond Beef.* New York: Plume, 1992.

Sanday, Peggy. *Female Power and Male Dominance: On the Origins of Sexual Inequality.* Cambridge, UK and New York: Cambridge University Press, 1981.

Schlosser, Eric. *Fast-Food Nation: The Dark Side of the All-American Meal.* New York: Harper Collins, 2002.

Schmelzer, Randi, and Axel Koester. "Raunchy Ranch." *Adweek* 46, no. 7 (2005): 24. Available at Business Source Premier database (accessed March 30, 2007).

Schneider, Kenneth, and Sharon Schneider. "Trends in Sex Roles in Television Commercials." *Journal of Marketing* 43 (1979): 79–84.

Senay, Emily, and Rob Waters. *From Boys to Men: A Woman's Guide to the Health of Husbands, Partners, Sons, Fathers, and Brothers.* New York: Simon & Schuster, 2004.

Sierra Club. "Clean Water and Factory Farms. Report and Fact Sheets from the Sierra Club." 2006. Available online at http://www.sierraclub.org/factoryfarms/factsheets/ (accessed April 1, 2007).

Singer, Peter, and Jim Mason. *The Way We Eat: Why Our Food Choices Matter.* New York: Rodale, 2006.

Sobal, Jeffery. "Men, Meat, and Marriage: Models of Masculinity." *Food & Foodways* 13 (2005): 135–58.

Strate, Lance. "Beer Commercials: A Manual on Masculinity." In *Men, Masculinity, and the Media*, edited by Steve Craig, 78–92. Newbury Park, CA: Sage, 1992.

Super Size Me. Written, produced, and directed by Morgan Spurlock. Film. Culver City, CA: Columbia TriStar Home Entertainment, 2004.

Van Dijk, Teun Adrianus. *Discourse, Racism, and Ideology.* La Laguna, Mexico: RCEI Ediciones, 1996.

Williamson, Judith. *Decoding Advertisements: Ideology and Meaning in Advertising.* New York: Marion Boyars, 1978.

Everything I Need to Know About Food, Eating and Culture I Learned from Tupperware

Afterword

BY LAWRENCE C. RUBIN

Be careful of your wishes! How prophetic these words became when, at a recent Tupperware party at my home, I asked the hostess to keep an eye out for vintage Tupperware. A few months later, her cryptic phone message directed me to the daughter of a fellow Tupperware lady who had recently passed away. Part of this woman's legacy was nine boxes of vintage Tupperware that her widower eagerly sold to me for a nominal fee.

Long story short, and with the pilgrimage behind us, my wife and I stood in daunted silence before a veritable wall of plastic (actually polyethylene) containers, cookware, and kitchen gadgets in every imaginable size, shape and color. A few short days later, our refrigerator and cupboards brimmed with neatly stacked plastic containers and we eagerly carted leftovers to school and work in loving and vacuum-sealed safety. Ever scouting the popular culture horizon for even the faintest beacons of discourse, my thoughts turned to food, eating and the many fascinating, insightful and provocative essays in this volume.

Tupperware, the actualized vision of futurist, chemical engineer, entrepreneur and accidental feminist Silas Tupper,[1] seemed to me a useful lens for focusing these seemingly disparate voices into a chorus of cultural significance. Scanning the Internet and a number of popular magazines from the last several decades, I found a trove of print ads for Tupperware with catchy slogans such as "When you lock in freshness, you set yourself free," "How many holiday gifts last a lifetime?" (alluding to Tupperware's lifetime guarantee), "Share Sunday's chicken Tuesday" and "What puts the mmm-mm-m in a midnight snack?" The accompanying images were similarly fascinating and more importantly, telling. Father and son rowed ashore from a treacherous fishing expedition while mother lovingly awaited them, her table brimming with overflowing Tupperware. A flustered bride-to-be, surrounded by her compassionate bridal entourage lamented that she could not say "I do" until she had her Tupperware. Plump meats and verdant veggies had brass locks and keys suggesting that with Tupperware's help, their freshness could be preserved. And, finally, neatly stacked "his" and "her" Tupperware containers preserved carefully gender-scripted items including pipe tobacco and camera for him, and cookies, fruit and bread for her.

What did my newfound trove of polyethylene treasures have to do with food, eating and culture as discussed in this book? Quite a lot, as it turns out. Tupperware was initially designed for food storage, plain and simple! By tapping into the well-established technology of mass production, the inevitably conspicuous consumption and the pervasive influence of advertising, it evolved from simple food container to a rich and organic repository for cultural discourse in the areas of sociology, politics, economics and cultural anthropology. Tupperware was not an anomaly, but a curious nexus of forces that coalesced in postwar America in the forms of suburbanization, gender re-balancing, the proliferation of the media, democratization and moralization of the marketplace, the ensconcement of modernity and the increasing power of science and technology to move man (and woman) kind closer to utopian visions. Perhaps, and at a much simpler level, Tupperware was about people, and its legacy was best stated by Brownie Wise, the pioneer of the home party who asserted, "if we build the people, they'll build the business."[2]

The essays in this volume have offered a rich smorgasbord of ideas and ways of looking at food and eating beyond the obvious; because beyond the obvious role of food and eating in sustaining life and building social relations, they are postmodern morsels of delicious discourse. Each of these essays offered a tantalizing taste of cultural fare, a glimpse into the many ways that food and eating practices do just what Tupperware did. They offer us a glimpse into ourselves; whether we are eating quickly or slowly, in prison or at 30,000 feet, dining in or dining out, snacking or gorging, supping alone or with others, using our hands or cleverly crafted objects, savoring chocolate or high cuisine, thinking locally or globally.

Notes

1. For a complete history of Tupper and Tupperware, see A. J. Clarke (1999), *Tupperware: The Promise of Plastic in 1950's America*. (Washington, DC: Smithsonian Institution Press).

2. Brownie Wise, vice president of the Tupperware Home Party division offered this quote, which appeared under her picture on the cover of *Business Week* (April 17, 1954). She was the first woman to appear on the cover of this magazine.

About the Contributors

Santiago Daydi-Tolson received his Ph.D. from the University of Kansas in 1973. Since then he has taught at Fordham University, the University of Virginia and the University of Wisconsin-Milwaukee. Presently he teaches Spanish, Latin American and comparative literature at the University of Texas in San Antonio. His academic publications include several books and numerous articles and book reviews. He is the founder and editor of the electronic journal *Convivium Artium,* devoted to the study of food representation in literature and the arts. He serves as faculty advisor of *Labrapalabra,* an electronic literary magazine in Spanish published by the Department of Modern Languages and Literatures at the University of Texas in San Antonio.

Guillaume de Syon teaches European history and the history of technology at Albright College in Reading, Pennsylvania. He is the author of *Zeppelin! Germany and the Airship, 1900–1939* (Johns Hopkins, 2002; paperback 2007). His research interests include the cultural history of aviation, cultures of travel and tourism, and European popular culture. He is completing a history of transatlantic flight.

Carrie Packwood Freeman is currently an Assistant Professor of Communication at Georgia State University. For nine years prior to pursuing graduate work, Carrie worked in both nonprofit public relations and in corporate leadership training. She has been active in the animal rights movement for fifteen years and founded local grassroots groups in both Florida and Georgia.

Dawn Gilpin is a doctoral student in Mass Media and Communication at Temple University in Philadelphia. Her research interests focus on the complex intersection between media, organizations and public policy, and organizational crises. Nearly twenty years spent living in Italy honed her appreciation of food and sparked her interest in its cultural dimensions. Since she tries to combine work and pleasure whenever possible, Dawn is currently writing her dissertation on organic foods discourse.

Simon Gottschalk is associate professor of Sociology at the University of Nevada, Las Vegas. He is the author of numerous articles and book chapters about topics such as youth subcultures, mass media, postmodernism, qualitative research methods, cultural studies, the sociology of mental illness, environmental identity, the social psychology of terrorism, the acceleration of everyday life.

Carlnita P. Greene is an assistant professor of Communication & Rhetoric in the Department of English at Nazareth College in Rochester, New York. Her specialization is the intersection of rhetoric, media, and cultural studies. In her current research, she is exploring the relationship between identity, rhetoric, and social style within a hypermediated, consumerist society.

Tina M. Harris received her Ph.D. from the University of Kentucky in 1995. She is an associate professor of Speech Communication at the University of Georgia. She is co-author of the leading text on interracial communication with Mark P. Orbe of Western Michigan University, *Interracial Communication: Theory to Practice*, the second edition of which will be released in August 2007 by Sage. She conducts research on interracial communication, interracial dating, race relations, racial representation and the media, classroom instruction and interaction regarding race, and the intersection of religious faith, health and genes. She has been and is currently at work on university- and federally-funded projects examining the impact of racial identity on communication about genes, race, and health.

John Shelton Lawrence is professor emeritus of Philosophy at Morningside College in Sioux City, Iowa. He currently lives near California's Gourmet Ghetto in Berkeley. His long-term interest in heroic mythologies, both classical and contemporary, led him, with Robert Jewett, to write *The Myth of the American Superhero* (2002) as well as *Captain America and the Crusade Against Evil* (2003). He has felt urgency about eating since birth and finds that fasting, a form of spiritual mastery for some, merely induces a feeling of entitlement for excessive amounts of food. As an eater, he has traveled widely, eating raw horse meat (*basashi*) during his most recent trip to Japan.

Heather Lee is a doctoral graduate student at Brown University. She previously lectured at the John F. Kennedy Institute, Free University, Berlin and at Freiburg University. She plans to write her dissertation on American restaurant culture.

Robert Lee is Malaysian Chinese and was educated in New Zealand, with a business background in restaurants, bars and cafés in Malaysia, New Zealand and Australia. His experience of Malaysian Hawker Food in the

Nyonya style of the Peranakan or Malay Straits people has led to an interest in fusion food, while his business experience across the Pacific Rim has produced an understanding of how much food culture contributes to "high-energy" urban development in the new information economy. His study of coffee bars in China is part of a larger project on fusion food within the Chinese Pacific diaspora, and its role in business promotion and business culture generally.

Debra Merskin received her Ph.D. from the S. I. Newhouse School, Syracuse University. She is head of the Communication Studies sequence in the School of Journalism & Communication at the University of Oregon. Her research on race, gender, and media appears in journals such as *The Howard Journal of Communication, Sex Roles, Feminist Media Studies, Peace Review*, and *Mass Communication & Society*. She has contributed chapters to *Bring 'Em on: Media and Politics in the Iraq War, Sex in Consumer Culture: The Erotic Content of Media and Marketing, The Girl Wide Web: Girls, the Internet, and the Negotiation of Identity*. She is currently writing a book for Blackwell on race, gender, and mass media portrayals.

Ellen E. Moore is a Ph.D. candidate at the Institute for Communications Research at the University of Illinois. She has worked extensively on an NSF study of media use and the public sphere, including research on the relationship between media consumption and perceptions of environmental issues. Her dissertation research focuses on the relationship between the use of secular popular culture in American evangelical churches and political mobilization. Ellen still eats and enjoys all kinds of chocolate, especially if it's Fair Trade and organic!

Megan Mullen is associate professor of Communication at University of Wisconsin-Parkside, where she also co-directs the interdisciplinary Humanities Program. Her research interests include cable television history and programming. Her publications include *The Rise of Cable Programming in the United States: Revolution or Evolution* (University of Texas, 2003) and the forthcoming *Television in the Multichannel Era* (Blackwell).

Hillary Murtha is a Fellow and Ph.D. candidate in the University of Delaware's program in American Civilization. She is a scholar of material culture, decorative arts and American history. Prior to entering the University of Delaware, she was the Curator of Exhibitions at the Cornelius Low House Museum in New Jersey, developing and mounting changing exhibitions. She has an MA in the history of decorative arts from the Bard Graduate Center for Studies in the Decorative Arts and an MA in history from the University of Delaware.

Dr. Mallay Occhiogrosso holds a bachelor's degree in American History from Harvard University and a medical degree from Cornell University. She is a former arts journalist who now works as an attending and instructor in psychiatry at Weill Medical College of Cornell University, where she is also a member of the History of Psychiatry department. Her research interest is in the history of psychiatry, particularly as it pertains to nosology and to perspectives on overeating and overweight.

Ming-Yeh T. Rawnsley was head of Chinese Studies and head of the Institute of Asia-Pacific Studies Ningbo, University of Nottingham Ningbo, China (UNNC) from 2005 to 2007. She is currently writing a book on *Cultural and Social Change in Taiwan: Society, Cinema and Theatre*, to be published by RoutledgeCurzon in 2008. She is also co-editing a book (with Gary Rawnsley and Julian Stringer) on *Hero: Culture, Politics and Transnational Chinese Cinema*.

Lawrence Rubin is professor of Counselor Education at St. Thomas University, in Miami, and a psychologist in private practice, where he works with children and families. His research interests lie at the intersection of popular culture and psychology. His first edited collection, *Psychotropic Drugs and Popular Culture: Essays in Medicine, Mental Health and the Media*, published by McFarland, won the 2006 Ray and Pat Browne Book Award by the Association for Popular Culture.

Jim Thomas, emeritus professor at Northern Illinois University, specializes in research on cultures of marginalized groups, including prisoners and Internet subcultures, and on ethnographic methods, especially research ethics. From 1980 to the present, he has periodically taught in Illinois prisons and is a prison monitor with the John Howard Association, Illinois' prison watchdog agency. He is currently completing two monographs: *Revising Critical Ethnograpy* (Sage, 2008) and *Communicating Prison Culture* (in progress).

Phillip Vannini is an assistant professor in the School of Communication and Culture at Royal Roads University. His research interests include the study of symbolic systems and symbolic interaction, the sociology of the body, technology and material culture, as well as media and popular culture. Together with Dennis Waskul he is editor of *Body/Embodiment* (Ashgate, 2006).

Doctoral Regents Scholar and Melbern G. Glasscock Stipendiary Fellow **Chris Westgate** is a graduate of Texas A&M University, Columbia University, and Cornell University. He studies the radio and music industries, Latino media, visual and material cultures, media technologies and critical-cultural theory. More specifically, he is interested in communicative acts of cultural commerce between Mexico and the U.S.; these acts include reciprocal radio broadcasts; resistant record and music texts; power dynamics between computers and communities; digitized realities of sight and sound contained in typographic imaginaries; producers of industry; circulators of identity; and consumers of policy. He has always been a serious food critic at heart.

Craig Wight is a researcher in the Moffat Centre within the Cultural Business Group at Glasgow Caledonian University. Craig has academic interests in the discourses of "dissonant" heritage sites in Eastern Europe and culinary tourism as an emerging concept. Craig is also a Project Officer within the Moffat Centre, undertaking business consultancy and commercial research into a diverse range of tourism topics nationally and internationally.

Index

303